UNITED NATIONS REFORM AND THE NEW COLLECTIVE SECURITY

The 2004 Report of the Secretary-General's High-Level Panel on Threats, Challenges and Change emphasized the links between economic development, security and human rights, and the imperative of collective action and cooperation between states. In a world divided by differences of power, wealth, culture and ideology, a central question in international law and organization is whether reaffirmation of the concept of collective security and a workable consensus on the means of its realization are possible.

In addressing these questions, this book considers the three key documents in the recent UN reform process: the High-Level Panel report, the Secretary-General's *In Larger Freedom* report and the 2005 World Summit Outcome document. The chapters examine the responsibilities, commitments, strategies and institutions necessary for collective security to function both in practice and as a normative ideal in international law and relations between state and non-state actors alike.

PETER G. DANCHIN is an Associate Professor of Law at the University of Maryland School of Law, where his academic areas of interest are international law, international legal theory and human rights.

HORST FISCHER is Professor of International Humanitarian Law at Leiden University, the Netherlands, Academic Director of the Institute for International Law of Peace and Armed Conflict at the Ruhr University Bochum, Germany, and Adjunct Professor at Columbia University's School of International and Public Affairs in New York.

UNITED NATIONS REFORM AND THE NEW COLLECTIVE SECURITY

PETER G. DANCHIN

and

HORST FISCHER

CAMBRIDGE
UNIVERSITY PRESS

CAMBRIDGE UNIVERSITY PRESS
Cambridge, New York, Melbourne, Madrid, Cape Town, Singapore,
São Paulo, Delhi, Dubai, Tokyo

Cambridge University Press
The Edinburgh Building, Cambridge CB2 8RU, UK

Published in the United States of America by Cambridge University Press, New York

www.cambridge.org
Information on this title: www.cambridge.org/9780521515436

First published 2010

Printed in the United Kingdom at the University Press, Cambridge

A catalogue record for this publication is available from the British Library

ISBN 978-0-521-51543-6 Hardback

CONTENTS

CONTRIBUTORS

GEORGE ANDREOPOULOS is Professor of Political Science at the John Jay College of Criminal Justice and a member of the doctoral faculty at the Graduate School and University Center, CUNY. Professor Andreopoulos studied history, law, and international relations at the Universities of Chicago and Cambridge. Before coming to CUNY, he taught for several years at Yale University, where he was the founding Associate Director of the Orville Schell Center for International Human Rights. He has written extensively on international security, international human rights, and international humanitarian law issues. His recent publications include *Non-State Actors in the Human Rights Universe* (with Zehra Arat and Peter Juviler); *Concepts and Strategies in International Human Rights* (with Peter Lang); *The Laws of War: Constraints on Warfare in the Western World* (with Sir Michael Howard and Mark Shulman); and *Human Rights Education for the Twenty-First Century* (with Richard Pierre Claude). Professor Andreopoulos is currently completing a book on Humanitarian Intervention, serves on the Editorial Board of *Human Rights Review*, and is currently President of the Human Rights Section of the American Political Science Association.

MAXWELL O. CHIBUNDU is Professor of Law at the University of Maryland School of Law where he teaches courses on US civil procedure, international civil litigation, international business transactions, public international law, and jurisprudence. He has published articles on issues relating to public international law, law and development, human rights, affirmative action, the civil jury and statutory interpretation. His current research interests are on matters of procedure, comparative jurisprudence and the intersections of international human rights and power.

PETER G. DANCHIN is Associate Professor of Law at the University of Maryland School of Law where he chairs the International and Comparative Law Committee. He has a B.A. and LL.B. (first class honors) from the University of Melbourne and a LL.M. and J.S.D. from Columbia

Law School. From 2000 to 2006, he was lecturer and director of the human rights program at Columbia University's School of International and Public Affairs. He teaches in the areas of international law, international human rights, and legal theory. This volume, co-edited with Horst Fischer, is the result of a visiting appointment in 2005 as an Erasmus Mundus Scholar at the Institute for International Law of Peace and Armed Conflict (IFHV) at the Ruhr University Bochum, Germany.

DENNIS DIJKZEUL is Junior Professor in the management of humanitarian crises at the Institute for International Law of Peace and Armed Conflict at the Ruhr University Bochum, Germany. He is also Adjunct Professor at the School of International and Public Affairs at Columbia University, New York, and regularly consults for international organizations in Africa, Central America, Europe, and the United States. His main interests concern the management of international organizations and the (non) participation of local population in humanitarian programs. His latest books are *Supporting Local Health Care in a Chronic Crisis: Management and Financing Approaches in the Eastern Democratic Republic of the Congo* (2005), *Between Force and Mercy: Military Action and Humanitarian Aid* (2004), and *Rethinking International Organizations: Pathology and Promise* (2003).

JEREMY FARRALL is a Research Fellow working on the project Building Democracy and Justice after Conflict at the ANU Centre for International Governance and Justice. He joined the Centre in 2006 from the University of Tasmania Faculty of Law, where he was a Post-Doctoral Research Fellow. Jeremy has considerable practical experience in International Law, Human Rights, and UN affairs. He worked for the United Nations from 2001 to 2006, serving as a policy adviser for the UN Mission in Liberia (2004–2006), on the UN mediation team that facilitated peace talks in Cyprus (2004), and as a political officer for the UN Security Council at UNHQ (2001–2004). He has also worked for the Quaker United Nations Office. Jeremy's research interests include UN sanctions, peacekeeping, peacebuilding, and the rule of law. He is the author of *United Nations Sanctions and the Rule of Law* (Cambridge University Press, 2007).

HORST FISCHER is Professor of International Humanitarian Law at Leiden University in the Netherlands, Academic Director of the Institute for International Law of Peace and Armed Conflict (Institut für Friedenssicherungsrecht und Humanitäres Völkerrecht/IFHV) at the Ruhr University Bochum, Germany, Adjunct Professor at Columbia University (SIPA), New York (2002–2006) and Lecturer in International Humanitarian Law, Humboldt University, Berlin (2003–2004) as well as Visiting Professor in Human Rights at University Robert Schuman in Strasbourg in 2005, and Visiting Professor in Human Rights at Widener Law School in 2003 and 2005. In 2002 he was elected as the first president of the European Inter-university Centre for Human Rights and Democratization in Venice and has been since 1999 the president of the NOHA University Association (Network on Humanitarian Assistance, Brussels) and of the Berghof Foundation Board in Berlin. He is the General Editor both of the *Yearbook of International Humanitarian Law* (The Hague) as well as of the journal *Humanitäres Völkerrecht – Informationsschriften* (*International Humanitarian Law Journal*) (Bochum). He has been co-editor of the *Bochumer Schriften zur Friedenssicherung und zum Humanitären Völkerrecht* (*Bochum Studies on Peace and Armed Conflict*) since 1988. His academic work has focused on international humanitarian law, humanitarian action, and questions related to the maintenance of international peace and security including disarmament law.

JAN KLABBERS is Professor of International Organizations Law at the University of Helsinki and director of the Academy of Finland Centre of Excellence in Global Governance Research, and has held visiting professorships at Hofstra Law School (New York) and the Graduate Institute of International Studies and Development (Geneva). He is the book review editor of the *International Organizations Law Review*, and his publications include *An Introduction to International Institutional Law* (2002) and *The Concept of Treaty in International Law* (1996). He has edited the volume on *International Organizations* for the Library of Essays in International Law series (2005), while a monograph on *Treaty Conflict and the European Union* is forthcoming.

LAURI MÄLKSOO is currently the head of international and EC law lectureship at the University of Tartu, Estonia. He studied law in Tartu (LL.B.) and Göttingen and obtained his master's degree at Georgetown University Law Center. He defended his doctoral thesis "Illegal Annexation and State Continuity: the Case of the Incorporation of the Baltic States by the USSR" at Humboldt University, Berlin. The thesis was published in 2003 in Erik Castrén Institute's monograph series of

Martinus Nijhoff. Beside working at the university, he has also served as the international and EC law adviser of the Legal Chancellor (ombudsman) of the Republic of Estonia. He is also serving as a member of the EU Network of Independent Experts on Fundamental Rights.

CARMEN MÁRQUEZ CARRASCO is Professor of Public International Law and International Relations at the University of Seville (Spain), and is currently the Program Director of the European Masters on Human Rights and Democratization at the European Inter-University Centre for Human Rights and Democratization in Venice, Italy.

J. PAUL MARTIN is Senior Scholar and was from 1978 to 2007 the Executive Director of the Center for the Study of Human Rights at Columbia University. He teaches and researches on religion, rights, and world community, rights and the role of multinational corporations in developing countries, and on human rights education. The Center promotes multidisciplinary human rights teaching and research at Columbia and engages in capacity building for human rights NGOs and university human rights programs in developing countries.

EJEVIOME ELOHO OTOBO is Director of Strategic Planning in the Peacebuilding Support Office (PBSO) at the United Nations Secretariat in New York. Prior to joining PBSO, Otobo was Deputy Director for Policy Analysis and Monitoring in the Office of the Special Adviser on Africa (OSAA) at the UN Secretariat, where he led the team that prepared several reports on the progress and challenges in the implementation of the New Partnership for Africa's Development (NEPAD). Before joining OSAA, Otobo served at the UN Economic Commission for Africa where he worked on issues concerning sub-regional dimensions of post-conflict reconstruction and development, institutional reforms, and governance. His main areas of research interest are business–government relations, development management, and strategic planning. He has contributed book chapters and published articles on such issues as public service management, institutional reforms, international trade, and economic and corporate governance. Otobo obtained his undergraduate education at the University of Lagos, Nigeria and did his graduate studies at the John F. Kennedy School of Government, Harvard University, Cambridge, Massachusetts.

ERIC ROSAND is a Senior Fellow at the Center on Global Counter-terrorism Cooperation and a non-resident fellow at NYU's Center on International Cooperation. Previously he was Chief of the Multilateral Affairs Unit in the Office of the Coordinator for Counter-terrorism at the US Department of State. Before that he served as the US Mission to the UN's counter-terrorism expert. He has published numerous articles and book chapters, and lectured widely, on the role of multilateral institutions in the fight against terrorism. He has a B.A. from Haverford College, a J.D. from Columbia University Law School, and an LL.M in International Law from Cambridge University.

ELIZABETH SALMÓN GÁRATE is Associate Professor in the Department of Law at the Pontifical Catholic University of Peru, academic coordinator of the Institute for Democracy and Human Rights and coordinator of the university's master's degree in human rights. Salmón has a doctorate in law from the University of Seville, Spain and has been a visiting professor at the International University of Andalusia and the Carlos III University of Madrid. She is a member of the Editorial Committee of the International Journal of the Red Cross and has served as an external adviser to the Ministry of Justice (during the transitional government), the International Committee of the Red Cross, the Truth and Reconciliation Commission, the Ministry of Defence and the United Nations. Salmón's publications include: *Introduction to International Humanitarian Law* (2004), *Encounters and Desencuentros: Peru and the International Humanitarian Law* (2001), *The International Criminal Court and measures for their implementation in Peru*, editor (2001), and *Peru's international obligations on human rights*, co-author (2000 and 2002).

DIRK SALOMONS is Director of the Program for Humanitarian Affairs at the School of International Public Affairs, Columbia University. Salomons focuses on the interaction between policy and management in humanitarian operations, and has a particular interest in the demobilization and reintegration of former combatants after armed conflict. Prior to joining the SIPA faculty in 2002, Salomons served from 1997 as Managing Partner of the Praxis Group, Ltd., an international management consulting firm based in the USA and Switzerland. From 1970 until 1997, Salomons served in a wide range of management, peace-building and policy advisory functions in several organizations of the United Nations system, including FAO, UNDP, UNAIDS, UNOPS, and the UN Secretariat. Salomons received a "Kandidaats" degree from the University of Amsterdam in 1964, and subsequently obtained his "Doctoraal," also at the University of Amsterdam, in 1967. He is the author of a wide range of United Nations documents and reports on management issues and humanitarian affairs.

BENEDICTO Q. SÁNCHEZ is the program coordinator of the Broad Initiatives for Negros Development (BIND), a local NGO based in Negros Occidental, Philippines. A former top cadre of the Maoist Communist Party of the Philippines, who did administrative, theoretical, propaganda, and united front and urban mass movement work, he is now involved hands-on in integrating development, peace and human rights work in the Negrense mountains. He represents BIND in the International Partnership for the Sustainable Development of Mountain Regions, actively promoting Chapter 13 of Rio's Agenda 21. An alumnus of Columbia University's 2005 Human Rights Advocacy Program focusing on economic, social, and cultural rights, he has assisted mountain communities to attain tenurial and natural resource use rights and has participated in national and international policy conferences on sustainable mountain development. A former stage actor who performed in the Philippines and Canada in the mid-1990s, he is also a journalist and a court-annexed mediator of the Philippine Supreme Court.

JOACHIM WOLF holds the chair of public law, with an emphasis on environmental law, administrative law, and planning law, at the Ruhr University Bochum and is managing director of the Institute for International Law of Peace and Armed Conflict (IFHV), which is a centralized institution of the Ruhr University. He is also a Director of the Institute for Development Research and Development Politics at the Ruhr University. Since 1995 Professor Wolf has worked as a permanent contributor to the Encyclopedia of Public International Law edited by Professor Rudolf Bernhardt of the Max Planck Institute for Public Comparative and International Law in Heidelberg, Germany. He is also a member of the German Commission of Disaster Prevention.

SERIES EDITORS' PREFACE

This book is the second in the new series of EIUC Studies in Human Rights and Democratization. The first book in the series was *Economic Globalization and Human Rights*, edited by Wolfgang Benedek, Koen de Feyter, and Fabrizio Marrella (Cambridge University Press, 2007). The European Inter-University Centre for Human Rights and Democratization (EIUC) in Venice, Italy is the principal European human rights and democratization center supported by almost 40 renowned European universities, the European Union, the Region of Veneto, the City of Venice and other strategic partners. Professors, researchers, teachers, and experts from all over Europe and from different scientific disciplines and partner organizations are active in the Centre's programs and teaching activities. One of the main objectives of the EIUC is to create a fertile environment for research and research cooperation and the transformation of the results of that cooperation into realistic policies. The EIUC studies aim to publish the best scholarly work on Human Rights and Democratization resulting from that process of academic cooperation in the Venice Centre and its member universities. The series is not limited to lawyers' discourse alone. It encompasses the scientific disciplinary and interdisciplinary dialogue on Human Rights and Democratization as practiced in research and teaching in the Centre's activities.

This second book reflects in approach and outcome the overall aim of the EIUC series to enrich the academic discourse on Human Rights and Democratization with innovative contributions which also facilitate the transfer of academic and institutional expertise into the public sphere. The contributions to the volume are the result of two international conferences, the first held in New York, USA on December 2–4, 2005 and the second in Venice, Italy on June 1–2, 2007, both jointly organized by EIUC, the Institute for International Law of Peace and Armed Conflict (IFHV) of the Ruhr University Bochum, Germany and the School of International and Public Affairs (SIPA) of Columbia

University in New York. The introduction and contributions by a diverse interdisciplinary group of authors seek to analyze the concept of collective security in contemporary international law and politics and to assess critically the latest attempts at United Nations reform in normative and institutional terms. EIUC owes gratitude to the volume editors and the authors of the present volume. The editors have been able together with the other EIUC, IFHV, and SIPA professors to collaborate successfully in the process of multidisciplinary research on a complex and fast-changing subject, setting a significant example for future cooperation in the field. We would like to express our sincere thanks to the EIUC Board and the EIUC Assembly members who have supported the project of a new series with dedication and patience.

The series would not exist without the support of Finola O'Sullivan of Cambridge University Press. We would like to thank her for her guidance, encouragement, and assistance.

Horst Fischer
Fabrizio Marrella
Florence Benoit-Rohmer
Michael O'Flaherty

PREFACE

In late 2004, the United Nations High-Level Panel Report on Threats, Challenges, and Change proclaimed that the central challenge for the twenty-first century is to fashion a broader understanding of the notion of "collective security." In addition to various far-reaching proposals for reform within the United Nations, the panel emphasized the linkages between economic development, security, and human rights, and the imperative of collective action and cooperation between states. In a world deeply divided by differences of power, wealth, and geography, a central question in the fields of international law and organization is whether reaffirmation of the concept of collective security, and a workable consensus on the means of its realization, is possible.

This book brings together a distinguished and diverse group of scholars and practitioners from Europe and the United States to examine these questions and to consider critically the findings and recommendations of the High-Level Panel and ensuing reports. The volume does so by assessing the various responsibilities, commitments, strategies, and institutions necessary for any meaningful conception of collective security both as a matter of practice and as a normative ideal in the fast-changing spheres of international law and organization and amongst a wide array of actors and interests.

The book is organized in four parts, each part considering a contested aspect of the current UN reform process. Part I begins by considering the current impetus for and likely success of UN institutional reform and, in particular, the place of collective security in international legal theory. Part II interrogates the concept of a "threat" to collective security and asks how such threats are to be addressed (and who decides). Part III analyzes the institutional innovations and potential limitations of the newly created Peacebuilding Commission and Human Rights Council, and questions how inclusive participation will be in these new international institutions. Given current and proposed conceptions of collective security, the chapters in this part address likely responses to urgent issues such as state failure, massive human rights violations, the activities of rogue states and non-state actors as regards terrorism and proliferation, and attempts to hold perpetrators to account for violations of international law. Finally, Part IV concludes by asking how any new collective security regime may affect developments on the ground, especially as viewed from practitioner and humanitarian perspectives.

We are proud that this is the second volume in the series initiated by the European Inter-University Centre for Human Rights and Democratization in Venice, Italy. We would like to extend our warmest thanks to Finola O'Sullivan of Cambridge University Press for her wisdom, guidance and unfailing encouragement in the course of this project. Peter Danchin would also like to thank his two research assistants, Lydia Nussbaum and Michael Melick, for their tremendously hard and diligent work during the editorial process and for their assistance during the Venice conference. Gratitude is further owed to Sylvia Dove, Garth Olcese, and Nishamarie Sherry, students of the University of Maryland School of Law, for their thorough and thoughtful copy-editing.

Peter G. Danchin
Horst Fischer

ABBREVIATIONS

AJIL	*American Journal of International Law*
CAC	Convention Against Corruption
COE	Concert of Europe
CFI	Court of First Instance
DRC	Democratic Republic of Congo
EJIL	*European Journal of International Law*
ECOSOC	Economic and Social Council
EU	European Union
EC	European Community
GA	General Assembly
GDP	Gross Domestic Product
GNP	Gross National Product
HLP	High-Level Panel Report on Threats, Challenges, and Change, *A More Secure World: Our Shared Responsibility*
HRC	Human Rights Council
ICC	International Criminal Court
ICJ	International Court of Justice
IAEA	International Atomic Energy Agency
ILF	*In Larger Freedom: Towards Development, Security, and Human Rights for All*
IMF	International Monetary Fund
LON	League of Nations
MONUC	Mission in the Democratic Republic of the Congo
NATO	North Atlantic Treaty Organization
NGO	Non-Governmental Organization
NPT	Nuclear Non-proliferation Treaty
OAS	Organization of American States
OAU	Organization of African Unity
ODA	Official Development Aid
OECD	Organization for Economic Cooperation and Development
OIC	Organization of the Islamic Conference
OHCHR	Office of the High Commissioner for Human Rights
OPCW	Organization for the Prohibition of Chemical Weapons

P5	Five permanent members of the Security Council
SCR	Security Council Resolution
TOC	Transnational Organized Crime
UNSC	United Nations Security Council
UNC	United Nations Charter
UN	United Nations
UNLS	United Nations Libyan Sanctions
UNMIK	Interim UN Administration Mission in Kosovo
UPR	Universal Periodic Review
UNPC	United Nations Peacebuilding Commission
UNTAC	UN Transitional Authority in Cambodia
UNTAES	UN Transitional Administration for Eastern Slavonia, Baranja, and Western Sirmium
UNTAET	UN Transitional Administration in East Timor
UNTAG	UN Transition Assistance Group in Namibia
World Summit Outcome	World Summit Outcome document, General Assembly Sixtieth Session (September 16, 2005)
WMD	Weapons of Mass Destruction
WTO	World Trade Organization

Introduction: the new collective security

PETER G. DANCHIN AND HORST FISCHER

Whether viewed as a socio-legal project gently civilizing states away from an older politics of diplomacy, deterrence, self-help and legitimate warfare,[1] or as an institutional project establishing a collective security system premised on the rule of law,[2] the primary purpose of the United Nations today remains the maintenance of international peace and security and the abolition of the "scourge of war." During the four long decades of the Cold War, the practice of the Security Council was shaped, and often thwarted, by superpower deadlock and the paralysis of veto. In nine major interstate uses of force between 1956 and 1982, the Council played only a marginal role.[3] But with the ebbing of the Cold War in the late 1980s, and with a revitalized Council unanimously condemning

[1] The idea of the function of international law as a "gentle civilizer of national self-interest" is from George F. Kennan, *American Diplomacy 1900–1950* (Chicago: University of Chicago Press, 1985), p. 54. For Koskenniemi, this quote reveals the *cultural* and *non-instrumental* aspects of international law as opposed to *realist* and *institutionalist* views which imagine the law as an "instrument for political purposes." Martti Koskenniemi, "The Place of Law in Collective Security," 17 *Michigan Journal of International Law* 455 (1995–1996), p. 489. Thus, "[e]ngaging in the formalism of the legal argument inevitably makes public the normative basis and objectives of one's actions and assumes the actor's communal accountability for what it is one is justifying. It is the antithesis of a culture of secrecy, hegemony, dogmatism, and unaccountability." *Ibid.*, 490. See also Martti Koskenniemi, *The Gentle Civilizer of Nations: The Rise and Fall of International Law 1870–1960* (Cambridge: Cambridge University Press, 2001).

[2] This notion is well captured by the legal formalism of Hans Kelsen: "By its very nature, collective security is a legal principle, while the balance of power is a principle of political convenience." Hans Kelsen, *Collective Security Under International Law* (New Jersey: The Law Book Exchange, 1954), p. 42.

[3] For example, Mark A. Weisburd identifies nine conflicts in his analysis: (1) the attack on Egypt by France, the United Kingdom, and Israel in 1956 (the Suez Crisis); (2) Indonesia's campaign against the Netherlands' territorial possession of New Guinea in the period 1960–1962 (the West Irian campaign); (3) India's conquest of the Portuguese colony of Goa in 1961; (4) Somalia's invasion of Ethiopia in 1975; (5) Tanzania's conquest of Uganda in 1978; (6) Vietnam's invasion of Democratic Kampuchea in 1978; (7) the

Iraq's invasion of Kuwait in August 1990, the possibility of collective security arose anew.

The 1990s thus witnessed major shifts in multilateral efforts to maintain peace and security. Seemingly unnoticed, the permanent five began working together on major issues. The Security Council approved enforcement actions on a non-originalist interpretation of "threats to peace," now read to include humanitarian considerations in principally internal conflicts. Following a modest record of authorizing force and employing sanctions, the Council greatly expanded its use of Chapter VII enforcement measures.[4] And over the grave of the moribund Trusteeship Council, the UN resurrected a series of modern trusteeships in the form of transitional administrations.[5] Bolstered by announcements of the End of History, confidence in the emergence of a "new world order" reached euphoric levels.[6]

Even during this period, however, there were warnings about the dark side of the end of Cold War "stability" and the volatile effects of economic and technological globalization. While security analysts warned of a chaotic world of rogue states and terrorists intent on acquiring weapons of mass destruction, political economists warned of a central paradox: economic globalization does not strengthen the current regime of global *laissez-faire*, but may in fact work to undermine it.[7] These warnings coalesced with a shattering reality when in September 2001 a non-state

Soviet Union's campaign in Afghanistan from 1979 through 1989; (8) Iraq's invasion of Iran in 1980; and (9) Argentina's attack on the United Kingdom's Falkland Islands colony in 1982. See Mark A. Weisburd, "The War in Iraq and the Dilemma of Controlling the International Use of Force," 39 *Texas International Law Journal* 521 (2004), p. 524.

4 Before 1990, the collective use of force was authorized only twice: first in Korea in 1950 (with the USSR absent from the Council), and second in the Congo in the 1960s. Comprehensive sanctions were also only implemented twice: first against Rhodesia in 1966, and second against South Africa in 1977.

5 See generally Simon Chesterman, *You, the People: The United Nations, Transitional Administration, and State-Building* (Oxford: Oxford University Press, 2005). Chesterman analyzes the following post-1990 UN transitional administrations: Interim Administration Mission in Kosovo (UNMIK), June 1999 to present; Transitional Administration in East Timor (UNTAET), October 1999 to May 2002; Transition Assistance Group (UNTAG) in Namibia, April 1989 to March 1990; Transitional Authority in Cambodia (UNTAC), March 1992 to September 1993; and Transitional Administration for Eastern Slavonia, Baranja and Western Sirmium (UNTAES), January 1996 to January 1998.

6 Francis Fukuyama, *The End of History and the Last Man* (London: Hamish Hamilton, 1992).

7 See, e.g., John Gray, *False Dawn: The Delusions of Global Capitalism* (New York: New Press, 1998), chs. 1–4 (arguing that global capitalism, as presently constituted, is inherently unstable; that free markets are the creatures of strong states; and that a global free market is not a necessary historical development but a political project that engenders

group operating from within a failed state appeared to turn the economic and military power of globalization against itself. In an instant, the world's single remaining superpower and the UN collective security regime alike were presented with a moment of simultaneous opportunity and peril.

Perhaps as never before in history, a worldwide consensus emerged following the September 11 attacks for collective action against a perceived global threat. Within a day, the Security Council had adopted a resolution unequivocally condemning the attacks, declaring them a "threat to international peace and security" and recognizing the "inherent right of individual or collective self defense in accordance with the Charter."[8] By the end of the month, the Security Council had unanimously adopted a Chapter VII resolution directed towards combating terrorists and any states which "support, harbor, provide safe haven to, finance, supply weapons to, help recruit, or aid terrorists," and requiring all member states to cooperate in a wide range of areas – from suppressing and financing of terrorism to providing early warning, cooperating in criminal investigations, and exchanging information on possible terrorist acts.[9] Resolution 1373 quickly established a comprehensive legal framework, backed by Chapter VII enforcement power, for states to address the threat of international terrorism through mutual cooperation and coordination of their criminal justice systems.

At the same time, by October the United States had initiated actions against Al-Qaeda terrorist training camps and military installations of the Taliban regime in Afghanistan asserting its "inherent right of individual and collective self-defense." Thus was born the "Bush doctrine" – the

new varieties of nationalism and fundamentalism even as it creates new elites); Amy Chua, *World on Fire: How Exporting Free Market Democracy Breeds Ethnic Hatred and Global Instability* (New York: Random House, 2003), pp. 123–175 (discussing the political consequences of globalization and arguing that the global spread of markets and democracy is a principal, aggravating cause of group hatred and ethnic violence throughout the non-Western world); and Joseph Stiglitz, *Globalization and its Discontents* (New York: W. W. Norton, 2003), pp. 23–52 (arguing that the problem lies not with globalization *per se* but with how it has been managed through international economic institutions which help set the "rules of the game" and suggesting that not only have the WTO, World Bank and IMF served the interests of the more advanced industrialized countries, they have approached globalization from particular narrow mind-sets shaped by a particular vision of the economy and society).

8 UN S.C. Res. 1368 of September 12, 2001.

9 UN S.C. Res. 1373 of September 28, 2001. The resolution also provided for the establishment of a new "terrorism committee" of the Security Council, consisting of all members of the Council, to which all member states were required to report within ninety days on the steps they had taken to implement the resolution.

asserted right of a state to use military force in "self defense" against any state which aids, harbors, or supports international terrorists or terrorist organizations.[10] Such an assertion of vigorous unilateralism posed two dangers, however, to the Charter-based collective security system. First, it suggested that when a state was the victim of a terrorist attack it was entitled to use *military* force in response (whether in the territory of other states or on its own territory) thus encouraging resort to violence rather than legal or other diplomatic measures short of the use of force. Second, it posited responses to international terrorism in an undefined new category beyond the traditional laws of war and peace paradigms thereby shifting the normative legal framework governing the conduct of states' anti-terrorist activities, a matter with potentially far-reaching consequences for international law.[11]

It is now a matter of history that in March 2003 the US and its allies invaded Iraq, a member state of the United Nations, in order to disarm it and change the regime of Saddam Hussein. In the months leading up to the invasion, a bitter struggle ensued in the Security Council as a "coalition of the willing" sought to justify the use of force on the basis of preexisting resolutions,[12] and a majority of member states – including a clear majority in the Council itself – insisted that, in the absence of express Security Council authorization,[13] the case for war had not been established. As reflected in the 2002 National Security Strategy of the United States,[14] the terrain of struggle was seen to have intensified and

[10] For discussion on how this proposition conflicts with a number of settled principles of international law, see Peter Danchin, "Human Rights: *Jus Ad Bellum*: The New 'Bush Doctrine'" in *A Global Agenda: Issues Before the General Assembly of the United Nations* (Lanham, MD: UNA and Rowman & Littlefield Publishers), pp. 1, 4–8.

[11] The idea of a "universal humanitarian war" was prefigured in Schmitt's argument that such a war "becomes a war of annihilation (*Vernichtungskrieg*), a global civil war where the enemy does not have the dignity of a State and resistance will appear as 'the illegal and immoral resistance of a few delinquents, troublemakers, pirates and gangsters'." Koskenniemi, *Gentle Civilizer*, p. 434 (*citing* Carl Schmitt, "Die Wendung zum totalen Staat" in *Positionen und Begriffe in Kampf mit Weimar-Genf-Versailles, 1923–1939* (Berlin: Duncker & Humbolt, 1988 [1940]), p. 43 n. 45).

[12] See, in particular, UN S.C. Res. 678 of November 29, 1990, 687 of April 3, 1991, and 1441 of November 8, 2002.

[13] UN S.C. Res. 1441 of November 8, 2002 declares that breaches must be reported to the Council for assessment, and that it "decides to remain seized of the matter and to take such further steps as may be required for the implementation of the present resolution and to secure peace and security in the area."

[14] President George W. Bush, "Prevent Our Enemies From Threatening Us, Our Allies, and Our Friends with Weapons of Mass Destruction," in *National Security Strategy of the United States of America* (September 2002), pp. 13, 15.

shifted from the question of "preemptive" war in Afghanistan to the question of "preventive" war in Iraq. In this respect, the war was a challenge not merely to multilateral institutions, but to the very idea of international order and collective security: "The war split the Security Council, divided the North Atlantic Treaty Organization (NATO), and prompted the creation of a high-level panel to rethink the very idea of collective security in a world dominated by US military power."[15]

These developments shook the United Nations and leading capitals around the world. Now visible to all was the tension between two competing visions of world order. On the one hand stood the old ideal of multilateral cooperation and collective security – a form of international politics defined by legal liberalism and premised on the *Grundnorm* of sovereign equality. On the other hand stood the world's undisputed military and economic superpower projecting an imperial political morality based on a good/evil dichotomy which divided the world into a Great Power patrolling a civilized core of democratic nations against a periphery of rogue states and non-state outlaws.[16]

Unsurprisingly, the stark incompatibility between these two visions prompted calls for reform within the United Nations. These calls encompassed two dimensions of the problem: one normative, the other institutional. First, was the structure of the Charter itself, and the body of international law on which it depends, still the correct framework by which to view and assess new and emerging threats in a post-September 11 world? Second, how could the 1945 UN peace and security architecture be made to work more effectively to respond to new threats and lessen the impetus for powerful states to "go it alone"?

As the post-invasion chaos of the Iraq War unfolded, these questions prompted Kofi Annan to convene in late 2003 a "high-level panel of eminent persons" charged with assessing current threats to peace and security, evaluating existing policies and institutions, and making recommendations for strengthening the UN "so it can provide collective security for all in the twenty-first century."[17] Having already set in

[15] Simon Chesterman, "Reforming the United Nations: Legitimacy, Effectiveness and Power After Iraq," 10 *Singapore Yearbook of International Law* 1 (2006), p. 2.

[16] The vernacular of Great Powers and rogue states is from Gerry Simpson, *Great Powers and Outlaw States: Unequal Sovereigns in the International Legal Order* (Cambridge: Cambridge University Press, 2004).

[17] Note by UN Secretary-General, A/59/565, December 2, 2004, para. 3. For the report of the Panel, see High-Level Panel on Threats, Challenges, and Change, *A More Secure*

motion an ambitious development agenda,[18] this would be followed in March 2005 with the Secretary-General's own *In Larger Freedom* report which joined human rights to the preexisting security and development agendas and, in sweeping and ambitious terms, attempted to establish the agenda for the upcoming sixtieth General Assembly and planned Summit of Heads of State in September 2005.[19] The Summit, in turn, would generate a report which selectively adopted certain proposals of the High-Level Panel and Secretary-General.[20]

This most recent of efforts to vanquish war and power politics through international law and organization is the subject of the chapters of this volume. The overarching questions the authors address are whether there is a compelling argument for a new collective security agenda, whether the eminent ones dreamed the right dreams and saw the right nightmares, and whether normatively and institutionally we are in fact moving towards a new collective security paradigm.

Structure of the volume

The book is organized in four parts, each part considering a contested element in the UN reform process. Part I addresses the impetus for and likely future success of institutional reform efforts and considers the place of international law in competing conceptions of collective security. Part II interrogates the concept of a "threat" to collective security and asks how such threats are to be addressed (and who decides). This analysis includes the questions of massive and systematic violations of human rights and so-called "nonmilitary" threats in areas such as the environment, disease, and technology. Part III analyzes the collective security innovations and potential limitations of the newly created Peacebuilding Commission and Human Rights Council, and asks how inclusive participation is in these new international institutions. Given

World: Our Shared Responsibility (Report of the High-Level Panel on Threats, Challenges, and Change), December 1, 2004, UN Doc A/59/565 (hereinafter High-Level Panel).

18 See Investing in Development: A Practical Plan to Achieve the Millennium Development Goals (Report of the UN Millennium Project to the Secretary-General), January 17, 2005, online: Millennium Project: www.unmillenniumproject.org/reports.

19 Kofi Annan, *In Larger Freedom: Towards Security, Development, and Human Rights for All*, UN Doc. A/59/2005 of March 21, 2005, online: www.un.org/largerfreedom (hereinafter *In Larger Freedom*).

20 2005 World Summit Outcome document, General Assembly Sixtieth Session, UN Doc. A/Res/60/1 of September 16, 2005, online: http://un.org/summit2005 (hereinafter World Summit Outcome).

current and proposed conceptions of collective security, each chapter in this part then addresses the likely responses to urgent issues such as state failure, massive human rights violations, the activities of rogue states and non-state actors as regards terrorism and weapons proliferation, and attempts to hold perpetrators to account for violations of international law. Finally, Part IV concludes by asking how any new collective security regime will relate to and influence developments on the ground as viewed from the perspectives of humanitarian practitioners and actors.

Law and politics in United Nations reform

In September 2003, following the United States' invasion of Iraq earlier that year, Kofi Annan forcefully addressed the UN General Assembly and argued that the international community had come to a "fork in the road":

> This may be a moment no less decisive than 1945 itself, when the United Nations was founded. At that time, a group of far-sighted leaders, led and inspired by President Franklin D. Roosevelt, were determined to make the second half of the twentieth century different from the first half. They saw that the human race had only one world to live in, and that unless it managed its affairs prudently, all human beings may perish. So they drew up rules to govern international behavior, and founded a network of institutions, with the United Nations at its centre, in which the peoples of the world could work together for the common good.

Annan thus suggested that we "face a decisive moment, in particular for the aspiration set out in the Charter to provide collective security for all." While pointing to deep divisions among states on the nature of threats to peace and security and the appropriateness of the use of force, he challenged member states to make the UN more effective.[21]

This is perhaps unsurprising. Major reforms in the international system have been driven historically by crisis, whether the creation of a League of Nations after the First World War or the founding of a United Nations after the Second World War.[22] But what kind of moment was

[21] Kofi Annan, "Secretary-General's Address to the General Assembly" (New York, September 23, 2003), online: www.un.org/apps/sg/sgstats.asp?nid=517.

[22] Developments in international humanitarian law have often occurred at similar crisis points. The Geneva Conventions of 1949, for example, were signed in the aftermath of the Second World War. In 1977, in the wake of the Vietnam War, the two additional protocols to the Geneva Conventions were added. Also, during the US Civil War, the US War Department instituted the Lieber Code.

this exactly? What kind of political space, consensus, and will was there among states for major changes to the international security architecture? What is now evident is that, rather than being the kind of moment following a catastrophe of sufficient gravity as to open political space for normative and institutional reformation, this reform cycle has been driven primarily by concerns about the role of the world's single superpower in the organization and, conversely, by US concerns regarding how best to protect and project its strategic and political interests.

To some at least, the post-Iraq invasion period presented the third great opportunity after the creation of the League and UN itself to get the "international order right." Gareth Evans, for example, the former Australian Foreign Minister and himself an eminent one, suggested that if the reform attempts failed this time "we might just be putting the same death sentence on the United Nations as was put upon the League of Nations by the utter failure of political statesmanship in the 1930s."[23] But to others, calls for radical changes were simply unrealistic in the wake of six decades of largely frustrated reform efforts. Professor Edward Luck, for example, has suggested that the organization has survived because of its capacity to make corrections and take on new agendas as the needs and values of its member states shift. It has adopted formal reforms, however, with great reluctance.[24] Furthermore, the Secretary-General's call for reform represented a serious misdiagnosis of the problems facing the UN.[25]

Still for others, especially those in the American foreign policy establishment, the solution was to be found elsewhere in new forms of "competitive multilateralism." Ruth Wedgwood thus argued that if the UN cannot reform, the US should rely more on regional organizations

[23] Gareth Evans, *A Make or Break Year for the UN: Reforming the 60 Year Old*, Lecture at Centre for International Studies, Dublin City University (June 24, 2005).

[24] Edward C. Luck, "How Not to Reform the United Nations," *Global Governance* 11 (2005), pp. 412–13. For Luck, the process "has tested the member states' commitment to the organization and found it to be fundamentally sound, if as shallow and self-serving as ever." Noting that member states continue to entrust the UN to take on more and more peacekeeping, humanitarian, and counter-terrorism missions, Mats Berdal has similarly observed that it is "clear that the [High-Level] Panel report firmly rejects the suggestion that the UN may be facing a fork in the road." See Mats Berdal, "The United Nations at 60: A New San Francisco Moment?," *Survival* 47 (Autumn 2005), pp. 7–31.

[25] For Luck, institutional reform will not address the underlying political difficulties confronting the UN. Expanding Security Council membership to achieve greater legitimacy, for example, would not increase and almost certainly would decrease the Council's effectiveness. Would an enlarged Council have agreed on what action to take in Iraq or other divisive issues? See Luck, "How Not to Reform the United Nations," p. 409.

that can deliver where the UN cannot or will not. As one example she advocated abandoning the search for consensus with "political thugs" at the UN Commission on Human Rights, and the provision of more US support to regional human rights organizations and groups. In this way, the stark choice between "going it alone or going to the United Nations" could be avoided.[26]

What is clear, however, is that anxiety resulting from US ambivalence over, and indeed outright hostility toward, the UN undergirded many of the calls for change.[27] This is visible in the Secretary-General's *In Larger Freedom* report which targets Washington overtly by invoking Roosevelt's "Four Freedoms" and echoing FDR's call for leaders to have "the courage to fulfill [their] responsibilities in an admittedly imperfect world."[28] The same sentiment literally bursts out of a controversial speech delivered in mid-2006 by the UN Deputy Secretary-General, Mark Malloch Brown, warning that without US leadership the UN's ability to respond to the increasing challenges the world is facing was weakened, and vice versa.[29]

[26] See Ruth Wedgwood, "Give the United Nations a Little Competition," *New York Times*, December 5, 2005. According to Wedgwood, the US should, however, continue to support the UN because it "remains the only all-inclusive political organization around" and because, as a member of the Security Council, "America enjoys prerogatives ... that would be hard to gain again." See also Ruth Wedgwood, "A Run for the Money: Spin-Offs, Rivals and UN Reform," *The National Interest* (Winter 2005/06).

[27] At the same time as unilaterally projecting increased military power, the US has repudiated a series of widely supported conventions and has rejected a long list of new treaties. These include the Kyoto Protocol on global warming, the ABM treaty on missile defence and the militarization of space, the Biological Weapons Convention prohibiting developing biological weapons, the Small Arms Convention, and the Land Mines Convention to name only the most prominent, while also seeking to exempt itself from, and indeed actively to undermine, the Rome Statute of the International Criminal Court.

[28] F. D. Roosevelt, "Annual Address to Congress: The 'Four Freedoms'" (Washington D.C., January 6, 1941), online: www.fdrlibrary.marist.edu/od4frees.html. Specifically in its sections on development and security, *In Larger Freedom* adopts Roosevelt's calls for freedom from want and from fear. It also combines Roosevelt's two other freedoms (freedom of speech and thought, and of worship) into a broader concept of freedom to live in dignity.

[29] Mark Malloch Brown, "Power and Super-Power: Global Leadership in the Twenty-First Century," speech delivered at the Century Foundation and Center for American Progress, June 6, 2006. As a result of constant American calls for "management reform," there is currently "a perception among many otherwise quite moderate countries that anything the US supports must have a secret agenda aimed at either subordinating multilateral processes to Washington's ends or weakening the institution, and therefore ... should be opposed without any real discussion of whether they make sense or not."

What is perhaps more curious, however, is that while the Panel's imagined collective security consensus is justified by the emergence of new threats, its report strongly reaffirms the preexisting multilateral framework and normative structure. It is also important to note that most of the recommendations the Panel *did* make were either substantially watered down through the intergovernmental process, or did not make it at all into the 2005 World Summit Outcome document. This tripartite sequence of idealistic Panel recommendations, policy endorsement or repackaging by the Secretary-General, and political rejection at the World Summit, can be traced in a number of areas.

Both the Panel Report and *In Larger Freedom* discuss in some detail the connections between economic and social issues on the one hand, and security on the other. Under the rubric of "freedom from want," for example, the Secretary-General discusses expansively the Millennium Development Goals (MDGs), the target of 0.7 percent of gross national income for developed states in official development assistance by 2015, and the need for a new round of multilateral trade negotiations. This builds on the Panel's endorsement of the MDGs and its call (at least indirectly) for a reduction in agricultural subsidies by the developed countries.[30] After fierce resistance by the US, the 2005 World Summit Outcome document finally did endorse the MDG goals but set no new commitments toward reaching the 0.7 percent target.

The Panel also looked critically at the role of the UN in ending civil conflicts, and in particular its failure to halt ethnic cleansing and genocide. In order to prevent and minimize future conflicts, the Panel broadly endorsed the use of the International Criminal Court (ICC) by the Security Council, suggested mechanisms to better govern the management of natural resources for countries emerging from or at risk of conflict, and called for better controls on small arms. The Summit Outcome document, however, makes no reference to the ICC, makes no connection between natural resource extraction and conflict, and fails to endorse the arms control recommendations of the Panel.

But perhaps the greatest disappointment of the Summit was its failure to reach agreement on disarmament and non-proliferation of weapons of mass destruction (WMD), despite the unambiguous call from both the Panel and Secretary-General for nuclear-weapons states to honor their obligations under the Non-Proliferation Treaty and to move

[30] High-Level Panel, para. 62.

towards disarmament.[31] This omission was due mainly to US opposition to the linking of non-proliferation to disarmament. The Summit also failed to establish a definition of terrorism while calling plaintively for a comprehensive terrorism convention.[32] On the nexus between WMD and terrorism then, the Summit Outcome document – influenced by the politics surrounding the "global war on terrorism" – focused almost entirely on the question of weapons falling into the wrong hands rather than their continued presence in and threatened use by those with the right hands.[33]

In addition to these normative questions, the Panel made several institutional reform proposals which, again, met with tepid reception at the Summit. The first involved the reshaping of the Economic and Social Council (ECOSOC)'s agenda away from administration and program coordination toward an agenda built around the Millennium Declaration.[34] The Outcome Document, however, simply reaffirmed ECOSOC's role "as a principal body for coordination, policy review, policy dialogue and recommendations on issues of economic and social development, as well as for implementation of the international development goals."[35]

The second involved reforms to the UN General Assembly. Here the Panel reached the conclusion that an "unwieldy and static agenda" had

[31] Kofi Annan labeled this omission at the time a "disgrace." See W. Hoge, "UN Adopts Modest Goals on Reforms and Poverty," *New York Times*, September 14, 2005.

[32] Approximately 109 different definitions of terrorism have been used in official documents between 1936 and 1983. See Alex Schmid, *Political Terrorism: A Research Guide to Concepts, Theories, Databases and Literature* (New Brunswick, New Jersey: Elsevier Science Ltd., 1983). Two issues, in particular, have divided states. The first is the volatile issue of the distinction between "terrorists" and "freedom fighters." The Organization of the Islamic Conference (OIC), for example, has stressed the need to distinguish terrorism from a people's struggle for "national liberation … and the elimination of foreign occupation and colonial hegemony as well as for regaining the right of self-determination." See OIC, Ninth Summit Conference (Qatar, 2000), Doha Declaration. Second is the highly political issue of the distinction between "state terrorism" (or terrorism promoted or tolerated by states) and "terrorism emanating from irregular armed groups and other groups and organizations" which is directed against the state. See UN Doc. E/CN.4/Sub.2/1997/SR.33, para. 42. As Rosand notes, the "General Assembly's inability to reach agreement on a definition of terrorism after more than three decades of discussions – with the unfortunate continuing relevance of the phrase 'one man's terrorist is another man's freedom fighter' – has limited the impact of its counterterrorism efforts." Eric Rosand, "Global Terrorism: Multilateral Responses to an Extraordinary Threat," *International Peace Academy* (April 2007), p. 13. See further Chapter 10 of this volume.

[33] The Panel also discussed means to combat transnational organized crime under the rubric of human and state security. While broadly endorsed at the Summit, the Panel's recommendations did not generate any binding obligations on states.

[34] High-Level Panel, paras. 275–279. [35] *Ibid.*, para. 155.

led to repetitive debates and proposed introducing smaller, more focused committees to sharpen and improve resolutions brought to the Assembly. While the Secretary-General tentatively embraced these ideas, the Summit rejected them and merely reaffirmed the position of the Assembly as the chief deliberative body of the UN system.[36]

Finally, the Panel proposed two bold institutional initiatives: a new Human Rights Council standing at the same level as the Security Council and ECOSOC to replace the discredited Commission on Human Rights; and the establishment of a new Peacebuilding Commission. The Summit Outcome document broadly endorsed the idea of a new Human Rights Council but left the details to be worked out at the sixtieth session of the General Assembly. Negotiations then began in earnest among states, with the criteria for membership being the central issue and with little debate regarding what the Council would actually do once created. Similarly, the Outcome Document endorsed the Panel's vision of a Peacebuilding Commission to "marshal and sustain" the efforts of the international community in post-conflict peacebuilding over whatever period may be necessary to decrease the odds that a country will relapse into conflict.[37] This constituted official recognition that no existing international institutions are well organized for this task and that what is needed is a "single intergovernmental organ dedicated to peacebuilding, empowered to monitor and pay close attention to countries at risk, ensure concerted actions by donors, agencies, programmes and financial institutions, and mobilize financial resources for sustainable peace."[38]

Each of the chapters in Part I discusses different aspects of these latest attempts at United Nations reform.[39] The first chapter by Peter Danchin provides an introduction to the analytical and historical aspects of the concept of collective security in international law. Taking the examples of Italy's invasion of Ethiopia in 1935 during the League of Nations and the complaint brought by Hyderabad against India at the very inception of the United Nations in 1948, the chapter traces the complex dialectics of normativity and concreteness in debates concerning collective security. Danchin observes that, mirroring the normative and institutional dilemmas underlying the two cases of Ethiopia and Hyderabad, the questions of "external threats" (or the threat or use of force between

[36] *Ibid.*, paras. 149–150. [37] *Ibid.*, para. 224. [38] *Ibid.*, para. 225.

[39] For a useful discussion and critique of the entire reform process, see Ramesh Thakur, *The United Nations, Peace and Security: From Collective Responsibility to Responsibility to Protect* (Cambridge: Cambridge University Press, 2006).

states) and "internal threats" (or what today is referred to as the "responsibility to protect") were the two most controversial issues in the post-2004 UN reform process. The High-Level Panel's recommendations in this respect should be seen as responses to a breakdown beginning in the early 1990s of the pragmatic compromise lying at the heart of the UN Charter. This can be seen in two directions: first, as a result of an instrumental *autonomy* argument which asserts that the sovereign right of self-defense includes the right to carry out preemptive strikes; and second, as a result of an instrumental *communitarian* argument which views sovereignty as an anachronistic obstacle to humanitarian objectives and thus outweighed by the need to protect fundamental human rights. In order to counter these two trends, the *non-instrumental* or *cultural* aspects of international law are indispensable for any robust account of collective security in relations between states.

In Chapter 2, Jan Klabbers argues that the responsibility to maintain or restore international peace is best vested in an institution rather than a single state in order to avoid abuses of power and to guarantee fairness in decision-making processes. According to Klabbers, when an institution fails to function as planned, the proposed cure is inevitably to change the institution's blueprint rather than to be critical of its actual functioning. Institutional reform, however, is an ambivalent process torn as it is between the idea of institutions as purposive, technical, managerial entities on the one hand (*universitas*) and as non-purposive, debating clubs (*societas*) on the other. For Klabbers, the UN is well-equipped to carry out its responsibility to maintain international peace and security and reform attempts, while ostensibly about improving the UN's functioning, are more often than not an emanation of politics – even to the point where reform processes in fact substitute for real decision-making. The chapter thus analyzes UN reform as a manifestation of the dual ambivalence of *universitas* versus *societas* on the one hand and instrumental versus political rationality on the other. Klabbers' analysis in this way seeks to discern whether UN reform has become more a symbolic event, aimed to portray an image of rationalization, instead of actually creating significant substantive change.

Chapter 3 by Lauri Mälksoo turns to the vexed issue of Security Council reform. Recalling Hans Kelsen's prophetic critique in 1950 of the Security Council, Mälksoo sets out the various criticisms of the High-Level Panel today – regarding, in particular, the Council's politicized agenda, its tendency to act according to double standards, and its hopeless inaction in the face of genocide and other grave threats to human security. Noting, like Danchin, the steady breakdown of the UN collective security system since the 1990s and especially since NATO's intervention into Kosovo in 1999, the chapter proceeds to evaluate the Panel's criticisms and its recommendations for institutional reform. Mälksoo concludes by arguing that the Panel focuses too heavily on issues of effectiveness while overlooking the more fundamental issues of the Council's structure (e.g. the veto power) and its lack of legitimacy, both products of the paradox lying at the core of the United Nations itself: "that in the age of democracy it is run by an oligarchy."

Defining "threats" to collective security

The most important claim in the High-Level Panel Report is that the central challenge for the twenty-first century is to fashion a broader understanding of what collective security means and of "all the responsibilities, commitments, strategies and institutions that come with it if a collective security system is to be effective, efficient and equitable." Pivotal to this broader understanding is a substantively expanded notion of what constitutes a "threat." The Panel's Report proposes a definition of threats as "any event or process that leads to large-scale death or lessening of life chances and undermines states as the basic unit of the international system."[40] The Report then identifies six "clusters of threats" organized as follows: (1) economic and social threats including poverty, infectious disease, and environmental degradation; (2) interstate conflict; (3) internal conflict such as civil war, genocide, and other large-scale atrocities; (4) weapons of mass destruction, including nuclear, radiological, chemical, and biological weapons; (5) terrorism; and (6) transnational organized crime.[41] The discussion that follows sets out briefly the Panel's vision of the scope and content of each of these clusters of threat.

1. *Economic and Social Threats.* Over fifty-four UN member states have seen average per capita income decline since 1990 with women and youth disproportionately affected by increased poverty.[42] When accompanied by ethnic or regional inequalities, poverty and its accomplices (a booming youth population, urbanization, and unemployment) foster grievances that fuel civil violence.[43] The "shockingly

[40] High-Level Panel. [41] *Ibid.*

[42] *Ibid.*, para. 44. Many donor countries still currently fall short of the 0.7 percent gross national product (GNP) target for official development assistance. *Ibid.*, para. 60.

[43] *Ibid.*, para. 45.

slow" and "shamefully ill-resourced" international response to HIV/AIDS has allowed the pandemic to continue and render states, especially those on the African continent, weakened by the reduced life-expectancy of their adult populations and an upsurge in orphaned children.[44] Increased food consumption by industrial countries, coupled with the loss of arable land, water scarcity, over-fishing, and deforestation, has aggravated food insecurity and led to greater competition for already scarce resources.[45] Furthermore, the environmental degradation resulting from attempts to feed a growing world population has enhanced the destructive potential of natural disasters, in some cases hastening their occurrence.[46]

2. *Interstate Conflict.* The Panel points to unresolved disputes between states in South Asia, North-East Asia and the Middle East as threats to international peace and security on two counts. First, these states are capable of using nuclear, biological, and chemical weapons against each other. Second, such interstate rivalry exacerbates civil conflicts also occurring in those regions.[47] Sanctions have failed to check interstate conflict because of ineffective targeting and weak enforcement of sanctions by the Security Council when such sanctions ran counter to the strategic interests of powerful states.[48]
3. *Internal State Conflict.* The vast majority of United Nations peace and security operations involve peacemaking, peacekeeping, and post-conflict peacebuilding in states undergoing civil war. However, interests of powerful states have disrupted sanctions enforcement and interfered with halting ethnic cleansing and genocide, which the Panel terms "the biggest failures of the United Nations in civil violence."[49]

[44] *Ibid.*, paras. 48, 49. "Although international resources devoted to meeting the challenge of HIV/AIDS have increased from about $250 million in 1996 to about $2.8 billion in 2002, more than $10 billion annually is needed to stem the pandemic." *Ibid.*, para. 64.

[45] *Ibid.*, para. 52.

[46] *Ibid.*, paras. 52, 53. The Panel notes that "entry into force of the Kyoto Protocol after ratification by the Russian Federation is a positive development ... yet problems remain ... Developing countries ... have been opposed to accepting any binding emission caps, which they perceive to be impediments to economic growth. Industrialized nations are likely to be more resistant to accepting costly reductions without increased developing-country participation." *Ibid.*, para. 72.

[47] *Ibid.*, para. 74. The Panel highlights the war and ongoing instability in Iraq and Palestine, noting that these conflicts "have fuelled extremism in parts of the Muslim world and the West." *Ibid.*, para. 75.

[48] *Ibid.*, para. 79.

[49] "The biggest failures of the United Nations in civil violence have been in halting ethnic cleansing and genocide. In Rwanda, Secretariat officials failed to provide the Security

4. *Weapons of Mass Destruction.* Nuclear weapons, radiological weapons, and chemical and biological weapons each pose a different set of threats to collective security. Accidental or deliberate use of nuclear weapons by a state or non-state actor threatens international peace and security because of the weapons' power to create human casualties and economic dislocation on a catastrophic scale.[50] In addition to their potential use, the Panel identifies the erosion of the legal and normative constraints of the non-proliferation regime, i.e. the International Atomic Energy Agency (IAEA) and the Non-Proliferation of Nuclear Weapons Treaty (NPT), as threats. Were this regime to collapse, the result could be a "cascade of proliferation," with countries entering into arms races and placing at risk the lives of millions.[51] While the immediate destructive effect of radiological weapons, or "dirty bombs," may be less than nuclear weapons, radiological weapons are equally capable of causing economic damage because they prompt public alarm and necessitate evacuation and decontamination of affected areas. Furthermore, radiological weapons are more likely to be used because of the ubiquity of radiological materials and crude requirements for detonating such a device.[52] Chemical and biological weapons can inflict mass casualties in a single attack and cause deliberate outbreaks of infectious disease that could ultimately prove more lethal than nuclear detonation.[53]
5. *Terrorism.* While global terrorism networks are identified as threats, the precise nature and definition of that threat remains unsettled.[54] The Panel describes terrorism in terms only of what it targets:

Council with early warning of extremist plans to kill thousands of Tutsis and moderate Hutus. When the genocide started, troop contributors withdrew peacekeepers, and the Security Council, bowing to United States pressure, failed to respond. In Bosnia and Herzegovina, United Nations peacekeeping and the protection of humanitarian aid became a substitute for political and military action to stop ethnic cleansing and genocide. In Kosovo, paralysis in the Security Council led the North Atlantic Treaty Organization (NATO) to bypass the United Nations. Only in one instance in the 1990s – in East Timor – did the Security Council, urged on by the Secretary-General, work together with national Governments and regional actors to apply concerted pressure swiftly to halt large-scale killing." *Ibid.*, para. 87.

50 *Ibid.*, para. 107. 51 *Ibid.*, paras. 109–112. 52 *Ibid.*, para. 113.

53 "Chemical agents are widespread and relatively easy to acquire and weaponize. There are almost 6,000 industrial chemical facilities worldwide, posing potential targets and opportunities for the acquisition of materials … There are countless fermentation, medical and research facilities equipped to produce biological agents. Meanwhile, the biological toxin ricin has been discovered in several terrorist workshops. Unlike anthrax, which can be treated by antibiotics, ricin has no antidote and is lethal to humans in quantities smaller than the size of a pinhead." *Ibid.*, paras. 114, 115.

54 The Panel Report does not provide a definition of terrorism. Instead it urges the General Assembly to form a consensus definition and rapidly complete negotiations on a comprehensive convention on terrorism. *Ibid.*, para. 163.

> Terrorism attacks the values that lie at the heart of the Charter of the United Nations: respect for human rights; the rule of law; rules of war that protect civilians; tolerance among peoples and nations; and the peaceful resolution of conflict. Terrorism flourishes in environments of despair, humiliation, poverty, political oppression, extremism and human rights abuse; it also flourishes in contexts of regional conflict and foreign occupation; and it profits from weak state capacity to maintain law and order.[55]

6. *Transnational Organized Crime.* This type of criminal activity erodes human security and states' primary obligation to provide for law and order. The persistence of organized crime, entrenched corruption, and the use of violence to protect criminal activities threatens state authority by undermining state weapons control and thwarting the rule of law.[56] Furthermore, the lucrative business of drug-trafficking fuels the spread of HIV/AIDS via intravenous drug use.

For the Panel, this substantively expanded notion of threats generates three basic conclusions or "pillars" upon which the case for a new security consensus rests. First, the interconnectedness of today's threats – which recognize no national boundaries – necessitates a collective response, not only at the global and regional levels, but also at the national level. Second, "no State, no matter how powerful, can by its own efforts alone make itself invulnerable to today's threats." And third, "it cannot be assumed that every State will always be able, or willing, to meet its responsibility to protect its own peoples and not to harm its neighbors."[57]

In emphasizing the interconnectedness and internal/external aspects of threats, the Panel thus sought to overcome the artificial dichotomy between Northern concerns regarding so-called "hard" threats of armed conflict and terrorism, and Southern concerns regarding so-called "soft" threats of poverty, disease, and environmental degradation. As David Hannay notes, the correlation between poverty and insecurity literally "leaps at you from the charts in the Panel's report."[58] Furthermore, in

55 *Ibid.*, para. 145.

56 *Ibid.*, para. 169. It is estimated that criminal organizations gain $300 to $500 billion annually from narcotics trafficking, their single largest source of income. In some regions, the huge profits generated through drug activity even rival some countries' GDP. The Panel points to the nexus between the financing of terrorist groups and profits from drug-trafficking, citing Afghanistan as the most visible example. *Ibid.*, para. 166.

57 *Ibid.*, synopsis.

58 David Hannay, "'A More Secure World: Our Shared Responsibility,' Report of the UN Secretary-General's High-Level Panel on Threats, Challenges, and Change," in Felix

areas such as terrorism and the proliferation of WMDs, there will always be genuine and difficult policy choices for states to make between unilateral and multilateral approaches. A "crude juxtaposition" conceals more than it reveals and the most effective response in many cases is "both/and" not "either/or."[59]

At the same time, the Panel was careful to observe that there is a great diversity of perceptions among states regarding the relative severity and imminence of threats thus recognizing that "differences of power, wealth and geography ... determine what we perceive as the gravest threats to our survival and well-being" and that such "differences of focus lead us to dismiss what others perceive as the gravest of all threats to their survival."[60] This recognition of different perceptions existing between often very differently situated states raises the conceptual question of a *hierarchy* of threats. To some, the reform process opened the possibility of a "grand bargain" between North and South: in order to secure greater support and cooperation for its counter-terrorism and counter-proliferation agenda, the wealthy Northern states could agree to provide countries in the South with greater development assistance and reform of agricultural subsidies. While the Panel ultimately decided not to embrace the grand bargain idea, and recognized instead the disparate ways in which different stakeholders perceive threats, both the Panel Report and *In Larger Freedom* bear "traces of this philosophy."[61]

In thinking about the fit between cause and cure in diagnosing threats to collective security, Maxwell Chibundu considers in Chapter 4 how to confront the complex and intertwined interests and institutions that make up the contemporary international system. The relationship between diagnosis and prescription is most important because of the real possibility that even the best-intentioned prescriptions create unintended consequences which may themselves constitute threats to the international order. Chibundu is critical, in particular, not only of the High-Level Panel's expanded definition of collective security, but also its recommendations regarding the increased use of coercive

Dodds and Tim Pippard (eds.), *Human and Environmental Security: An Agenda for Change* (London: Earthscan, 2005), p. 9.

59 State intelligence and law-enforcement capabilities are essential for any effective response and cannot be replaced. However, multilateral organizations have wider scope and can organize cooperation on a wide-ranging basis to deal with threats that do not respect national boundaries that have "seized on globalization as an ally in the pursuit of their objectives." What is needed then is a "judicious blend" between the national and the international. *Ibid.*, p. 10.

60 *Ibid.* 61 Chesterman, "Reforming the United Nations," p. 7.

but nonmilitaristic responses to threats (i.e. collective economic sanctions) which seek to preserve order through ostracism rather than inclusion.[62] He suggests instead that coexistence rather than assimilation, and cooperation and collaboration rather than coercion, should be the operational norms of collective security. Given that the point and effect of collective security under Chapter VII of the UN Charter is to indicate instances in which state sovereignty must yield involuntarily to assertions of international power, Chibundu's analysis points towards a less all-encompassing and more concrete definition of collective security and less, rather than more, centralization in the international system.

Following Chibundu's elegant conceptual analysis, the next two chapters address two of the major "new threats" identified by the High-Level Panel. In Chapter 5, George Andreopoulos addresses the notion of "Responsibility to Protect" and analyzes the threat emanating from massive and systematic violations of human rights. His chapter first examines the nature of this threat in the context of a transition from the older idea of "humanitarian intervention" to the more recent notion of responsibility to protect. Second, he examines some of the similarities between "humanitarian intervention" on the one hand and the "war on terror" on the other, and explores some of the key issues addressed in these debates. Finally, Andreopoulos examines the implications of the Responsibility to Protect for the viability of collective security itself.

In Chapter 6, Joachim Wolf then discusses the challenges that the High-Level Panel's inclusion of nonmilitary threats to collective security may pose for the UN Security Council. The definition of a "threat to collective security" under the UN Charter has historically referred only to threats that can be responded to with force and under the direction of a "Commander in Chief" Security Council. The reform movement's addition of new substantive criteria to the definition of threat creates a number of challenges. First, the new definition is imprecise – it refers to *any* process or event that poses a challenge to the existing system and does not require the source of that threat to be an identifiable entity. Second, broadening the definition of threat to include nonmilitary situations calls into question the Security Council's authority as the sole responder to threats. The Council as it currently exists is unprepared to respond to nonmilitary threats and an expansion of its power to enable it to have the competency to respond to such nonmilitary threats may well not be in the best interests of the United Nations.

[62] The same line of argument is pursued and further developed by J. Farrall in Chapter 9.

Prevention and responses

The final section of the Secretary-General's directive instructed the Panel to make recommendations for strengthening the UN collective security system for the 21st century. The Panel Report thus responded to each of the six clusters of threats by suggesting various institutional and normative reforms,[63] as follows.

1. *Economic and Social Threats.* To address the threats of poverty, infectious disease, and environmental degradation the Panel called upon wealthier member states to fulfill their pledges to meet the Millennium Development Goals.[64] Donor countries need to provide greater debt relief and improved access to global markets by lowering agricultural subsidies at home. Furthermore, these wealthier member states should collaborate in a new global initiative to rebuild local and national public health systems throughout the developing world.[65] The Panel noted the gap between the promise of the Kyoto Protocol and its performance, placing responsibility for the gap on the shoulders of both industrial nations and developing countries that lack the political will to affect change.[66] The Panel urged all states to re-engage on the pressing problem of global warming and to discuss long-term strategies for reducing global warming beyond 2012, the expiration of the Kyoto Protocol. As previously noted, while the Panel endorsed the MDGs and indirectly called for a reduction in agricultural subsidies by the developed countries,[67] the 2005 Summit Outcome document set no new commitments to reaching the 0.7 percent target.

[63] For an early comprehensive discussion of these suggested reforms, see *Reforming the United Nations for Peace and Security*, Proceedings of the Workshop to Analyze the Report of the High-level Panel on Threats, Challenges, and Change, Yale Center for the Study of Globalization (New Haven: Connecticut, March 2005).

[64] High-Level Panel, para. 60. During the debates leading up to the World Summit in October 2005, US Ambassador John Bolton sought to remove any reference to the Millennium Development Goals from the Outcome Document. See W. Hoge, "Clash By Diplomats at UN over Reform Bares Divisions," *New York Times*, September 10, 2005.

[65] High-Level Panel, paras. 63, 67.

[66] "The United States, which accounts for about one quarter of world emissions of greenhouse gases, refuses to ratify the Protocol. At the same time, developing countries, which now account for almost half of today's net emissions of greenhouse gases (but only one tenth of per capita emissions), have been opposed to accepting any binding emission caps, which they perceive to be impediments to economic growth." *Ibid.*, para. 72.

[67] *Ibid.*, para. 62.

2. *Interstate and Internal Conflict.* The Panel recommended a four-pronged regulatory and normative approach to preventing the use of force between and within states. First, the Panel stated that the Security Council needed to make greater use of the International Criminal Court (ICC) by referring all cases of crimes against humanity and violations of the laws of war to the Court.[68] Second, further legal mechanisms are required to regulate natural resources to prevent states from going to war over them.[69] Third, the UN should work closely with regional organizations like the Organization of American States (OAS) and the African Union (AU) that have done significant work to set normative standards for conflict prevention.[70] And fourth, member states must comply with the UN's own Register of Conventional Arms by reporting on the sale and purchase of conventional weapons and existing weapons holdings, as well as defense postures, policies, and doctrines.[71] As noted above, the Summit Outcome document made no reference to the ICC, made no connection between natural resource extraction and conflict, and failed to endorse the arms control recommendations of the Panel.

The difficult question of the relationship between the Security Council and the International Criminal Court is taken up by Carmen Márquez Carrasco in Chapter 11. Opening her analysis with the tension between the Council's objective of maintaining peace and the ICC's goal of obtaining justice, Carrasco explores the origin of the problem by tracing the evolution of the institutions' relationship. The chapter examines, in particular, the conflicting logics of coordination and subordination which underlie this relationship. First, Carrasco reveals how the Council's power to refer cases to the ICC and its role in ensuring state cooperation with the Court demonstrate attempts to coordinate the institutions' respective objectives. Second, she proceeds to describe how the Council's power of deferral and recent proposals regarding both institutions' roles in determining the crime of aggression tend to prioritize the Council's pursuit of peace over the objectives of the ICC. Carrasco concludes with a few preliminary assessments of these conflicting conceptions of

68 *Ibid.*, para. 90.

69 E.g., the efforts to stem the illicit diamond trade contributed to ending the civil wars in Sierra Leone and Angola. *Ibid.*, para. 91.

70 Both the OAS and the AU agree on the need to protect elected governments from coups. *Ibid.*, para. 94.

71 *Ibid.*, para. 97.

the relationship in the context of the UN collective security system. She particularly notes the uneasy coordination of these objectives in practice and the difficulties confronting the Court as its goal is subordinated to that of the Council. Carrasco does emphasize, however, the important role that member states and the General Assembly should play in supporting and controlling each institution, thereby ensuring the furtherance of both peace and justice regardless of the strained relationship between the Council and the ICC.

3. *Weapons of Mass Destruction*. Proposed responses to the threat of nuclear, radiological, chemical, and biological weapons address the demand and supply of weapons production and require greater action from international organizations. The Panel recommended incorporating confidence-building measures and steps towards disarmament into negotiations to resolve regional conflicts, especially in the Middle East and South Asia, with the ultimate goal of establishing nuclear-weapon-free zones similar to those established for Latin America and the Caribbean, Africa, the South Pacific, and South-East Asia.[72] The Security Council should support the Non-Proliferation Treaty by explicitly pledging "to take collective action in response to a nuclear attack or the threat of such attack on a non-nuclear-weapon State."[73] International organizations such as the International Atomic Energy Agency (IAEA) and the Organization for the Prohibition of Chemical Weapons (OPCW) should also have greater powers to investigate non-compliance with international non-proliferation and safeguards standards and the Security Council needs to be prepared to act in cases of serious concern over non-compliance with those standards.[74]

[72] *Ibid.*, paras. 123, 124. The US staunchly opposed equating disarmament with non-proliferation and introduced provisions to remove language placing the terms side by side. This stance was an apparent rejection of the NPT obligations for nuclear powers to disarm themselves. See Chesterman, "Reforming the United Nations," p. 12.

[73] High-Level Panel, para. 122.

[74] *Ibid.*, para. 129. One of the unexpected outcomes of the 2003 Iraq War, and the failure to find any evidence of WMDs in Iraq, is support for the view that aggressive multilateral inspection regimes such as UNMOVIC can be effective in ensuring compliance with non-proliferation and disarmament obligations. See, e.g., Hans Blix, "Let Us Inspect Everywhere," *The Wall Street Journal*, May 16, 2003 (arguing that long-term monitoring is "more easily accepted – and more credible – if managed by authorities which are independent of the states which assist them, for instance, by providing intelligence" and that "[u]sed in this manner, inspection and long-term monitoring through international organizations could provide an important element in the prevention of the spread of weapons of mass destruction in the Middle East, on the Korean peninsula and elsewhere").

4. *Terrorism.* According to the Panel, the first step in responding to the threat of terrorism requires member states to agree on a definition of terrorism. Only when all states reach consensus on what constitutes a terrorist act or a terrorist network can the UN develop a strategy to combat terrorism.[75] The Panel identified two sticking points in discussions of what "terrorism" actually means. The first is the question of whether states' use of armed forces against civilians can be considered terrorism. The second is the claim that peoples under foreign occupation have a right to resistance that should not be included within a broad definition of terrorism. The Panel dismissed both of these objections as not "weighty enough to contradict the argument that the strong, clear normative framework of the United Nations surrounding state use of force must be complemented by a normative framework of equal authority surrounding non-state use of force. Attacks that specifically target innocent civilians and non-combatants must be condemned clearly and unequivocally by all."[76] Interestingly in its later discussion of transnational organized crime, the Panel distinguished terrorists from criminals by citing financial gain as an objective of criminals only.[77]

Many of these issues are taken up by Eric Rosand in Chapter 10 in his discussion of the various anti-terrorism measures taken to date by the Security Council, the Secretariat, and the General Assembly in an attempt both to illuminate the political in-fighting which plagues much of the UN's work in this area while also analyzing the efficacy of the various anti-terrorism policies and procedures which have actually been developed. In considering the Panel's call for a broad-

[75] The Panel identified four elements to be included in the definition of terrorism: (1) "recognition, in the preamble, that State use of force against civilians is regulated by the Geneva Conventions and other instruments, and, if of sufficient scale, constitutes a war crime by the persons concerned or a crime against humanity"; (2) "Restatement that acts under the 12 preceding anti-terrorism conventions are terrorism, and declaration that they are a crime under international law; and restatement that terrorism in time of armed conflict is prohibited by the Geneva Conventions and Protocols"; (3) "Reference to the definitions contained in the 1999 International Convention for the Suppression of the Financing of Terrorism and Security Council Resolution 1566 (2004)"; and (4) Description of terrorism as "any action, in addition to actions already specified by the existing conventions on aspects of terrorism, the Geneva Conventions and Security Council resolution 1566 (2004), that is intended to cause death or serious bodily harm to civilians or non-combatants, when the purpose of such an act, by its nature or context, is to intimidate a population, or to compel a Government or an international organization to do or to abstain from doing any act." High-Level Panel, para. 164.

[76] High-Level Panel, paras. 160, 161. [77] *Ibid.*, para. 174.

based response to terrorism at both the normative and institutional levels, Rosand concludes by suggesting that the global counter-terrorism framework encapsulated in the UN strategy could best be implemented by creating a new UN counter-terrorism body which would provide the kind of institutional support necessary to make the UN a more truly effective collective security regime.

5. *Transnational Organized Crime.* The Panel suggested that collective response to transnational organized crime depends on the consolidation and strengthening of the international treaty framework.[78] Member states need to sign, ratify, and resource the 2000 Convention against Transnational Organized Crime and its three Protocols and the 2003 Convention Against Corruption. Furthermore, the free movement of organized crime groups across state borders can be stopped by forging legal cooperation between states, such as the exchange of evidence between judicial authorities, mutual legal assistance among prosecutorial authorities, and the enforcement of extradition requests.[79] The Summit broadly endorsed the Panel's recommendations but did not create any binding obligations on states.

In addition to identifying responses tailored to the six clusters of threats, the Panel also discussed extensively the use of force under the UN collective security regime. As a general matter, the Panel found little to fault with the existing legal framework which restricts the use of force in all situations except genuine cases of self-defense (Article 51) or military measures authorized by the Security Council (Chapter VII). While the Panel stated that it did not favor the rewriting or reinterpretation of Article 51, it did proceed to identify the article's language as "restrictive" and in need of broader interpretation.[80] The Panel thus argued for a looser reading of Article 51 which would allow for "military action as long as the threatened attack is *imminent*."[81] Under this interpretation, "anticipatory" but not "preventive" self-defense is lawful under the Charter. A state wishing to use force preventively would therefore have to receive express authorization from the Security Council so as not to violate international law.[82] The World Summit Outcome document confined itself to reaffirming existing obligations and noting that "the relevant provisions of the Charter are sufficient to address the full range of threats to international peace and security."[83]

[78] *Ibid.*, para. 172. [79] *Ibid.*, para. 173. [80] *Ibid.*, paras. 188, 192. [81] *Ibid.*, para. 188.
[82] *Ibid.*, para. 190. [83] World Summit Outcome, para. 79.

The legal standard for the Security Council to use force under Chapter VII was also identified by the Panel as adequate to address the full range of threats to global security.[84] The Panel did find as lacking, however, a perception that Security Council decisions to use force are legitimate. In order to increase the Council's legitimacy in the eyes of all member states, the Panel thus advanced five criteria to guide its decision-making processes.[85] Both self-defense and collective use of force under Chapter VII are discussed by Danchin in Chapter 1.

In addition to its recommendations on ECOSOC and the UN General Assembly discussed above, the Panel made three major institutional reform proposals regarding first, the Security Council; second, a proposed new Human Rights Council; and third, a proposed new Peacebuilding Commission.

Security Council reform

While the Panel agreed that the Security Council needs to be enlarged to improve its credibility, it failed to come to a consensus as to how to reach this goal.[86] They agreed that any changes must meet certain basic criteria: (1) that member states which contribute financially, militarily, and diplomatically need increased involvement in the decision-making of the Council; (2) that the Council needs broader membership, especially in relation to states from the developing world; (3) that any changes to membership cannot impair the effectiveness of the Council; and (4) that the Security Council should be made more democratic and accountable.[87]

To satisfy these requirements, the Panel floated two plans, Model A and Model B.[88] Neither model, however, would alter the existing veto

84 High-Level Panel, para. 198.

85 *Ibid.*, para. 204. The Security Council needs to consider (i) the seriousness of the threat, (ii) the purpose of using force, (iii) whether all other alternatives have been explored and found to yield no chance of success, (iv) the proportionality of the response, and finally (v) whether the consequences of inaction outweigh the consequences of an action using force. *Ibid.*, para. 207.

86 The Panel suggested that the effectiveness and the willingness of the Security Council to act had improved since the end of the Cold War. However, the Security Council's decisions have "not always been equitable," nor has the Security Council "acted consistently or effectively in the face of genocide or other atrocities." *Ibid.*, para. 246.

87 *Ibid.*, para. 249.

88 Both models distribute seats between four major regional areas: "Africa," "Asia and Pacific," "Europe," and the "Americas." Model A provides for six new permanent seats, with no veto being created, and three new two-year term non-permanent seats. Model B provides for no new permanent seats but creates a new category of eight four-year

rights of the permanent five members or expand the veto to new members. The only way to temper the effects of the veto would be through a system of "indicative voting," which allows any member to call upon fellow members to provide a public indication of their positions on any relevant issue before the Council.[89] Unfortunately, the World Summit Outcome document did not address any of the Panel's recommendations and remained silent on the question of Security Council reform.[90]

Human Rights Council

Concerned that states had been seeking membership on the former Commission on Human Rights in order to deflect criticism from their own human rights records or simply to criticize the records of others, the Panel proposed universal membership as a means to "de-politicize" the UN's human rights work and to underscore the commitment of all member states to promote human rights.[91] The only other substantive difference between the two bodies is the position of the Council relative to other UN bodies. Rather than being a subcommittee of the Economic and Social Council, the new Human Rights Council is a subsidiary organ of the General Assembly.[92]

At the World Summit, the General Assembly endorsed the establishment of the Council but left all the details to be worked out at the sixtieth session of the General Assembly. Subsequent negotiations centered on the issue of membership. The US pushed for election of members by a two-thirds majority of the General Assembly and automatic exclusion of any state subject to coercive measures imposed by the Security Council for gross human rights violations or acts of terrorism. When these proposals were defeated, the US voted against the draft resolution. The resolution itself was finally adopted on March 15, 2006 by a vote of 170 in favor, four against.

renewable-term seats and one new two-year non-permanent (and non-renewable) seat. *Ibid.*, paras. 251, 252.

89 The Panel hoped this voting system would create more transparency in the Security Council's voting process and also force the permanent members to be held accountable for the threat or use of the veto function. *Ibid.*, para. 257.

90 For analysis of the various Security Council reform proposals, see Nico Schrijver, "Reforming the UN Security Council in Pursuance of Collective Security," *Journal of Conflict and Security Law* (2007), pp. 1–11.

91 *Ibid.*, paras. 283, 285.

92 High-Level Panel, paras. 283, 285.

Peacebuilding Commission

The Panel's call for a new Peacebuilding Commission arose from recognition of a glaring institutional gap: "there is no place in the United Nations system explicitly designed to avoid state collapse and the slide to war or to assist countries in their transition from war to peace."[93] The proposed Peacebuilding Commission's four core functions accordingly were (1) to identify countries which are under stress and risk sliding towards state collapse; (2) to organize, in partnership with national governments, proactive assistance in preventing that process from developing further; (3) to assist in the planning for transitions between conflict and post-conflict peacebuilding; and (4) in particular, to marshal and sustain the efforts of the international community in post-conflict peacebuilding over whatever period may be necessary.[94]

Perhaps anticipating pressure from governments who themselves were wary of coming under scrutiny, the Secretary-General's version of the Peacebuilding Commission removed any suggestion of an early warning function. While this had the effect of eviscerating the first two of the Panel's four functions, Kofi Annan proceeded to set out a range of functions which the Commission would be tasked to perform including planning for sustained recovery in the immediate aftermath of war, helping to ensure predictable financing for early recovery activities, improving the coordination of the many UN post-conflict activities, and providing a forum in the UN for all stakeholders to share information.[95] The Summit Outcome document generally endorsed the Secretary-General's more limited view of the Peacebuilding Commission as restricted to mobilizing resources for post-conflict reconstruction.[96] As Chesterman observes, if the Panel had seen the Commission as assisting in the "planning" for transition from conflict to post-conflict, the Secretary-General limited it to "improving United Nations planning for sustained recovery." By the time of the Summit, the Commission was reduced to "advis[ing] on and propos[ing] integrated strategies."[97]

In Chapters 7 and 8, Dirk Salomons and Ejeviome Eloho Otobo address respectively many of the key normative and institutional aspects of the new Peacebuilding Commission architecture. While Otobo is optimistic about the Commission's likelihood for success, Salomons argues that the Commission is a disappointing conclusion to a long

[93] *Ibid.*, para. 261. [94] *Ibid.*, para. 264.
[95] *In Larger Freedom*, para. 115. [96] See World Summit Outcome, para. 98.
[97] Chesterman, "Reforming the United Nations," p. 22.

process which, at certain times, had considerable promise. In his chapter Salomons describes the historical trajectory which led ultimately to the Peacebuilding Commission, specifically the way in which the UN's development arm evolved from a post-colonial extension of the "imperial model" into an organizational network which has a unique array of skills and insights to support countries in transition. In so doing, he points out some of the intellectual landmarks which shaped the process and discusses various precursors of the newly established Commission.

For his part, Otobo provides a helpful description of the design and functions assigned to each of the three components of the new Commission (the Commission itself, the Support Office, and the Fund). This is followed by a brief discussion of the selection process and characteristics of the Commission's recent efforts in Burundi and Sierra Leone, including an examination of the nature and scope of the Commission's engagement in those two countries. Otobo thus presents his analysis of the challenges facing the peacebuilding structure, highlights its present and potential added value, and concludes with an explanation of how the new structure may respond to various tests of relevance.

Responsibility to protect

As noted above, one of the key normative ideas contained in the Panel's recommended reforms was the notion that states, as equal members of the international community, have a responsibility to protect. This was said to be an emerging norm "exercisable by the Security Council authorizing military intervention as a last resort, in the event of genocide and other large-scale killing, ethnic cleansing or serious violations of international humanitarian law which sovereign Governments have proved powerless or unwilling to prevent."[98] The Panel rejected the idea that global security is best preserved by either a balance of power or by any single, "benignly motivated," superpower.[99] Referring to "the wider international community," the Panel called on all states, as sovereign equals, to take responsibility and intervene when people are suffering "from avoidable catastrophe."[100] The Panel thus posited a transition

[98] High-Level Panel, para. 203. [99] *Ibid.*, para. 187.

[100] *Ibid.*, para. 201. Avoidable catastrophes include humanitarian disasters in Somalia, Bosnia and Herzegovina, Rwanda, Kosovo, and Darfur, Sudan.

away from the idea that sovereign equality could be used to justify the immunity of state governments.

For some, one of the few "successes" of the World Summit was its endorsement of the notion of a responsibility to protect, although again in diluted form as compared to its original articulation by the Panel. In his report, Kofi Annan limited the threshold for intervention to those situations where a government is unwilling or unable to prevent "genocide, ethnic cleansing and crimes against humanity,"[101] thus omitting "large-scale killing" and serious violations of international humanitarian law from his proposals. While the World Summit Outcome document restored "war crimes" to the list of actions warranting international concern, it limited those situations to times where national authorities are "manifestly failing to protect the population."[102] Despite a further raising of the intervention threshold, the Secretary-General described this aspect of the Outcome document as a "revolution in international affairs."[103] For others, however, especially states in the global South, endorsement of the responsibility to protect doctrine (while rejecting all proposals regarding development aid and assistance) opened the door to a new but equally unjustified form of neocolonialism and imperialism.[104]

It should be noted that the leaders at the World Summit also decided formally to amend the Charter to reflect the new normative approach to global security by deleting references to "enemy states" in the Charter.[105]

UN Sanctions reform

Finally, in Chapter 9, Jeremy Farrall traces the evolution of recent attempts at UN sanctions reform starting with the High-Level Panel

[101] *In Larger Freedom*, Annex, para. 7(b). [102] World Summit Outcome, paras. 138–139.

[103] Kofi Annan, Speech at the Conclusion of the High-level Plenary Meeting of the General Assembly, UN Doc. A/60/PV.9 of September 17, 2005.

[104] See, e.g., Thakur, *The United Nations, Peace and Security*, p. 360 (noting that the two major sets of controversies dividing industrial from developing countries in the context of UN policy have been the "relative priority to be accorded to development and security," and the "circumstances in which sovereignty can be suspended in order to honor the collective responsibility to protect").

[105] "Taking into account General Assembly resolution 50/52 of 11 December 1995 and recalling the related discussions conducted in the General Assembly, bearing in mind the profound cause for the founding of the United Nations and looking to our common future, we resolve to delete references to 'enemy States' in Article 53, 77 and 107 of the Charter." See World Summit Outcome, para. 177.

report, moving through the Secretary-General's response *In Larger Freedom*, and ending with the results of the General Assembly's deliberations in the World Summit Outcome document. Farrall begins by surveying post-Cold War developments in UN Security Council sanctions practice and identifies some of the major shortcomings of collective sanctions from both human-rights and rule-of-law perspectives. The chapter then traces the progression of sanctions-related observations in the above reports, considers the likely long-term impact of this progression on sanctions practice, and argues that the battle for sanctions reform is far from over. Farrall concludes by contending that efforts to promote further Security Council sanctions policy reform *via* external regulation, whether by normative or institutional innovation, are unlikely to succeed in the near future and suggests that meaningful sanctions regulation must come from within the Council itself.

Perspectives on the ground

Each of the final three chapters in the collection ask how any new collective security regime may influence or impact developments on the ground, especially as viewed from practitioner or humanitarian perspectives. In Chapter 12, Dennis Dijkzeul analyzes the UN Mission in the Democratic Republic of the Congo (MONUC) as a concrete example of collective security in action. The chapter thus examines the closely related difficulties of creating a collective security system and improving security in the context of a chronic conflict. Within the DRC, Dijkzeul focuses especially on the Sud Kivu province, where the conflict changed significantly after a haphazard peace process, the entrance of armed peacekeeping by the UN Mission in 2005, and democratic elections in 2006. With the success of MONUC's actions contested by both the local Congolese and non-governmental organizations (NGOs) present in the war zones, it is within this ambiguous context that Dijkzeul offers concrete examples of the difficulties of collective intervention. In asking whether and how the recent UN reform process will change MONUC's functioning, he concludes by offering a grounded critique, using empirical examples, of international decision- and policy-making concerning collective security.

In Chapter 13, Elizabeth Salmón discusses whether the replacement of the Human Rights Commission with the Human Rights Council may lead to the better protection of human rights. She argues that the recent UN reform process has pursued a comprehensive human rights-based approach to the concept of collective security and that

NGOs will be central to the successful functioning of the new Human Rights Council. This is because NGOs can serve as a supranational and international civil society with greater flexibility than states. Salmón is optimistic that the close involvement of NGOs in the new Human Rights Council will help to restore the UN's credibility and effectiveness in the area of human rights protection and enforcement.

In the concluding chapter, J. Paul Martin and Benedicto Q. Sánchez explore collective security and UN reform from the perspective of "villages," the authors' metaphor for poor communities with little influence over the external forces and powers that shape their lives. Martin and Sánchez together examine the major security threats to such communities and explain the roles of institutions, such as international and local NGOs, foreign and national governments, and the local communities themselves, in minimizing these threats. The authors argue that the collective security paradigm presents a more inclusive view of development and the involvement of these various institutions than alternative models based on national security or focused on economic and political development. They particularly consider the UN's unique position to develop this paradigm to the advantage of local communities. As a first step to implementing their vision for the collective security model at the village level, the authors propose a collective security index which identifies threats to local communities and evaluates local capabilities while promoting the participation of villagers in their own development. In conclusion, Martin and Sánchez recommend that while implementing its reforms, the UN should use its powers to enhance institutions' abilities to combat these threats because threats to villages are relevant to collective security everywhere.

PART I

Law and politics in United Nations reform

1

Things fall apart: the concept of collective security in international law

PETER G. DANCHIN

> Turning and turning in the widening gyre
> The falcon cannot hear the falconer;
> Things fall apart; the centre cannot hold;
> Mere anarchy is loosed upon the world.
>
> W. B. Yeats, "The Second Coming" (1920)

Introduction

In June 1919, a year before Yeats penned his sorrowful lament to the collapse of European order and Christian civilization in the First World War, Article 16 of the Covenant of the League of Nations came into force. Article 16 encapsulated the theory implicit in the Covenant and the Pact of Paris that war is illegitimate as an instrument of policy or of justice, or indeed for any purpose, except individual or collective defense against a state which has already resorted to or is immediately threatening war.[1] It provided, in part, as follows:

> Should any Member of the League resort to war in disregard of its covenants ... it shall *ipso facto* be deemed to have committed an act of war against all other Members of the League, which hereby undertake immediately to subject it to the severance of all trade or financial relations, the prohibition of all intercourse between their nationals and the nationals of the covenant-breaking State, and the prevention of all financial, commercial or personal intercourse between the nationals of the covenant-breaking State and the nationals of any other State, whether a member of the League or not.

[1] See, e.g., Quincy Wright, "The Meaning of the Pact of Paris," *AJIL* 27 (1933); "The Concept of Aggression in International Law," *AJIL* 29 (1935).

> It shall be the duty of the Council in such case to recommend to the several Governments concerned what effective military, naval or air force the Members of the League shall severally contribute to the armed forces to be used to protect the covenants of the League.[2]

It would be fifteen years before these provisions would meet their first decisive test when Italy invaded Abyssinia (Ethiopia) on October 3, 1935.[3] On March 17 and again on September 5, Ethiopia formally requested the League Council to consider the dispute with Italy in terms of the conciliatory procedure under Article 16. With this having failed, a Committee of six states – Portugal, Great Britain, France, Chile, Denmark, and Romania – presented their conclusion to the Council on October 7 that Italy had resorted to war in violation of the League Covenant.[4] All members of the Council accepted this finding, except Italy. The Italian government continued to insist that such a case could not be settled by the means provided in the Covenant "[s]ince this question affects vital interests and is of primary importance to Italian security and civilization." Thus, Italy "would be failing in its most elementary duty, did it not cease once and for all to place any confidence in Ethiopia, reserving full liberty to adopt any measures that may become necessary to insure the safety of its colonies and to safeguard its own interests."[5]

In his speech to the Assembly on October 10, the Italian representative Baron Aloisi advanced an array of arguments in favor of his country's position: these included: (1) the League had paid insufficient attention to Italy's grievances against Ethiopia; (2) it had not applied Article 16 in the Manchurian and Chaco disputes; (3) Italy had "done much more for civilization than Ethiopia"; (4) Ethiopia, "because of its backwardness and failure to live up to the conditions on which it was admitted to the League" had either ceased to be a member or should be ejected from the

[2] Covenant of the League of Nations, June 28, 1919, Article XVI, 1 *Hudson International Legislation* 1 (1931).

[3] Previously, the League had varying degrees of involvement in the Graeco-Bulgarian crisis in 1925, the Chaco dispute in 1928, and the invasion of Manchuria in 1931. But no enforcement measures or collective sanctions under Article 16 were applied in these crises.

[4] Quincy Wright, "The Test of Aggression in the Italo-Ethiopian War," 30 *AJIL* 45, 47 (1936). For the history of the League deliberations, see John H. Spencer, "The Italian-Ethiopian Dispute and the League of Nations," 31 *AJIL* 614 (1937).

[5] League of Nations, Dispute between Ethiopia and Italy, Memorandum of the Italian Government, I Report, II Documents (1935, VII, 11). Italy raised various arguments alleging the necessity of self-defense in response to Ethiopia's "aggressive attitude" which was said to have become an "immediate danger, obliging Italy to adopt adequate measures of a military character." See Wright, "The Meaning of the Pact of Paris," 27 *AJIL* 42 (1933).

League, or placed under a mandate; (5) Italy's interests in Ethiopia had been expressly recognized in treaties with France and Great Britain; (6) the League could not "force the course of history" but must balance the parts of the Covenant which relate to "evolution" with those which relate to "conservation" by a greater "elasticity"; and that (7) the League should recognize Italy's expression of this "imperative necessity of life."

> Caught as she is ... in the tide of her full spiritual and material development, but confined by historical vicissitudes and international restrictions within territorial limits which are stifling her, Italy is the country which must make her voice heard in this assembly of the States as the voice of the proletariat calling for justice.[6]

Rejecting these arguments and overriding Italian intransigence, a Coordination Committee soon recommended sanctions against Italy, including arms and credit embargoes and import and export boycotts, and called for mutual assistance among those sanctioning Powers adversely affected by such measures. These sanctions, however, fell well short of those envisaged in Article 16. The main reason was British and French vacillation in light of their strategic, political, and economic interests with Italy. In the end, the export embargo did not include coal, steel, or oil, the commodities most critical to the Italian economy, and with British, French, and Russian fears of war with Italy increasing, the general oil embargo was never adopted. Faced with the obvious inadequacies of the sanctions regime, the League refused to take any further measures. The first real test of the post-war collective security regime – an order premised on the international rule of law prohibiting aggression by one member state against another, and formally abolishing war as an instrument of either national policy or of justice – thus ended in failure.[7] For John Spencer, the former adviser to the Ethiopian Ministry of Foreign Affairs, this outcome was not the result of any bureaucratic or procedural failure within the League, but rather

[6] Records, 16th Assembly, 15th Plenary Meeting, cited in Wright, "The Test of Aggression in the Italo-Ethiopian War," pp. 53–54.

[7] The question of whether a breach had occurred, or whether there was an obligation to apply economic sanctions under Article 16(1), was ultimately dependent on each member's view of the situation. Thus, "[m]ilitary sanctions could be recommended by the Council, but the decision on whether to apply them rested with each member." D. W. Bowett, *The Law of International Institutions*, 4th edn., Library of World Affairs (London: Sweet & Maxwell, 1982), pp. 17–18.

> was due clearly to its inability, on the one hand, to give precedence to the procedure which it had adopted for the settlement of the dispute, over the attempts made outside the League with a view to conciliation, and, on the other, to pursue consistently any one course of procedure once adopted by itself.[8]

It is now a matter of history, as events turned in the widening gyre – first with the German march into the Rhineland in 1936, then Austria in 1938, and Czechoslovakia in 1939; then with the Soviet Union's invasion of Finland in 1939; and then finally with the German invasion of Poland in 1939 – that things would fall apart, that the League would not hold. As soon as 1945, however, against the backdrop of catastrophic moral horror and the death of over sixty million people, a "new world order" was instituted. Under Article 2(4) of the new post-war Charter, the "threat or use of force against the territorial integrity or political independence of other states in any manner inconsistent with the purposes of the United Nations" was outlawed. While Article 51 confirmed that the new regime of collective security did not impair the "inherent right of individual or collective self-defense if an armed attack occurs," under Article 24 and Chapter VII a newly created Security Council was given the authority to determine the existence of any threat to the peace, breach of peace or act of aggression, and the primary responsibility to decide what collective measures were to be taken to maintain or restore international peace or security in conformity with principles of international law.

No sooner had the delegates returned home from San Francisco, however, than a cablegram, dated August 21, 1948, arrived for the President of the Security Council regarding the "question of Hyderabad." The relevant section read as follows:

> The Government of Hyderabad, in reliance on Article 35, paragraph 2, of the Charter of the United Nations, requests you to bring to the attention of the Security Council the grave dispute which has arisen between

[8] Spencer, "The Italian-Ethiopian Dispute and the League of Nations," p. 640. As regards the various efforts made outside the League first to avert hostilities and later to bring them to an end, Spencer notes the statement by Sir Samuel Hoare to the House of Commons on December 19, 1935:

> I have been terrified with the thought – I speak very frankly to the House – that we might lead Abyssinia on to think that the League could do more than it can do, that in the end we should find a terrible moment of disillusionment in which it might be that Abyssinia would be destroyed altogether as an independent State.

307 Parl. Deb., at 2013, cited *ibid.*, p. 641.

> Hyderabad and India, and which, unless settled in accordance with international law and justice, is likely to endanger the maintenance of international peace and security. Hyderabad has been exposed in recent months to violent intimidation, to threats of invasion, and to crippling economic blockade which has inflicted cruel hardship upon the people of Hyderabad and which is intended to coerce it into a renunciation of its independence. The frontiers have been forcibly violated and Hyderabad villages have been occupied by Indian troops. The action of India threatens the existence of Hyderabad, the peace of the Indian and entire Asiatic Continent, and the principles of the United Nations.[9]

But by September 13, a later cablegram informed the Secretary-General that India had invaded and conquered Hyderabad.[10] Sir Benegal Rau, the representative of India, justified India's actions the following May on the grounds that Hyderabad was "not a State in the international sense … and cannot be one at any time in the future if India is to live. We cannot defy or ignore geography." Accordingly, not only was this not an "international dispute" for the purposes of the Charter, but Hyderabad was not competent to appear before the Security Council and the matter had properly been dealt with by the Government of India as a "matter of domestic concern."[11] Although the case of Hyderabad would soon be forgotten in the pages of history, for commentators at the time it represented the worst failure, viewed in either political or legal terms, of the Security Council since it

[9] UN Doc. S/986, Security Council, Official Records, 3rd Year, Supp., September 1948, at 5. Hyderabad stated that it was a State, albeit a "State not a Member of the United Nations," and it accepted for the purposes of the dispute the obligations of pacific settlement provided in the UN Charter. This included its intention to adhere to the Statute of the International Court of Justice in conformity with Article 93(2), and to sign the Optional Clause in Article 36 of the Statute. Despite India's objections, the Head of the Hyderabad Delegation, Nawab Moin, was received and heard by the Security Council.

[10] UN Docs. S/998 and S/1000, *ibid.*, at 6, 7.

[11] S.C., O.R., 4th Year, No. 28, 425th meeting, at 7. As noted by Eagleton, these arguments ignored the effect of the Indian Independence Act which "authorized independence for the Princely States if desired … Nor does it follow from the facts of geography that Hyderabad should legally be regarded as a domestic concern by India." Clyde Eagleton, "The Case of Hyderabad Before the Security Council," 44 *AJIL* 277, 281 n. 7 (1950). As the President of the Council, Sir Alexander Cadogan of the United Kingdom, himself replied to a request of the Soviet delegate: "I can inform the Security Council that on August 15, 1947 the suzerainty of the Crown in the United Kingdom over Hyderabad, and all other Indian States, came to an end. None of the powers previously exercised by the Crown was transferred to the Government of the two new Dominions, that is, India and Pakistan." S.C., O.R., 3rd Year, No. 109, 357th meeting, September 16, 1948.

> was not due, as in other cases, to uncertainty as to legal rights, or to the extrinsic difficulties of the problem. The legal rights were embarrassingly clear; and a satisfactory political settlement could have been agreed upon with little difficulty. In all other cases, the Council has tried, and has frequently achieved a solution; in this case it did not even try.[12]

Writing in 1950, Eagleton suggested that the case of Hyderabad raised the question whether the United Nations was to be a "constitutional system or not."

> Thus far, its trend has been away from law; the Security Council (and the General Assembly as well) has overridden the restrictions set by the Charter where it has desired to take an action, and has disregarded both its obligations under, and the principles of, the Charter when it did not desire to take action … It is in this connection that the case of Hyderabad deserves study by those who are interested in achieving a system of international law and order in the world.[13]

In seeking to respond to Eagleton's question, how do we understand the two cases of Ethiopia and Hyderabad? What might they reveal about the problems and prospects today of achieving a "system of international law and order in the world"? What, in other words, are the purposes of international law and how do they relate to any notion of collective security? It is to these conceptual questions which this chapter now turns.

The concept of collective security

The concept of collective security is notoriously difficult to define. Like democracy, human rights and the rule of law, the term is associated with a loose set of assumptions and ideas and its continued existence rests in no small measure on its remaining an essentially contested concept. In

[12] Eagleton, "The Case of Hyderabad Before the Security Council," pp. 301–302. As Eagleton notes, apart from questions of law, the strategic and economic implications in the case were obvious. An Indian Government White Paper on Hyderabad stated in 1948: "India could live if its Moslem limbs in the North-West and North-East were amputated, but could it live without its heart?' Cited in *ibid.*, p. 277 n. 1. An Editorial in the Karachi newspaper, *Dawn*, stated on November 12, 1949 (*ibid.*, p. 302 n. 71):

> The Hyderabad complaint remains on the agenda of the Security Council and India has been rewarded for her "police action" with a seat on that body – a reward that the Dutch could not have expected in their wildest dreams for their repeated "police actions" in Indonesia. Inscrutable, indeed are the ways of Western democracy – and of its most boosted compeer, the Indian.

[13] Eagleton, "The Case of Hyderabad Before the Security Council," p. 302.

basic terms, we might define collective security as an agreement between states to "abide by certain norms and rules to maintain stability and, when necessary, band together to stop aggression."[14] This definition captures three distinct ideas: the purpose or end of stopping "aggression"; the reliance on legal norms to determine both the meaning of that term and the appropriate form of response; and the rejection of self-help in favor of collective action. Collective security thus rests on the idea of institutionalizing the legal use of force "to reduce reliance on self-help as a rather crude instrument of law enforcement."[15] Bringing these ideas together, the concept of collective security may be further defined as:

> an institutionalized universal or regional system in which States have agreed by treaty jointly to meet any act of aggression or other illegal use of force resorted to by a member State of the system.[16]

The concept is thus primarily directed against the illegal use of force *within* the group of states forming the collective security system rather than against an external threat. This idea is well captured in Johnson and Niemeyer's definition of collective security as constituting:

> a system based on the universal obligation of all nations to join forces against an aggressor state as soon as the fact of aggression is determined by established procedure. In such a system, aggression is defined as a wrong in universal terms and an aggressor, as soon as he has been identified, stands condemned. Hence the obligation of all nations to take action against him is conceived as a duty to support *right* against *wrong*. It is equally founded upon the practical expectation that the communal solidarity of all nations would from the outset make it clear to every government that "aggression does not pay."[17]

In order to understand the underlying logic, it is useful to distinguish collective security from two closely related terms: *balance of power* and *global government* (or, in more anti-formal terms, *global governance*). A balance of power arrangement between states rests on the idea of decentralization, a kind of *laissez-faire* within a sphere of power politics. States act as separate units without subordinating their autonomy or sovereignty

[14] Charles A. Kupchan and Clifford A. Kupchan, "The Promise of Collective Security," *International Security* 20 (Summer 1995), pp. 52–53.

[15] Jost Delbruck, "Collective Security" in Bernhardt, R. (ed.), *Encyclopedia of Public International Law* (1992), p. 646.

[16] *Ibid.*, p. 647.

[17] Howard C. Johnson and Gerhart Niemeyer, "Collective Security: The Validity of an Ideal," *International Organization* 8 (1954), pp. 19–20.

to any central agency established for the management of power relations. In this way, states function as "coordinate managers" of the power situation. Thus, "[s]ingly or in combinations reflecting the coincidence of interests, [s]tates seek to influence the pattern of power distribution and to determine their own places within that pattern."[18] Under this conception, states may form defensive alliances such as under the NATO Treaty against actual or perceived *external* threats. These sorts of flexible alliances allow for recurrent shifts of alignment to take place. The promise of order lies in the expectation that competing claims to power will somehow balance and thereby cancel each other out to produce "deterrence through equilibration."[19]

On the other hand, global government or notions of "global constitutional order" posit the creation of a centralized institutional system superior to individual states with a monopoly on power and the use of force akin to that of a well-ordered national state. This conception rests on depriving states of their "standing as centers of power and policy, where issues of war and peace are concerned," and superimposing upon them "an institution possessed of the authority and capability to maintain, by unchallengeable force so far as may be necessary, the order and stability of a global community."[20] Global government is thus a normative vision of political community under a universal law which does not currently, and arguably is unlikely ever to, exist.

The concept of collective security sits uneasily between and incorporates elements of both these ideas functioning as a dialectical notion of "order without government"[21] in an effort to manage the problem of power relations between states by "superimposing a scheme of partially centralized management upon a situation in which power remains diffused among national units."[22] This hybrid system involves a centralization of *authority* over the use of force to the extent that states are deprived of the *legal right* to use violence at their own discretion. That states give up this discretion and agree to follow objective rules governing

[18] Inis L. Claude, Jr., "The Management of Power in the Changing United Nations," *International Organization* 15 (Spring 1961), pp. 219–221.

[19] *Ibid.*, p. 222. [20] *Ibid.*

[21] The term is from Inis L. Claude, Jr., "Comment on 'An Autopsy of Collective Security'," *Political Science Quarterly* 90 (Winter 1975–6), p. 715. Koskenniemi also suggests a dialectical view of the competences of the UN which "seeks to accommodate concerns of power [order] and of authority [justice]". Martti Koskenniemi, "The Police in the Temple: Order, Justice and the UN: A Dialectical View," *EJIL* 6 (1995), p. 328.

[22] Claude, "The Management of Power in the Changing United Nations," p. 221.

the threat and use of force requires an international organization with authority not only to determine when a resort to force is illegitimate but also to require states to collaborate under its direction in suppressing such use of force. This system of collective security falls short of creating an institution with a centralized monopoly of force in the full sense implied by world government. The power wielded by a hybrid collective security system thus can reach no further than that given to it by the sovereign will of its members.

Given its dialectical nature, such a conception of international law and organization has two fundamental purposes which simultaneously rely on and deny each other.[23] We can see this, for example, in the paradoxical structure of the Charter of the United Nations. On the one hand, Article 2(1) of the Charter states that the Organization is based on the "sovereign equality of its members." The Charter is thus based on a presumption of initial state freedom, but as soon as states are regarded as members of an *international community* this initial freedom is limited by the normative demands of the "equal" freedom of other states. The Charter in this sense posits a *social ethics* expressing the freedom of each state as a function of community values and justice. In the absence of a world government or global sovereign, however, it constructs a collective security system intended to foster collaboration and cooperation rather than competition between states.

On the other hand, Article 2(7) provides that "[n]othing contained in the present Charter shall authorize the United Nations to intervene in matters which are essentially within the domestic jurisdiction of any state." While international law is normatively universal and binding on all states, and while Chapter VII of the Charter provides the Security Council with extensive enforcement powers, both the law and its enforcement are held to be limited by the factual existence and unique "internal" identity (sovereignty) of each state. In this respect, the Charter posits an *individualistic morality* which expresses the international community as a function of each state's unique identity and awareness. Given the inevitability of conflict and violence between states, the Charter's collective security system is intended to ensure peaceful coexistence by obliging states to band together to halt aggression and thus imagines a solidarist international community with the authority to constrain state egoism, but only on the basis of and in accordance with objective law and procedure.

[23] See David Kennedy, "Theses about International Law Discourse," *German Yearbook of International Law* 23 (1980), p. 364.

In this picture, we can recognize the essential paradox of the liberal structure of international law itself.[24] Koskenniemi describes the distinctive "double-bind" of international legal argument in the following terms:

> In the one case, community is interpreted as negative collectivism and autonomy (independence, self-determination) is presented as the normative goal. In the other, autonomy is interpreted as negative egoism and community (integration, solidarity) as what the law should aim at. Neither community nor autonomy can be exclusive goals. To think of community as the ultimate goal seems utopian: as there is no agreement on the character of a desirable community, attempts to impose it seem like imperialism in disguise. To think of autonomy as the normative aim seems apologist: it strengthens the absolutist claims of national power-elites and supports their pursuits at international dominance.[25]

The international legal project of collective security is driven by this dialectic which creates a dynamic of contradiction and constant oscillation between patterns of argument seeking to legitimate social order against individual state freedom. The result is that international law – and its application and practice in and by international organizations – provides a site of deliberation and hegemonic contestation by which "international actors routinely challenge each other by invoking legal rules and principles on which they have projected meanings that support their preferences and counteract those of their opponents."[26]

From this conceptual structure, we can isolate three necessary but insufficient conditions for the effective functioning of any collective security system. The first is a certain degree of political solidarity or consensus among member states.[27] The second is a sufficiently strong peacekeeping force which, at a minimum, is strong enough to "balance the military power of the aggressor(s) in order to render military success for the aggressor impossible," or be "stronger than the strongest single

[24] Martti Koskenniemi, *From Apology to Utopia: The Structure of International Legal Argument* (Helsinki: Finnish Lawyers' Publishing Company, 1989), reissued as *From Apology to Utopia: The Structure of International Legal Argument: Reissue with a new Epilogue* (Cambridge: Cambridge University Press, 2005).

[25] *Ibid.* 424. (1989 edition).

[26] Martti Koskenniemi, "International Law and Hegemony: A Reconfiguration," *Cambridge Review of International Affairs* 17 (2004), p. 199. Contestation is "hegemonic" because the goal of the contestants is "to make their partial view of that meaning appear as the total view, their preference seem like the *universal preference.*" *Ibid.*

[27] Thus, if a "great number of member States should not live up to their obligations to join in collective action against an aggressor, the system as a whole would be doomed to failure." Delbruck, "Collective Security," p. 648.

military force mobilized by an aggressor, or … group of aggressors."[28] And the third element is sufficiently determinate criteria to enable the objective determination of when an act constitutes "aggression" or "self-defense."

At the same time, however, once the purposes of collective security are joined together with the elements necessary for such a system actually to function in practice, an inherent tension is immediately visible. The more the control of force and enforcement of the law is centralized, the greater the restrictions on the preexisting autonomy and sovereignty of states will be and the greater the danger that the collective security system itself will be seen as an aggressor. Conversely, the more the control of force and enforcement of law remains decentralized, the greater the potential danger of the outbreak of war and interstate aggression and the more difficult it will be to mobilize effective and consistent collective action. Thus, the "key question is whether regulated balancing predicated upon the notion of all against one, or unregulated balancing predicated upon the notion of each for his own, is more likely to preserve peace."[29] Competing conceptions of collective security provide different answers regarding how best to mediate these contradictory forces.[30]

Finally, it is important to observe that collective security systems are premised to some extent on the so-called "domestic analogy" – the assumption that principles considered valid for interpersonal relationships may also have application to interstate relations.[31] If states are viewed as subjects of international law in much the same way as individuals are held to be subjects of domestic law ("States-as-Individuals,") then sovereignty may be seen to play an equivalent function at the international level as that played by rights at the domestic level. Thus, international law allows a state the right to act *externally* in self-defense or to protect its anterior liberty from external domination; at the same time it protects a certain *internal* autonomy for a state's people to conduct its own affairs free of interference. The former is the international equivalent of the individual's natural or "fundamental" right to self-defense and liberty; the latter is the mirror image of the distinction between public and private

[28] *Ibid.* [29] Kupchan and Kupchan, "The Promise of Collective Security," p. 53.

[30] See further below, note 114 and accompanying text.

[31] The domestic analogy can be seen, for example, in Hobbes, Rousseau, and Locke. Thomas Hobbes, *Leviathan*, C. B. Macpherson (ed.), (Harmondsworth: Penguin, 1982), pp. 187–188; Jean-Jacques Rousseau, *The Social Contract*, Maurice Cranston (trans.), (New York: Harper & Row, 1986), bk. I, ch. 7, 63; John Locke, *Two Treatises of Government* Second Treatise (W. S. Carpenter (intr.), 1984), sect. 183, 211 (London). See Koskenniemi, *From Apology to Utopia*, p. 68, n. 66.

spheres.[32] "State sovereignty" in this sense mediates between the claims of legal subjects *inter se* in a public international community while at the same time demarcating a private national sphere.[33]

Finally, however, we should observe a critical distinction between the domestic and international levels. As a matter of history, natural rights evolved at the domestic level in large response to the *factual absolutism* of the Hobbesian Leviathan, which increasingly came to be seen as a threat to individual freedom. As the centralization of state power and the monopoly on the use of force was consolidated (and exercised) within nation states, it was doubted whether life in such circumstances was really preferable to the *bellum omnium* which the sovereign was intended to replace.[34] At the international level, however, the situation is normatively similar but factually inverse. Advocates of collective security regard the absence of any equivalent to the Hobbesian Leviathan as guaranteeing an ever-present danger to the freedom and autonomy of states. Similarly, the perceived weakness and partiality of balance of power alliances in opposing aggression are often seen to necessitate the move towards the greater inclusiveness and legal objectivity of a collective security system. In this respect, the defining feature of any collective security project is the need to justify *limitations* and impose *constraints* on the unrestricted power of state sovereignty in the name of political community. We should thus take care to ensure that the domestic analogy's equation of sovereignty to fundamental rights does not obscure the inverse correlation between facts and norms in the two cases.[35]

32 For discussion of the distinction between non-interference and non-domination in international legal theory, see Philip Pettit, "A Republican Law of Peoples," *European Journal of Political Theory* (forthcoming). See generally Quentin Skinner, *Liberty Before Liberalism* (Cambridge: Cambridge University Press, 1998).

33 I further develop this theme in "Whose Public? Which Law? Mapping the Internal/External Distinction in International Law," in J. Farrall and K. Rubenstein (eds.), *Sanctions, Accountability and Governance in a Globalized World* (Cambridge: Cambridge University Press, 2009), pp. 27–52.

34 We see this in the rights theories of Locke and Rousseau which sought to guarantee liberty within social order and for whom "consent is not only an initial authorization but also a continuing constraint on power." Koskenniemi, *From Apology to Utopia*, p. 63.

35 See, e.g., Robert Jackson, *Quasi-States: Sovereignty, International Relations and the Third World* (Cambridge: Cambridge University Press, 1990), p. 29 (suggesting for these reasons that "international liberalism is more contradictory and ambivalent than domestic liberalism"). See also Richard Tuck, *The Rights of War and Peace: Political Thought and the International Order from Grotius to Kant* (New York: Oxford University Press, 2001), p. 9 (arguing that the liberal politics of Locke and Vattel in international society was compatible with "international adventurism and exploitation" as the "model of the independent moral agent upon which their liberalism was based was precisely the belligerent post-Renaissance state").

The historical evolution of collective security

These general theoretical ideas find their historical origins in the gradual evolution of both conceptual and institutional forms of collective security from the late-seventeenth century onwards. In normative terms, the term can be traced back to the various schemes for perpetual peace proposed by William Penn, Abbé de Saint-Pierre and Immanuel Kant. Penn's *Essay Towards the Present and Future Peace of Europe* in 1693 and Abbé de Saint-Pierre's *Projet pour rendre la paix perpetuelle en Europe* in 1713 each advocated, for example, a legal organization of the European powers in a League comparable to modern international organizations such as the League of Nations and the United Nations.[36] A century later, Kant's famous essay *On Perpetual Peace* argued in 1795 that peace was an aim that mankind could realize, but only incrementally. In each of these works, the essential ideas of collective security began to take shape: in the absence of a central authority for the enforcement of law and the maintenance of peace, it was necessary to provide a substitute solution; a substitute can only be created by organizing the common defense of all states against the illegal use of force; and the right of states to use force as a form of self-help or law enforcement must be reduced to a minimum or limited as an interim measure.

These ideas drew on deeper currents and shifts set in motion by the classicism born in the wake of the 1648 Peace of Westphalia which sought to justify normative order by building on the equal right to sovereignty and independence of states.[37] This moment in history is said to mark the "great epistemological break" when religious medieval unity under Pope and Emperor gave way to a secular system of plural, territorially limited sovereign states. Between the sixteenth and eighteenth centuries, this shift led to the emergence of what Koskenniemi has termed the "liberal doctrine of politics" in international legal thought, the driving force of which was the attempt to "escape the anarchical conclusions to which loss of faith in an overriding theologico-moral world order otherwise seemed to lead."[38] In this process, just war doctrine was transformed from the ethical to the formally *legal* as the use of force was recast in legalistic terms as a self-help remedy of last resort.

36 Delbruck, "Collective Security," p. 646.

37 As Kennedy notes, traditional scholarship in the post-Grotian era "sprang from the ruins of primitive scholarship" and [r]ather than assuming social order, it allows for disorder and conflict." David Kennedy, "Primitive Legal Scholarship," *Harvard International Law Journal* 27 (1986), p. 97.

38 Koskenniemi, *From Apology to Utopia*, p. 52.

The institutional origins of collective security may be traced to the efforts of the European powers to maintain peace and security within the nineteenth-century international system known as the Concert of Europe. The Concert provided not only for the common defense against *external* dangers in the classical form of a defensive alliance, but also for collective action by the European Great Powers against any potential enemy *within* their own ranks.[39] As this structure gradually collapsed, the peace movement began to advocate at the turn of the century for renewed conceptions of collective security. Walter Schucking, for example, a leading German international lawyer, was a prominent advocate of an institutionalized peacekeeping machinery which "he visualized as a universal organization of states for the purpose of collective action and responsibility in the maintenance of international peace and security."[40]

It was not until after the First World War, however, that an institutionalized system of collective security was realized by the formation in 1919 of the League of Nations. The creation of the League built on longstanding efforts since the late nineteenth century to reduce the effects of war on belligerents and civilians alike by adopting new rules of humanitarian law and outlawing war and interstate aggression under international law.[41] While intended to be a collective security arrangement, the League was in reality closer to a balance of power arrangement as it lacked a coordinated, centralized decision-making procedure capable of applying sanctions against aggressors internal to the system itself.[42] As discussed above, the

[39] The Congress System or Concert of Europe comprised the Holy Alliance between Austria, Prussia and Russia and the Quadripartite Alliance between Austria, Britain, Prussia, and Russia, with France entering in 1818 via the Treaty of Aix-la-Chapelle. F. Knipping, H. von Mangoldt and V. Rittergerger, *The United Nations System and its Predecessors* (Oxford: Oxford University Press, 1997), pp. 7–9.

[40] Delbruck, "Collective Security," p. 647. [41] *Ibid.*, p. 649.

[42] The League was effective in the 1923 Corfu crisis between Greece and Italy; Great Britain and Turkey over Mosul (in the British mandate of Iraq); Greece and Bulgaria over border incursions by both parties; and Lithuania and Poland. The only deployments of League of Nations Forces were in the 1935 Saarland Plebiscite and in a 1933–34 Colombian Force acting under League authority in the upper Amazon. In each of these cases, the League was able to bring about a successful resolution without recourse to actively coercive measures. However, these "successes were due, in no small part, to the fact that the disputes were of a relatively minor nature and either concerned two weak states which lacked powerful allies within the League Council, or alternatively involved one party with such a preponderance of power that the other had no practical alternative but to acquiesce in a settlement which the League felt able to endorse." H. McCoubrey and J. C. Morris, "International Law, International Relations and the Development of European Collective Security," *Journal of Armed Conflict Law* 4 (1999), 195, 199–200.

inability of the League to prevent Italy from invading Ethiopia in 1936 provides the classic illustration of this deficiency.[43]

After the League's failure in the period before and during the Second World War, the United Nations emerged in a renewed effort to realize the idea of collective security. The United States, the United Kingdom and the Soviet Union, united in political terms as the victorious powers emerging from the war, sought to overcome the weaknesses of the League of Nations through two main innovations: first, through the drafting of a new Charter that completely prohibited the use of force except as a means of individual and collective self-defense; and second, by creating a new Security Council with the authority to determine whether an act of aggression had occurred and what measures ought to be taken by its member states in response.[44] These improvements in the legal framework of collective security were soon diminished, however, by the onset of the Cold War and ensuing collapse of whatever political solidarity had previously existed between the Soviet Union and the West.

This brief history allows us to make four tentative observations. First, the historical development of the idea of collective security can variously be interpreted and is not the product of any simple or singular process. The development of international legal norms pertaining to collective security in Europe and more generally should rather be seen as a succession of responses to war crises with which existing normative structures have adequately failed to cope. As McCoubrey and Morris observe, this process "may be traced historically through the traumas, *inter alia*, of the Thirty Years War, the French revolutionary and Napoleonic wars and the First and Second World Wars."[45] In this respect, the most recent efforts of United Nations reform are part of a far longer historical continuum of normative and institutional change occurring in the immediate aftermath of catastrophe.

Second, even though the United Nations was intended to be a new collective security arrangement remedying the various deficiencies of the

[43] Thus, the lesson drawn from the failure of the League was that without a "centralized authoritative determination of whether an act of aggression has occurred or not, and of the measures to be taken against an act of aggression, collective security may not become effective." Furthermore, it was "essential that the use of force be completely outlawed, except for the purpose of self-defence, in order to exclude any possibility for a State legally to assume an aggressive policy." Delbruck, "Collective Security," pp. 650–651.

[44] See Ruth B. Russell, "Review: 'The United Nations and Collective Security: A Historical Analysis' by K. P. Saksena," *AJIL* 69 (1975), p. 928.

[45] McCoubrey and Morris, "International Law, International Relations and the Development of European Collective Security," p. 196.

League of Nations, its structure retained central elements of the balance of power paradigm. We see this most clearly in the veto rule which allows each of the permanent five Great Powers the capacity to prevent any Chapter VII enforcement measures directed towards either themselves or any state which they choose to support or protect, or in any other case in which they prefer not to participate or to have others participate in enforcement measures under UN auspices. The veto provision, in short, "renders collective security impossible in all the instances most vital to the preservation of world peace and order."[46] In this respect, the United States declared openly that "if a major power became the aggressor the Council had no power to prevent war."[47] As Claude thus suggests, the UN Charter is "a curious amalgam of collective security, dominant in ideological terms, and balance of power, dominant in terms of practical application."[48]

Third, the concept of global government has always figured as a distant and unrealizable ideal in the articulation and realization of collective security. Woodrow Wilson and other early advocates of collective security rejected world federation. In this respect, World Federalists and advocates for other forms of supranational organization have long attacked collective security "precisely because it neither anticipates nor promises to bring about the drastic reduction of the role of the nation-state in the international system."[49] As we shall see, despite great changes in international relations and the emergence of new types of threat in an age of increasing interdependence and globalization, the United Nations

[46] Claude, "The Management of Power in the Changing United Nations," p. 224. The P5 members can veto/block decisions regarding (1) the determination that aggression has taken place, (2) the designation of the guilty party, and (3) the decision to use sanctions (whether military or other). Each of these decisions is fundamental to the operation of any collective security system.

[47] UN Information Organizations and US Library of Congress, *Documents of the United Nations Conference on International Organization* (New York, 1945), p. 514. Note also the statement of the National League of Women Voters:

> If a great power becomes an aggressor, the United Nations Organization will not be able to act, and the situation will have to be handled outside the Organization. This is because we are still in the experimental stage of collective security, and world opinion has not yet developed to the point where nations are willing to delegate sufficient authority to an international organization to make it capable of coercing a great power.

The Charter of the United Nations, Hearings before the Committee on Foreign Relations, US Senate 79th Congress, 1st Session (Washington, 1945) p. 422.

[48] Claude, "The Management of Power in the Changing United Nations," p. 229.

[49] Claude, "Comment on 'An Autopsy of Collective Security'," p. 716.

and its associated organs (including the High-Level Panel) continue to view the nation-state as the dominant actor in international affairs.

Fourth, and finally, the idea of collective security is premised at some level on the efficacy of the idea of the rule of law in international relations. Without determinate and objective means to interpret agreed rules governing the use of force, collective security soon collapses into the very politics it portends to transcend. State A claims that its use of force is self-defense while state B's use of force is aggression; state B claims the exact reverse. The hope of a system of collective security – a hope deeply premised on modern variants of the rationalist philosophy of the Enlightenment – is that some version of the Rule of Law in international relations can resolve this clash of interests in an objective and determinate way.[50] Whether this is a hope in vain is a critical question addressed by the chapters in Parts I and II of this volume.

Collective security in international law

Once we recognize that debates over the role of law in a system of collective security presuppose the acceptance of a form of international legal liberalism, it becomes apparent that the various contradictions and binary oppositions lying at the heart of the discipline are the same as those lying at the core of liberal theory.[51] The most basic claim of liberalism is that political and social order should be based on individual consent. The liberal tradition thus assumes the separateness of individuals from each other and denies the existence of a natural, objective social order which preexists man's entry into it.[52] In the absence of a controlling natural order, it logically follows that individuals are both free and equal in some essential sense. It has been in pursuit of this claim that varying ideas of social contract have evolved over the last three centuries in order to justify

[50] See, e.g., Sean D. Murphy, "The Security Council, Legitimacy, and the Concept of Collective Security after the Cold War," *Columbia Journal of Transnational Law* 32 (1994), p. 252 (arguing that "when an act of aggression occurs, corrective action is to be taken regardless of who the aggressor is or who the victim is, and the system is to respond automatically and reliably"). More generally, see Simon Chesterman, "An International Rule of Law?," *American Journal of Comparative Law* 56 (2008), pp. 331–361.

[51] Koskenniemi, *From Apology to Utopia*. For David Kennedy, the opposition between sovereign authority and community membership is the *controlling contradiction* which is then transformed into the various different opposing doctrines at other levels of argument. See Kennedy, "Theses About International Law Discourse," *German Yearbook of International Law* 23 (1980), p. 353, pp. 361–362.

[52] Koskenniemi, *From Apology to Utopia*, pp. 55–56.

principles of justice – whether "sovereignty" or "human rights" – whose primary function is to guarantee liberty within social order.

In this way, competing conceptions of statehood, self-determination, independence, consent, the rule of law, authority, legitimacy, obligation, etc. turn on the justifiability of (liberal) assumptions about the relationship between social description (facts) and political prescription (norms). This opposition characterizes the dilemmas of liberal theory:

> How to guarantee that States are not coerced by law imposed "from above"? How to maintain the objectivity of law-application? How to delimit off a "private" realm of sovereignty or domestic jurisdiction while allowing international action to enforce collective preferences or human rights? How to guarantee State "freedom" while providing the conditions for international "order"?[53]

The liberal response to these conflicts involves a form of paradox: "To preserve freedom, order must be created to restrict it."[54] The basic logic of the argument is as follows: in order to avoid apologism, international law must be objective and normative such that it can bind states regardless of their behavior, interest, or consent. In order to justify the objectivity of international norms, it therefore becomes necessary to invoke a normatively justifiable or "descending" pattern of argument. Whether expressed in terms of justice, common interests, progress, the nature of international community, or other similar ideas, the critical assumption here is that there is a "normative code" which is either anterior or superior to state behavior, will, or interest. But any argument advancing a natural morality or objective theory of justice is immediately vulnerable to familiar objections voiced against "formalism" or "naturalism." At the same time, this normative

[53] As Koskenniemi notes, "[t]hese are all distinctly liberal problems, whose connection to domestic issues concerning the legitimation of social order against individual freedom appear evident." *Ibid.*, p. xvii.

[54] This idea is well captured in Kant's conception of Hobbes's state of nature:

> As Hobbes maintains, the state of nature is a state of injustice and violence, and we have no option save to abandon it and submit ourselves to the constraint of law, which limits our freedom solely in order that it may be consistent with the freedom of others and with the common good of all.

Immanuel Kant, *Critique of Pure Reason* (Edinburgh: Palgrave Macmillan, Norman Kemp Smith trans., 1933), pp. 601–602. In similar terms, Duncan Kennedy has observed the "fundamental contradiction" that "coercion of the individual by the group appears to be inextricably bound up with the liberation of the same individual," and that "relations with others are both necessary to and incompatible with our freedom." Duncan Kennedy, "The Structure of Blackstone's Commentaries," 28 *Buffalo Law Review* 205 (1979), pp. 211–213.

justification conflicts with the principles of subjective consent (which itself provides the justification for the Rule of Law) and the subjectivity of values. Thus, in order to avoid utopianism, international law must turn to a concrete or "ascending" justification which provides a link to the subjective acceptance and actual will of states.[55] But, as soon as the acceptance of states is what counts – the notion that state behavior, will, and interest are *determining of* the law – then the law risks losing its objectivity and normativity. The result is that neither set of arguments can consistently be preferred.[56]

> Adopting a descending pattern will seem political and subjective either because it assumes the existence of a natural morality or because it creates an arbitrary distinction between States. An ascending pattern will seem political and subjective because it cannot constrain at all. It simply accepts as law whatever the State will choose to regard at any moment. Both must be included in order to make law seem objective, that is, normative and concrete and, as such, something other than politics.[57]

The continuing quest for the primacy of the Rule of Law in relations between states, a refrain reiterated in United Nations resolutions, is in this respect "another reformulation of the liberal impulse to escape politics."[58] But due to the logic of this conceptual structure, international legal doctrines remain at all times open to attack on two fronts. For one group of critics, usually those representing or sympathetic to the interests of smaller or weaker states, international law is too political because overly dependent on states' political power, an infinitely flexible and manipulable "façade for power politics." For another group, usually representing or sympathetic to the interests of bigger or more powerful states, international law is too political because founded on "speculative utopias," and thus too far removed from the factual realities of politics to

[55] "Only an ascending argument can give expression to the principles of subjectivity of value, freedom of the State, sovereign equality and the Rule of Law." Koskenniemi, *From Apology to Utopia*, p. 45.

[56] "Any doctrine, argument or position can be criticized because either utopian or apologist. The more it tries to escape from one, the deeper it sinks into the other. This will explain why familiar disputes keep recurring without there seeming to exist any way of disposing of them permanently. Law is contrasted to discretion, 'positivism' to 'naturalism,' consent to justice, sovereignty to community, autonomy to organization and so on." *Ibid.*, p. 46.

[57] *Ibid.* This dynamic has thus prompted the turn in the modern era away from theory and towards pragmatism in legal reasoning.

[58] Martti Koskenniemi, "The Politics of International Law," *European Journal of International Law* 1 (1990), p. 6. See, e.g., UN G.A. Res. 44/23, November 15, 1989 (declaring the period 1990–1999 as the "United Nations Decade of International Law").

At the same time, this approach is vulnerable to two major criticisms. First, the assumed formal doctrine of sources is unable to exclude either political considerations or discretion given persistent (and good faith) disagreement regarding both the correct tests of pedigree and the means by which to construct applicable legal rules.[67] Second, the idea of an objective theory of law is vulnerable to familiar charges leveled against doctrinal utopianism and its disconnectedness from state practice given that the actual application of the law requires constant balancing, interpretation, and evaluation resulting in a blurred and indeterminate law/politics distinction.[68]

Policy anti-formalism

The second approach defines itself in response to the criticisms of the first. The real lesson of the failure of the League of Nations, and before that the Congress system in the nineteenth century, was the naïve belief in the "ideas of legality and collective intervention."[69] Following Politis, Scelle and Pound, international law should be conceived not in terms of abstract rules but social ends, and should be linked more closely to the social necessities of international life. On this view, it is the effectiveness of standards – their "capacity to further social goals" – rather than their "formal validity" or "binding force" which is the relevant consideration.[70] What matters, for example, is not whether Article 16 of the Covenant or Article 2(4) of the Charter is legally binding, but rather what substantive values and policy goals are realized by and lie behind these norms.

[67] Thus, positivists tend to emphasize treaties and custom while naturalists include within their idea of sources both general principles and community values. Koskenniemi, *From Apology to Utopia*, p. 160.

[68] Whenever formal rules are applied, the need arises to delimit the disputing states' freedoms. But the law is devoid of criteria for preferring between conflicting freedoms. The construction of any solution will entail looking beyond the formal notion of "freedom" to some material criteria by which to make a preference or determine the relevant limits. "How to integrate such material criteria into the overall image of an objective law is a central problem" for the rule approach. As Koskenniemi notes, "Kelsen himself admits that the choice between a State-centered and an international community-centered systematics is a *political* choice." *Ibid.*, pp. 28–29.

[69] Wilsonian idealism is seen to have produced the League of Nations and the Kellogg–Briand Pact, but the idea that international law and organization could vanquish war and power politics was later "held responsible for the failure to prevent a host of interventions in the 1930s before eventually being implicated in the rise of Hitler and the Second World War. Idealism's failure became realism's ascendance." Simpson, "The Situation on the International Legal Theory Front," p. 449.

[70] Koskenniemi, "Politics of International Law," pp. 10–11.

The strength of the "policy" approach – with its rule-skepticism, emphasis on processes of authoritative decision-making and close connection between legal norms and state behavior (effectiveness) – is its embrace of value-dependent policies and processes to construct a teleological jurisprudence thus ensuring the wide scope and relevance of international law. But this closer connection between law and policy is achieved at the cost of what is arguably distinct about legal doctrine. If law is viewed merely as a technique of social engineering and as a function of bureaucratic management skills by technocratic experts, this ignores what H. L. A. Hart once described as the "internal aspect" of rules, the fact that decision makers concern themselves with questions of formal validity. Two major criticisms of anti-formalism logically follow.

First, if law is judged only in terms of its instrumental effectiveness, it soon becomes no more than an apology for the interests of powerful states. If ends are described in terms of community values, this fails to guarantee the protection of the rights of states or peoples when social effectiveness or overall utility argues for overruling them. We see this, for example, when peace between European powers was held to be more important than the freedom of Ethiopia, or when the independence and territorial integrity of India was held to be more important than an internal humanitarian crisis and a minority people's claim to self-determination.

Second, by emphasizing concreteness and effectiveness in this fashion, the law risks losing its objectivity and binding force altogether. As argued by Italy in response to the League's invocation of Article 16 measures against it, international law may in this way legitimize force as "enforcement" in a manner that conflicts directly with the belligerents' self-understanding. To correct this, the policy approach resorts to tacit naturalistic or material ideas of justice (e.g. certain "goal values of international human dignity") which international law is held to advance. But this returns the policy approach, paradoxically, to the problem it had sought to overcome by invoking the basis on which legal formalism had itself initially been criticized.[71] The problem then becomes how to justify the correctness of certain base values, especially when they come into conflict. Why, for example, in the case of Hyderabad was the decision not

[71] Base values in this way become, in effect, the equivalent to the rule approach within the system of anti-formal norms and processes. But the indeterminacy affecting the law/politics distinction is equally present in the human dignity value/actual decision distinction. This raises the charge of subjectivism in any account of goal or community values. Koskenniemi, *From Apology to Utopia*, p. 175 n. 163.

to take collective action against India premised on community prescriptions regarding peace (order) as opposed to social goals regarding the protection of fundamental human rights (justice)?

Realist skepticism

Faced with the apparently Sisyphean oscillation between these two approaches, the third approach adopts a thoroughly skeptical view that international law is neither normatively controlling nor widely applied in practice. Following the "collapse of the law of Geneva," this position is epitomized in the turn from international law towards the realism of international relations theory in the work of Hans Morgenthau.[72] While the formalism of the rule approach may have succeeded in putting some distance between itself and early modern naturalism, the anti-formalism of the policy approach – in an effort to bridge the metaphysical nature of legal rules with sociological, ethical and other factors – resulted in international law having little binding force. In the absence of enforceable sanctions, international legal rules such as Article 16 of the Covenant and Article 2(4) of the Charter thus amount to no more than subjective wishes.[73] The failure of the League to act in the case of Ethiopia was due to the unbridgeable gulf between Article 16 on the one hand and the national interests of Britain and France in avoiding war with Italy on the other. Similarly, the failure of the Security Council to act in the case of Hyderabad was due to the distance between Chapter VII's formal conception of collective security and the actual security interests of the Great Powers in a newly independent India.

This critique of collective security is premised on both interpretive and causal theses.[74] What is problematic about the skepticism of the realist

[72] See, e.g., Hans Morgenthau, "Positivism, Functionalism and International Law," 34 *AJIL* 260, 264 (1940).

[73] Note that the key element for the skeptic is the "enforceability" of sanctions. Under the formal rule approach of a jurist such as Kelsen, "sanction is a matter of the existence of a rule providing for sanctions. For the skeptic, this is a matter of observable fact." Koskenniemi, *From Apology to Utopia*, p. 168. While sharing the rule approach's domestically influenced "legalistic" idea of law, for the skeptic binding force emerges directly from factual coercion and law is merely an aspect of power politics. *Ibid.*, p. 169.

[74] The *interpretive* thesis is that collective security does not involve rule application in any way distinct from hegemonic or balance of power policy resulting in selective action taken according to the interests of hegemonic powers. The *causal* thesis is that peace and security do not depend on the presence or absence of rules, but rather on the use of power by states in a position to advance their interests. Martti Koskenniemi, "The Place of Law in Collective Security," 17 *Michigan Journal of International Law* 455 (1995–1996), p. 463.

position, however, is that it is premised on assumptions derived "outside the system itself" and thus from an external point of view. Skepticism does not consider the *internal* or *situated* aspect of rules, the "feeling with many statesmen and diplomats that rules exist and are binding upon them and their States."[75] By assuming that legal rules will always be overridden when vital state interests are at stake, skepticism overlooks how international law often protects and constructs state interests and identities.[76] It further overlooks how all Security Council action constantly refers to and invokes normative codes, rules, or principles creating specific modes of discourse and justification between states.[77] It thus misses what law most contributes to collective security: a form of *social* or *situational* ethics encompassing not just rules and principles but "a fairness of process, an attitude of openness, and a spirit of responsibility that implicitly or expressly means submission to critique and dialogue with others about the proper understanding of the community's principles and purposes – in a word, its identity."[78]

Idealism

The fourth and final position simply *assumes* as a matter of course both the law's binding force as well as its correspondence with developments in international practice. Embodying the modern program in its original form, this is the position towards which both rule and policy approaches are constantly drawn. While classical positivism is regarded as being excessively formalistic, reliance on naturalistic "policies" is seen as either a "powerless form of moral criticism" or "reactionary imperialism."[79] The idealist argument assumes that law is both a reflection of society, assuring its material scope, while at the same time being critical of existing structures of international dominance, assuring its normative nature. The problem, however, is that these two assumptions contradict

[75] Thus by simply looking at behavior, skepticism fails to "answer the relevant question of whether and to what extent legal rules worked behind that behavior (at the level of motivations, by structuring decision-contexts, delimiting alternative ways of action etc.)." Koskenniemi, *From Apology to Utopia*, p. 170.

[76] See, e.g., Friedrich V. Kratochwil, *Rules, Norms, and Decisions: On the Conditions of Practical and Legal Reasoning in International Relations and Domestic Affairs* (1989).

[77] Koskenniemi, "The Place of Law in Collective Security," p. 468. The *authority* of the Council thus rests not on factual or power-dependent but normative considerations.

[78] *Ibid.*, p. 478. [79] Koskenniemi, *From Apology to Utopia*, p. 179.

each other.[80] This forces idealism to collapse ultimately back into either a rule or policy approach, or to succumb to the siren call of skepticism.

Thus for the idealist, who sees social life among states in terms of common needs and solidarity values, Article 16 of the League Covenant may be *assumed* to reflect the will, interest and consent of League members while at the same time providing an objective means by which to assess and criticize the conduct of any member state which violates its terms. But as soon as Italy has actually invaded Ethiopia, the argument dissolves into contradiction. Our idealist must explain, for example, whether it is Ethiopia which has been the subject of unlawful aggression or whether it is Italy which has exercised its inherent right to self-defense and, either way, why the League's interpretation of these issues is any more objective than that of Ethiopia or Italy, or indeed of any other member state. In so doing, she will have assumed a rule approach viewing international social life through a formal doctrine of "sources."

Conversely, our idealist may explain the failure of the League to act on the grounds that Article 16 does not closely enough reflect the objective interests, needs and behavior of the League's member states (viewed together as an "international society"). In so doing, she will have assumed a policy approach constructing what counts as "processes of authoritative decision" by an "anterior criterion of authority, base-values and relevance." Of course, even if Article 16 were better to reflect the actual interests and "wants" of states in protecting collective security – e.g. by increasing the effectiveness of its sanctions and enforcement regime by allowing a right of veto to a sub-set of powerful states as in the UN Security Council – our idealist will have difficulty explaining why this is not merely an instrumental façade by which certain states seek to protect and project their vital policy interests.

Faced with these partial solutions and contradictions, each vulnerable to valid criticism from the others, our idealist may finally be tempted to adopt a skeptical position seeing the behavior of states as part of a continuing pattern of self-interested violence. In this way, each of the four conceptual schemes

[80] The first element resembles the policy approach: as law mirrors society, it reflects changes in international social life and thus corresponds to the "objective character (interests, needs etc.) of the international society." But this runs the risk of apologism and appears to foreclose any critical vantage point. A second element then is needed to explain law as a mechanism of change. But this will immediately contradict the first element. *Ibid.*, pp. 185–186.

> bases its superiority on its capacity to describe more accurately the social environment of international politics ... Using apparently neutral (descriptive) language they hope to preserve the liberal theory of politics. But in their mutual criticism, they reveal the material theories of justice hidden in them.[81]

What this account reveals is that, while on the one hand the *actual* political interests, preferences, and policies of states are both widely divergent and often in conflict, on the other hand there is no *external* or *objective* normative ideal that can be invoked to bring them into harmony. In his more recent writing, Koskenniemi has referred to this as the "paradox of objectives." It is important we recognize that this is not a "technical problem that could be disposed of by reflecting more closely on the meaning of words such as 'peace', 'security', or 'justice' or by carrying out more sophisticated social or economic analyses about the way the world is." Rather, we should realize that the founding Westphalian myth of the system

> lay the basis for an agnostic, procedural international law whose merit consisted in its refraining from imposing any external normative ideal on the international society. The objectives of that society would now arise from itself: there were no religious or other transcendental notions of the good that international law should realize. If there is an "international community", it is not a teleological but a practical association, a system not designed to realize ultimate ends but to coordinate practical action to further the objectives of existing communities.[82]

A system of international legal liberalism based on these premises will automatically give rise to two main conceptual problems which, unsurprisingly, have been strikingly evident in debates over the role of law in collective security following September 11, 2001. The first dynamic involves questions of identity and recognition: Who is the subject of the law? What is a "state" and why is it that only "state objectives" count? Why, for example, did the League Council recognize Ethiopia as a state while the Security Council refused so to recognize Hyderabad? On account of difficulties such as these, the state-centrism of the international system has long been a target of critique in the modern era. Further, the disaggregating forces of globalization and the burgeoning role of subjects apart

81 *Ibid.*, pp. 189–190. (1989 edition).

82 Martti Koskenniemi, "What is International Law For?," in Evans, M. D. (ed.), *International Law* (Oxford: Oxford University Press, 2003), p. 89. This explains the easy application of Kantian ethics to international law: "an ethics of universalizable principles of *right action* rather than as instrumental guidelines for attaining the Good." *Ibid.*, p. 90, n. 1.

from states (individuals, peoples, nations, minorities, international organizations, transnational corporations etc.) have now led to new theories of "global" or "cosmopolitan" justice which it is said international law should encompass.[83] This trend has only accelerated in the post-September 11 context of "global terrorism," and the threat not of traditional state but *non-state* actors using weapons of mass destruction.[84] It is also reflected in the extent to which informal networks and epistemic communities today influence international politics well beyond the Westphalian state model.[85] Nevertheless, despite these vast economic, technological, and cultural "globalizing" processes the sovereign state has maintained its status as the central subject of the international legal order.[86]

The second conceptual problem is that of sovereignty: What freedom do states have and how exactly are conflicting state freedoms to be reconciled in a world deeply divided by differences of power, wealth, and geography? As High-Level idealism in the Lauterpachtian mold[87] is confronted with Morgenthau-style skepticism, international lawyers have responded to this question in two ways. Some have accepted the diminished role that law can play in a single-superpower world and have sought instead to reconceive the United Nations collective security

[83] Koskenniemi, "What is International Law For?," p. 94. For a useful discussion, see Thomas W. Pogge, "What is Global Justice?," unpublished manuscript, Oslo, September 11, 2003 (noting the recent shift in terminology from older notions of "international justice," "international ethics," and the "law of nations," to the new concept of "global justice"). In a similar vein, see Amartya Sen, "Justice Across Borders" in Ciaran Cronin and Pablo De Grieff, eds., *Global Justice and Transnational Politics* (Cambridge, Mass.: MIT Press, 2002) pp. 37–51.

[84] The High-Level Panel Report refers to these as "threats without boundaries": High-Level Panel Report, paras. 17–23.

[85] Hillary Charlesworth, "International Law: A Discipline of Crisis," 65 *Modern Law Review* 377 (2002) (noting that what constitutes a "threat" in the international system is determined by a completely Western-dominated process). Accordingly, it is difficult to justify the attention and resources allocated to the "war against terrorism" after the death of nearly 3,000 people in September 2001 while "simultaneously six million children under five years old die annually of malnutrition by causes that could be prevented by existing economic and technical resources." Koskenniemi, "What is International Law For?," pp. 95–96.

[86] See, e.g., High-Level Panel Report, synopsis p. 11: "If there is to be a new security consensus, it must start with the understanding that the front-line actors in dealing with all the threats we face, new and old, continue to be individual sovereign States, whose role and responsibilities, and the right to be respected, are fully recognized in the Charter of the United Nations."

[87] United Nations, *A More Secure World: Our Shared Responsibility*, Report of the Secretary-General's High-Level Panel on Threats, Challenges, and Change, UN Doc. A/59/565 (2004) (hereinafter the High-Level Panel Report).

apparatus and other international legal regimes as "variables dependent on a central power."[88] Alternatively, they have developed "purely instrumental accounts of the use of law in the defense of particular interests or preferences."[89] Both positions adopt variants of the policy approach.

Others, relying on a background conception of a "harmony of interests" which international law is to realize in conflicts between states, have advanced more sophisticated "interdependence" or "globalization" theories. Jürgen Habermas, for example, has argued for a "global domestic politics without a world government" which combines an "empowered United Nations responsible for securing peace and promoting human rights at the *supranational* level with governance institutions based on cooperation among the major world powers to address urgent problems of regional and global concern at the *transnational* level."[90] The combined rule and idealist approaches are again here apparent.

Collective security under the United Nations Charter

Let me illustrate these two dynamics in terms of the collective security system established under the UN Charter. In the late 1980s, Stanley

[88] Hedley Bull, "The Grotian Conception of International Society," in H. Butterfield and M. Wight (eds.), *Diplomatic Investigations: Essays in the Theory of International Relations* (London: Allen & Unwin, 1966), p. 51 (arguing for a "pluralist" rather than "solidarist" conception of international relations under which international society "will be able to enforce its law only if it can mobilize superior power in its support" and where international law "leave[s] room for the operation of those political forces, beyond the control of law, on which the existence of international society also depends"). For a classic account of this view, see George W. Keeton and Georg Schwarzenberger, *Making International Law Work* (London: Stevens & Sons, 2nd edn., 1946).

[89] United States Institute of Peace, *American Interests and UN Reform: Report of the Task Force on the United Nations* (2005) (suggesting, *contra* the findings of the High-Level Panel on the use of force, that "there is nothing exclusive about the United Nations as regards American interests" and that the "United Nations is one of the tools that America, our allies, and other democracies use cooperatively on the basis of our shared values"). See also Ruth Wedgwood, "Unilateral Action in the UN System," 11 *EJIL* 349, 353 (2000) (arguing that "when push comes to shove, waiting for unanimity may sometimes fail to protect other values at stake"); Michael J. Glennon, "Platonism, Adaptivism, and Illusion in UN Reform," 6 *Chicago Journal of International Law* 613 (2005–2006), pp. 613–614 (describing the recent UN reform process as a "useful project" and arguing that even if "the objective were merely to advance individual states' national interests, the UN might be a useful tool for doing so"). See also Michael J. Glennon, "Idealism at the UN," *Policy Review* (February and March 2005).

[90] Jürgen Habermas, *The Divided West*, Ciaran Cronin trans. and ed. (Cambridge: Polity Press Ltd., 2006), p. xi.

Hoffmann assessed the prospects of the emergence of an international order governed by the rule of law and collective security as follows:

> Nobody seems to believe anymore in the chances of collective security; because of its constraining character, it is too contrary to the freedom of judgement and action implied by sovereignty; and … it is in conflict with the imperatives of prudence in the nuclear age, in which the localization or insulation of conflicts appears far preferable to their generalization.[91]

Writing in the twilight of the Cold War, Hoffman's pessimism can today be seen to reflect the deep disillusionment of most statesmen, policy makers, and international lawyers with a Charter-based collective security regime that had been paralyzed for the better part of four decades by the balance of power strategies of the two superpowers. That system, grounded as we have seen in a post-war vision of a new international order determined to overcome the "scourge of war," is premised on two basic elements: first, the prohibition under Article 2(4) on the threat or use of force between states; and second, the establishment of a Security Council bearing "primary responsibility for the maintenance of international peace and security" and thus empowered under Chapter VII, on behalf of all member states, to enforce a regime of collective security.[92]

Each element finds its justification in the basic assumption of *sovereign equality* – the equal "sovereignty" of all "states" as the subjects of a putative legal order. The obligation not to threaten or use force applies equally to all states and thus generates a correlative right to non-interference under Article 2(7). Again, in this structure, we see the basic paradox of liberal doctrine: the attempt to reconcile what seem like opposing demands for state freedom and social order. This normative dilemma presents itself in the opposing demands of state autonomy (sovereignty) and international

91 Stanley Hoffmann, "Is There an International Order?," in *Janus and Minerva Essays in the Theory and Practice of International Politics* (Boulder: Westview Press, 1987), p. 117.

92 Traditionally, this regime was concerned with interstate violence but more recently it has tackled large-scale violence and civil war within states. Boutros Boutros-Ghali, *An Agenda for Peace: Preventative Diplomacy, Peacemaking and Peace-Keeping: Report of the Secretary-General*, UN GAOR, 47th Sess., UN Doc. A/47/277 (1992). During the 1990s, the question arose whether threats to international peace and security may also include nonmilitary sources of instability in the economic, social, humanitarian, or ecological spheres in such a way as to trigger the Council's competence under Chapter VII. Such developments suggest an image of the Council as a "post-Cold War Leviathan" presiding over a new world order. Koskenniemi, "The Place of Law in Collective Security," p. 460. See Part II of this volume for discussion of the notion of "threats" to collective security.

community (collective security) mediated by the international equivalent of Mill's "harm principle" set out jointly in Articles 2(4) and 51. But how is this reconciliation meant to occur?

In the case of the former, each state's sovereignty is said to include an "inherent" right to individual and collective self-defense under Article 51. States are under a duty to refrain under Article 2(4) from the threat or use of force in their interstate relations, *except* when harmed or imminently threatened by an "armed attack" by another state or group of states. In such a case, the unilateral use of force is permitted by the law to the extent necessary to repel the attack or until such time as the Security Council assumes its institutional responsibility to impose a range of collective security measures. In the case of the latter, the determination and enforcement of any collective security measure is premised on the consent, real or imagined, of all member states. The collective use of force is thus permitted by the law but only under such terms, both procedural and substantive, as provided in Chapter VII.

Interpreting the meaning of the Charter's harm principle conjoined in Articles 2(4)/51 and applying some normative reconciliation in a world of diverse and hostile sovereign states is clearly a Herculean interpretive task. On account of these difficulties, the only imagined and just solution has been thought to be the establishment of some impartial decision maker with the authority to interpret and enforce a set of neutral and objective "legal" rules which, simultaneously, protect the preexisting autonomy and liberty of states *and* constrain that liberty in the name of the liberty of all, the collective security of the community of states. Of course, as between the principle of sovereign equality and a Security Council with five permanent members wielding the right of veto over all other member states, the realist compromise of idealism with the post-war balance of power is evident.[93]

The relationship between the prohibition on the threat or use of force in Article 2(4) and its two exceptions in Article 51 (unilateral self-defense) and Chapter VII (collective security) was the most controversial issue in the post-2004 UN reform process. The High-Level Panel identified two concerns, in particular, which mirror the issues underlying our

[93] This well illustrates the interdependence in the Charter regime between order (power) and justice (authority): "Justice as a means to uphold order, order as a means to realize justice." Koskenniemi, "The Police in the Temple," p. 329. Unlike the League, the Charter collective security system is "based on the co-option of overwhelming power." *Ibid.*, p. 338.

older two cases of Ethiopia and Hyderabad. The first was the traditional Charter concern of "external threats" and the threat or use of force between states. Following the 2003 US-led invasion of Iraq, the critical question here was that of "anticipatory self-defense" and the lawfulness under the Charter of the Bush administration's new national security policy which expands the notion of "preemptive" war to encompass "preventive" war.[94] On this score, the Panel did not favor rewriting or reinterpreting the formal terms of Article 51:

> [I]f there are good arguments for preventive military action, with good evidence to support them, they should be put to the Security Council, which can authorize such action if it chooses to. If it does not so choose, there will be, by definition, time to pursue other strategies, including persuasion, negotiation, deterrence and containment – and to visit again the military option.[95]

At the same time, the Panel immediately qualified the formalism of this position on the unilateral use of force with five anti-formal "criteria of legitimacy"[96] said to be necessary in the case of collective action because

[94] President George W. Bush, "Prevent Our Enemies From Threatening Us, Our Allies, and Our Friends with Weapons of Mass Destruction," in *National Security Strategy of the United States of America* (September 2002), pp. 13–15:

> We must adapt the concept of imminent threat to the capabilities and objectives of today's adversaries … The greater the threat, the greater is the risk of inaction – and the more compelling the case for taking anticipatory action to defend ourselves, even if uncertainty remains as to the time and place of the enemy's attack.

[95] High-Level Panel Report, para. 190. The Panel justified its preference for "collective endorsed action" on the basis of the risk to the "global order and the norm of non-intervention on which it continues to be based" of unilateral preventive action. "Allowing one to so act is to allow all." *Ibid.*, para. 191.

[96] In considering whether to authorize or endorse the use of military force, the Security Council should address at least five basic criteria of legitimacy: (a) *seriousness of the threat* (is the threatened harm to a State or human security of a kind, and sufficiently clear and serious, to justify prima facie the use of force); (b) *proper purpose* (is it clear that the primary purpose of the proposed military action is to halt or avert the threat in question, whatever other purposes may be involved); (c) *last resort* (has every nonmilitary option been explored, with reasonable grounds for believing that other measures will not succeed); (d) *proportional means* (are the scale, duration, and intensity of the proposed military action the minimum necessary to meet the threat); and (e) *balance of consequences* (is there a reasonable chance of the military action being successful in meeting the threat, with the consequences of action not likely to be worse than the consequences of inaction). *Ibid.*, para. 207. The Panel further suggests that it would be "valuable if individual Member States, whether or not they are members of the Security Council, subscribed to them." *Ibid.*, para. 209.

> [t]he *effectiveness* of the global security system, as with any other legal order, depends ultimately not only on the legality of decisions but also on the common perception of their *legitimacy* – their being made on solid evidentiary grounds, and for the right reasons, morally as well as legally.[97]

Thus if the Security Council is to "win the respect it must have as the primary body in the collective security system," it must adopt and address such a set of agreed guidelines "going directly not to whether force *can* legally be used but whether, as a matter of good conscience and good sense, it *should* be."[98]

Noting the increased effectiveness of the Security Council in regulating international conflict since the end of Cold War paralysis, the Panel seamlessly wove these two positions together: on the one hand, the balance between unilateral use of force and collectively authorized force was said to have "shifted dramatically" since the 1990s with the result that today, in accordance with the rules of the Charter, there is an "expectation that the Security Council should be the arbiter of the use of force."[99] On the other hand, although the Council did not actually deter war in Iraq, it provided a "clear and principled standard with which to assess the decision to go to war."[100]

Unsurprisingly, commentators have criticized the Panel both for its formalism regarding Article 51 and its anti-formalism in the application of Chapter VII. Michael Glennon, for example, has argued that the Panel's recommended limitation on the use of force in the case of a "serious and likely threat until it becomes imminent … is not a reasonable limit on state power." It is not imminence, but the gravity of the threat and the probability of its occurrence that are the key factors. Accordingly, no "responsible policymaker, knowing that some rogue state or terrorist group is planning a nuclear strike, would recommend sitting tight until the attack

97 *Ibid.*, para. 204 (my emphasis).

98 *Ibid.*, para. 205 (emphasis in original). As opposed to a constitutionalist, rule-based approach, this is rather a mindset of "virtue ethics" – the "sensibility to do the right thing, to act on proper motives". Jan Klabbers, "Kadi Justice at the Security Council," *International Organizations Law Review* (2007), p. 7.

99 High-Level Panel Report, para. 81. The failure of the Security Council to deter the US and its allies from invading Iraq does not undermine the legal rule that the Charter prohibits unilateral preventive action. Indeed, the Panel notes, "Superpowers have rarely sought Security Council approval for their actions" and because this is not a "time-honoured principle … what is at stake is a relatively new emerging norm, one that is precious but not yet deep-rooted." *Ibid.*, para. 82.

100 *Ibid.*, para. 83.

becomes imminent."[101] In the case of Chapter VII, the Panel has adopted the core assumption of just war theory: "All right-thinking people, everywhere, will somehow identify in unison, 'sufficiently clear and serious' threats to 'State … or human security' and can in addition determine as with one mind the 'primary purpose' of a given military action." Glennon has thus criticized the Panel for what he terms its "radical adaptivism" – a "free-wheeling, outcome-oriented mode of analysis that abandons all fidelity to limitations set out in the text, views interpretation and amendment as interchangeable, and exhibits a lack of commitment to the notion of limited power and the rule of law." Where, he asks, does the Panel "extract its universally 'valuable' legitimacy criteria? Right reason? The Bible? The Koran?"[102]

The second dominant concern of the Panel was "internal threats" and what is today referred to as the "responsibility to protect."[103] While the Panel insisted that "genocide anywhere is a threat to the security of all and should never be tolerated," this did not *per se* generate a right to unilateral humanitarian intervention. In the event of humanitarian catastrophes, the issue is "not the 'right to intervene' of any State but the 'responsibility to protect' of *every* State."[104] Accordingly, the Panel endorsed an "emerging norm" that there is

> a collective international responsibility to protect, exercisable by the Security Council authorizing military intervention as a last resort, in the event of genocide and other large-scale killing, ethnic cleansing or serious violations of international humanitarian law which sovereign Governments have proved powerless or unwilling to prevent.[105]

Here, again, Glennon has criticized the Panel for its unjustifiable mix of legal formalism and policy anti-formalism. On the one hand, reading the UN Charter formally to preclude unilateral humanitarian intervention, and thus placing sole responsibility in the hands of the Security Council with its

[101] Glennon, "Platonism, Adaptivism, and Illusion in UN Reform," p. 615. As Glennon astutely notes, the Panel's own criteria "seem to suggest that using defensive force under such circumstances would be legitimate." Further, and paradoxically, the Panel's endorsement of the notion of "imminence" is itself a departure from the plain text of Article 51 which requires an *actual* "armed attack." Having taken the initial anti-formal step from "actual" to "imminent," why not continue to "preventive"? *Ibid.*, p. 620.

[102] *Ibid.*, pp. 614, 617.

[103] The term derives from the report of a group of experts convened by the Canadian government in 2000: Gareth Evans and Mohamed Sahnoun, *The Responsibility to Protect: Report of the International Commission on Intervention and State Sovereignty* (2001).

[104] High-Level Panel Report, para. 200. [105] *Ibid.*, para. 203.

ever-present risk of deadlock or inaction, implies that genocide and ethnic cleansing *can* sometimes be tolerated and allowed to continue. On the other hand – under the Panel's own five anti-formal criteria of legitimacy – interventions in cases such as Vietnam in Cambodia to end the killing fields, Tanzania in Uganda to halt Idi Amin, or NATO in Yugoslavia to prevent ethnic cleansing in Kosovo, can themselves make a case for legitimacy.[106] As regards the former we should recall our case of Hyderabad,[107] while as regards the latter we may point to examples such as India's "humanitarian intervention" in 1971 into East Pakistan (Bangladesh).[108]

The Panel's recommendations on the use of force in relation to both external and internal threats in this way raise a host of difficult questions regarding the place of law in the UN collective security system. In general, they represent a response to the breakdown since the early 1990s of the pragmatic compromise of the Charter system in two directions. First, according to an anti-formal communitarian argument which views sovereignty as an anachronistic obstacle to humanitarian objectives and thus outweighed by the need to protect fundamental human rights. This argument is best illustrated by the discourse seeking to justify military intervention by NATO in Kosovo in the late 1990s (and which today seeks military intervention in Sudan in response to the humanitarian crisis in Darfur).[109] Second, according to an anti-formal autonomy argument which asserts that the sovereign right of self-defense includes the right of preemptive strikes.[110] This position was asserted most directly by the US following the terrorist attacks of September 11, 2001. The first represents a shift from a formal statist conception of collective security to a new anti-formal individualistic "responsibility to

106 Glennon, "Platonism, Adaptivism, and Illusion in UN Reform," p. 615.

107 See, e.g., Omar Khalidi, ed., *Hyderabad: After the Fall* (Wichita, Kan.: Hyderabad Historical Society 1988) (describing a catalogue of massacres, looting, rape, and abduction as India's armed forces broke the resistance of the Hyderabadi army and Muslim irregulars and sent 200,000 people fleeing to Pakistan by 1950).

108 Pakistan used military force in its eastern province in March 1971 to eliminate the Bengali movement for autonomy. In what is widely regarded as a genuine case of humanitarian intervention, and despite its clear strategic and moral interests, India unilaterally intervened to stop the slaughter. Michael Walzer, *Just and Unjust Wars: A Moral Argument with Historical Illustrations* (New York: Basic Books, 1977), p. 105 (arguing that India's actions were a "*rescue*, strictly and narrowly defined" and that thus "circumstances sometimes make saints of us all").

109 Christine Chinkin, "Kosovo: A 'Good' or 'Bad' War?," 93 *AJIL* 841 (1999). On Darfur, see Alex de Waal, "Darfur and the Failure of the Responsibility to Protect," 83 *International Affairs* 1039 (2007).

110 Koskenniemi, "International Law and Hegemony," pp. 202–203.

protect."[111] The second represents the danger of Great Power hegemony in a system predicated on sovereign equality. Three main difficulties bear observing in light of the Panel's responses to these challenges.

First, the Panel's reliance on armed collective action by the Security Council in cases of external aggression or internal violence is contradicted not only by history, but by the structure of the Charter itself. As a matter of history, the Cold War prevented the Council from ever negotiating the special Article 43 agreements needed to provide the "constabulary power before which barbaric and atavistic forces will stand in awe."[112] The Council has thus never had at its disposal standing forces provided by member states to respond to breaches of the peace.[113] Structurally, the duty of member states to make armed forces available for the purposes of enforcing Security Council resolutions in response to threats to peace and security is one requiring special negotiation and consent.[114] This distinguishes the Charter-based conception of collective security from mutual security treaties such as NATO and the Rio Pact which are explicitly based on the notion that an "attack on one is an attack on all."[115] Given this cooperation-based and voluntarist conception of member state duty to the Council, how exactly is collective action to be taken in cases where powerful state interests are threatened (e.g. as against Russian military action in Chechnya) or, worse, where they are not directly implicated at all (e.g. as against Sudanese military action in Darfur, Moroccan military action in Western Sahara, or in the Congo generally)?

Second, the hopeful notion that humanitarian crises in one state are a threat to the security of all states is not a position borne out in state practice. As Glennon notes, the "reason states often do not respond to such humanitarian catastrophes is that they do not believe that such events really *are* threats to their own security."[116] The failure of the Council to

[111] Compare Ramesh Thakur, *The United Nations, Peace and Security: From Collective Responsibility to Responsibility to Protect* (Cambridge: Cambridge University Press, 2006), p. 256 (arguing that while military intervention for human protection purposes "takes away the rights flowing from the status of sovereignty," this does not "in itself challenge the status as such").

[112] Winston Churchill, Chancellor's Address at the University of Bristol, July 2, 1938, cited in Glennon, "Platonism, Adaptivism, and Illusion in UN Reform," p. 621.

[113] *Ibid.* [114] See United Nations Charter, Article 43, para. 1.

[115] Glennon, "Platonism, Adaptivism, and Illusion in UN Reform," p. 622.

[116] *Ibid.* p. 623. The Panel correctly observes, however, that the "interrelatedness" of threats arising from situations of massive state failure and gross human rights violations such as disease, internal displacement and refugee flows is increasingly becoming recognized as a threat to collective security.

respond effectively to the disastrous humanitarian situation in Congo over the last five years is one example among many. Further, the concept of "responsibility to protect" raises formalist and anti-formalist difficulties of its own: on the one hand, the formal structure of the Charter itself does not envisage internal threats – if they were thought about at all – as threats to peace and security. The dramatic rise of the (anti-formal) universal human rights discourse in the UN Charter era has shattered the formal notion of *domain reservé* in Article 2(7) with both unintended and anti-pluralist consequences. On the other hand, the idea that the responsibility to protect now gives rise to a far-reaching right of collective action in cases of massive internal violence remains a contested question among states, especially among post-colonial countries wary of manipulation – unilateral *or* multilateral – of humanitarian criteria for imperial motives.

Third, despite the Panel's protestations to the contrary, it is not clear as a matter of historical record whether realist balances of power have been less effective in maintaining peace and stopping the scourge of war as compared to collective security regimes premised on the international rule of law. This remains an issue of vigorous argument among international relations and legal scholars and is the subject of a voluminous literature.[117] Conversely, as an empirical matter looking to the future, it is not obvious whether loosening the strictures on preemption and humanitarian intervention will result in more instability in the global order. This, too, is a question of current interest for scholars seeking to understand the empirical patterns of interstate conflicts.[118]

Conclusion

These competing positions help to explain the conceptual positions adopted by the High-Level Panel Report and its critics. Each point of

[117] It is difficult to see the 150 million people killed in war during the twentieth century – vastly more than during the balance of power dynamics of the nineteenth century – as a sign of the effectiveness of legalistic multilateralism. Glennon, "Platonism, Adaptivism, and Illusion in UN Reform," p. 626.

[118] Ryan Goodman, "Humanitarian Intervention and Pretexts for War," *AJIL* 100 (2006) (arguing on the basis of empirical studies of unintended constraints on state action that legalizing unilateral humanitarian intervention "holds the prospect of restraining some aggressive wars"); John C. Yoo, "Force Rules: UN Reform and Intervention," *Chicago Journal of International Law* 6 (2006), p. 661 (arguing that reform of the UN Charter's use of force rules "should begin by modifying the rules to produce higher levels of desirable uses of force" and advocating an "international public goods" approach which will "produce positive externalities to the international system by ending rogue states, flushing out international terrorist groups, or ending human rights disasters").

view seeks to offer interpretations of *both* the objective meaning of the UN Charter (i.e. the textual or formal rules) and the objective reasons that lie behind and justify these rules (i.e. relevant social goals and ethical principles). For the Panel, Article 51 should be read loosely enough to *imply* a right of preemptive self-defense, but formally enough to preclude a right to preventive self-defense. This is in line with the original intent of the drafters of the Charter to outlaw war (Article 2(4)) while allowing for force only in genuine emergencies or when agreed through collective decision. Similarly, the Chapter VII collective enforcement measures should be read loosely enough to *imply* a collective duty to protect in situations of genocide and ethnic cleansing, but still formally enough to require explicit authorization for any use of force (whether in self-defense or for humanitarian purposes). Thus, the non-interference aspect of sovereignty in Article 2(7) remains a bar to unilateral action, but not to legally justified collective action. This is in line with the objective meaning and purposes of the Charter to ensure both peace and justice.[119]

Conversely, from the perspective of its critics the formal and anti-formal considerations are reversed. Even if it allows narrowly for preemptive action, Article 51 remains an unreasonable formal constraint and should be read more loosely to allow for preventive action against grave and gathering threats to state security. This is in line with the objective meaning and purpose of the Charter to protect states from violence and destruction. Similarly, Chapter VII should be read narrowly not to create a collective duty to act in cases of gross human rights violations. This is in line with the original intent of the drafters of the Charter who were primarily concerned with situations of interstate conflict. At the same time, Article 2(7) and the notion of non-interference should be read broadly enough not to bar *unilateral* humanitarian intervention in cases of true tyranny and oppression by a state of its people (as in the case of Serbia regarding Kosovo or Sudan regarding Darfur).

The differences express the different social objectives and ethical principles of the two starting positions. The High-Level Panel recommendations are premised on a preference for and bias towards multilateralism and the perceived needs of the "international community" – on whose behalf the Panel portends to speak. Critics of collective security – whether states or

[119] This is a classic liberal internationalist view of how to reconcile issues of legality and legitimacy. For such a view, see Richard A. Falk, "Kosovo, World Order, and the Future of International Law," 93 *AJIL* 847 (1999).

their apologists – premise their views on a preference for and bias towards unilateralism and the protection of national interests and values. It is not a simple matter then of the Panel illuminating the formal law of the Charter and the critics their preexisting policy preferences. Both sides rely on the formal/anti-formal dichotomy in an oscillating fashion to articulate their background biases. The critical point to observe, however, is that it is the formality of the Charter itself, and of international law in general, which allows us to critique the positions of both the Panel and its most ardent critics.[120]

Why, for example, does the Panel believe itself capable of accessing the true or objective purposes of the international community in some politics-independent way? Who exactly are the eminent ones? What are their identities, backgrounds and interests? What is the source of their authority to speak on behalf of humanity? As Glennon suggests, the Panel's findings appear as another form of moral naturalism (he uses the term "Platonism and radical adaptivism") and, to the extent they are contrary to either powerful state interests or competing views of the *true purposes* of international law, a utopian illusion. On the other hand, why are the United States' or Glennon's own interpretations of the Charter not merely instrumental justifications seeking to realize their own purposes and policy objectives? Even, and perhaps especially, when articulated in universal terms[121] – e.g. to promote democracy, human rights, or the rule of law – why should we assume that these are the *right objectives* and not simply façades for powerful states or other actors to achieve their imperial ends?

As Koskenniemi powerfully argues, this dynamic reveals the indispensability of the *non-instrumental* or *cultural* aspects of law in international politics:

> Every standard is always formal and substantive at the same time. The very ideas of treaty and codification make sense only if one assumes that at some point there emerges an agreement, an understanding, a standard that is separate from its legislative background … The point of law is to

[120] Following the 2003 invasion of Iraq, Richard Perle stated that we should "thank God for the death of the UN," and, in particular, the idea that "only the UN Security Council can legitimize the use of force." Richard Perle, "Thank God for the Death of the UN," *The Guardian*, March 23, 2003. Even for the world's superpower then, the mere existence of the UN Charter and its rules limiting the use of force create the need for normative justification and objective reasons.

[121] "Whoever invokes humanity wants to cheat." Carl Schmitt, *Der Nomos der Erde im Völkerrecht des Jus Publicum Europaeum,* 3rd edn. (Berlin: Duncker and Humbolt, 1988), p. 54.

> give rise to standards that are no longer merely "proposed" or "useful" or "good", and therefore can be deviated from if one happens to share a deviating notion of what in fact is useful or good. Instead, they are assumed to possess "validity."[122]

This validity indicates a formal property of legal norms – a "'flat substanceless surface' [which] expresses the universalist principle of inclusion at the outset and makes possible the regulative ideal of a pluralistic international world." This is absolutely critical as the form of the law

> constructs political adversaries as equals, entitled to express their subjectively felt injustices in terms of breaches of the rules of the community to which they belong no less than their adversaries – thus affirming both that inclusion and the principle that the conditions applying to the treatment of any one member of the community must apply to every other member as well.[123]

These two qualities – law's validity and its inclusive and pluralist ideals – are pivotal to understanding the dialectics between formalism and instrumentalism in the post-2003 UN reform debates and for assessing the policy arguments of the Great Powers formulated to deal with a new gallery of rogue states and non-state outlaws.[124] While for realists and institutionalists international law may be *external* and *instrumentalist* – a means by which to realize certain political interests and values – the concept of collective security in international law requires an understanding of the *internal* or *engaged* aspect of the law which "acts as a spirit or an attitude that involves recognizing the communal situatedness of the

122 Koskenniemi, "What is International Law For?," p. 102. See also Anne Orford, "The Gift of Formalism," *EJIL* 15 (2004) (arguing that the formality of the UN Charter's rules on the use of force offers "resistance to imperialism (specifically of the American variety)," but also that the "notion that the UN Charter embodies an international legal order that is free of the desire for empire is complicated if we turn to those sections … that support the trend towards constituting the UN as the manager of problems in the developing world.")

123 Koskenniemi, "What is International Law For?," pp. 102–103. In any decision to attach meaning to legal norms, sovereign equality means that states can articulate their interpretations on conditions of equal standing. They are thus included in the "normative universe as subjects of rights and duties or carriers as distinct identities." It is only because a regime comprises noninstrumental rules (i.e. "understood to be authoritative independent of particular beliefs or purposes") that the freedom of its subjects to be different becomes possible. Terry Nardin, "Legal Positivism as a Theory of International Society," in D. R. Mapel and T. Nardin (eds.), *International Society: Diverse Ethical Perspectives* (Princeton: Princeton University Press, 1998), p. 31, cited in Koskenniemi, "What is International Law For?," p. 102.

124 Gerry Simpson, *Great Powers and Outlaw States: Unequal Sovereigns in the International Legal Order* (Cambridge: Cambridge University Press, 2004).

speaker: hence its curious, yet typical, ability to engage the practitioner in political action while seeking distance from anyone's idiosyncratic interests."[125] It is this distancing of political actors from their preferences which constitutes them as members of a self-creating legal and political community, itself a necessary but insufficient condition for any coherent conception of collective security.

[125] Koskenniemi, "The Place of Law in Collective Security," pp. 489–490.

2

Reflections on the politics of institutional reform

JAN KLABBERS[1]

Whenever there are goods to be allocated, human beings devise institutions to do the allocating. Whether it concerns the distribution of donor kidneys among kidney patients, the allocation of scholarships among PhD students, the organization of social security in the welfare state, or the maintenance of peace in an anarchic world, some institution will be devised to organize, implement, manage, or oversee the activity. Leaving it to a single individual, *à titre personnel*, to decide on scholarships is, after all, not terribly satisfactory; she might decide to sponsor nieces and nephews first, or people working in the same discipline, or people of the same ethnic descent. In short, we tend to think that leaving such decisions to an individual is usually not a good idea.[2] When such issues, like the allocation of goods, cannot be settled judicially, an institution offers better guarantees for fairness in the decision-making process, than leaving things to the whims and preferences of individuals.[3]

By the same token, giving a single state the responsibility (or privilege) to maintain or restore international peace is bound to provoke outcries of protest. What if the state ignores aggression by its allies? Or only acts upon aggression committed by some, but not by others? Or, worst of all perhaps, uses its elevated position to commit aggression itself? Again, creating an institution is deemed to be the most obvious way to prevent abuse.

[1] Many thanks to Horst Fischer and Peter Danchin for inviting me to the conference where an earlier version of this paper was first presented and to the participants for their commentaries.

[2] See Lon L. Fuller, "The Forms and Limits of Adjudication," *Harvard Law Review* 92 (1978), pp. 353–409.

[3] See in general Jon Elster, *Local Justice: How Institutions Allocate Scarce Goods and Necessary Burdens* (New York: Russell Sage Foundation, 1992).

Yet, institutional design, and by extension institutional reform, is an ambivalent topic, forever torn between two sets of competing sentiments. The first set of competing sentiments stems from the tension between action, on the one hand, and reflection or debate on the other. The philosopher Michael Oakeshott has pioneered the idea that states and their institutions derive from the tension between two different conceptions of association: purposive (he calls this *universitas*), and non-purposive (*societas*).[4] In the field of international organizations, this translates into a tension between organizations as technical, managerial entities on the one hand, and debating clubs on the other.[5] And it is between those poles that institutional reform plays out, in part: Should organs become more effective, thus highlighting the managerial approach? Or should organs be more inclusive, more representative, more geared towards deliberation than toward action? Related, if perhaps somewhat subordinate, is a tension between instrumental rationality and political rationality. Instrumental rationality taps into the idea of making an institution more effective, while political rationality concentrates on the political effect of the institution's actions. Political rationality looks at whether others appreciate the attempt, even if it may make no difference in instrumental terms. A sub-theme of this chapter will be that many reform proposals oscillate between instrumental and political rationality.[6]

The second set of competing sentiments stems from the tension between the substantive morality of the institutions, and the morality of the individuals in the institutions. On the one hand there is the idea, perhaps best formulated by Lon Fuller, that the right institutions will more often than not produce the right results. As Fuller suggests, proper institutional design (he speaks of the internal morality of law) obviates the need to include substantive morality in the rules of the institution concerned and the substantive morality between the people in the institution.[7]

[4] See in general Michael Oakeshott, *On Human Conduct* (Oxford: Clarendon Press, 1975).

[5] See Jan Klabbers, "Two Concepts of International Organization," *International Organizations Law Review* 2 (2005), pp. 277–293.

[6] For application of the same idea in a different setting, see Jan Klabbers, "Compliance Procedures," in Daniel Bodansky, Jutta Brunnée, and Ellen Hey (eds.), *The Oxford Handbook of International Environmental Law* (Oxford: Oxford University Press, 2007), pp. 995–1009.

[7] See Lon L. Fuller, *The Morality of Law*, revised edition (New Haven CT: Yale University Press, 1969); see also Michael Oakeshott, "The Rule of Law," in *On History and Other Essays* (Indianapolis: Liberty, 1999), p. 173. This is further elaborated by T. R. S. Allan, *Constitutional Justice: A Liberal Theory of the Rule of Law* (Oxford: Oxford University Press, 2001). A useful introduction to Fuller is Robert S. Summers, *Lon L. Fuller* (London: Edward Arnold, 1984).

On the other hand, experience also suggests that even the best designs can be abused by unscrupulous individuals. All the checks and balances of the US Constitution did not prevent the Watergate scandal, the Iran-Contra affair, or alleged cronyism and awarding of reconstruction contracts in post-war Iraq.[8] By the same token, all the rules of the Brussels bureaucracy (of which there are quite a few) are unable to tame corruption, or prevent the appearance of nepotism in appointments. As the great British constitutionalist Ivor Jennings expressed in the midst of a world war, "the psychology of government is more important than the forms of government."[9] What matters is not only how procedures are organized, how powers are distributed, or which checks and balances are in place. Instead, what matters is that people in responsible positions behave responsibly. Even the best possible system can be nullified by irresponsible administration and any organizational blueprint ought to be complemented by an insistence on individual virtue.[10]

The present chapter aims to analyze UN reform as yet another manifestation of the dual ambivalence of *universitas* versus *societas* and instrumental versus political rationality. I will pay less attention to the importance of individual virtues – partly for the reason that individual virtue does not lend itself very easily to a discussion in terms of generally applicable principles or rules, or blueprints and reform proposals.[11] It will be my general argument that the UN, in its present form, is quite well equipped to perform its tasks; however, UN reform is also a political

8 A devastating critique of the latter is Naomi Klein, *The Shock Doctrine* (London: Penguin, 2007).

9 See W. Ivor Jennings, *The Law and the Constitution*, 3rd edn. (London: University of London Press, 1943), p. xxxi.

10 This might be increasingly difficult to achieve; it may not be a coincidence that Sennett can note that much political leadership has become "a form of seduction," in which the "modern charismatic leader destroys any distance between his own sentiments and impulses and those of his audience, and so, focusing his followers on his motivations, deflects them from measuring him in terms of his acts." See Richard Sennett, *The Fall of Public Man* (New York: Norton, 1977), p. 265.

11 A philosophical attempt to construct a deontological approach while taking virtue ethics seriously is Onora O'Neill, *Bounds of Justice* (Cambridge: Cambridge University Press, 2000). For a possible application to the UN, see Jan Klabbers, "Kadi Justice at the Security Council?" *International Organizations Law Review* 4 (2007), pp. 293–304.

matter and it is important to address the political rationality of UN reform rather than see reform as a mere technical way to improve the UN's effectiveness.

This is so because none of the sentiments mentioned above are unproblematic; thus they automatically become contested. Advocacy of inclusiveness and representativeness leads into issues as to the basis of inclusion. The quest for effectiveness, in turn, raises issues about the purpose of effectiveness, what it achieves, and what purposes it serves. Moreover, *universitas* and *societas* tend to lapse into each other or, at the very least, provoke each other. Too much debate will generate a call for more action while too much action by small groups of like-minded actors will result in a call for more reflection, legitimacy, and accountability.

In the end institutional reform is best treated as an intensely political process, with actors who stand to benefit and others who stand to lose out. So too with the latest plans for UN reform; those launched by the Secretary-General in the spring of 2005,[12] following the recommendations of the High-Level Panel published in December 2004, should also be treated as an intensely political process.[13] In what follows, I will briefly discuss three of the perhaps most eye-catching proposals: those to reform the Security Council, create a Human Rights Council, and create a Peacebuilding Commission, respectively, after which I will subsequently address the curious silence surrounding the role of the Sanctions Committees.

The Security Council

It has become commonplace to complain about the composition of the Security Council and to suggest "improvements," usually boiling down to an expansion of the number of permanent members.[14] The overriding rationale is that somehow the Council, as presently composed, is not "representative." This raises two related questions: what is the Council's membership supposed to represent and, granted that some form of representation might be warranted, what is the Council's task? The two

[12] See his report *In Larger Freedom: Towards Development, Security and Human Rights for All*, UN Doc. A/59/2005.

[13] See *A More Secure World: Our Shared Responsibility*. Report of the High-Level Panel on Threats, Challenges, and Change, UN Doc. A/59/565.

[14] For a brief overview, see Bardo Fassbender, "On the Boulevard of Broken Dreams: The Project of a Reform of the UN Security Council After the 2005 World Summit," *International Organizations Law Review* 2 (2005), pp. 391–402.

questions are related because the Council's main tasks will determine, at least to some extent, how it ought to be composed.

As is well known, the Council's composition, with five permanent members all possessing a right of veto, stems from the painful experiences with the League of Nations (which, for most of its time, did not include the United States and the Soviet Union among its members, and failed to indicate whether anyone should bear special responsibility for the maintenance of peace and security).[15] The four Great Powers emerging from the Second World War, with France added for good measure, appointed themselves permanent members of the Council with, importantly, a right of veto.[16] Incidentally, France proved initially reluctant to accept a permanent membership,[17] perhaps signifying that, for the French, permanent membership represented a responsibility rather than a privilege.[18]

The Great Powers were not chosen (or self-appointed, to be more accurate) because of their achievements on the football pitch (or soccer field), nor for producing the best painters, the best violinists, for having the largest GDP, or the biggest populations – let alone any notion of democracy. Instead, the permanent five (P5) were appointed, by and large, according to their military capacities and potential, based on the notion that one could hardly expect the member states of the UN to send troops to the various corners of the world if the ones making that decision would not themselves be capable of helping out. Nicholas

[15] English diplomat, politician and writer Harold Nicolson provides a memorably succinct analysis of the League's downfall in a letter to his wife in 1936 after Germany invaded the Rhineland: "If we sent an ultimatum to Germany she ought in all reason to climb down. But then she will not climb down and we shall have war. Naturally we shall win and enter Berlin. And what is the good of that? It would only mean communism in Germany and in France and that is why the Russians are so keen on it. Moreover the people of this country absolutely refuse to have a war. We shall therefore have to climb down ignominiously and Hitler will have scored. But it does mean the final end of the League and that I do mind dreadfully. Quite dreadfully." See Nigel Nicolson (ed.), *The Harold Nicolson Diaries 1907–1963* (London: Weidenfeld & Nicolson, 2004), p. 139.

[16] An excellent discussion of the acceptance hereof by the smaller powers is contained in Ian Hurd, *After Anarchy* (Princeton: Princeton University Press, 2007).

[17] See Stephen C. Schlesinger, *Act of Creation: The Founding of the United Nations* (Boulder: Westview, 2003), pp. 101–102.

[18] The Great Powers were equally reluctant at first to invite France, but eventually did so to prevent France from becoming a nuisance by possibly establishing itself as the leader of the smaller powers. See Gerry Simpson, *Great Powers and Outlaw States: Unequal Sovereigns in the International Legal Order* (Cambridge: Cambridge University Press, 2004), p. 173.

described this concept in his classic study of the UN: "Force would be put at the service of law, and even law itself would be obliged to serve and not to obstruct the overriding concern of a post-war world with peace and security."[19]

The underlying logic is that of street credibility. In much the same way as it is easier to accept instruction in chess from a grandmaster than from someone who might know the theory but has never played a match, so too was it deemed necessary to have the military power of states backing up the military activities of the UN.[20] Historian Paul Kennedy nicely sums up the underlying sentiment: "Small nations ought ... to cease carping about the unfairness of the veto and be grateful that the Great Powers were now going to take their international responsibilities seriously."[21]

It is telling, perhaps, that much of the debate in 1945, and already earlier at the Yalta Conference,[22] was cast in terms of the responsibilities of the permanent members for maintaining and restoring peace and security. Membership of the P5 was not considered a privilege so much as a burden that only the strong could carry.[23] Tellingly, when in April 1947 the Military Staff Committee presented its report on the possibility of UN armed forces under Article 43 of the Charter, it found that the permanent members should contribute the majority of those armed forces.[24]

In other words if the Council's composition is representative of anything, it is of military prowess. China's inclusion amongst the great powers illustrates this; while neither the UK nor the USSR wished to include China, the US insisted on having the Chinese as "policing

[19] See H. G. Nicholas, *The United Nations as a Political Institution*, 3rd edn. (Oxford: Oxford University Press, 1967), p. 70.

[20] A P5 consisting of Belgium, Botswana, Belarus, Belize and Burma would be representative in two ways at least (geographical, and in terms of diversity of political outlooks) as well as pleasantly alliterating, but would probably not inspire the same confidence in terms of keeping the peace.

[21] See Paul Kennedy, *The Parliament of Man: The Past, Present, and Future of the United Nations* (New York: Random House, 2006), p. 29.

[22] James Byrnes, who would later become US Secretary of State, was present at Yalta, and recalls: "Where the decisions might require the use of force, we felt justified in placing the permanent members in a special position, since they would have to bear the principal responsibility for such action." See James F. Byrnes, *Speaking Frankly* (New York: Harper, 1947), pp. 34–35.

[23] Compare the discussion as reflected in G. Simpson, *Great Powers and Outlaw States*, pp. 182–184.

[24] See Nicholas, *The United Nations as a Political Institution* 3rd edn., p. 70.

again play the geographical card. Geographical representation would seem to be the only criterion that is acceptable to many, precisely because it does not tap into substantive talents or qualities. But, as a result, there is no particular reason to suppose that Egypt would be better at doing the job than, say, France; or that Brazil would be a better P5 member than Russia. In other words, the Security Council might become representative this way, but not necessarily more effective – perhaps the opposite.[33]

In addition (but by no means secondary), it is useful to remember that merely changing the composition of the Council is no guarantee against unpalatable acts. Indeed it is here that Jennings' words, quoted earlier, come to the fore, to the effect that responsible authority requires responsible authorities.[34] The Council's mission creep[35] results from a "the end justifies the means" attitude, and as long as such an attitude prevails among the members of the UN at large, no reform will be able to quell anxieties.[36]

The Human Rights Council

Institutional reform can easily become a symbolic event, aimed to portray an image of rationalization where, in effect, none takes place. States can score diplomatic victories by proposing reform of this body or that, while evading more difficult discussions on substance. Arguably, the substitution of the Human Rights Council for the erstwhile Commission on Human Rights falls into this category.

The Commission on Human Rights had, for many years, been regarded as a problematic body. Its members were elected from amongst the members of the General Assembly, and notoriously, their human rights credentials did not generally play a huge role in the composition of

[33] Likewise, merely expanding the number of members – with or without veto – cannot be expected to enhance effectiveness. See Nico J. Schrijver, "The Future of the Charter of the United Nations," *Max Planck Yearbook of United Nations Law* 10 (2006), p. 33.

[34] Interestingly, even authors insisting that the Security Council apply the principle of legality have a hard time resisting the "end-justifies-the-means" mentality that is part of the problem. An example is Kenneth Manusama, *The United Nations Security Council in the Post-Cold War Era: Applying the Principle of Legality* (Leiden: Martinus Nijhoff, 2006).

[35] See Frederic L. Kirgis, Jr., "The Security Council's First Fifty Years," *AJIL* 89 (1995), pp. 506–539.

[36] In principle all UN member states are implicated, for two reasons. First, some of the Council's decisions warrant budgetary support, and the power of the purse rests with the General Assembly. Second, it is difficult to believe that the Council would be able, or even willing, to push measures in the face of overwhelming resistance from a majority of the member states.

the Commission. Thus, members with debatable human rights track records found themselves on the Commission, while members that considered themselves more worthy may not have been elected.[37] In a word, the Commission was politicized,[38] leading to Kofi Annan's somewhat bemused observation that "States have sought membership of the Commission not to strengthen human rights but to protect themselves against criticism or to criticize others."[39]

In order to remedy the situation, the High-Level Panel, in December 2004, proposed a fairly radical solution: the membership of the Commission on Human Rights should be expanded to universal membership. In other words, a body usually considered as being already too huge and ineffective should be expanded, so as to underscore "that all members are committed by the Charter to the promotion of human rights."[40] Eccentric as it may seem, the High-Level Panel did have a point. With universal membership of the Commission on Human Rights, membership would no longer be seen as a trophy, and attention could focus once again on substantive human rights rather than on the highly divisive formalities of voting rights.[41] The drawback would be that a Commission with universal membership might turn out to be little more than a debating club; but it can be argued that there is nothing wrong with establishing fora for the discussion[42] rather than the solution (or dissolution) of international

[37] There is also the issue (not open for discussion in polite company perhaps) of the individuals representing the members. Brian Simpson vividly details the way the UK government selected its first delegate Geoffrey Wilson, bypassing established authorities such as Hersch Lauterpacht in the process. In the end, Simpson writes, "the United Kingdom came to be represented by a retired trade unionist, whose mind was unencumbered by the least knowledge of international law, assisted by a junior civil servant, who in all probability knew little more. Thus did the Foreign Office exhibit its commitment to the cult of the gifted amateur." See A. W. Brian Simpson, *Human Rights and the End of Empire: Britain and the Genesis of the European Convention* (Oxford: Oxford University Press, 2001), pp. 351–352.

[38] That is not a novel development, of course. Already Eleanor Roosevelt, the US delegate on the Commission in its early years, noticed the conduct of politics at the Commission, and quite possibly added some to it when innocently observing that Soviet officials "display such stubborn unfriendliness toward Western ideas." See Eleanor Roosevelt, *The Autobiography of Eleanor Roosevelt* (Boston: Hall & Co, 1984), p. 312.

[39] See *In Larger Freedom*, para. 182. The language was borrowed verbatim from that of the High-Level Panel, para. 283.

[40] See High-Level Panel, para. 285. [41] *Ibid.*

[42] Nicholas puts it nicely when describing plenary bodies such as the General Assembly as "meeting grounds at which acquaintances are made or maintained and awareness of other styles of thought and behavior is – however reluctantly – cultivated." Nicholas, *The United Nations as a Political Institution*, p. 98.

issues.[43] Doing so would have implied, however, an open acknowledgement of the particularist nature of human rights, at loggerheads with the usual presumption that human rights are universal.

Hence, the Secretary-General opted for a different approach when proposing his smaller Human Rights Council,[44] and the establishment of a Council was endorsed in the World Summit Resolution.[45] Without much clarity on what the Council would look like, the president of the General Assembly was asked to start negotiations "with the aim of establishing the mandate, modalities, functions, size, composition, membership, working methods and procedures of the Council."[46] In other words, everything was still out in the open.[47]

Eventually, the General Assembly decided to establish the new Human Rights Council in the spring of 2006, and early experiences suggest that the Council continues where the Commission left off. Nothing much has changed in terms of membership, in the sense that the Council's current membership reflects the wide variety of views (and practices) available on the scope and authority of human rights. It comprises, amongst others, Nigeria, Saudi Arabia, China, and Pakistan, although both Sudan and the United States of America are not, at present, included. Early experiences also suggest that political divisions on human rights are not immediately overcome by the new Council. A resolution on globalization and human rights, stressing a central role for development, was adopted by a highly divided Council, with the West against, and the South in favor.[48] And one can only marvel at the Council's desire to turn the philosophically highly problematic notion of truth into a human right.[49]

43 For such an argument, see Klabbers, "Two Concepts of International Organization," pp. 277–293.

44 See *In Larger Freedom*, para. 183.

45 See UN Doc. A/Res/60/1, paras. 157–160.

46 *Ibid.*, para. 160.

47 Corell notes that a document circulating in August 2005 contained "fairly elaborate provisions" on the Council, but that these provisions did not find their way into the summit resolution. See Hans Corell, "Reforming the United Nations," *International Organizations Law Review* 2 (2005), p. 385.

48 See Resolution A/HRC/4/L.16, on Globalization and its Impact on the Full Enjoyment of Human Rights. The resolution was adopted by 34 in favor and 13 against, with no abstentions which, if nothing else, signifies that politicization has already entered the Council's work.

49 See the Council's Report on the Second Session, A/HRC/2/9, of March 22, 2007, at 17. In particular in politics, truth is a difficult notion, as already realized by Hannah Arendt. See her essay "Truth and Politics," reproduced in Hannah Arendt, *Between Past and Future* (New York: Penguin, 1968) pp. 227–264. Arendt's main point is that truth claims in politics tend to be despotic in nature, unable to tolerate competing claims. See also Jan Klabbers, "Commissioning the Truth," *Ius Gentium* 8 (2002), pp. 57–67.

Ironically, the main result that the substitution of the Council for the Commission on Human Rights has had so far is a reappraisal of the Commission. The Commission, after all, has decidedly changed the normative landscape by creating a more or less universal set of human rights standards through the Universal Declaration and the two covenants, and has by the creation of all sorts of reporting mechanisms ensured that human rights are never far from the spotlights and that states can be approached and reproached for their human rights records. The post-war human rights revolution, in other words, owes much to the Commission on Human Rights. In the words of one commentator, attempts to replace the Commission with a new Council, before making sure that such a plan would be viable, has "severely damaged the credibility of the current Commission."[50] Perhaps the Commission on Human Rights was little more than a badly composed talking shop; but surely, no instrumental purpose is served by replacing it with another badly composed talking shop.

The Peacebuilding Commission

Thus far possibly the most eye-catching proposal to come out of the High-Level Panel's reform plans is the creation of a Peacebuilding Commission, which the General Assembly established in December 2005.[51] That is not to say that the High-Level Panel's plan was carried out in all detail; the current Commission is a diluted version of what the Panel had in mind.[52]

The High-Level Panel had recommended that the Commission be established by the Security Council, under Article 29 of the Charter. An implication hereof would have been that the Commission be endowed with great political clout, perhaps to the point of interfering in the domestic affairs of states without their consent. This now is no longer the case. Under the terms of Resolution 60/180, the tasks of the Commission are limited to providing a forum for discussion and to

[50] See Nico Schrijver, "UN Reform: A Once-in-a-Generation Opportunity?," *International Organizations Law Review* 2 (2005), pp. 271–275, at 275. Elsewhere, Schrijver speaks of new wine in old bottles, and invokes the maxim of the baby and the bathwater. See his inaugural address "Bij een zestigste verjaardig. De toekomst van het Handvest van de Verenigde Naties," dated October 24, 2005 (on file with the author).

[51] See UN Doc. A/Res/60/1 para. 197.

[52] On its genesis, see Carsten Stahn, "Institutionalizing Brahimi's 'Light Footprint': A Comment on the Role and Mandate of the Peacebuilding Commission," *International Organizations Law Review* 2 (2005), pp. 403–415.

recommending on coordination of activities. This *Werdegang* nicely illustrates the tensions between the *universitas–societas* poles mentioned above; while the High-Level Panel favored an exercise in managerialism, the General Assembly (the UN's membership, lest this be forgotten) was more interested in creating a clearing house for information and knowledge.

The Commission comprises a standing Organizational Committee, which includes permanent members of the Security Council,[53] members of the Economic and Social Council, financial and military donor states, and an additional seven members. In addition, the composition of the Commission will depend on the situation, comprising the state concerned and its neighbors, relevant regional institutions, and so on. No doubt this will involve, at each and every occasion, a political struggle as to who exactly is to be included – and who is to be excluded from participation. Indeed, this mirrors one of the bigger problems with thinking in terms of "stakeholders" generally: those who are deemed to have nothing at stake are left without a voice; democracy (such as it is) is therewith eroded from within.

Perhaps the most relevant effect of the establishment of the Peacebuilding Commission is twofold. One is that it renders any discussions on whether territorial administration is a legitimate task for the UN (given the absence of any reference in the Charter) irrelevant. While the establishment of the Commission does not in itself create the legal power to administer territory, it does create a political *fait accompli*. The Commission's creation must mean that the UN's membership feels that territorial administration falls properly within the competences of the UN. Second, it also suggests that the UN has "primary responsibility," to borrow a phrase, in the matter. Attempts by regional actors (EU, NATO) to create post-conflict fiefdoms will, arguably, have to meet with the approval of the UN. Although primary responsibilities can always be circumvented (NATO's acts over Kosovo being a case in point), the establishment of the Peacebuilding Commission would seem to create a presumption that the UN gets the first chance at running things.

More practical effects may not be all that easily forthcoming. The Commission's mandate is limited to providing advice and information, and decision making within the Commission shall take place, "in all matters," by consensus.[54] There is little, if anything, on the substance of

[53] The text is ambiguous, possibly on purpose, on whether all permanent members will be represented. See High-Level Panel, para. 4(a).

[54] *Ibid.*, para. 18.

peacebuilding. For example, there is no mention of what law to apply in times of transition, how to actually run a peacebuilding mission, how to administer territory, or how to prevent peacebuilders from engaging in criminal activities. There is not even a reference to the necessity of taking human rights into account. There are some of the usual buzzwords (civil society, gender perspective, private sector, sustainable peace, and development), but fairly little that would be of immediate use on the ground in, say, Kosovo, East Timor or Iraq.[55] Blissfully, though, modern communication technology has reached the UN; the Commission is encouraged to use such devices as videoconferencing.[56]

Silence on the Sanctions Committees

The recent efforts at reforming the UN have produced voluminous heaps of paper, yet on one issue most of the papers remain silent: what to do with the Sanctions Committees.[57] The problems are familiar, and were highlighted by a number of decisions of the Court of First Instance (CFI) of the European Community (EC).[58] In the first of these cases, individuals complained that due to UN sanctions, their accounts had been frozen, depriving them of their property and, given how Sanctions Committees work, depriving them of the right to a fair trial as well. Indeed, the fact that they felt compelled to address the CFI was, in itself, telling because it showed that there exists no judicial procedure available at the UN level. Hence, those individuals did the next best thing and complained before the courts of the entity implementing UN sanctions into their domestic legal order, the EC.

This resulted in the unpleasant spectacle of the CFI having to defend (or feeling such an obligation) the sanctions policies of the Security

[55] Understandably so, of course, as there is no blueprint to achieve peace (deterrence by means of an arms build-up may be effective; then again, so may disarmament), and no blueprint to achieve national unity either. On the latter, see Jan Klabbers, "Redemption Song: Human Rights Versus Community-building in East Timor," 16 *Leiden Journal of International Law* (2003), pp. 367–376.

[56] See the High-Level Panel, para. 19.

[57] The Sanctions Committees are decidedly under-analyzed in the literature, attracting little attention. Exceptions are Martti Koskenniemi, "Le Comité de Sanctions (crée par la résolution 661 (1990) du Conseil de Sécurité)," *Annuaire Français de Droit International* 37 (1991), pp. 119–137, and Michael P. Scharf and Joshua L. Dorosin, "Interpreting UN Sanctions: The Rulings and Role of the Yugoslavia Sanctions Committee," *Brooklyn Journal of International Law* 19 (1993), p. 771–827.

[58] See Case T-306/01, *Yusuf & Al Barakaat* v. *Council & Commission*, and Case T-315/01, *Kadi* v. *Council & Commission*, judgments of September 21, 2005, nyr.

Council, and proclaiming that the right to property is not violated if accounts are merely frozen and that the existence of a highly politicized procedure to get individuals taken off the blacklists is compatible with the demands of a fair trial. Most disturbingly, perhaps, the CFI ended up advocating balancing the rights of the individuals thus affected with, in dramatic terms, the violation of the right to life of the victims of terrorism. Surely, that is an impossible balance to achieve, potentially justifying each and every limitation of human rights in the aftermath of a terrorist attack or incident.

In short, if there were anything to reform in the UN system, it would be the way sanctions are implemented and monitored; the rule of law, however defined, demands nothing less.[59] Yet, the reform efforts retained a deafening silence. While all reports habitually stress the importance of the rule of law, none seemed overly bothered by the sanctions mechanisms. The one exception was the High-Level Panel, which noted that the manner in which people or entities are blacklisted "and the absence of review or appeal for those listed raise serious accountability issues and possibly violate fundamental human rights norms and conventions." Accordingly, it advocated the creation of a process for reviewing cases.[60]

In Kofi Annan's report, *In Larger Freedom*, this had all but vanished. Instead, Annan advocated the creation of a special human rights *rapporteur* to report "on the compatibility of counter-terrorism measures with international human rights law,"[61] leaving aside whether this would cover measures taken by national governments or whether it would also cover the activities of the Security Council. None of the sections of *In Larger Freedom* dealing with sanctions,[62] with the rule of law,[63] and with human rights[64] address the issue. In the World Summit Outcome, the High-Level Panel's laudable intentions had been turned into a bland paragraph in which the General Assembly calls upon the Security Council "to ensure that fair and clear procedures exist for placing individuals and entities on sanctions lists and for removing them, as well as for granting humanitarian exemptions."[65]

[59] For a fine recent study proposing a thin version of the rule of law in this context, see Jeremy M. Farrall, *United Nations Sanctions and the Rule of Law* (Cambridge: Cambridge University Press, 2007).

[60] See High-Level Panel, paras. 152, 182. [61] See *In Larger Freedom*, para. 94.

[62] *Ibid.*, paras. 109–110. The current rapporteur is Martin Scheinin.

[63] *Ibid.*, paras. 133–139. [64] *Ibid.*, paras. 140–147.

[65] See UN Doc. A/RES/60/1, para. 109.

In short, the entire reform attempt displays precious little attention for the Sanctions Committees, and the most obvious explanation is no doubt that monitoring the human rights of people suspected of terrorist activities, or at least terrorist sympathies, is not considered a worthy cause. Human rights are for the innocent, not for the guilty or those who look guilty. The guilty do not deserve a fair trial because, after all, they do not respect human rights themselves. Or do they? The end, the fight against terrorism, therefore justifies the means and if innocent people get hurt in the process, well, that is, in fitting military terms, merely collateral damage; you cannot make an omelet without breaking some eggs.

The political rationality of reform

Reform of institutions is a highly ambivalent process, an emanation of politics even to the point of having reform processes substitute for real decision making. There may be occasions where reform attempts and discussion turn out to be a substitute for action on issues where no agreement is to be found, and it is no exaggeration to say that issues such as global poverty, debt relief, AIDS, and others have been overshadowed by the attempts at reforming the UN. This carries, of course, its own justifying theory that a reformed UN will be better placed to help combat poverty, to reach a consensus on debt relief, and to push back AIDS. It is in this light, no doubt, that many speak about progress in the reform process.[66]

Much of this sort of thinking is premised, though, on a highly contestable notion: the idea that the UN should somehow be likened to a world government; the global equivalent of the welfare state, exercising all sorts of more or less governmental tasks and taking decisions on all sorts of topics in a more or less democratic manner. The General Assembly, on this resilient view, somehow resembles a parliament, while the Security Council forms the nucleus of a government, however embryonic still.[67] The type of decisions made is less relevant; what matters is that policies are made internationally rather than locally. As David Kennedy once commented, many of those working on, in, or with international organizations "seem simply to be working in an alternative political universe,

[66] For example, see Schrijver, "UN Reform: A Once-in-a-Generation Opportunity?" p. 275.

[67] A hint to this effect was contained in the advisory opinion of the World Court in *Legality of the Use by a State of Nuclear Weapons in Armed Conflict*, [1996] ICJ Reports 66, where the ICJ suggested that the precise powers of the World Health Organization were dependent, to some extent, on the WHO's role within the UN "family."

in which commitment to the *level* of government has displaced concern about its outcomes."[68]

All politics is instrumental, and as such there is nothing wrong with attempts to reform the UN; there is even nothing particularly wrong with trying to hide the political nature of the reform attempt behind a veneer of neutral, objective technocracy geared towards ever-increasing progress. Whether it will actually work, though, is another matter. It is by no means certain that the world will be a better place with a different Security Council, with a Human Rights Council instead of the Commission of Human Rights, or with a new Peacebuilding Commission. Much will depend on what those institutions eventually do, on the substantive decisions they take and the policies they develop, which will in turn depend in part on the quality, trustworthiness, and integrity of the individuals composing those organs, elusive as such factors might be.[69] And as noted, there are other factors too. There is the lingering sentiment that decent institutions will help produce decent outcomes even if one cannot control whom the member states will send. At least the institutions and organs should develop decent working procedures, focusing on such things as transparency, consistency, and accountability.

There is also the tension between thinking of organizations and their organs as talking shops on the one hand, or as effective result-oriented decision-making machines on the other. The Security Council is, at present, probably more effective than ever;[70] small wonder then that concerns arise about the legitimacy of its acts, translated into arguments about representation. And once this is fixed (if ever), arguments will no doubt start to emphasize how the effectiveness of the Council has been reduced.

The same applies, *mutatis mutandis*, to the Peacebuilding Commission and the proposed Human Rights Council: these too will lead to discussions

68 See David Kennedy, "A New World Order: Yesterday, Today, and Tomorrow," *Transnational Law and Contemporary Problems* 4 (1994) 1–47, at 9 (emphasis in original).

69 They are also difficult to measure, which might help explain their virtual absence from the more systematically inclined literature. A good example of missing this dimension is Barbara Koremenos, Charles Lipson, and Duncan Snidal (eds.), *The Rational Design of International Institutions* (Cambridge: Cambridge University Press, 2001).

70 It is perhaps worth recalling that until the 1990s, its level of inactivity was usually bemoaned: even Secretary-General Waldheim acknowledged a lack of confidence in the Council's "capacity for even-handed and effective action." As quoted in Thomas M. Franck, *Nation Against Nation* (Oxford: Oxford University Press, 1985), pp. 132–133. Tellingly, a leading textbook on international law published in the mid-1980s contained no index reference to the Security Council, as if to underline its practical irrelevance. See Antonio Cassese, *International Law in a Divided World* (Oxford: Clarendon, 1986).

oscillating between effectiveness and representation; these too will lead to discussions oscillating between working procedures and the individual characteristics of the individuals actually sitting on those bodies. And the same applies even to the Sanctions Committees, although so far they have been considered first and foremost in light of their contribution to the fight against terrorism. Nonetheless, the advocacy (however lukewarm perhaps) of some modicum of fairness and humanity in applying sanctions in the *World Summit Resolution* is an indication that the limit of effectiveness has been reached.[71]

David Kennedy once observed that international lawyers typically do not advocate a return to original plans. Where an organization does not function as planned, the proposed cure is inevitably to change the blueprint, rather than be critical of the functioning.[72] This presupposes that there is a close fit between the blueprint and its execution; yet it is precisely this presumption that may not survive closer scrutiny unscathed as, typically, organizations and their organs engage in activities they were never scheduled to engage in, following procedures that have grown and developed beyond recognition and bending over backwards to accommodate the issue of the month, from incident to incident. The very idea of institutional reform, moreover, while ostensibly about improving the functioning of an institution, more often than not is based on a political rationality. Very few instrumental results are to be expected, as discussed above, from a reformed Security Council, from the new Human Rights Council and the Peacebuilding Commission, never mind the Sanctions Committees. Such reform proposals as have been floating, though, suggest the prevalence of a political rationality: being seen to be actively engaged, being seen to be taking steps, being seen to help improve the world. In the meantime, though, the various reform proposals run the risk of creating the general sentiment that nothing functions as it should, and that those who are less keen on some of the proposals be castigated as obstructive.[73] They also run the risk of creating a climate of mistrust and distrust, and that, surely, cannot be good from either a political or an instrumental rationality perspective.

[71] Note also that the Office of Legal Affairs has commissioned an independent study into some aspects of the work of the Sanctions Committees. See Bardo Fassbender, *Targeted Sanctions and Due Process* (Berlin: Humboldt University, 2006).

[72] See Kennedy, "A New World Order: Yesterday, Today, and Tomorrow," p. 32.

[73] Hints to this effect can be discerned in Joachim Müller (ed.), *Reforming the United Nations: The Struggle for Legitimacy and Effectiveness* (Leiden: Martinus Nijhoff, 2006), p. 93.

3

Great Powers then and now: Security Council reform and responses to threats to peace and security

LAURI MÄLKSOO

The United Nations Security Council is widely regarded as having legitimacy problems but there are serious disagreements about what exactly is at the root of these problems. In 1950, Hans Kelsen identified the veto power of the five permanent members ("the P5") as the greatest likely source of future challenges to the legitimacy of the newly created UN Security Council. His quite prophetic thoughts are worth quoting here at a greater length:

> The Security Council has almost the character of a governmental body. Hence the political measurements used for forms of government are applicable to it. The question of democracy and of autocracy becomes unavoidable. The veto right of the five permanent members of the Security Council, which places the privileged powers above the law of the United Nations, establishes their legal hegemony over all the other members of the Organization and thus stamps on it the mark of an autocratic or aristocratic regime. This is all the more critical as the United Nations presents itself ideologically as the crowning of a war waged for a victory not only of arms but of ideals, especially of the ideal of democracy. If the Security Council by its voting procedure was to be elevated by the rank of a government at all, only a democratic form of government, that is to say, the majority vote principle without veto rights of privileged members, was adequate ... There is an open contradiction between the political ideology of the United Nations and its legal constitution. And this contradiction may completely paralyze the great advantage that the Charter tried to gain over the Covenant by conferring upon the Security Council a power almost equal to that of a government.[1]

[1] H. Kelsen, *The Law of the United Nations. A Critical Analysis of Its Fundamental Problems* (New York: F. Praeger, 1950), pp. 275–276.

Notwithstanding the critiques of Kelsen and others, the UN Security Council has functioned with the veto power of the P5 for over sixty years. How well, however, is open to debate. Kelsen would probably point to the Council's unresolved legitimacy deficit as having played a significant part in the Council's Cold War paralysis. He would also probably tie it to more recent failures to make any progress toward reaching comprehensive peace in the Middle East, as well as to its impotence in dealing with questions of nuclear proliferation in North Korea and Iran, and its inability to alleviate the suffering of hundreds of thousands in intrastate conflicts, such as the ongoing conflict in Darfur, Sudan. In 2004, the High-Level Panel on Threats, Challenges, and Change, convened by the UN Secretary-General Kofi Annan, recognizing that the UN Security Council has legitimacy problems, concluded that the Security Council needed "greater credibility, legitimacy and representation to do all that we demand of it."[2]

In its report, the High-Level Panel expounded on the factors that most diminish support for Council decisions. Among those listed were institutional problems, such as inadequate representation of board membership, and the normative failures of the Council to: (1) adjust to changes in the international distribution of power; (2) react to the changing international threatscape; and (3) adequately empower bodies created to address specific international threats with proper mandates, fund and provision them adequately, and offer them the proper support and political determination necessary for them to succeed.[3]

The Panel found a general improvement in the Council's effectiveness since the end of the Cold War, but noted that several facets of the Council's behavior over the last two decades have continued to damage its credibility and undermine international confidence in it.[4] First, the Council may no longer be paralyzed by the P5 veto, but the P5 have nevertheless shown a remarkable ability to keep critical issues of peace and security off the Security Council's agenda.[5] Second, the Council has often acted inequitably, brazenly applying double standards to different states in similar situations.[6] Third, the Council has not acted consistently or effectively to confront genocide and other atrocious affronts to human security.[7]

[2] Report of the United Nations Secretary-General's High-Level Panel on Threats, Challenges, and Change, *A More Secure World: Our Shared Responsibility* (New York: United Nations, 2004), synopsis.

[3] High-Level Panel, para. 245. [4] *Ibid.*, para. 246. [5] *Ibid.* [6] *Ibid.* [7] *Ibid.*

The Panel outlined that the goals of any reform to the Council should be the increase of both its effectiveness and its credibility, and, paramount to all else, the enhancement of its capacity and willingness to act in the face of threats. Meeting those goals, it determined, first requires "consensus on the nature of today's threats, on the obligations of broadened collective security, on the necessity of prevention, and on when and why the Security Council should authorize the use of force."[8] Then it requires greater contributions from those imbued by the Charter with special decision-making authority, as well as greater efforts to include all those who contribute substantially, and more consultation between the Council and the bodies charged with implementing its decisions.[9]

Finally (and specifically related to Hans Kelsen's concerns) the High-Level Panel concluded by criticizing the veto mechanism as anachronistic and unsuited to an increasingly democratic international system, but were resigned to the fact that there is no realistic way of altering the veto powers of the P5, and thus endorsed a next-best program of reform.[10] The Panel implored that the veto be reserved for those truly rare circumstances where vital interests are genuinely at stake, and entreated members of the P5 to pledge themselves to refrain from using the veto in cases of genocide and large-scale human rights abuses.[11] It also advocated immediate discussion on enlargement of the number of permanent members of the Security Council.[12]

The Panel further explained that the enlargement, as reform altogether, should satisfy several criteria. It should increase the involvement in decision making of those who contribute most to the UN financially, militarily, and diplomatically. The Panel suggested that "among developing countries, achieving or making substantial progress towards the internationally agreed level of 0.7% of GNP for ODA should be considered an important criterion for contribution."[13] It should bring countries more representative of the broader membership (particularly from the developing world) into the decision-making process in a way that increases the democratic and accountable nature of the Council without impairing its effectiveness.

This chapter will analyze and evaluate the criticisms and the suggested reforms of the High-Level Panel. In proper form, it will first critically examine the High-Level Panel's diagnosis and prognosis of the factors ailing the Security Council and diminishing its legitimacy, before turning

[8] *Ibid.*, para. 248. [9] *Ibid.* [10] *Ibid.*, para. 256. [11] *Ibid.*
[12] *Ibid.*, para 250. [13] *Ibid.*, para 249.

to its recommended course of treatment. After giving a second opinion, it will conclude with the author's recommendations for positive change.

Great Powers and the trouble with international egalitarianism

The Panel's criticism of the Security Council begins by charging that the Security Council has not adapted quickly enough to changes in the international environment, but the Panel's report does not address the antecedent questions of why the Council was created, how and why it might change, and what key interests it would consider before making any decision to change. The essence of the Security Council is privilege over egalitarianism. While probably truly interested in creating an international body that could act to preserve peace and stability, the victorious Great Powers also took great care to grant themselves special superior status and special privileges within the new body they helped create. This power play was probably motivated by a general, though not necessarily correct, belief that international stability and total equality of states were mutually exclusive and also by an irresistible desire to accumulate as much power in the new body as possible. To better understand the motivations of the P5 in 1945 and now, it is useful to briefly examine how the idea of the special status of the Great Powers gained prominence in international normative thinking.

In the late nineteenth century, several British writers on international law started to demand that the higher status of the Great Powers would be recognized in international law.[14] The idea gained popularity among writers from other European Empires as well. For example, in 1912 Vladimir Hrabar (1865–1956), one of the most outstanding international law scholars in late-Tsarist Russia and a specialist in the history of international law, published an article advocating the idea that the special status of the Great Powers – and in that sense, a formal hierarchy of states – should be more clearly recognized in international law.[15]

14 See, e.g., Hortense Ute Demme, *Hegemonialstellungen im Völkerrecht: Der ständige Sitz im Sicherheitsrat der Vereinten Nationen* (Frankfurt: Peter Lang, 2006), p. 206.

15 V. E. Hrabar, "Nachalo ravenstva gosudarstv v sovremennom mezhdunarodnom prave," in V. Kirschbaum (ed.), *Izvestia Ministerstva Inostrannych Del* (St. Petersburg: V. Kirschbaum, 1912). See further L. Mälksoo, "1912 and 2005: the Theory of the Legal Inequality of States of the Russian International Law Scholar Vladimir Hrabar (1865–1956)," in *Proceedings of the 99th annual meeting of the American Society of International Law,* Washington, DC, 2005, pp. 310–312 and "The Science of International Law and the Concept of Politics: the Arguments and Lives of the International Law Professors at the University of Dorpat/Iur'ev/Tartu 1855–1985," 76 *British Year Book of International Law* (2005), pp. 383–502.

Hrabar argued that rather than relying on the utopian theory of juridical equality of Great Powers and small states, international law should become more realistic and recognize that there is a hierarchy between states. Hrabar derided scholarly writers from small states such as Switzerland, Greece, and Belgium, arguing they defended formal equality of states simply because they wanted to defend their respective countries. A then-recent case demonstrating the inequality of states to Hrabar was the Austro-Hungarian Empire's ability to force the Serbian government to declare that it would give up its "protesting and hostile attitude." What "juridical equality of States" could one talk about in such circumstances, Hrabar asked rhetorically.[16]

Not long after Hrabar's article, another exchange between the subjects of his snide illustration of inequality was not resolved so humorously, but instead precipitated the First World War. After approximately four years and 40 million casualties, the first universal international organization, the League of Nations, was created in 1919. The history of its impotence, ineptitude, and of its failure to avert the very thing it was created to prevent, a second and much deadlier world war, is widely known.

When the United Nations was created in 1945, the Dutch delegate in San Francisco commented that the League of Nations failed because of the "exaggerated equality between great and small Powers" that characterized the consensus rule in the League's Council, notwithstanding the special status of the Principal Allied and Associated Powers.[17] The delegates, seeking to avoid repeating the same mistakes, employed ideas from the Hrabar school of thought and created an unequal arrangement that afforded a special enhanced legal status to the victors of the Second World War. While reaffirming the principle of sovereign equality of states, the Charter simultaneously created a special and unequal enforcement authority in the Security Council and gave the Council's permanent members a veto power so powerful, that its use by any one member could totally derail any resolution.[18] The resulting imbalance of power is so great that, according to M. J. Peterson, "member governments have always regarded the Security Council as the aristocracy and the General Assembly as the masses."[19] In addition to granting the P5 the

[16] See footnote 15.

[17] Edward C. Luck, *UN Security Council: Practice and Promise* (London and New York: Routledge, 2006), p. 10.

[18] UN Charter Article 27.

[19] M. J. Peterson, *The UN General Assembly* (London and New York: Routledge, 2006), p. 105.

veto power, the Charter also charged the Security Council with "primary responsibility for the maintenance of international peace and security." This capacity gives the Council authority to determine the existence of a "threat to the peace," a "breach of the peace," or an "act of aggression."[20]

Most commentators agree this blend of the powers to collectively identify threats and act to maintain peace, and the power to unilaterally block any action, was a recipe for inaction during the stalemate years of the Cold War, primarily because of the extensive use of the veto power by the two superpowers, the Soviet Union and the United States. While the Council has been more active since the end of the Cold War, some argue that now Britain and the United States are overusing the veto.[21] Thus, the High-Level Panel's charge that the Security Council has been "slow to change" may be an accurate reflection of facts on the ground, but it fails to take into account that the United Nations was designed specifically to avoid the pitfalls of consensus rule that had plagued the League of Nations. To facilitate the maintenance of international peace and security the Security Council was empowered to make binding decisions for all UN members. The Great Powers would have been disinclined to support a system which could result in enforcement action against them, so such a grant of power was only possible with the "price" of the P5 veto. In other words, some built-in rigidity was the price paid for centralizing such tremendous collective security power in such a small organization, and it is not surprising that the members of the Security Council seem reticent to recalibrate it in a way that may jeopardize their privileged status.

The High-Level Panel observed that the Council has "not always been equitable in its actions" and that "decisions taken and mandates given have often lacked the essential components of realism, adequate resources and political determination to see them through."[22] Again, this is not surprising. International politics is not, or not only, about fairness. As Danilo Türk, the former Assistant Secretary-General of the UN from (and currently President of) Slovenia, has suggested, "... the Council is a political body. It applies and creates law, but its authority is essentially political, as are all the problems and remedies towards which its decision-making is directed."[23]

20 UN Charter Article 24.

21 R. Thakur, *The United Nations, Peace and Security. From Collective Security to the Responsibility to Protect* (Cambridge: Cambridge University Press, 2006), pp. 307–308.

22 High-Level Panel, para. 245.

23 D. Türk, "Improving Decision-making in the UN Security Council," in Roy S. Lee (ed.), *Swords into Ploughshares: Building Peace Through the United Nations* (Leiden/Boston: Martinus Nijhoff, 2006), p. 7.

Nevertheless, at the end of his analysis, Professor Türk joins the chorus of mainstream critical suggestions with respect to the Security Council and he asserts that there exists "… the need for the Security Council's actions to be credible, predictable and reliable. The Council needs to act in a consistent manner and avoid the impression of applying double standards … The stature of the Security Council will suffer if it acts in some cases and ignores others."[24] The analysis essentially admits that the Council's historical record is full of power politics and double standards but charges that in the future this should change.

There is a something in this kind of analysis that makes it either wishful thinking or propaganda in favor of putting one's trust in the Security Council. It is not cynical but responsible to ask: Why would the Council change? If its existence is ruled by the primacy of the political, why not intellectually recognize that double standards and inconsistencies are a constant in the politics of the Security Council? Perhaps rather than imagining that in some sort of future these aspects will disappear we should recognize that they are part of the political system and concentrate on finding checks and balances against the misuses of power?

Hypocrisies and double standards are a natural part of domestic policies, in democracies and dictatorships alike. Most democracies face the challenge of constraining the economically richer and politically more powerful minorities in the population. In domestic politics we often witness how more powerful segments of the population are capable of implementing and successfully "selling" policies that logically could not be in the interest of the poorer segments of the voters, e.g. lowering of taxes. In the opinion of many victims and analysts, the US government's response to hurricane Katrina was neither adequate nor "fair." Which parts of an urban area get money for the development of infrastructure, and which parts remain disadvantaged or even become ghettoized, may be a matter of conscious political choices and priorities; however, these types of choices are usually explained in a hypocritical manner.

As to equity of action, no matter what the Panel may suggest the Council will never become truly "equitable in its actions," because no matter what the promise, as long as the P5 members retain their privileged status, the temptation and opportunity for their abuse of that power will exist. To clarify, the veto power is only one institutionalized "window of opportunity" for the P5 to misuse their power and impose their will against the majority. The nature of their status as permanent

[24] *Ibid.*, p. 9.

members of the Security Council is another tremendous power which can be misused. Great Powers also have power outside of the Council, which in tandem with their veto ability makes them virtually immune from sanction. For example, the United States' decision to abandon efforts to resolve the Iraq problem through the Council and invade Iraq unilaterally undoubtedly factored in America's ability to veto any potential sanction or collective security resolution against it.

The creation of the Security Council: history debunked

Having examined why the Council naturally resists changes in its structure, how double standards and politicization of global security are natural outgrowths of the arrangement of the Council, and how a system designed around a bias toward Great Power privilege breeds inequity, we turn now to the issue of how much we can or should trust the Great Powers (individually or collectively) to reform the Council in a principled manner for the benefit of the greater UN membership. The South Centre, representing positions of the global South, commented on the topic of Security Council reform in 1996: "Institutional change can be used either to increase the power of wealth over people, or the power of people over wealth."[25] This critical perspective of developing countries about the developed ones can be rephrased to express the less powerful states' point of view concerning Great Powers: institutional change can be used either to back up the principle of the equality of states or to further undermine it.

The historical record of the Security Council is replete with instances of ignoble motives behind apparently noble actions. In fact, looking back to its founding, the architecture of the P5 veto belied any claims of desires to ensure either equity or fairness in the new international order. In 1945 the P5 members neither represented the five most powerful states, nor the five most cooperative and peace-loving. Over time, we have started to obscure this fact in our minds, and we have increasingly come to see the Security Council as having been a natural forum for all the Great Powers concerned with maintenance of international peace to meet; but we should nevertheless be aware that we are talking about the *victorious* Great Powers, some of whom have had less than perfect records as stewards of international peace.

[25] South Centre, *For a Strong and Democratic United Nations: A South Perspective on UN Reform* (Geneva: Imprimerie Idéale, 1996), p. 46.

There were other Great Powers in 1939, fascist Germany and imperial Japan; however, these powers were defeated in the war and thus lost their right to argue for a seat at the table of post-war power. Is it any surprise that whenever suggestions for increasing the permanent membership of the Council arise, both Japan and Germany routinely make the short list of candidates? Though we may prefer to think of the San Francisco Conference as a first-ever meeting of its kind, with international participants focused on how to create a stable world order, in truth that was the object of the Treaty of Versailles in 1919, and the Treaty of Paris at the end of the Napoleonic Wars. In all such earlier instances, as at San Francisco, the victorious powers asserted that they were peace-loving/"good" while the defeated were characterized as aggressive/"evil." Had Napoleon Bonaparte not lost the battle of Waterloo, the afterworld may well have learned about him as the heroic creator of the new world order, rather than as the principal evildoer of his day that German and Russian texts claimed he was. Likewise, had Germany emerged victorious from the Second World War, we would have probably heard about the war of preemptive self-defense that the *Reich der Mitte* led against Bolshevist Russia and the Komintern, perhaps even in defense of "European values."

The point is not to justify or criticize Napoleon or Hitler, the point is in the question whether victorious powers are also capable of committing crimes against peace (as they were defined, for example, for the purposes of the Nuremberg trials in 1945). This is not an argument in support of some extreme historical relativism to say that any claim of self-defense, legality, or justness in matters of war and peace would be equally presentable and thus "valid" had history turned out differently. It may indeed very well happen that the law-abiding powers win and the ones that triggered the military confrontation lose a war. However, there is no guarantee that the winning powers are always objectively peace-loving or "good." The Second World War, its aftermath, and the creation of the UN happen to illustrate this all too well. The Soviet Union was a victor of the Second World War and one of the founders of and permanent members on the UN Security Council; but was the USSR a "peace-loving" country when, on the eve of the war, it concluded the Molotov–Ribbentrop Pact of August 23, 1939? Was it "peace-loving" when it coordinated an invasion of Poland with the Nazis or when it celebrated its successful joint dismemberment of Poland with a common military parade in Brest? How about when it attacked Finland on November 30, 1939 and was subsequently expelled from the League of

Nations? It simply cannot be refuted that in 1939 the USSR's actions made it a threat to international peace. In light of all this, the Soviet foreign minister Vyacheslav V. Molotov's comments giving during the San Francisco conference of 1945 must surely be read with an ironic smile:

> [The League of Nations] betrayed the hopes of those who believed in it. It is obvious that no one wishes to restore a League of Nations which had no rights or power, which did not interfere with any aggressors preparing for war against peace-loving nations and which sometimes even lulled the nations' vigilance with regard to impending aggression.[26]

The example above is not presented in order to point an accusing finger in particular at the USSR, who has not been the only Great Power to act in a way contrary to international peace and comity of nations. The point is rather to emphasize that one should be careful to analyze critically the rhetoric offered by powerful states in support of their foreign policy actions.

The P5 have the power to effect much positive change internationally while adhering to the values of multilateralism, transparency, accountability, and good governance they promote; however, the vast quantities of hard power they command present an ever-present temptation for P5 states to do what is expedient for their citizens in a *Realpolitik* sense, rather than what is best for the global community. For example, the real post-war constitution of Eastern Europe could have been resolved in the summer of 1945 in San Francisco by delegates from all over the world. Instead the fate of millions was scribbled down on the back of a paper napkin by Churchill and Stalin during a private meeting in the fall of 1944, and then finalized by Churchill, Stalin, and Roosevelt at Yalta in early 1945. In the end, the three Baltic states lost their independence and were integrated into the Soviet Union until the end of the Cold War. The remaining states of Southern and Eastern Europe – with the exceptions of Yugoslavia, Albania, and Greece – were allocated to Moscow's sphere of influence. Though technically "independent," they were compelled to elect Soviet-sponsored communist governments, or face the kinds of violence and repression seen in Hungary in 1956, Czechoslovakia in 1968, and Poland in 1981. The hypocrisy of this politically expedient condemnation of Eastern Europe to vassal status vis-à-vis Communist Moscow should not be forgotten or smoothed over. Both the United

[26] Quoted in Luck, *UN Security Council: Practice and Promise*, p. 1.

needed, better than the autocratic hegemony of a single superpower? Moreover, does not modern democratic thinking tell us that a democratic system of governance, in which "everyone has some say" (at least to the extent that this is technically possible and practically feasible) is more commendable than either autocracy or oligarchy? Understanding that a negative answer to the first question or an affirmative answer to this last question would constitute an acknowledgment that the Security Council and in some ways the UN itself were built upon an inferior model of global governance, it seems natural that the High-Level Panel would want to make the Security Council as strong, proactive, and effective as possible.

For almost all of its existence the Security Council has performed inadequately because of paralyzing differences among its members, and because of the use of veto power those differences provoked.[32] In the early 1990s there was a brief period of "new thinking" in the P5 and the Security Council, marked by the Council's unanimous response to the Iraqi occupation and annexation of Kuwait in 1990. This period of short-lived unity among the P5 started to fade around the mid-1990s, and is best characterized by the totally inadequate response to an outbreak of genocide in Rwanda that could have likely been prevented with only limited intervention,[33] resulting in the deaths of hundreds of thousands, and in a failure to follow through on a promise to protect thousands of Bosnians who were massacred at a UN safe zone in Srebrenica after UN troops retreated in the face of a Serbian attack. Any signs of effective cooperation were totally gone by 1999 when NATO countries bombed Serbia, which had not attacked any NATO members, without prior authorization from the Security Council to use military force. Two permanent members of the Security Council, Russia and China, had opposed a military solution against Serbia; Russia was particularly adamant that force not be used.

Carl Schmitt defined sovereignty – a *mutatis mutandis* equivalent in international relations would probably be hegemony – as the power to decide when to declare a state of emergency. In that spirit, the NATO

[32] For en exhaustive yet occasionally somewhat idiosyncratic history of the use of veto, see Anjali V. Patil, *The UN Veto in World Affairs, 1946–1990: A Complete Record and Case Histories of the Security Council's Veto* (Sarasota, Fla.: UNIFO Publishers/London: Mansell, 1992).

[33] For a full discussion of what could likely have prevented violence, see Romeo Dallaire, *Shake Hands with the Devil: The Failure of Humanity in Rwanda* (Canada: Random House, 2003).

countries hurried to affirm that one was not supposed to look for a legal "precedent" in the Kosovo intervention. The enlightened public in the Western world tended to believe that the reason the Security Council failed to act was because of Russia's illegitimate quest to support Serbia, an historic ally, no matter what.[34] Whatever the merits of the Western argument that intervention in Kosovo "may have been illegal but in the given circumstances was nevertheless legitimate"[35] it eroded the authority of the UN Charter and the Security Council. Although the 1999 use of force against Yugoslavia (Serbia and Montenegro) eroded the Council's authority, it was not yet perceived as a fatal blow to the organization. The incident could be, it was hoped, dismissed as a *sui generis* case explained by the stubbornness and hurt prestige of a former superpower. Many argued that in terms of legitimacy at least, Russia did not have the veto power in this kind of humanitarian crisis. In any case, it was easier to act in a way that violated the charter right to a veto of certain Security Council members when the violation did not affect the West, but only a weakened Russia and a totalitarian China.

After the Kosovo intervention, the government of Canada launched the "responsibility to protect" project, the main idea of which apparently was to avoid future UN Security Council stalemates in situations like Kosovo. The advocates of this new concept maintained that in cases of genocide and ethnic cleansing, the international community had a duty to intervene. The idea was not so much to find new legitimacy for unilateral humanitarian interventions but rather to establish a norm that in such cases the Security Council *was obliged* to act. In other words, the "responsibility to protect" project was as much an effort to justify NATO's actions in Kosovo and thereby repair the damage to the image of the UN as an effective collective security institution, as it was an effort to prevent future genocides. It cleared the consciences of NATO countries for their violation of Article 2, paragraph 4 of the UN Charter, intimating that obviously they had acted responsibly in a way that justified their means.

The twin ideas of intervention to prevent genocide being a responsibility and of NATO being the military vanguard of the UN gained

[34] The interesting thing about this belief that Russia and Serbia are longtime allies is that it is absolutely unsupported by historical fact. Other than offering some material assistance during Serbia's struggle for independence from the Ottoman Empire, Russia has never risked backing Serbia, unless it stands to gain something concrete.

[35] See, e.g., Anne-Marie Slaughter, "Good Reasons for Going Around the UN," *New York Times*, March 18, 2003.

support. Then the terror attacks of 9/11 happened and, in response, the US and UK used military force against the Taliban regime in Afghanistan. In continental European scholarly circles, the US justified its actions both by claiming it was acting in self-defense and therefore in accordance with customary international law if not with the letter of the UN Charter as interpreted by the International Court of Justice (ICJ) in the *Nicaragua* decision, but also by claiming Afghanistan was the type of failed state in which the international community had a responsibility to act.[36] Although these arguments were received with some uneasiness, most experts in international law gave the US the benefit of the doubt, and the UN Security Council approved the use of force in Afghanistan.

Then came the US-backed invasion of Iraq. Whether the invasion of Iraq was part of a wider strategy, a hawkish-Messianic, realist-idealist plan to use military force in order to remake the Islamic world, or a legitimate policy decision based upon hard evidence, is debatable. An increasing number of scholars, including this author, are leaning towards the former position, as are an increasing number of former White House officials, such as former White House Press Secretary Scott McClellan.[37] There is no need to weigh in on that subject here, nor is there a need to retell the events that led to the highly divisive war of the US-led "coalition of the willing" against Iraq. These events are still very fresh in our memories and the military occupation of Iraq by the US-led coalition is still ongoing.

It is important to note that the Iraq debate in the United Nations presented a unique challenge to the Council. Rather than an East–West debate, the West was suddenly divided. On one side was the hawkish alliance of the United States and the United Kingdom. On the other stood the highly influential EU behemoths, P5-member France and then elected member of the Security Council Germany. Both questioned America's motives and both pressed for continued inspections and further negotiation with Iraq. To be clear, both China and Russia also voiced concern over the wisdom of invading Iraq.

The American decision to circumvent the United Nations' collective security process and to act alone, or rather with its coalition of the willing, from which the majority of the UN Security Council was

[36] US Department of Justice Memo on Interrogation Methods that do not Violate Prohibitions against Torture. From Deputy Assistant Attorney General John Yoo to Alberto R. Gonzales, White House Counsel (August 1, 2002).

[37] Scott McClellan, *What Happened* (United States: Public Affairs 2008).

noticeably absent, seriously weakened the UN's perceived power and legitimacy. The hortatory messages of the Secretary-General, Kofi Annan, suddenly sounded somewhat hollow, because the organization no longer enjoyed the support or backing of its chief founder and most economically and militarily powerful member. The impression was amplified by the nomination of John Bolton as the US ambassador to the UN. Even before his nomination for the position he had repeatedly made the case against multilateralism and international law and had been quoted as saying "There's no such thing as the United Nations. If the UN secretary building in New York lost 10 stories, it wouldn't make a bit of difference." Though certainly not the type of behavior from Washington that the rest of the West would have liked, they should not have been surprised. The seeds for unilateral action were sown when the West advocated a NATO use of force without first securing UN approval.

Those two crises – Kosovo 1999 and Iraq 2003 – clearly involved the use of military force against the letter of the UN Charter and created the immediate context in which we should read the policy paper produced by the High-Level Panel convened by Secretary-General Annan. The panel of course implies that its report is about saving the world;[38] in reality it is about saving the UN and rationalizing its Charter with the age in which we now live. Specifically, it is about reinvigorating the Great Power oligarchic approach to global governance and about combating the rise of the alternative – enlightened US hegemony, supported by a de facto US veto power over the veto power of the rest of the P5. Even if oligarchy is preferable to autocracy, the Security Council is not that different from previous Holy Alliances and other Great Power "directorates of European/world affairs."[39] Likewise, while a more inclusive Security Council may be preferable to the closed and relatively undemocratic Council of today, the motivations behind a quest to become a member on an enlarged Council, such as international prestige, are anything but altruistic, and are not fundamentally different from the historical quests of states to be recognized as global leaders.[40]

[38] High-Level Panel, paras. 1–43.

[39] See Gerry Simpson, *Great Powers and Outlaw States. Unequal Sovereigns in the International Legal Order* (Cambridge: Cambridge University Press, 2004).

[40] See H. Triepel, *Die Hegemonie. Ein Buch von führenden Staaten* (Stuttgart/Berlin, 1943).

The High-Level Panel's suggestions: the dangers of a further-empowered Security Council and why enlargement and legitimacy don't mix

Commentators on the High-Level Panel's work have mostly concentrated on the question of how to reform the Security Council, concentrating specifically on issues of enlargement and reform. This focus on Council enlargement overlooks more fundamental structural problems, such as abuse of the veto power. It also fails to flush out a detailed answer to the antecedent questions of what the Panel wants the reformed Security Council to achieve, and how enlarging it will help. Finally, such an approach does not squarely address the issue of the Security Council's perceived lack of legitimacy.

The High-Level Panel advocates the idea that the Security Council should become more proactive in the future. This flows naturally from its main thesis that the types of threat that merit a collective security response should be broadened to include things other than traditional interstate war or intrastate conflict. The result of that would be an extension of the Security Council's legal authority and moral duty to act in a wider variety of scenarios. The Panel recognizes that an empowered Security Council would have an even greater need to be seen as legitimate in order to enjoy the cooperation of UN member states. Its approach seems to imply that enlarging the Council and reducing the existing legitimacy deficit are separate though thoroughly intertwined issues, essential to an effective, empowered Security Council.

Thinking that legitimacy and effectiveness of such an oligarchic and unrepresentative organ as the Security Council are highly correlated issues that could be promoted on the same ticket is absurdly idealistic. It overlooks the fact that further empowerment may negate a need for legitimacy, since a beefed-up Council of Great Powers may have the ability to authorize unilateral action of its powerful P5 members. In general, one cannot blame the members of the High-Level Panel for lacking a sense of realism on this issue. After all, such an extensive reform effort requires walking a narrow line between the need to reform and the political realities of that which is doable. In the case of the Security Council, however, the emphasis has gone too much in one direction. Notwithstanding much lip-service paid to the Council's legitimacy deficit, the ultimate priority seems to have been to improve the effectiveness of the Security Council to act independently.

In choosing to focus on effectiveness, the members of the Panel have demonstrated an uncritical and overly optimistic attitude toward both the Security Council as a concerned advocate for the rest of the UN member states' interests, and toward the motivations and intentions of the Great Powers on the P5. Did the Panel get carried away with the ultimate fantasy of a benevolent and altruistic Security Council, working as a quasi-global government entrusted and empowered to deal with emerging threats? Or was the report the natural, self-interested action plan of states asked to critique themselves? After all, would a bias in favor of aggrandizement be that shocking, considering that the High-Level Panel was to an important extent made up of individuals from P5 member countries and long-time aspirant countries, such as Brazil, India, and Japan? Its research directors were citizens of the United States and Canada and, quite exotically, the research team even included a German descendant of Otto von Bismarck.[41]

The High-Level Panel's ideas about widening the competences of the Security Council should not be accepted uncritically. First, the historical record of the Security Council and of Great Power politics simply does not warrant additional grants of trust and power, unless checks to the veto power are created or the veto mechanism itself is made more fair. Otherwise the international community faces a prospect even worse than that of entrusting its collective security to an oligarchy of five self-interested powers that vote or veto resolutions first and foremost based on whether they stand to make individual relative power gains in a given situation. Now one of the five, the United States, has discovered the recipe for total freedom to act unilaterally – the hard power to make war individually and the juridical power to veto any potential retributive resolution from the Council.

Second, the optimistic and somewhat uncritical emphasis that the High-Level Panel puts on strengthening the Council may be problematic in the light of the UN Charter, which emphasizes sovereign equality between the states.[42] The South Centre, representing the viewpoints of the global South, has critically commented on the attempts to expand the notion of threats to international peace and security: "Nowhere in the span of Chapters VI, VII and VIII of the Charter's mandates to the Council is there reference to any dispute or situation that should engage it other than one between states."[43] Even if that statement does not mean that the UN Charter may not be

[41] See www.un.org/secureworld and www.europeandynasties.com (last accessed June 8, 2008).

[42] For a discussion, yet also the conclusion that by and large the SC has not acted *ultra vires*, see Kenneth Manusama, *The United Nations Security Council in the post-Cold War Era: Applying the Principle of Legality* (Leiden: Martinus Nijhoff Publishers, 2006).

[43] South Centre, *For a Strong and Democratic United Nations: A South Perspective on UN Reform*, p. 130.

reinterpreted, simply expanding its authority without addressing the issues of Security Council legitimacy is not acceptable.

Turning specifically to legitimacy, the Council's legitimacy deficit will not be reduced by enlargement of the permanent membership. The Council is not viewed as illegitimate because it is "unrepresentative." Even if it were, would adding four new permanent members (Germany, Japan, India, and Brazil) make the Council suddenly democratic? Not really. The main impediment to legitimacy is quite clearly systemic and far-reaching, and it stems from the fact that Council members and (non-members alike) continue to promote a never-ending game of classical realist international politics. The game creates structural winners and losers, and it allows winners to draft the peace treaties and write the histories. It is telling that in the case of Security Council enlargement, the most vehement resistance to adding Germany, Japan, Brazil, and India as permanent members has come from regional rivals who have not felt "represented" at all by the aspirant countries – even notwithstanding common EU membership as in the case of Germany and Italy.

Looking back to the Council's formation, the body took its legitimacy not from being representative and "democratic" but from being the exclusive club of the powerful victorious powers.[44] It is a well-known fact that in 1945, the veto power was created by a "take it or leave it"-style ultimatum given to the smaller nations at the Convention. Since those beginning moments, the Council has been a political body, and political bodies do not normally act out of altruism.

The frontlines of the next international order: United Nations or American hegemony?

In 1946, Hans Kelsen warned that the future of the SC might look like this:

> The members which have no [veto] right may be induced to secure for themselves the friendship and protection of one of the five great powers ... The veto right of the five permanent members may lead to a political system of more or less open clientage, that is to say, to a dismemberment of the Organization into five groups of states each of them taking advantage of the privilege of its patron.[45]

[44] Edward Luck recounts that President Roosevelt stressed in 1943 that the post-war organization must be built on a clear foundation of power politics, not welfare politics or wishful thinking. See Luck, *UN Security Council: Practice and Promise*, p. 11.

[45] Hans Kelsen, "Organization and Procedure of the Security Council of the United Nations," *Harvard Law Review* 59 (1946), p. 1120.

While the worst expectations and warnings have not come true, Kelsen's analysis contains some truth. The 1999 Kosovo crisis was, at least pretextually, about Russia voting like the patron of Serbia. The same could be said about Russia's position regarding Kosovo's recent declaration of independence. When the US invaded Iraq in 2003, Eastern European countries supported the decision uncritically, lining up with the hegemon rather than the Security Council, a collegial aristocratic organ of the United Nations. Could this have been a show of support for a new patron without whose support the former Soviet satellites could not have acceded to and attained the protection of NATO?

The choice today is actually not as complex as Kelsen predicted. Primarily due to imbalances in the economic and military powers of the individual members of the P5, the choice today is a binary choice. One can opt for a world order dominated by a hegemonic United States, audacious but foolhardy, idealistic yet classically realist, and unwavering in its commitments to its stupendously ill-thought-out adventures. Or one can throw one's lot in with the United Nations, an organization struggling to balance efficacy against autocracy and an organization paralyzed by a paradox at its core: that in the age of democracy it is run by an oligarchy. American conservative scholars have already started to make their arguments in favor of the US hegemony – it might not be so bad after all.[46] If history has taught anything to the Eastern Europeans, it has taught them to remain skeptical of ideological claims of moral supremacy. It seems that the rule of aristocracy is better than the rule of a hegemon – at least one would hope that the aristocrats would sometimes balance each other. At the same time, we should not simply take for granted that the current moment in history is the end of the principle of the equality of states. A "democracy" (in terms of an international normative order) that takes into account the interests of both Great Powers and small states has not become an outdated normative ideal. In that sense, "democracy" is preferable to the rule of aristocracy. There are compelling reasons to remain skeptical about the fantasy of increasing the power of the Security Council at the cost of the General Assembly, especially under conditions that do not reform the veto power of the permanent members.

[46] See in particular, R. Kagan, "End of Dreams, Return of History," *Policy Review* (August–September 2007).

PART II

Defining "threats" to collective security

of collective security concerns.[5] It required the unusual cataclysm of genocide, or a multinational confrontation in an especially resource-rich country such as the Democratic Republic of the Congo (then known as Zaire) for international society, outside of the continent itself, to become especially perturbed. The wars in the Balkans, waged in an arena that had become a persistent and perennial source of conflagrations among European empires, caused a good deal more consternation. But even there, the Great Powers, restrained by a history of accumulated errors and uncertainties as to the transference of those experiences into the management of the fluid world of the 1990s, initially hesitated and equivocated as to the nature and scope of international intervention.

The management of events in the Middle East furnished a lodestar. The chief pariah state of the region, Iraq, was effectively brought under the thumb of the Security Council, which used its Chapter VII powers to rigorously enforce a thoroughgoing sanctions regime. In the Balkans and in Africa, the Security Council was seen to have learned from the mistakes of the 1990s and to have become a more effective body, highly interventionist in wrestling with the political disorders and human rights violations evident in what had come to be termed "failed states." To be sure, the conflicts between Palestine and Israel remained far from being resolved, and the Security Council had been divided over NATO's war in Kosovo; but even in those situations, the disagreements had not led to the sort of vituperative clashes between the big powers that a decade earlier would have been expected as *de rigueur*.

All in all, as the new century began, the United Nations system, largely under the direction and control of its most prominent member and sole superpower, the United States, seemed poised to establish a world governance system that could effectively herd, tame, and check the proclivities of nation states to insist on their right to act independently of any binding supervisory authority. It seemed this new regime could be held together through the affirmation of core neoliberal principles, notably those of "democracy," "human rights," "rule of law," and "free markets."

This euphoria over the existence of an allegedly effective international "legal" order contrasted sharply with the apparent incapacity of the

[5] The massive European wars of the post-1848 world, ranging from the national conflicts among the Germans and the French to the proxy colonial wars of the English, French, and Italians and the proxy ideological wars of the United States and the Soviet Union, involving, as they invariably did, reasonably organized interstate armies, were quintessential examples of what the international system had in mind when it spoke of "threats to collective security."

system during the first thirty-five years of its existence to come anywhere close to the high aspirations for a just, peaceful, and ordered world that had been so eloquently articulated in the founding document of the United Nations system.[6] The launch of a permanent International Criminal Court, the flaming-out of the much-dreaded "y2k" catastrophe, the remarkable economic recoveries from the Asian and Russian contagions, the seemingly unstoppable boom in financial markets across the globe, successful development of democracy in Central and Eastern Europe, exemplary "non-racial" politics of South Africa, the touted universal acclaim for "human rights," and the sense that we all now marched to a single drumbeat, all gave a glorious tinge to the commencement of a new decade.

So, when heads of states and governments from around the globe gathered in New York in 2000 at a "millennium" summit, the focus was on the limitless future possibilities for humankind, rather than on reconstructing a demoralized civilization from the ashes of its self-destruction, as it had been in 1945. These leaders could focus on the ideals of "preventive diplomacy," "millennium development goals," "primary education," "nation-building," "sustainable development," the environment, economic development, and similarly broad agendas, rather than confront the messiness of specific regional crisis, or address the creaky machinery of the international system.

In particular, the 2000 conference could afford to suspend addressing the numerous calls for reform of the system that had emerged following the collapse of the bipolar world system. These calls in large measure could be (at least temporarily) dispensed with because of the unchallenged dominance of Western ideals, interests, institutions, and concerns in the corridors of power. The seeming unassailable position of the United States during the 1990s effectively converted Western preferences into global policy. International agreement seemed not to be necessary because Washington could be expected to decide for all.

Three years later, however, international society faced a quite different landscape. The euphoria and triumphalism of "peace enforcement" was stalemated (if not checked) by the costs of nation-building. The efficacy of the neoliberal economic order, which had in part underwritten the unassailable position of the West in the 1990s, had been frayed by numerous financial crises, first in the so-called "emerging markets," and then in the dominant capital markets of North America and Europe. The confidence of the "sole superpower" in its ability to direct

[6] See, e.g., Preamble to the Charter of the United Nations; see also Article 1 of the Charter.

the affairs of the globe had been shaken dramatically by the September 11, 2001 attacks on symbols of its financial and military prowess. Notwithstanding the sympathy generated by those attacks, the confidence of much of the world in the leadership capacities of the United States in turn had been undercut by the shortsighted unilateralism that underpinned many of the responses to those attacks. Most consequentially, and partly as differing responses to those attacks, the Great Powers vigorously and vituperatively disagreed in public about the role of the UN Security Council in bringing Iraq to heel. In particular, these powers, whose self-confident exercise of authority in the 1990s had transformed the United Nations Security Council into a forceful baton-wielding orchestrator of international law and politics, now disagreed among themselves as to the appropriate steps for compelling Saddam Hussein's Iraq to abide by longstanding Security Council decrees. Outmaneuvered by France, the United States and the United Kingdom, with minimal pretext of legality, dispensed with demands for Security Council benediction of the invasion and overthrow of the government of a member state of the United Nations system. In the acrimony that followed, a re-elected Secretary-General, whose organization had just won the ultimate accolade – the Nobel Prize for Peace – felt sufficiently emboldened to appoint a panel to revisit the long-overlooked demands for reform. The High-Level Panel Report was the result.

Given the rapid and kaleidoscopic changes in the moods and realities of international society just described, one cannot help but be empathetic to the daunting task faced by the members of the High-Level Panel. To be sure, they shared the attribute of all being drawn from the most privileged cadres of their national societies, and they were of necessity committed to multilateral internationalism. Yet they had to give voice to the claims and interests drawn from highly diverse socio-economic and political cultures, and to do so through complete consensus. It's hardly surprising, then, that the Report at best is an amalgam of ideas that are held together only by the most elastic of principles. The Report proclaims that:

> individual sovereign states whose role and responsibilities, and right to be respected, are fully recognized in the Charter of the United Nations must form the backbone of any reform to collective security. But threats recognize no national boundaries ... No State, no matter how powerful, can by its own efforts alone make itself invulnerable to today's threats. And it cannot be assumed that every State will always be able, or willing,

> to meet its responsibility to protect its own peoples and not to harm its neighbours.[7]

What constitutes a threat? The Panel's working definition is "[a]ny event or process that leads to large-scale death or lessening of life chances and undermines states as the basic unit of the international system."[8] These are grouped into six clusters: (1) economic and social threats including poverty, infectious diseases, and environmental degradation; (2) interstate conflict; (3) internal conflict, including civil war, genocide, and other large-scale atrocities; (4) nuclear, radiological, chemical, and biological weapons; (5) terrorism; and (6) transnational organized crime.[9]

In evaluating the Panel's Report, it must be acknowledged that it identifies genuine and persistent problems with which contemporary humanity must wrestle. To acknowledge the existence of problems, however, is not the same as treating those problems, *mutatis mutandis*, as threats to collective security. Comprehensiveness is clearly the watchword of the Report, but it might also be its primary shortcoming. It suggests that all threats are of equal weight, and in doing so, it avoids the hard task of providing grounds for prioritizing the expenditure of the surely limited resources available to the system. Moreover, this grab-bag approach avoids having to confront the possible trade-offs that may exist among threats, and between threats and prescribed cures. What relationships, for example, may exist between poverty, internal conflicts, and terrorism, and does addressing one or the other of these threats increase the likelihood of the other?

Here, we are met with a second related shortcoming. Despite the well-crafted arguments of the Report, and the volumes of back-up data, the criteria for the selection of purported particular threats are far from being transparently principled. To be sure, in virtually any circumstance, interstate warfare and genocide self-evidently implicate the likelihood of large-scale death and the lessening of life chances and clearly pose challenges of a collective nature to international order; but such clarity of threat (using the Report's own definition) is surely less evident in cases of terrorism or transnational organized crime. This is not to argue that these latter problems should not be of international concern, but what elevates them to more international solicitude or concern than, for example, "socio-economic discrimination" or inadequate access to

[7] High-Level Panel Report, Synopsis, p. 1. [8] *Ibid.*, Part 2 Synopsis, p. 23. [9] *Ibid.*

conciliation, recommendations, and moral suasion to avert the looming conflict. In the event of failure, the problem could be escalated and under Chapter VII, the Security Council was fully empowered to take coercive measures, including the use of collective military force to bring a determined wrongdoer to heel.[12]

One of the shortcomings of the United Nations system between 1945 and 1990 was the hesitation with which it resorted to the use of the Chapter VII powers. That hesitation grew out of the polarized politics of the Cold War. The collapse of the Soviet Union as a reflexive rival center of power inaugurated a new era in which the Security Council was afforded the opportunity to weigh on their own merits claimed threats to collective security, and to take preventive measures in a dispassionate manner. But the manner of the exercise of these powers over the next decade and a half disclosed two obvious flaws in such optimism.

In the first place, the hoped-for objectivity proved to be forlorn. The decision as to the exercise of Chapter VII powers depended almost exclusively on the political preferences of the United States; preferences that are configured by the country's domestic interest groups rather than any sense of a shared common wellbeing for the so-called "international community." Secondly, the absence of counterweights in the Security Council meant that any perceived threat was almost always dealt with under the coercive authority of Chapter VII. Use of the more conciliatory instruments of Chapter VI atrophied. The resulting gravitation of power to the Security Council laid bare its undemocratic structures, and precipitated questions of its legitimacy. Many of these questions could and were avoided until the sharp disagreements first over Kosovo and later over Iraq made ignoring them less and less tenable.

A consequence of the reliance on Chapter VII was the need to flesh out its preventive tools. In the aftermath of the Second World War, coercive military force had been contemplated as a last resort, and the United Nations Charter extensively provided the criteria for such use of military force, as well as the means and manner for its organization. Actual Cold War practice had rendered these charter provisions effectively moot. In the wake of the return to the exercise of power under

UN Secretary-General's Mission of Good Offices in Cyprus, 1999–2004 (Oxford: Hart Publishing, 2005) and David J. Ludlow, "Preventative Peacemaking in Macedonia: An Assessment of UN Good Offices Diplomacy," *Brigham Young University Law Review* 761 (2003).

12 See generally United Nations Charter, Articles 39, 42.

Chapter VII, little of precedent could be called upon. Much of the subsequent behavior was dictated as much by ad hoc considerations of cost and expedient politics as by any principled resort to Charter provisions or established legal rules.

Coercion by military force can be both financially and politically expensive. Early Chapter VII operations in Iraq, Somalia, Haiti, and the Balkans brought these realities home. The system adapted quite readily. Coercion through economic sanctions became the more favored tool. This approach had two radical effects that must be considered in any evaluation of the treatment of sanctions in the High-Level Panel's Report. In the first place, precisely because sanctions, unlike military force, impose relatively insignificant costs on those who seek their use, the tendency to advocate their use is much greater. Secondly, because their effects are concentrated on weak and vulnerable societies, their use magnifies the distributive inequalities in the system and the troubling issues of legitimation raised by the unrepresentative structure of the Security Council. In what follows, I explore how the High-Level Panel Report confronts these two questions. I then go on to suggest alternative responses to these twin deficits of accountability and legitimacy.

Sanctions and collective security

Dr. Jeremy Farrall, in his contribution to this volume, has thoughtfully canvassed the occasional strengths and many weaknesses of the implementations of the United Nations' sanctions regimes.[13] I do not wish here to rehearse many of his cogently made points. What I do want to do is to examine the use of sanctions as a systemic policy for furthering collective security. Under such an inquiry, enforceability and efficacy of specific regimes, while relevant, is not the subject of study. Rather, the primary theme that I wish to pursue here is the value of sanctions as instruments of policy, both in terms of the specific justifications for them advanced by the High-Level Panel (and other members of the international intelligentsia) and the overlooked discordant notes that sanctions may present for an order based on the principle of collective security. In so doing I am interested in the resort to sanctions not simply as a coercive

[13] See Jeremy Farrall, "The World Summit Process and UN Sanctions Reform: Between Rhetoric and Force," below, Chapter 9; Jeremy M. Farrall, *United Nations Sanctions and the Rule of Law* (Cambridge: Cambridge University Press, 2007).

policy tool in and of itself, but for its symbolic value in the international system's pursuit of collective security.[14]

The basic argument for economic sanctions (and by "sanctions," we almost always mean "economic sanctions") is straightforward.[15] It is seen as a middle point between doing nothing and using military force.[16] The creators of the United Nations system carefully orchestrated the role of the Security Council as a graduated ratcheting-up of the General Assembly's non-binding recommendations to Security Council recommendations under Chapter VI and then ultimately binding action under Chapter VII. They also provided for a graduated and symmetrical response under Chapter VII from a simple finding and declaration of threats to or breach of international peace and security under Article 39, to the use of sanctions under Article 41, culminating of course in the outright use of force under Article 42.

On its face the analysis for determining the legal legitimacy of a sanctions regime would appear to be fundamentally no different from that for deciding upon the use of force under Chapter VII. Upon closer scrutiny that syllogism exhibits its failing as an analytical tool in matters of policy. Because of the substantial costs that it entails, the use of force is rarely employed as a policy solution. Specifically, the use of force requires that member states be willing and able to raise and finance armies. Furthermore, it requires that the international system be willing to justify the all-too-visible consequences of waging war.[17] There are thus

[14] For book-length discussions of the United Nations Sanctions regimes in the post-Cold war world, see Farrall, *United Nations Sanctions and the Rule of Law*; David Cortright and George A. Lopez, *The Sanctions Decade: Assessing UN Strategies in the 1990s* (Boulder, Colorado: Lynne Rienner, 2000).

[15] The United Nations sanctions ostensibly have come in several varieties including diplomatic isolation, travel bans, and outright refusals to deal. See, e.g., Farrall, *United Nations Sanctions and the Rule of Law*. These on their face are either obviously counter-productive, or can be seen as being effective only in the light of their economic effects. Further, use of economic sanctions under Chapter VII should be distinguished from the imposition of arms embargoes. The latter legitimately can be seen as working *in pari passu* with coercive military force. For this reason, the arguments presented below are intended to be considered within the context of economic sanctions rather than of embargoes on the shipment of arms and ammunitions into areas in which the existence of conflict is determined by the Security Council to constitute threats to international peace and security.

[16] See, e.g., High-Level Panel, para. 178; See also Kofi Annan, *In Larger Freedom: Towards Security, Development and Human Rights for All*, A/59/2005 (March 21, 2005).

[17] Difficulties in staffing UN peacekeeping efforts illustrate this point. To avoid these difficulties, the Security Council has simply either contracted out war waging under

substantial extralegal checks on the use by the Security Council of force as a policy tool.

Before accepting resort to economic sanctions as the lesser evil of two legally permissible tools, it is worth reflecting on the extent to which similar extralegal considerations may influence – whether for better or for worse – decision making regarding the use of sanctions. It is unfortunately an issue that has not received much attention. The instinctive understanding being to believe that since sanctions seemingly pose lesser intrusiveness or apparent social costs than the outright use of force, they must necessarily be preferable. But sometimes a supposedly lesser evil is not necessarily preferable.[18]

As a jurisdictional matter, the Security Council's legal authority to impose economic sanctions is triggered only by a determination that there exists a "threat to the peace, breach of the peace, or act of aggression, and that sanctions are necessary to remove such related threats to international security, or to maintain or restore international security."[19] These determinations are lodged exclusively in the Council itself. Neither the Charter nor any extant authoritative text or interpretative decisions – judicial or otherwise – have furnished any persuasive, let alone binding determinations of the scope of this jurisdictional verbiage.[20] One is thus forced to rely on reading the tea leaves of the highly politicized and

Chapter VII, as in the case of the "Gulf War" (see Security Council Resolution 678), or stood on the sidelines while the war is waged only to provide its imprimatur after the war (compare Security Council Resolution 1244 (after the Kosovo War), and Security Council Resolution 1511 (following the US-led invasion and occupation of Iraq)).

[18] See, e.g., David J. Lektzian and Christopher M. Sprecher, "Sanctions, Signals, and Militarized Conflict," *American Journal of Political Science* 51 (April 2007), pp. 415–431 (empirically demonstrating that resort to sanctions often does not obviate the use of military force).

[19] UN Charter, Article 39.

[20] The extent to which these determinations may be subject to dispositive legal rules has generated much discussion. See, e.g., *Prosecutor* v. *Tadic*, Case No. IT-94-1-T, Opinion and Judgment, May 7, 1997; see also *Questions of Interpretation and Application of the 1971 Montreal Convention Arising from the Aerial Incident at Lockerbie* (*Libya* v. *UK*; *Libya* v. *US*), Provisional Measures (Orders of April 14, 1992), *ICJ Reports* (1992), p. 32 (Judge Shahabuddeen, separate opinion), p. 64 (Judge Schwabel, Separate Opinion), p. 65 (Judge Weeramantry, dissenting opinion). Compare Thomas M. Franck, "Powers of Appreciation: Who is the Ultimate Guardian of UN Legality?," 86 *AJIL* 519 (1992) (analogizing the ICJ's authority to review the "political" decisions of the Security Council to the famous US case of *Marbury* v. *Madison*, which enshrined the doctrine of judicial review of legislative and executive actions within US domestic law). An interesting development with potentially far-reaching possibilities for bringing under review and ultimately cabining Security Council exercise of coercive power is the willingness of domestic and regional courts to review for consistency with domestic law the exercise of

The disclosure of the pervasive financial corruption within the sanctions regime took a while to receive confirmation, but its existence was hardly doubted.[35]

These failings, which differed from those experienced by other sanctions regimes only in their magnitude, would nonetheless have been overlooked but for two additional failings. First, the utter failure of sanctions to obtain any of the sought-for objectives was simply too glaring to be ignored. The frequent use of military force by the United States and the United Kingdom as backup coercive measures showed the shallowness (if not outright falsity) of the claim that the international system was faced with an either/or proposition between military force and economic sanctions. While Iraqis were being subjected to the penalties of economic sanctions, United States citizens were also being asked to bear the cost of a low-intensity war for which the nation had not been mobilized. The ordering of a sustained bombing campaign by the President of the United States at a time when he faced likely impeachment for lying about his sexual escapades could not but illuminate the moral and political failings of the reliance on sanctions as a means of keeping Iraq in check.

Second, the weaknesses of the sanctions regime were magnified when, following the cessation of the bombings, both the United States and the Security Council appeared entirely at a loss as to how to follow up. Both meekly accepted Iraq's ordering out of the United Nations arms inspectors, who had supposedly been charged with monitoring Iraq's compliance with the terms of Resolution 687.[36] Yet, the sanctions continued. But for what purpose? The world thus seemed poised for an indefinite sanctions regime with no means for telling when they should be considered a success or a failure. That dilemma illustrated a significant and devastating challenge for the use of sanctions. No state or society can remain in a perpetual state of siege. Military force has at least one important check on its use: namely that at some point, one side or both give up and sue for peace. Given the asymmetrical structure of sanctions, it is conceivably possible for one country to maintain sanctions for an

[35] See generally the multi-volume Report of the Independent Inquiry Committee into the United Nations Oil for Food Program (The "Volcker committee"), available at: www.iic-offp.org/.

[36] See generally Scott Ritter, *Iraq Confidential: The Untold Story of the Intelligence Conspiracy to Undermine the UN and Overthrow Saddam Hussein* (London: Tauris, 2005).

indefinite period of time.[37] This was precisely what the Iraqi sanctions regime seemed to foreshadow.

It was thus hardly surprising that by 2002 much of the world had lost patience with the Iraqi sanctions regime. As with the Libyan sanctions regime, many countries outside of the Western world were beginning to see Security Council sanctions less as a device for collective security and more as a means for punishing independent-minded governments that operated outside of the West's orbit. The United States seemed to understand this and tried to alter the dynamics of the discourse by calling for "smart sanctions." Unable to obtain the requisite consensus, it ultimately chose the outright waging of war, and thereby gave the coup de grace to the sanctions regime.

Considering the above, a resort to sanctions should not be viewed with pacific equanimity. Sanctions may on their face appear as an attractive alternative to the use of force by a hegemonic Security Council.[38] They certainly act as a salve to the conscience of humanity. But this alternative has its own – and by no means insignificant – costs. As evident from the brief discussion just presented, these include the following: First, there are the genuinely humanitarian and social costs that are disproportionately born by the poorest and weakest individual members of those societies that sanctions seek to ostracize from what passes as an international community of states. Second, like any politically induced regulatory regime, the administration of sanctions regimes invariably appears to harbor the seeds for far-reaching corruption of the administering authorities. Third, while it might be hoped that sanctions work in the sense of coercing the preferred behavior from those on whom they are imposed, there can be no assurance that they will so work. Indeed, history suggests otherwise. What seems indisputable is that when they do fail, the international political system is left with two bleak and equally unpalatable choices: to employ the force that sanctions originally were intended to avoid, or to capitulate in abject surrender to the detested evil.

Perhaps these shortcomings can be ignored if the likelihood of sanctions succeeding is the norm rather than the exception. Notwithstanding the enthusiastic support of sanctions, there is in fact virtually no history

[37] The United States has maintained a more or less complete boycott of Cuba for almost fifty years. Its boycott of North Korea has been longer, and its use of sanctions against Iran has been ongoing for almost thirty years.

[38] Compare José E. Alvarez, "Judging the Security Council," 90 *AJIL* 1 (1990); José E. Alvarez, "Hegemonic International Law Revisited," 97 *AJIL* 873 (2003).

to support such optimism. Indeed, it is virtually impossible to come up with any instance in which sanctions can be said to have had unqualified success.[39] These systemic shortcomings, although scrupulously avoided during discussions of sanctions regimes, are all too obvious to policy makers. Attempts to address them by such tactical changes of policy as those embodied in so-called "targeted" or "smarter" sanctions that aim to narrow the range of persons, products or services covered may reduce the interest groups that are affected, but they are unlikely to address the systemic shortcomings just discussed. More significantly, such expediencies are as likely to reduce the practical effectiveness of a sanctions regime as to improve their moral acceptability.

That the illusion of sanctions as an effective tool of collective security was so unquestioningly embraced by the hard-headed diplomats, politicians, academics, and statesmen of the High-Level Panel speaks as much to the seeming absence of alternatives as to anything else. That the table is so barren of choices may be as much a testimonial to the failings of human imagination in the age of power and glory as it is to the triumph of idealism. What then is to be done? It is to this question that the concluding part of this chapter turns.

Rethinking the concept of collective security

The focus on the use of sanctions, it should be remembered, has been for the purpose of exploring one of the several tools chosen by the High-Level Panel (and, by extension, the United Nations system) to address the demands for collective security in the international order. Although in thinking about sanctions and the other tools available to the system the default approach is to evaluate their efficacy, it should not be forgotten that it is just as improper to consider sanctions as an end, in and of itself, as it would be to think of the use of force in this manner. After all, the resort to sanctions, even if effectively applied, is already a statement about the failure of the system to provide the necessary security to at least some of those for whose benefit the system supposedly exists. Unfortunately, this tendency to substitute means for ends is all too

[39] The example typically adduced in support of sanctions is its use against the apartheid system in South Africa. For a variety of reasons, the discussion of which is beyond the scope of and space permitted by this chapter, the example is inapposite. That the South African example has superficially underpinned the moral case for sanctions cannot be denied. The international system might do well, however, to treat it as *sui generis*.

pervasive in contemporary thinking about international law. The costs that this tendency poses for international law should not be overlooked, and it is with some reflections on them that this chapter closes.

The collapse of communism at the end of the 1980s and early 1990s offered liberal states an unparalleled opportunity to reshape the world order. The balance of power system that de facto had structured international relations during the Cold War was swept away, leaving the scene open for the implementation of the collective security norms that had formed the foundations of the San Francisco Charter. Under the Charter, collective security was framed in two dimensions. On the one hand, it was assumed that there were interests common to all peoples and states and that, in the interest of peace and justice, all member states of the United Nations system would strive for their realization.[40]

Those transcendent interests were framed in unexceptionable terms; they needed to be because of the second feature of the Charter's conception of collective security. That feature assumed the existence of shared interests, but it was also grounded in the view that societies and their political orders can be and frequently are different. Coexistence, cooperation and collaboration, rather than assimilation or coercion, should be the operational norms of collective security. The implementation of collective security thus demanded a healthy respect by member states of the United Nations and the organization itself for those differences.[41] This view that the concept of collective security requires bifurcation between transcendent ends and practical means, between shared universal goals articulated through deliberation and consensus, on the one hand, and implementation through highly restricted means on the other, is embedded in the structure of the system. The diffusions of representations and power between the General Assembly, the Security Council, and the functional agencies (including the International Court of Justice) exemplified the cooperative contractarian view of the maintenance of international order through the concept of collective security. Collective security, as envisioned by the Charter, was thus not a super-norm to be achieved at all costs. Rather, it was accepted under the San Francisco Charter as being viable only if the ends were shared, and the means achieved through cooptation and consensus.

The Cold War experience challenged the effectiveness of the system that had been thus created. The bipolarity of the conflict between

[40] See United Nations Charter, Preamble and Article 1.
[41] See generally UN Charter, Article 2.

Communist and market-based societies and the pressures put on so-called "nonaligned" states within the system undermined the claims of shared norms and frustrated the means for their realization. Indeed, far from resting on the concept of collective security, the international order of the Cold War seemed to be a reversion to the discredited balance of power arrangement with which both the League of Nations and the United Nations had been intended to dispense. Understandably, then, the triumphant liberal states of the post-Cold War order did not simply want to return to the original interpretation of the San Francisco Charter. Adopting a posture that is perhaps innate in victors, they emphasized those ideals that were more consonant with their own domestic systems, and did so with little regard for their effects on societies that differed from theirs.[42] The search for universal justice rather than for peace was to be the defining goal, in the service of which guaranteeing the proclaimed rights of the individual, whether in the political or the economic sphere, was to be privileged over the promotion of the complex network of group interests that euphemistically is referred to as "self-determination." More controversially, coercion (by economic or judicial means, when feasible, but military force, when otherwise necessary) rather than cooperation and persuasion became the accepted means for achieving these ends.

The Security Council, whose enforcement powers had lain dormant, was the one preexisting institution that could be pressed into service. It did suffer from one not insignificant shortcoming: its lack of representativeness of the peoples over whom it lorded. Lack of representativeness is of course not

[42] One of the most egregiously exaggerated supposed virtues of democracies that somehow gained mythological sanctity in the 1990s was that liberal democracies are inherently pacific, and therefore are immune from the misuse of power. Lord Acton, who coined the aphorism that "power corrupts, absolute power corrupts absolutely" was of course himself a denizen of a liberal democracy when those were indeed extremely rare. Both William Jefferson and John Stuart Mill were all too aware of the possibility that majorities can be tyrannical. Indeed, it is precisely to check the propensity for abuse of power even in a democratic society that foundational documents such as national constitutions and the United Nations Charter serve pivotal roles in constraining the potential for abuse of power. What is true about power relationships within the internal structures of liberal democracies is even more so when the governments of those democracies are not answerable to the people over whom they wield their power. In modern times, some of the most aggressive forms of European colonization and coercive subjugation of non-European peoples were superintended by two quintessential liberal democracies: Victorian England and the French Third Republic. See, e.g., Anthony Anghie, *Imperialism, Sovereignty and the Making of International Law* (Cambridge: Cambridge University Press, 2004); Jennifer Pitts, *A Turn to Empire: The Rise of Imperial Liberalism in Britain and France* (Princeton: Princeton University Press, 2005).

necessarily fatal; however, since the dominant post-Cold War liberal order had come to see democracy as the birthright of all peoples, its absence from an institution that increasingly exercised powers of life and death over the least privileged members of the international society clearly created a dissonance between asserted norms and the actual functioning of power and politics. This was the milieu in which the High-Level Panel was created, and within which its report was formulated.

The High-Level Panel Report is in many ways an attempt at balancing the preferences of the dominant post-Cold War intelligentsia for individualized and universalist claims with the realities of practical politics in which the focal points of international order continue to revolve around state power and domestic politics. To appease the desires of the former group, the Report proposed a wide-ranging laundry list of claimed challenges to collective security that, if taken seriously, would convert the vast majority of socio-economic and political problems into issues of international concern, and thereby extinguish virtually any line of demarcation between the functions of the state and those of international society. Of course, given the constellations of hard power and the composition of the panel, the Report did not and could not seriously intend such an outcome. In such an environment, the Report opted for the means that appeared the least threatening to the role of the state within the international system. The result is a lack of fit between the broad sweep of claimed threats to collective security, and the very modest means chosen to realize those objectives. The one significant reform that might have made a difference, the radical reconstitution of the Security Council, was underplayed by the Panel Report, even as it invoked the Chapter VII powers of the Council as the core of the new order that it proposed. The best that the Panel Report could do was to restate two models of Security Council reform that had been under consideration for at least a dozen years, and which, even if adopted, would only minimally improve upon the current unrepresentative character of the Security Council, and would do virtually nothing to address the power (rather than law) orientation of the decisions of the Council.[43]

This disjuncture between asserted threats and recommended means for addressing them, while easy to understand, is nonetheless imprudent for the maintenance of international order – that is, for collective security, properly understood. The inclination of the panel in its analysis of the

[43] For a perceptive analysis of the effect of Security Council composition on membership reform, see Farrall, *United Nations Sanctions and the Rule of Law*.

Humanitarian intervention and the "war on terror"

The attempt to shift the normative discourse from intervention to responsibility, not an easy task under any circumstances, was rendered more problematic due to the challenges posed by the 9/11 attacks and their aftermath. In fact, the timing of the Responsibility to Protect report coincided with the unleashing of the "global campaign against terror" and led several commentators to view the Responsibility to Protect as a concept dead on arrival. This view considered the ongoing debate of the previous decade on the use of force for human protection purposes as the high point of the human rights era;[38] an era eclipsed by the exigencies of the "war on terror." In this context, the Responsibility to Protect, as the successor concept, suffered an irrevocable blow at its inception.

While few would dispute that human rights issues acquired a higher profile during the 1990s, drawing a sharp contrast between the two decades misses important and troubling continuities. The argument made here is that considerable overlap exists between the human rights discourse (especially in its humanitarian intervention variant) and the "war on terror" discourse.[39]

The first facet of this overlap relates to the endorsement, albeit with reservations, of UNSC activism by organizations and groups in the human rights and humanitarian communities.[40] The opening up of the security discourse came at a price. It provided those actors in the international system most capable and willing to project military force with an increasing array of opportunities for doing so, as well as a forum (UNSC) capable of legitimizing the relevant initiatives. In this context, the human rights discourse, by its very nature subversive of authority structures, increasingly intersected with the language of diplomacy and statecraft. In the process, it strengthened the United States' role in this activist agenda by

[38] Typical is the view of Michael Ignatieff, "Is the Human Rights Era Ending?" *The New York Times*, February 5, 2002, p. A25.

[39] Parts of this section follow George Andreopoulos, "The Human Rights/Humanitarian Framework in the Age of Terror" (unpublished manuscript), and Andreopoulos, "The Challenges and Perils of Normative Overstretch."

[40] George Andreopoulos, "Pathways to Intervention: The Changing Nature of Threats" (unpublished manuscript). The use of force for human rights protection purposes has often generated heated debates both within, as well as among organizations in these two communities. For a good overview of the relevant issues, see International Council on Human Rights Policy, *Human Rights Crises: NGO Responses to Military Interventions* (Geneva, 2002).

providing the remaining superpower with continuous opportunities to "incorporate human rights concerns into its operational goals."[41]

The continuing appeal of human rights became apparent in the course of the military actions against Afghanistan and Iraq. One of the reasons cited to justify military action against the Taliban was the situation of women and girls in the country. Then-Secretary of State Colin Powell argued that "the recovery of Afghanistan must entail the restoration of the rights of Afghan women."[42] In a similar vein, in the case of Iraq, the Joint Resolution authorizing the use of force cited both Iraq's continuing "brutal repression of its civilian population" and its "willingness to use weapons of mass destruction against … its own people."[43] It is instructive to note here that some neoconservative analysts felt, on the aftermath of the weapons of mass destruction fiasco, that human rights arguments should have figured more prominently in the Administration's case for "regime change" in Iraq.

The second facet refers to the changing lens through which the terrorist threat is perceived. In the pre-9/11 period, the main focus was on places which harbored groups with an anti-Western agenda and the capacity to engage in transnational acts of violence.[44] Now, the angle of vision may have widened "to include places where prevailing conditions can foster or facilitate terrorism."[45] The transition from a focus on groups harbored by states to any disintegrating/failed or "rogue" state, a terrain potentially hospitable to all forms of abusive conduct, clearly shifts the parameters of the debate. The emerging post-9/11 consensus seems to be that these types of state constitute an inviting terrain for the intersections between human rights protection and counter-terrorist initiatives and, in the process, widen the menu of available discourses and policy options at the disposal of the interveners.

The above-mentioned case of Afghanistan constitutes a telling example of these intersections. As the National Security Strategy document (NSS) noted, the US "will continue to work … to provide the

[41] Expression used by Tom Farer, "Humanitarian Intervention before and after 9/11: legality and legitimacy," in J. L. Holzgrefe and R. O. Keohane (eds.), *Humanitarian Intervention: Ethical, Legal and Political Dilemmas* (Cambridge: Cambridge University Press, 2003), p. 84.

[42] Anne Orford, *Reading Humanitarian Intervention* (Cambridge: Cambridge University Press, 2003), p. 202.

[43] Joint Resolution to Authorize the Use of United States Armed Forces Against Iraq, October 2, 2002; www.whitehouse.gov/news/releases/2002/10/20021002-2.html.

[44] Farer, "Humanitarian Intervention before and after 9/11," p. 85. [45] *Ibid.*

humanitarian, political, economic and security assistance necessary to rebuild Afghanistan so that it will never again abuse its people, threaten its neighbors, and provide a haven for terrorists."[46] There is a seamless, discursive transition from the NSS to the report issued by the Secretary-General's High-Level Panel on Threats, Challenges, and Change which, in addressing the preventive use of force, stated: "In the world of the twenty-first century, the international community does have to be concerned about nightmare scenarios combining terrorists, weapons of mass destruction and irresponsible states … which may conceivably justify the use of force, not just reactively but preventively."[47] Thus, under certain circumstances state irresponsibility, by raising the specter of apocalyptic consequences, renders even preventive action necessary.

If these remarks are tolerably accurate, humanitarian intervention bequeathed a troubled legacy to the Responsibility to Protect even before the tensions inherent in the latter concept began to manifest themselves. In particular, the increasing cooptation of human rights and humanitarian arguments by those actors most capable and willing to act, and the notion of the failed/irresponsible state as the terrain where massive human rights abuses can and do intersect with terrorist activities, have demarcated a troubling interface between human protection and the preventive uses of force.

Taking human protection seriously

If the debate on human protection is to move forward, there are certain issues that need to be addressed. Key among them is the vulnerability of the Responsibility to Protect concept and the concomitant need to build communal credibility for human protection initiatives. It is the argument of this section that credibility can only be built by focusing on certain benchmarks of responsible global citizenship as an entry point to the Responsibility to Protect-related initiatives. One of the most common criticisms leveled at the Responsibility to Protect is that "it means too many things to too many different people."[48] Jose Alvarez, for example, has listed six different ways in which the Responsibility to Protect has

[46] *The National Security Strategy of the United States of America*, September 2002, p. 7.
[47] *A More Secure World*, p. 64.
[48] Jose Alvarez, "The Schizophrenias of the Responsibility to Protect," Panel Presentation at the 2007 Hague Joint Conference on Contemporary Issues of International Law: Criminal Jurisdiction 100 Years After the 1907 Hague Peace Conference (The Hague, Netherlands, June 30, 2007).

been cited that include a duty to protect national artifacts, the justification of the 2003 invasion of Iraq, a duty to prevent state and non-state actors from acquiring WMDs, and a duty to implement the Security Council's various counterterrorist measures under Chapter VII.[49]

To be sure, this susceptibility to manipulation is not unique to the Responsibility to Protect. As noted above, the doctrine of humanitarian intervention has been used or alluded to in various contexts during the previous decade, as well as during the early phases of the "war on terror," when the Responsibility to Protect seemed stuck in a state of limbo.[50] The critical issue here is not an allegation of overextension, something to which both humanitarian intervention and the Responsibility to Protect are vulnerable, but an examination of variations of overextension within specific issue areas. Let us briefly examine two of the issue areas discussed by Alvarez: sovereignty and protection.

Sovereignty

In the Responsibility to Protect lexicon, sovereignty implies responsibility.[51] This has been part and parcel of the effort to shift the focus from state-centered security to human security, an effort that began in earnest in the immediate aftermath of the Cold War. *An Agenda for Peace*, the first major UN document on peace and security in the post-Cold War era, is littered with references pointing to an evolving discourse on sovereignty. While the report acknowledges that "respect for [the state's] fundamental sovereignty and integrity [is] crucial to any common international progress," it also notes that "the time of absolute and exclusive sovereignty ... has passed; its theory was never matched by reality." In this context, "it is the task of leaders of States today to understand this and to find a balance between the needs of good internal governance and the requirements of an even more interdependent world."[52] By linking good internal governance to interdependence, the report reflected an emerging view that made membership in the community

[49] *Ibid.*

[50] One of the fascinating research questions here is how the fortunes of the Responsibility to Protect have shifted within the short span of three years: from being considered a concept grounded by the exigencies of 9/11 and its aftermath in 2001, to its designation as an "emerging norm" in the High-Level Panel Report in 2004.

[51] Alvarez, "The Schizophrenias of the Responsibility to Protect."

[52] *An Agenda for Peace. Preventive diplomacy, peacemaking and peace-keeping* A/47/277–S/2411, June 17, 1992.

degradation, disease, weapons technology, and biotechnology became the new, twenty-first-century enemies of global security and the UN needed to be better equipped to address them.

Although general opinion accepts that these trends clearly pose threats to international security, the way in which the global community should respond to these threats lacks equivalent clarity. To begin, the idea of globalized threats of a nonmilitary character transcends all familiar and historic concepts of international security of states. While the UN Charter broadly defines a threat to collective security as "any threat to the peace," the specific powers of response outlined by the Charter assume the threats can be credited to a single national government with which one can mediate, negotiate, arbitrate, or engage militarily.[4] Thus, the threats to collective security must originate with a state government and be controllable by a state government.

The new definition of a threat to collective security, as developed by the High-Level Panel, explodes the Charter's state-centric model for maintaining global peace and security. Environment, disease, and weapons technology are multidimensional and multifaceted: they are free of national boundaries, resistant to government control, impossible to sit down with in a room for negotiations, and indomitable against military force. What these threats do share in common is that they lead "to large-scale death or lessening of life chances" and undermine "States as the basic unit of the international system."[5]

Redefining a threat to global peace and security as any event or process that undermines the existing international political system[6] creates problems for the UN collective security response machinery. First, the Security Council serves as a UN "Commander in Chief" empowered with special privileges for addressing state-based threats of a military nature. It is not obvious that the UN Security Council is the right platform to deal with non-state threats requiring a nonmilitary response. Second, expanding the Security Council's powers to give it the competence and capacity to address these non-state threats requires equipping the UN Security Council with new, far-reaching competencies not covered by the existing UN Charter.[7] Due to the shared impact environment, disease, and technology have on global economic order and

[4] Charter of the United Nations, Chapter VI, Article 33 and Chapter VII, Article 39.
[5] High-Level Panel Report, synopsis p. 12. [6] *Ibid.*
[7] See Nico J. Schrijver, "The Future of the Charter of the United Nations," *Max Planck Yearbook of United Nations Law* 10 (2006), p. 31.

development, these competencies have to include restrictions on states' domestic policies. It is unrealistic to expect that such restrictions will be accepted without serious negotiations on a worldwide scale.[8] Allowing the Security Council to exercise its top-down decision-making power over the economic and social activity of member states would radically alter the balance of power between the branches of the UN and could destroy the current collective security system. On the other hand, such discussions initiated by the reform process in the realm of emerging nonmilitary threats may not be so destructive. As experience since the Second World War has shown, discussion over expansion or limitation of the United Nations can serve in many ways as inspiration for the creation of new international power systems or as a push factor for other global developments both within and outside the existing UN system.[9] What is certain is that without new theories of global security and evolving security strategy,[10] global security of a nonmilitary character can hardly be implemented or accommodated within the framework of the United Nations.

The subsequent sections will discuss the difficulties posed by the nonmilitary threats to collective security. First, the focus will be on documented positions in the UN reform process with regard to redesigning the collective security system of the Security Council in order to introduce possible responses to nonmilitary threats (as far as such responses can be derived from the content of the documents). Second, the documented positions will be analyzed in the context of the institutional, substantial, and conceptual dimension of the threat–response relationship. At the center of the discussion are the theoretical frameworks employed to approach each of the nonmilitary threats. These frameworks include sustainable development and human security, both of which give substance to complex global developments and inherent security threats. Finally, the aim is to present a conceptual idea for a global model based on the presumption that institutional and procedural dimensions of reform have to be developed alongside the substantive

[8] *Ibid.*

[9] John C. Yoo, "UN Reform. Force Rules: UN Reform and Intervention," 6 *Chicago Journal of International Law* (2006), p. 641; Kirsti Samuels, "UN Reform: Post-Conflict Peace-Building and Constitution-Making," 6 *Chicago Journal of International Law* (2006), p. 663; William Maley, "UN Reform: Democratic Governance and Post-Conflict Transitions," 6 *Chicago Journal of International Law* (2006), p. 683.

[10] See *inter alia* the new dimension of Human Security in: "Towards the UN Reform: New Threats, New Responses," *The Warsaw Report* (2004), p. 15.

the present UN reform process. There are basically three difficulties which have frustrated the responses to new nonmilitary threats to global security.

First, contrary to the views of the UN, a new system of collective security cannot be developed from a vague concept of a threat cluster. Such threats should first be analyzed thoroughly. One can only speak of a global threat once a state fails to get such a threat under control, and when regional and transnational systems also fail to resolve the problem. Once this has been determined, states start to consider appropriate responses.

Second, responses to new global threats will only lead to the realization of a new security concept when the financial and political burdens are listed and acceptable rules are worked out to spread the burden. A transparent determination of burdens and burden sharing is central to a new system of collective security. However, a vague global threat scenario hampers the creation of a new security concept rather than paving the way. States are willing to accept collective responsibility and share burdens in the future when they, too, are at risk. However, experience has shown that states are less willing to accept to share burdens for past developments for which they are vaguely held liable.

Third, the theory that places global development risks into the system of collective security is not suitable. A good example is the notion of a "common but differentiated responsibility of states," which was adopted at the 1992 Earth Summit Conference.[30] The aim of this formula was global responsibility for foreseeable future developmental economic and environmental risks. In terms of this formula, the industrial states carried the main responsibility and, through a transfer of technology to developing countries, they had to secure sustainable development. Meanwhile this concept landed on the rocks for two reasons: (a) the responsibility for sustainable development was primarily loaded on the shoulders of industrial nations without the willingness to negotiate new goals in the interest of all states; and (b) the concept "common but differentiated responsibility" lacked inspiring incentives for all states, including industrial states, to recognize global risks as a reality that also affects their national interests.[31]

[30] Joachim Wolf, *Die Haftung der Staaten für Privatpersonen nach Völkerrecht* (Berlin: Duncker and Humbolt, 1997), p. 580.

[31] Compare David Bishop, "Lessons from Sars: Why the WHO Must Provide Greater Economic Incentives for Countries to Comply with International Health Regulations," 36 *Georgetown Journal of International Law* (2005), p. 1173.

Responding: who and how

Since the development politics of the UN during the 1990s failed to succeed in convincing any group of member states to take responsibility for having created nonmilitary threats or for responding to nonmilitary threats, what should be done to respond to these emerging nonmilitary risks?

From the UN reform discussions, the outcome of the 2005 World Summit, and literature on the subject it has become clear that there are two different dimensions from which responses could be determined. First, the institutional dimension prompts the question whether the UN Security Council or rather a different UN organ is the appropriate organ to determine responses for a new collective security system. A second dimension to consider is of a more conceptual nature. Legal, economic, and political theories on global security with regard to nonmilitary threats should be considered and applied. Considerations with regard to a "road to responses" has pointed the way ahead and has shown which pitfalls should be avoided to be able to develop realistic and acceptable theoretical concepts.

The institutional dimension

The question "Who can best deal with nonmilitary global threats?" was never discussed in detail, neither within nor outside the United Nations. For most states and international organizations it was obvious that only the UN Security Council had the power to respond effectively. The primary reason for this perception can be traced to the system of collective security as set out in the UN Charter and the global security still expected from this system. Consequently it was just natural for most to think that the UN security system could also be extended to cover nonmilitary threats.

However, a close scrutiny of the goals of the UN as set out by Article 1 of the UN Charter and the responsibility of the UN Security Council for world peace and international security (in terms of Article 24 read with Chapter VII of the Charter) makes clear that the Security Council's power is limited to peace and security matters. It concerns cases of breach of the peace and a threat to security by states' powers in international relations, especially if military force is deployed. States are bound by the strict norm of a prohibition of using force, which has been laid down in Article 2(4) of the UN Charter. The UN Charter's collective security system therefore cannot simply be extended to nonmilitary threats because there is no substantive legal norm to this expansion of Security Council power. For this reason the UN Security Council is not the appropriate forum to deal with new nonmilitary threats. If the UN Security Council should be adapted to these new goals, this means that a new UN Charter should first be drafted to accommodate this new concept of global security.

A better option would be to consider a reorganization of the UN Economic and Social Council (ECOSOC) with the goal to extend its present functions to include responding to nonmilitary threats of a global nature. Another reason why this option makes sense is that all nonmilitary risks relating to the cluster of "environment, disease, technology" have an economic background to some extent. However, this option does not make for ready-made solutions either. The legal competencies attached to nonmilitary threats in the case of ECOSOC lead to a similar ambivalence and difficulties as in the case of the Security Council.

According to the current legal position, the competences of ECOSOC to make recommendations or to implement binding resolutions, which have a bearing on states and private persons, are restricted to a regional level and do not have a global impact. The range of ECOSOC's competencies is too restricted in its current form to be a global player that can effectively address nonmilitary threats. If ECOSOC's competencies were extended to include responses to nonmilitary threats, the likely result would be a conflict of competencies with the UN Security Council.

The conceptual dimension

The great success of the UN is not its system of collective security. Rather, the greatest success of the UN is the principle that the state is determined by a negotiated system of economies of scale. Almost all states today, including most developing countries, recognize that free trade is in the interest of economies of scale that secure growth and wealth. However, these states have paid a price for free trade: reductions in state security systems and control mechanisms in order to facilitate open borders for trade purposes. Additionally, risky technologies have proliferated. This has all been done with the aim of a growth in wealth and prosperity. It is therefore no coincidence that the world now faces new kinds of nonmilitary threats. It also explains why many states do not take note of such nonmilitary threats or discuss them. They are afraid of economic losses and a loss of wealth and prosperity.

Responses to nonmilitary threats of a global nature can be achieved when one accepts the reality of world politics and faces the consequences flowing from the discussions in and out of the UN on nonmilitary threats. Acceptable solutions to nonmilitary threats can only be of a preventative nature. We know from experience that states are not willing to subject their political and economic achievements to burdens in service of global security. This is the first consequence. The second consequence is that it is almost impossible to find effective solutions to such global threats resulting from a global economic system because it is simply too complex. The following overview of important global concepts and universal principles might lend weight to this perception.

The Earth Summit Conference showed that "sustainable development" is not a viable means for arriving at responses to nonmilitary global threats. The outdated message of sustainable development is that justice among rich and poor countries with regard to global development is laid down in the interconnected relationship of economic, ecological, and social development of the world with none of these elements superseding the other in importance for the system as a whole. Obviously, this "magic triangle" has done little to move the great world powers and therefore cannot serve as a realistic basis for responding to new emerging global threats. In order to bring wealthy nations on board, a different and more pragmatic concept is needed – one that emphasizes global security, not global development.

Another idea used to draw support for a collective response to nonmilitary global threats is "human security," a concept employed in the UN reform documents. The concept entails a fundamental shift from the security of states to the security of individual human beings. This move from state to individual complements the new, non-state-centric definition of threats to collective security.[32] However, as a new system "human security" would be incompatible with the existing world order conceptualized in terms of the United Nations Charter. The concept contradicts the basic premises of the UN where only sovereign states are subjects of international law.

While the Charter did not build into the UN a mechanism for responding to threats to individuals, there are classic rules of state responsibility that could form the basis for UN intervention. For example, the rule prohibiting states to tolerate activities by non-state actors on

[32] Reframing the subject of the response mechanism is particularly effective for addressing the situations of people living in failed states or failing states.

their territory if this has a detrimental transborder effect for other states or their inhabitants.[33] This rule is well-suited to cover all nonmilitary threats. Environmental, disease, and technology as new emerging threats cannot spread globally without having a local cause. Why such classic rules of state responsibility are not suitable as responses to global nonmilitary threats has less to do with legal grounds and more with economic and political circumstances. With a strict prohibition of transborder detrimental effects, especially economic activities causing environmental pollution, global economic development would not have been possible. States therefore implicitly agreed to tolerate a substantial amount of transborder environmental pollution. This caused inroads into classic rules of state responsibility. In this respect states have already waived effective legal responses to nonmilitary threats at an early stage when the problem is not yet of such an acute nature.

All threats are not created equally: the particular challenge of technology

In contrast to environmental degradation of a global scale and infectious diseases, "technology" as such is not easily understandable as a concept defining nonmilitary threats. The main reason technology stands apart is that technology can be harnessed for good. Surely, the development, expansion, and access to technology can imply both new threats to global security, but it can also provide the means to effectively respond. The UN reform documents do not explore the dual role played by technology in the effort to forge a more effective collective security.[34]

More can be done to explore the way in which technology can be employed as an effective response to nonmilitary threats. For example, technology can be used to avoid or minimize environmental harm: reducing harmful emissions, improved detection of seismic activity, and more effective alert and evacuation systems. Similarly, industrial

[33] *Texas Cattle Claims*, decision by the American Mexican Claims Commission 1942, Whiteman, *Digest of International Law* (Washington, DC: US Government Printing Office, 1967), vol. 8, 749 ff.; Trail Smelter Case, *USA* v. *Canada* (1941), RIAA 3, p. 1905, see also *RIAA* 3 (1949), p. 1903; Corfu Channel Case, *Great Britain* v. *Albania*, ICJ Reports 1949, p. 4 ff.

[34] In its discussion of the variety of technological threats (the technology involved in nuclear, radiological, chemical, and biological weaponry that has become increasingly accessible to both state and non-state actors), the High-Level Panel does make one reference to the double-edged potential of biotechnology: the ability to cure diseases as well as increase the opportunity for the development of new, deadlier diseases.

nations are seen to be much more effective at controlling infectious diseases like HIV/AIDS, malaria, tuberculosis, and other epidemics than other, less developed nations. Central to this capacity to control disease is the availability of effective medicine to cure such diseases and minimize their spread. The use of technology in developing and distributing medicine is therefore a key element in the response to the threat of infectious diseases.[35]

The flipside is, of course, that technological developments can also be risky and could enhance threats to global security. Global transport networks, as well as the liberalization of labor and new commoditizing markets, play into the hands of potential global security threats. It is beyond dispute that infectious diseases have become more risky because they spread easily and in a less controllable manner due to greater flexibility of the labor market, free trade, globalized travel, increasing democratization, and the opening of borders. Fast global transport and connections are the perfect means to spread a pandemic.[36]

Previously, the UN focused predominantly on development politics in order to combat poverty. In order to reduce poverty, development-needy countries argued for the transfer of wealth from the rich countries to the poor ones in the form of development aid (0.7 percent of their GNP).[37] However, rich countries, in particular the United States, blocked this wealth distribution proposal at the 2005 World Summit. The international community disagrees on whether development politics should concentrate on how the nonmilitary threats impact those individuals living in poor states or how these phenomena interact more generally at the regional and global levels.

The division in the international community is part of the reason why "technology" as a global threat remains ambiguous. Those who want to concentrate on individuals tend to see technological development as an asset that, once fostered, can improve standards of living around the world. This camp is populated by economists who are of the opinion that it is exactly the development of information technology that enabled the enormous increase in wealth, which is also responsible for the increasing

35 Uche U. Ewelukwa, "Centuries of Globalization; Centuries of Exclusion: African Women, Human Rights and the 'New' International Trade Regime," 20 *Berkeley Journal of Gender Law and Justice* (2005), p. 75.

36 According to Robert J. Rhee, "Catastrophic Risk and Governance after Hurricane Katrina: A Postscript to Terrorism Risk in a Post-9/11 Economy," 38 *Arizona State Law Journal* (2006), p. 581, p. 592, "globalization is a two-faced Jekyll and Hyde."

37 A request echoed in the High-Level Panel Report, para. 60.

gap of wealth between the rich and the poor countries that came about in the second part of twentieth century and the beginning of the twenty-first century.[38] On the other hand, those who want development to operate at the regional and global levels view technology as a risk rather than an asset. This camp is populated by academics that focus on the negative impacts of modern information technology. For example, information technology has made former labor-intensive branches redundant, which in turn directly affects general distribution of wealth.[39] There is a possible correlation between high technology risks and the global structural changes caused by technological developments linked to the political debate on development aid. The debate in the UN on responses to nonmilitary threats has not yet made this link.

[38] See Robert Shiller, "Jede Menge Instabilität," *Der Spiegel* 23 (2007), p. 54.

[39] See Yossi Yardi, an Israeli entrepreneur: "The more successful the high-tech sector, the more frustrated and unhappy the rest of society could become," in "Face Value: The Social Technologist," *The Economist* (January 5, 2008), p. 55; see also "China: Gift für den ganzen Erdball," *Der Spiegel* 4 (2007), p. 124.

PART III

Prevention and responses

7

On the far side of conflict: the UN Peacebuilding Commission as optical illusion

DIRK SALOMONS

The past as prologue

On October 24, 2005, sixty years after its creation, the General Assembly of the United Nations adopted a voluminous resolution, A/RES/60/1, reflecting the outcome of a lengthy process that culminated in a World Summit meant to bring the United Nations into the twenty-first century. One of the main features of this resolution was the establishment of a Peacebuilding Commission "as an intergovernmental advisory body."[1]

While this, at first blush, would seem to be a major accomplishment, it is in fact a disappointing ending to a long process that at certain times carried considerable promise. The decisions that led to the creation of a Commission with only a fraction of its potential were driven by the politically charged concept of "UN reform."

As a rule, organizations develop organically, and if they don't adapt to external changes they either die, as the League of Nations did, or they become a historical relic functioning on the margins, like the symphony orchestra – dressed up in the symbols of a bygone era. Those who see the UN as a viable institution, and therefore fear its ability to set global standards and make sovereignty into a relative term, would like to see its powers diminished. They hope to achieve this by depicting the organization as a corrupt and outdated entity that requires "reform," much as a delinquent is sent away to an institution where a few decades of austerity and hard labor will drive out the evil spirits. The UN, in fact, has been evolving and adapting continuously, and it has done so quite effectively, particularly when it comes to its ability to support peace processes and help countries recover from conflict. Most of the tools and mechanisms at its disposal to do so were not even there ten years ago.

[1] World Summit Outcome, para. 97.

In this chapter, I will describe how the UN's development arm evolved from a post-colonial extension of the "imperial model" into an organizational network that has a unique array of skills and insights to support countries in transition. In doing so, I will point out some of the intellectual landmarks that shaped this gradual reversal, and discuss the various precursors of the current newly established Peacebuilding Commission.

Common system coordination in the early years

The beginnings of the process that eventually led to the creation of the Peacebuilding Commission occurred in the mid-1960s, when Sir Robert Jackson conducted the so-called "Capacity Study." In 1970, this study led to the creation of the United Nations Development Programme (UNDP) out of the Special Fund and the Expanded Program for Technical Assistance in charge of managing UN development aid.[2] The Study was done at the request of donors, who wondered why there were so many UN system agencies independently operating in the developing world, each advocating its own programs, each with its own counterparts in governments, each with a governing structure of its own, each with its own funding and resource mobilization mechanism, and yet with no system in place to coordinate these various actors and moving parts.

The UNDP was originally designed to serve as the central funding agency for all UN system development aid, including the activities of specialized agencies. Donors gave all their money to the UNDP and the UNDP became the sole interlocutor with governments of recipient countries, worked with the ministry of planning to make an inventory of the country's needs, and planned how the UN system could help serve those needs. Projects then were allocated by the UNDP to the specialized agencies and the UN's Technical Assistance Program; the UNDP paid these agencies upon completion of their work and, by having a tight grip on the purse, the UNDP could enforce coordination.

This arrangement came to an end in 1976 when the UNDP made commitments well beyond its means and had to close down or cancel $40 million worth of projects already in the pipeline.[3] The specialized agencies, led by the Food and Agriculture Organization (FAO), rebelled and

[2] A Study of the Capacity of the United Nations Development System, DP/5, UN Geneva 1969, followed by General Assembly resolution GA 2688 (XXV) of December 11, 1970.

[3] Craig N. Murphy, *The United Nations Development Programme: A Better Way?* (Cambridge: Cambridge University Press, 2006), pp. 158 ff.

convinced donors that the central control exercised by the UNDP was a bad thing. Rather than give money to the UNDP, donors were asked to place funds in trust directly with the specialized agencies, giving far more control over funds to these agencies. Chaos returned and earmarked funds replaced needs-based planning. The UNDP was left behind, forced to invent a new role for itself.

These early efforts at field coordination, and their dramatic demise, all happened in the context of "development cooperation," a process rooted in the very same mechanisms whereby the colonial powers in the past built capacity in the countries they administered. In particular, those colonial powers that managed their wards through "indirect rule" used existing national structures as their tools, giving advice and guidance from behind the scenes. Much of the expertise of the UN system in the 1960s and 1970s in fields such as tropical agriculture or medicine came from colonial expertise and many of the colonial administrators returned to the South wearing UN hats, but maintaining the values and attitudes of their previous incarnations. The fact that so many post-colonial regimes in the developing world in fact were hand-picked by their former masters, or financially dependent on them, meant that very few countries receiving UN system technical assistance questioned the underlying premise of Western superiority.

Filling the vacuum after the Cold War

The situation changed completely when the Cold War came to an end at the beginning of the 1990s. As a result, the grip of the Western and Eastern blocs on their client states loosened. Former proxy wars (Afghanistan, Cambodia, Angola, Mozambique, and nations in Central America) now became vicious intrastate conflicts, while new wars erupted where the iron grip of the big powers relaxed and left a vacuum. The case in the Balkans, in parts of the former Soviet Union, and in large parts of Africa, such as the Democratic Republic of Congo, serve as illustrations.

For the UN, the end of the Cold War and the resultant new crises that developed brought about a completely new role incompatible with old, cozy post-colonial values. Suddenly the UN was drawn into the business of nation building. Peacekeeping, the traditional purely military effort to monitor peace accords (in the Middle East, Cyprus, and along the India/Pakistan line of demarcation in Kashmir) became a mandate to create viable states. In quick succession, between 1989 and 1994, the UN helped

Namibia make the transition from South African "protectorate" to independent country, set up a transitional administration in Cambodia (UNTAC), and carried out a holistic peace process in Mozambique (ONUMOZ).

These three missions forced the UN to introduce an entirely new set of competencies into its arsenal. The UN now had to support complex political peace negotiations, carry out the military demobilization of former combatants (and their reintegration into society), plan and conduct elections, monitor human rights, train police, design strategies for economic recovery, help local media find their voice, clear landmines, and address the humanitarian needs of populations caught in the crossfire of violent conflicts.

An analysis of the missions in Namibia, Cambodia, and Mozambique shows that all the issues now shaping the debate about the substance of "peacebuilding" were already on the table in the early 1990s. The UN improvised brilliantly in those days; the results were consolidated in new organizational units within the UN Secretariat, such as the current Mine Action Service, the Electoral Assistance Division, the Office for the Coordination of Humanitarian Affairs, and a strengthened Department of Political Affairs. Within the Department of Peacekeeping Operations (DPKO), the increased UN capacity also led to enhanced multidisciplinary fields of mission support capacity, strengthened logistics and procurement, and a more sophisticated military *cum* civilian policing doctrine. Indeed, the concept of "integrated missions" was born with Marti Ahtisaari's design of the Namibia mission, way back in 1989, a decade before the term was coined in the so-called "Brahimi Report" (about which more will follow).[4]

At the same time, it became very clear that the lack of coordination among the resident agencies at the country level, caused by the UNDP's loss of financial control, was unacceptable to donors and recipients alike. This was a time when the UN system suddenly had to respond to the needs of governments that were seeking solutions that were indigenous and structures that reflected local cultures and values. No longer constrained by the shackles of the Cold War, the UN was now challenged to provide support that was credible, unbiased, and with few strings attached. It was not prepared to do so.

[4] "Comprehensive review of the whole question of peacekeeping operations in all their aspects", UN Doc. A/55/305 of August 21, 2000.

The era of sweeping reform proposals

In response to this gap in system capacity, many proposals came forward, both from inside and outside the UN, regarding how it should adapt to its new context and mandates.

In 1991, Denmark, Finland, Norway and Sweden launched their report "The United Nations in Development: A Nordic Perspective."[5] They recommended the creation of an "International Development Council" that would give overall policy guidance for the UN's operational activities for development, and they advocated a complete overhaul and simplification of the UN's organizational structure.[6] The various operational funds and programs of the UN[7] could be brought into one framework, with a joint governing body, and become "in essence one organization," with a consolidated budget of some $4 billion annually, a 2,000-strong professional staff, and some 6,000 local staff. This would result in a unified career system, a unified representation at the field level, with one single Resident Coordinator heading the country teams, located in a common office.[8] At the time, the various programs protested fiercely, but many elements of the "Nordic" proposal have in fact been introduced in the last fifteen years. The most recent efforts by a high-level panel to develop recommendations on the creation of a more coherent UN system, presented in 2006 in a report entitled "Delivering as One," is in fact little more that a resurrection of the Nordic proposal, long considered dead and buried.[9]

Also in the early 1990s, the Ford Foundation sponsored a consultative process on the state of the UN system, which led to a series of four reports, issued between 1990 and 1994, driven by the intellectual leadership of Sir Brian Urquhart and Erskine Childers, who had both served successfully in the UN in senior capacities earlier in their careers. These studies addressed questions of leadership, the structure and functions of the Secretariat, the system's humanitarian emergency machinery, and reform of the overall UN system. The final volume, "Renewing the United Nations System," concluded, when it came to operational

[5] *The Nordic UN Project* (Stockholm: Almquist & Wiksell International, 1991). [6] *Ibid.*

[7] Such as the United Nations Development Programme (UNDP), the United Nations Children's Fund (UNICEF), the United Nations Population Fund (UNFPA), the United Nations World Food Programme (WFP), and the International Fund for Agricultural Development (IFAD).

[8] *Ibid.*, p. 57.

[9] *Delivering as One*, Report of the United Nations Secretary-General's High-Level Panel on UN System-wide Coherence, New York, November 9, 2006.

activities in the field, that "mere centralization at the global level is not the answer." The authors instead recommended that the system be decentralized with a shift of resources and structures to the regional and country level. They concluded that the separate identities of the UN funds and programs were not sacrosanct and that they all existed "solely to serve the temporary needs of the peoples of developing countries." The report stated that the "special influences through financing" should be brought to an end, and that there should only be one UN system office in any developing country, "headed by a UN Coordinator" with no allegiance to any one program. At the global level, all funds and programs should be brought under the authority of the Deputy Secretary-General (a post that did not exist at the time, but which the authors considered essential).[10] Once again, the executive heads of these programs staunchly resisted such an extreme makeover.

At the same time that discussions were going on about the future framework for the traditional development-oriented activities of the UN, the then Secretary-General, Boutros Boutros-Ghali, presented an "Agenda for Peace" in 1992 that drew previously underexposed connections between peacemaking, peacekeeping, and economic development. The "Agenda" foresaw an era of peace as the Cold War came to an end and mapped out opportunities to link peace enforcement, conflict resolution, introduction of the rule of law, development assistance, and support for state formation along a seamless continuum that spanned from one extreme of violent conflict and disarray to the other extreme of stability and prosperity. While this Messianic vision was soon discredited by the developments in Rwanda and Srebrenica, the conceptual connection between peacekeeping and peacebuilding had been made, and it remains valid to this day.[11]

The meaning of post-conflict recovery was further developed in the 1994 "Agenda for Development." This document foreshadowed the later work done by the Commission on Human Security because it defined development as a fundamental human right and stressed the strong links between peace, economic development, the environment, society, and democracy. In this context, Secretary-General Boutros-Ghali mapped out what we now call "post-conflict reconstruction" as a key challenge for the UN.[12]

[10] Erskine Childers and Brian Urquhart, *Renewing the United Nations System* (Uppsala: Dag Hammarskjold Foundation, 1994), p. 87 ff.

[11] *Agenda for Peace: Preventive diplomacy, peacemaking and peace-keeping*, UN Doc. A/47/277-S/2411 of June 17, 1992.

[12] *Agenda for Development: Report of the Secretary-General*, UN Doc. A/48/935 of May 6, 1994.

In retrospect, these developments in the UN system were part of a larger trend, a move away from a traditional development assistance model, dating from the post-colonial era, to an approach in which development no longer is a goal by itself, but a strategy for reaching human security, dignity, or in other words, human rights. This shift, in turn, shaped the later debate on the nature of collective security. While the World Bank took over the UN's old franchise of classical development, working with middle income countries, the UN has become the caretaker for the forty lowest ranking countries on the UNDP Human Development Index, and those countries identified by the Crisis Group as most at risk for conflict, or already at war.

The twenty-first century: an end to innocence

Since September 11, 2001, a new set of considerations has been added to this already complex matrix of forces driving international development assistance. The fear of terrorism and uncontrollable migration has become the lowest common denominator shaping the motivation of the international community to address global poverty and instability. Compassion and solidarity (if they ever were drivers for political action) have now largely made way for security concerns. The need to diversify the industrialized countries' access to natural resources, particularly oil, has only added impetus and urgency to the renewed global efforts to mitigate conflict and build peace.

I would therefore argue that one cannot detach peacebuilding from the broader challenge of overall poverty alleviation. This position holds true whether one is motivated by moral concerns or by pragmatic calculations of national interest. Peacebuilding, therefore, should not just be reactive, repairing the damage after conflict, but it should be proactive, stepping in before massive human rights violations and exclusionary policies create violent and desperate outbursts. Instability does not pay.

In light of all we have learned in the past fifteen years, we should be able to define some criteria for a successful global peacebuilding mechanism. Central to this is the ability to identify crises before they erupt, and to act in a timely and forceful manner to prevent them from escalating. The new structure should have the power to convene all potential actors, build consensus on steps to be taken (both politically and practically), allocate tasks among the key agents, draw on sufficient funding, and plan for the decades ahead, not simply the near future, to gradually strengthen national capacity.

How far have we come?

Ten years ago, on September 29, 1998, the Security Council adopted a Presidential Statement on peacebuilding that encouraged the Secretary-General to "explore the possibility of establishing post-conflict peace-building structures as parts of efforts by the United Nations system to achieve a lasting solution to conflicts."[13] This suggestion fell on deaf ears.

Shortly thereafter, however, appalled by a series of failed peacekeeping missions during much of the 1990s, ranging from Somalia and Rwanda to the Balkans, the General Assembly asked for a study to examine how peacekeeping operations should be restructured to reflect the reality of complex, multidimensional missions. This led to the establishment of a Panel on UN Peace Operations, chaired by Ambassador Lakhdar Brahimi, which reported its findings and recommendations in a lapidary and remarkably undiplomatic document now known as the "Brahimi Report."[14] This appeared in August 2000, just before the General Assembly was to begin its fall session, and its impact was both immediate and massive. It challenged the member states to invest more in order to "build the United Nations capacity to contribute to peace-building, both preventive and post-conflict, in a genuinely integrated manner," and argued that peacekeeping was only one component of an inseparable quadrant: conflict prevention, peacemaking, peacekeeping, and peace-building.[15] None of these could function alone. Preparations for peace operations had to involve all partners, and "integrated mission planning" was the new shorthand for a collaborative interagency approach.

Towards an organizational framework for peacebuilding

In his report, Brahimi defined peacebuilding as "activities undertaken on the far side of conflict to reassemble the foundations of peace and provide the tools for building on those foundations something that is more than just the absence of war."[16] These tools, Brahimi argued, included the demobilization and reintegration of former combatants, the establishment of the rule of law, training police, building respect for human rights, providing electoral assistance, supporting free media, resolving latent conflicts, combating corruption, clearing landmines, and combating

[13] Cited in "Comprehensive review of the whole question of peacekeeping operations in all their aspects," UN Doc. A/55/305 of August 21, 2000, para. 35.
[14] *Ibid.* [15] *Ibid.*, para. 6(f). [16] *Ibid.*, para. 13.

infectious diseases. In fact, these were exactly the activities that had made the operations in Namibia, Cambodia, and Mozambique so effective ten years earlier.

The Brahimi Report then mapped out the capacities that had to be developed or strengthened within the UN Secretariat to support such complex multidimensional operations, and advocated for the creation of a Peacebuilding Support Unit, located within the Department for Political Affairs, and working closely with the UNDP, under the guidance of the Secretary-General's Executive Committee on Peace and Security.[17]

Though the Report did not explicitly say so, these proposed changes would have provided a much needed counterweight to the Department of Peacekeeping Operations, which would be limited to supporting the military and logistical components of peace operations. The Brahimi Report thus saw no need for a new political organ, but defined all that had to be done in purely operational terms. It was tacitly assumed that the Security Council would be the driving political force.

Around the same time, during the summer of 1999, the Brookings Institution in Washington hosted a series of meetings to discuss the "relief to development gap," bringing together the UN system agencies, key donors, and non-governmental organizations. A discussion paper commissioned for these meetings, prepared by New York University's Center on International Cooperation, identified gaps in the international community's ability to conduct joint needs assessments, and argued for pooled start-up funds, a long-term planning timeline, clearer aid coordination, less conditionality, more coherence at the field level, more focus on national capacity building, and more accountability through the monitoring of aid flows. To spearhead these efforts, the NYU team recommended the establishment of an independent Post-conflict Recovery Facility, located outside of the UN system as a neutral joint venture of multilateral, bilateral and civil society actors, with convening authority, executive powers, and central control of funding. The Brookings "process," however, remained inconclusive.[18]

The next landmark in the peacebuilding debate was the report of the Commission on Human Security, entitled "Human Security Now,"

17 *Ibid.*, paras. 46, 239.

18 Shepard Forman and Dirk Salomons, "Meeting Essential Needs in Societies Emerging from Conflict," Working Paper prepared for the Brookings Roundtable on the Relief to Development Gap, NYU Center on International Cooperation, New York (2000). Available at: www.cic.nyu.edu.

which came out in 2003.[19] This Commission was jointly chaired by Sadako Ogata (a prominent Japanese banker) and Amartya Sen (the well-known Indian economist); Ambassador Lakhdar Brahimi was one of the Commission's most active members. The report addressed the special needs of countries emerging from conflict, and stressed the links between political, social, and economic action. In doing so, it noted security gaps, governance gaps, international response gaps, and resource gaps. To remedy these shortcomings, the Commission identified several human security clusters that need to be covered simultaneously after conflict – public safety, humanitarian relief, rehabilitation and reconstruction, reconciliation and coexistence, governance and civil society empowerment. To facilitate this approach, the Commission recommended the establishment of a separate transition fund for each post-conflict situation. This would be managed with participation of the national authorities in order to set priorities and ensure ownership, but other parties to a given conflict were to be included as well. The Commission noted that pledges of aid were unreliable, that the quality of charity was uneven, that compassion fatigue had a paralyzing effect, and it concluded that "greater coherence is required in planning, budgeting and resource mobilization for countries emerging from conflict."[20] As positive examples, it cited the 1994 Johan Jorgen Holst Peace Fund for donor support to the Palestinian National authority, as well as Japan's Peace Building Grant Aid.

The genesis of the Peacebuilding Commission: too little, too late?

All of a sudden, the pace of the discussions began to accelerate. The Secretary-General saw the forthcoming sixtieth anniversary of the United Nations as an opportunity to set a new course for the Organization, and he commissioned the High-Level Panel to map out how the UN system could best channel its energies.[21] In its report, the Panel paid considerable attention to the need to preserve or restore peace through nonmilitary means. It noted the void created by an institutional gap, as no agency had a primary mandate in the field of early recovery, and it stressed that the United Nations system could play a unique role in filling that void. In order to strengthen the United Nations' capacity for

[19] Commission on Human Security, "Human Security Now," New York (2003). Available at: www.humansecurity-chs.org/finalreport/English/FinalReport.pdf.

[20] *Ibid.*, p. 69. [21] High-Level Panel.

peacebuilding, covering a continuum from early warning through preventive action to post-conflict recovery, it recommended the establishment of a Peacebuilding Commission.[22] This Commission was to serve as an organ of the Security Council, to be established in consultation with ECOSOC, acting under Article 29 of the UN Charter, which says that the Security Council "may establish such subsidiary organs as it deems necessary for the performance of its functions."[23]

We now come to an interesting crossroads. The Commission serves as yet one more proposal to institutionalize the UN system's peacebuilding capacity by consolidating numerous ideas launched earlier. The proposal to create the Commission did not, however, take into account the changes in the UN's operational environment since the end of the Cold War. By 2004, the reality of the United Nations capacity on the ground had already changed fundamentally. While clamoring for UN reform over and over again, member states did not give sufficient credit to the incremental but essential changes made from within.

To begin, field coordination had seen considerable strengthening with the increased use of the Resident Coordinator system. Joint planning had progressed to the point that the UN country team in each program country prepared a Common Country Assessment and all the UN actors participated in formulating a UN Development Assistance Framework, drawn up in collaboration with the government. At the same time, the World Bank prompted governments to produce Poverty Reduction Strategy Papers. A UN Development Group established by UN funds and programs provided joint planning and programming tools, as well as support for the Resident Coordinator system. Above all, the UN gained considerable experience in addressing post-conflict challenges, having dealt with Afghanistan, Sierra Leone, Liberia, Kosovo, Eastern Slavonia, and the Democratic Republic of Congo in quick succession. The learning curve had become steeper.

Moreover, the international community discovered that long-term support was key to recovery. In both Cambodia and Mozambique, for example, the donors provided close to $1 billion, year after year, to sustain the momentum created by the initial peacekeeping operation. After most successful peacekeeping operations, voluntary funding sustained the momentum long after the UN had left.[24]

22 *Ibid.*, p. 83. 23 Charter of the United Nations, Article 29.

24 See Dirk Salomons and Dennis Dijkzeul, *The Conjurer's Hat, Financing Peace Operations* (Oslo: Fafo Institute and New York: New York University Center on International Cooperation, 2002).

The crucial development of a joint, post-conflict needs assessment methodology brought together UN system actors, international financial institutions, and key NGOs. Resource mobilization occurred effectively through coordinated UN donor meetings and World Bank Roundtables. Funding mechanisms such as dedicated multi-donor country trust funds flourished. Pooled funding models were piloted. Lessons learned were captured and disseminated. The Millennium Development Goals were used as benchmarks to measure progress. Was there really still a need for an overarching political institution as envisaged by the High-Level Panel?

The High-Level Panel was ambitious. It saw as the Peacebuilding Commission's core functions the responsibility "to identify countries which are under stress and risk sliding towards state collapse; to organize, in partnership with the national government, proactive assistance in preventing that process from developing further; to assist in the planning for transitions between conflict and post-conflict peacebuilding; and in particular to marshal and sustain the efforts of the international community in post-conflict peacebuilding over whatever period may be necessary."[25]

The Commission would have a broad membership, bringing together representatives of the Security Council, ECOSOC, the IMF, the World Bank, regional development banks as well as ad hoc invitees such as national representatives, principal donor countries, troop contributing countries, and relevant regional and subregional entities. This made sense in the context of the robust mandate proposed by the High-Level Panel. In addition, the Commission would obtain operational backing from a well staffed and resourced Peacebuilding Support Office, taking over some of the tasks of DPKO. This proposal, again, was grounded in a solid needs assessment reflective of stakeholder consensus. If this proposal had indeed been implemented, it might have added value to the existing mechanisms, particularly at the political level.

For the Secretary-General, however, these recommendations were too bold, and in his own *In Larger Freedom* report to the sixtieth session of the General Assembly he presented a diminished version of the Commission.[26] To fend off all controversy, the Secretary-General introduced his proposal with the statement that "I do not believe that such a body should have an early warning or monitoring function."[27] Instead of the robust, preventive, and proactive mandate envisaged by the High-Level Panel, the Secretary-General limited the Peacebuilding Commission's

[25] High-Level Panel, p. 83. [26] *In Larger Freedom.* [27] *Ibid.*, para. 116.

tasks to a few activities to be undertaken only after war. The Commission's responsibilities would be to improve planning, help ensure financing, provide a forum, improve coordination, review progress, and make sure that international attention would remain focused on countries coming out of crises.[28] In fact, all these tasks seemed remarkably similar to the work already done quite effectively by the newly reorganized UN system. Having the Commission report "in sequence" to both the Security Council and to ECSOC did not appear to strengthen its clout.

In the summer of 2005, there was considerable diplomatic activity to prepare an "outcome document" for the General Assembly's sixtieth anniversary session that would be bold, forward looking, and strong enough to serve as a blueprint for UN priorities in the twenty-first century. The drafting process was often tense because developing countries were wary of the industrialized powers' intentions. Weaker countries did not want reform measures to be used as a Trojan horse that would shift decision-making powers from the General Assembly to the Secretariat, thus rendering issues of development uncontrollable. In this climate, the discussions about the creation of a Peacebuilding Commission proved acrimonious and adversarial.

When the dust settled, the General Assembly decided to establish a Peacebuilding Commission as "an intergovernmental advisory body," with a core task of "[bringing] together all relevant actors to marshal resources and to advise on and propose integrated strategies for post-conflict peacebuilding and recovery."[29] It would "focus attention," "provide recommendations to improve coordination," "develop best practices," and help "to ensure predictable financing."[30] Its membership would be broad and diffused, and an Organizational Committee would serve as the *de facto* core, again with a broad and diverse membership. Most importantly, the Commission "should act in all matters on the basis of consensus of its members."[31] This proposed structure more or less guaranteed that only the lowest common denominator would prevail and that potential spoilers would have extra-ordinary powers.[32] Furthermore, by requiring the Commission to report to the General Assembly, the Commission was placed into a political "second tier." A "small peacebuilding support office" was to draw on the best expertise available, but had no operational responsibilities.[33]

[28] *Ibid.*, para. 115. [29] World Summit Outcome, para. 98.
[30] *Ibid.* [31] *Ibid.* [32] *Ibid.* [33] *Ibid.*, para. 104.

In addition, the General Assembly decided to create a Peacebuilding Fund, under the control of the Secretary-General, not the Commission, funded by voluntary contributions. This Fund was to ensure "the immediate release of resources needed to launch peacebuilding activities and the availability of appropriate financing for recovery."[34] The General Assembly failed to address the question of how the Fund would relate to the tools already in existence, except noting that it should take "due account of existing instruments."[35]

For good measure, the Security Council three months later passed a resolution once more establishing the Peacebuilding Commission, reiterating the functions and structure already adopted by the General Assembly, but giving far more specifics about the composition and the working methods of the Organizational Committee.[36] A key new feature was the requirement that the Peacekeeping Commission only place issues on its agenda at the specific request of the Security Council, the Secretary-General, or in exceptional circumstances, at the request of the ECOSOC or the General Assembly.[37] As an afterthought, through a subsequent resolution, the Security Council made sure that all its permanent members would be guaranteed a seat on the Organizational Committee.[38]

Off to a timid start

In February 2006, the Secretary-General submitted a detailed proposal to the General Assembly for the mandate and staffing of the Peacebuilding Support Office, describing as its core tasks "to facilitate coherence, identify gaps, recommend ways in which these gaps may be addressed and ensure that the Peacebuilding Commission is able to draw … on the expertise and capacities of the United Nations system as a whole as well as on the outside expert networks, regional organizations and other institutions."[39] For this purpose, fifteen posts would be required, of which eight had to be filled through redeployment or secondment (at the expense of the UN agencies), and seven to be charged to the new Peacebuilding Fund, to "ensure the full management of the resources received."[40] This was a far cry from the robust operational entity foreseen by the Brahimi Report or the High-Level

[34] *Ibid.*, para. 103. [35] *Ibid.*
[36] UN Doc. S/Res/1645 (2005) of December 20, 2005. [37] *Ibid*, para. 12.
[38] UN Doc. S/Res/1646 (2005) of December 20, 2005.
[39] UN Doc. A/60/694 of February 23, 2006. [40] *Ibid.*

Panel. Thematically, there seems to be considerable overlap with the tasks of the UN Development Group and the Lessons Learned Unit in the Department of Peacekeeping Operations (DPKO). The General Assembly, however, accepted the proposal and the Office was created, headed at the Assistant Secretary-General level.

Later that year, in August, the General Assembly received the Secretary-General's proposal outlining detailed arrangements for establishing a Peacebuilding Fund, with its key objective "to support interventions that are considered critical to the peacebuilding process."[41] The Fund, managed by the Peacebuilding Support Office and administered by UNDP, would be allowed to charge a management fee of 11 percent to cover costs incurred. Funds could go to any country "reviewed by the Peacebuilding Commission," and the allocation of resources would be "informed by an analysis of critical gaps in peacebuilding that would be conducted by the national authorities and the United Nations presence in the country concerned."[42] This gave a "dual key" control to governments and the Secretariat.[43]

While the composition of the Commission as a whole did not receive much further attention, the role of the Organizational Committee took on a larger dimension than initially foreseen. The Organizational Committee became the *de facto* decision-making body by bringing together seven members selected by the Security Council, seven elected by ECOSOC, five top financial contributors, the five top troop-contributing countries, and seven members elected by the General Assembly – a total of 31 members. Four institutional donors, the World Bank, the IMF, the European Community and the Organization of Islamic Conference received a standing invitation to participate.[44] A first annual report was expected by the end of June 2007.

In June 2006, the Security Council invited the Peacebuilding Commission to take on its first assignment, focusing its attention on Sierra Leone and Burundi. In early 2007 the Commission conducted field visits to both countries to see how it could support the peace process there. At the same time, the Peacebuilding Fund made allocations of $35 million to Sierra Leone[45] and $25 million to

41 UN Doc. A/60/984 of August 22, 2006, Annex: Terms of Reference for the Peacebuilding Fund.

42 *Ibid.* 43 *Ibid.* 44 See General Assembly Press Release PBC/12, dated May 16, 2007.

45 See UN News Centre, "UN grants Sierra Leone $35 million to help it build up institutions for peace," March 1, 2007. Available at: www.un.org/apps/news/story.asp?NewsID=21721&Cr=sierra&Cr1=leone%20.

Burundi[46] to meet perceived gaps. This led to a series of joint reports to the General Assembly and the Security Council that may be indicative of the Commission's lack of long-term potential for success.

One example may be cited to illustrate the projected downward trend. In its report on its field visit to Sierra Leone (in which nine diplomats participated), the Commission gave an analysis of the peace process there that closely followed the reports already regularly provided by the Department of Political Affairs and by the UN peacebuilding mission in Sierra Leone (UNIOSIL). It stressed the importance of addressing the lack of employment opportunities for young people, emphasized the need for good governance, security sector reform, and similar issues, and it observed, with some disappointment, "a generally limited awareness among all partners in Sierra Leone about the work of the Peacebuilding Commission as separate from the Peacebuilding Fund. Many stakeholders in the country remain primarily focused on the disbursement of the $35 million allocated to Sierra Leone by the Peacebuilding Fund."[47]

Conclusion

This one paragraph, while only providing anecdotal evidence, may in fact be construed as the epitaph of the Peacebuilding Commission. This chapter identified earlier the key criteria for establishing a Peacebuilding Commission with added value. Here, the Commission falls short on all counts. Where independent analysis is needed to identify countries at risk, the Commission has been muted by the General Assembly. Where a proactive and preventive mandate is required to initiate interventions, its functions are merely contemplative. Where a strong coordinating capacity at the country level is required, the UN system has already built its own, without waiting for a political body to take the initiative. The Commission can only observe from the sidelines. Where robust funding is needed, the new Peacebuilding Fund, limited in scope, has been cleverly rerouted from the Commission's control to that of the Secretariat. Where new policies, methodologies, or strategies have to be developed to meet the specific demands of post-conflict reconstruction, the UN Development Group is well ahead of the game. Where strong political advocacy could focus

[46] See UN News Centre, "UN Peacebuilding Commission unveils plans for first grants to Burundi, Sierra Leone," December 13, 2006. Available at: www.un.org/apps/news/storyAr.asp?NewsID=20976&Cr=peacebuild&Cr1=%20.

[47] UN Doc. A/61/901-S/2007/269 of May 14, 2007, para. 8.

international attention, one spoiler can shut down or reduce the Commission's voice to a whisper. In fact, one may wonder whether the creation of this intergovernmental body has not just added one more layer of bureaucratic resistance. All in all, the newly minted Commission may well prove to be an optical illusion, suggesting reforms while in fact representing a hindrance to post-conflict reconstruction and development.

What could rescue the Commission? The appointment of a charismatic and competent High Commissioner for Peacebuilding, giving a face and a voice to the needs of countries in transition; the mandatory assessment of 1 percent of member states' defense budgets to beef up the Peacebuilding Fund to a level with real clout; the revision of the Commission's terms of reference in accordance with the High-Level Panel's original design specifications; the transfer of key operational responsibilities from the Department of Peacekeeping Operations to the Peacebuilding Support Office. Short of such drastic measures, the prospects of the Commission are bleak.

8

The new peacebuilding architecture: an institutional innovation of the United Nations

EJEVIOME ELOHO OTOBO[1]

Filling an institutional gap

The decision to create a new peacebuilding architecture was one of the key outcomes of the World Summit held at the United Nations Headquarters in September 2005.[2] The prelude to that decision started with the report of the High-Level Panel on Threats, Challenges and Change[3] which recommended the establishment of a Peacebuilding Commission within the United Nations. In the Secretary-General's *In Larger Freedom* report, that recommendation was slightly modified.[4] The Secretary-General eliminated the High-Level Panel proposal to give the Peacebuilding Commission an early warning or monitoring function in conflict situations.[5]

As a follow-up the to the World Summit, the General Assembly and the Security Council concurrently adopted identical resolutions in December 2005[6] establishing the Peacebuilding Commission, the Peacebuilding Support Office, and the Peacebuilding Fund. This new peacebuilding architecture is an important institutional innovation in the history of the United Nations. It builds on longstanding efforts by the United Nations, dating back to the 1992 report of the Secretary-General entitled "An Agenda for Peace,"[7] to develop a coherent approach linking conflict prevention, peacemaking and peacekeeping to post-conflict peacebuilding and development.

[1] The views expressed are those of the author and do not necessarily represent those of the United Nations or the Peacebuilding Support Office.

[2] World Summit Outcome. [3] High-Level Panel, p. 85.

[4] *In Larger Freedom*, pp. 31–33. [5] *Ibid.*, para. 115.

[6] See United Nations General Assembly Resolution, UN Doc. A/RES/60/180 of December 20, 2005 and Security Council Resolution, UN Doc. S/1645 (December 20, 2005).

[7] Security Council Summit Meeting, January 21, 1992, *An Agenda for Peace: Preventive Diplomacy, Peacemaking and Peacebuilding*, UN Doc. A/47/277-S/2411 (June 17, 1992).

While "An Agenda for Peace" made an important conceptual contribution to the debate on peacebuilding, the report of the Panel on United Nations Peace Operations (the Brahimi Report)[8] provided additional impetus for the peacebuilding effort by highlighting its importance. The report also proposed the creation of a focal point for peacebuilding within the United Nations Secretariat, a reform that ultimately did not materialize. Meanwhile, instances of relapse into conflict,[9] especially in countries with United Nations peacekeeping operations, pointed to the need to intensify efforts in countries emerging from conflict to sustain their transition from war to post-conflict recovery and development.

The creation of the new peacebuilding architecture thus reflects international recognition that, despite decades of efforts, the United Nations and the broader international community have not succeeded in addressing post-conflict peacebuilding, in particular ensuring that countries do not relapse into conflict. Indeed, the Secretary-General observed that there had been a "gaping hole in the United Nations institutional machinery: no part of the United Nations system effectively addresses the challenge of helping countries with the transition from war to lasting peace."[10] The establishment of the new peacebuilding architecture is meant to close that gap.

Nearly two years have elapsed since the establishment of the various components of the new peacebuilding architecture. The Peacebuilding Commission was inaugurated in June 2006, the Peacebuilding Support Office was established in June 2006 and the Peacebuilding Fund was launched in October 2006. This is a short period in the life of any institution, but long enough to make preliminary assessments of its performance. In this chapter, I will argue that in spite of some challenges here and there, the new peacebuilding architecture is off to an encouraging start[11] and, more

8 Report of the Panel on United Nations Peace Operations, UN Doc. A/55/305-S/2000/809.

9 For an interesting discussion on portraits of such relapse, see Carolyn McAskie, "The International Peacebuilding Challenge: Can New Players and New Approaches Bring New Results," lecture delivered at Simon Fraser University School for International Studies, Vancouver, British Columbia, Canada, October 19, 2007.

10 *In Larger Freedom*, para 114.

11 This assessment finds echoes in two recent reports by two reputable NGO groups. See ActionAid, CAFOD, and CARE International, "Consolidating the Peace?: Views from Sierra Leone and Burundi on the United Nations Peacebuilding Commission" (June 2007) at www.actionaid.org/assets/pdf/peace_consolidating_the_final.pdf (last accessed August 6, 2008); see also Security Council Report, "Special Research Report No. 2: Peacebuilding Commission" (October 2007) at www.securitycouncilreport.org (last accessed August 6, 2008). (Note: The Security Council Report is the name of a non-governmental organization, not a report of the UN Security Council.)

crucially, it is adding value in incremental steps to international peacebuilding efforts and has much potential value added over the long term.

This chapter provides a description of the design and functions assigned to each of the three components of the peacebuilding architecture (the Peacebuilding Commission, the Peacebuilding Support Office, and the Peacebuilding Fund). This is followed by a brief discussion of the selection process and characteristics of the Peacebuilding Commission's recent efforts in Burundi and Sierra Leone, including an examination of the nature and scope of the engagement of the Peacebuilding Commission with those two countries. In addition, I will present an analysis of the challenges facing the peacebuilding architecture; highlight its present and potential added value, and present conclusions explaining how the new architecture responds to some crucial tests of relevance.

The Peacebuilding Commission

The Peacebuilding Commission is an intergovernmental advisory body. Its mandated functions include: bringing together all relevant actors to marshal resources; supporting the development of integrated strategies in order to lay the foundation for sustainable development; focusing on reconstruction and institution-building efforts necessary for recovery from conflict; providing recommendations and information to improve the coordination of all relevant actors within and outside the United Nations; developing best practices and helping to ensure predictable financing for early recovery activities; and extending the period of attention paid by the international community to post-conflict countries.[12]

The Peacebuilding Commission consists of 31 member states drawn from five categories of countries. Seven come from the General Assembly, seven from the Security Council, seven from the Economic and Social Council, five from among the highest troop-contributing countries to United Nations peacekeeping operations, and five from the highest financial contributors to the United Nations.[13] Mark

[12] See United Nations General Assembly Resolution, UN Doc. A/RES/60/180 (December 20, 2005), para. 2, and Security Council Resolution, UN Doc. S/1645/2005 (December 20, 2005).

[13] The current 31 members are China, France, Russian Federation, United Kingdom, United States plus Belgium and South Africa from the Security Council; Angola, Brazil, Czech Republic, Guinea-Bissau, Luxembourg, Indonesia, and Sri Lanka from the Economic and Social Council; Burundi, Chile, Egypt, El Salvador, Fiji, Georgia, and Jamaica from the General Assembly; Germany, Italy, Japan, the Netherlands, and Norway from the category of major UN financial contributors; and Bangladesh, Ghana, India, Nigeria, and Pakistan from the category of major troop-contributing countries.

Malloch Brown has noted that the last two criteria were designed to reflect "global good citizenship."[14]

The Peacebuilding Commission conducts its work in three configurations:[15] the Organizational Committee; the country-specific meetings; and the working group on lessons learned. The Organizational Committee serves as the forum for discussions on strategy and procedural issues. The country-specific meetings serve as the forum for deliberations and decisions on engagement with the countries under consideration. The working group on lessons learned provides a vehicle for review of experiences from other post-conflict situations and their potential application to countries currently under consideration.

The Peacebuilding Support Office

The Peacebuilding Support Office (PBSO) is headed by the Assistant Secretary-General for Peacebuilding Support, who performs her functions under the direction and authority of the Secretary-General.

The main functions of the PBSO are to support the work of the Peacebuilding Commission in developing peacebuilding strategies for countries under its consideration, develop and document best practices and lessons learned in post-conflict peacebuilding, and help to gather and analyze information on financial resources available for peacebuilding. An important aspect of the work of the PBSO is to bring together the entities of the UN in order to improve the coherence and coordination of its peacebuilding activities. The practical expressions of this role are reflected in the two groups convened by the PBSO: the Senior Policy Group on Peacebuilding, which consists of Assistant Secretaries-General/Directors from several Departments and Offices, and the Peacebuilding Contact Group at the working level. These mechanisms, together with its participation in various inter-departmental and inter-agency processes, enable the PBSO to undertake discussions on strategic peacebuilding priorities and options for the purpose of developing integrated peacebuilding strategies.

[14] Mark Malloch Brown, "Holmes Lecture: Can the UN be Reformed?," annual meeting of the Academic Council on the UN System (ACUNS) (June 7, 2007), p. 7.

[15] The word configuration is synonymous with committee and is also used interchangeably with meeting. Thus in the parlance of the Peacebuilding Commission, there is country-specific configuration or country-specific meeting.

The Peacebuilding Fund

The Peacebuilding Fund, as stated in its terms of reference,[16] aims to address the immediate needs of countries emerging from conflict. The scope of the activities of the Fund will include:

(a) "Activities in support of the implementation of peace agreements;
(b) Activities in support of efforts by countries to build and strengthen capacities that promote coexistence and the peaceful resolution of conflict;
(c) Establishment or re-establishment of essential administrative services and related human and technical capacities;
(d) Critical interventions designed to respond to imminent threats to the peacebuilding process."[17]

The Fund was designed to provide catalytic funding to reinforce funding by other agencies and donors and to address critical funding gaps and support interventions directly related to immediate peacebuilding efforts.

The Fund has exceeded the initial funding target of $250 million, having received a total contribution of $269.2 million as of June 2008. Financial assistance from the Fund is organized around three windows: countries under the consideration of the Peacebuilding Commission are supported from the first window; countries that the Secretary-General determines might be on the verge of lapsing or relapsing into conflict benefit from support from the second window; and countries that require access to immediate funding in order to respond to unforeseen threats to the peace process receive assistance from the emergency window, although the financial outlay for such purposes cannot exceed $1 million per project. The name and number of countries that have received from the three windows of the Fund are provided in the last section of this chapter, as part of discussing the tests of relevance of the peacebuilding architecture.

The Peacebuilding Commission: the selection process and the characteristics of the countries under consideration

The General Assembly and Security Council resolutions establishing the Peacebuilding Commission stipulate that countries shall be referred for

[16] The Terms of reference are annexed to *Arrangements for establishing the Peacebuilding Fund*, report of the Secretary-General, UN Doc. A/60/984 (August 22, 2006).
[17] *Ibid.*

the consideration of the Peacebuilding Commission on the request of the Security Council or the Secretary-General. Burundi and Sierra Leone, the first two countries to be placed on the agenda of the Peacebuilding Commission as well as Guinea-Bissau and Central African Republic were referred to it by the Security Council. In addition, the General Assembly, the Economic and Social Council, or the concerned member state can request for referral. These entities can only do so in situations where a country is on the verge of lapsing or relapsing into conflict. In each case, the concerned member state must give consent to the referral to the Peacebuilding Commission.

The first two countries under consideration by the Peacebuilding Commission, Burundi and Sierra Leone, both underwent similar processes before reaching peace. In both, the conflicts were brought to an end after lengthy negotiations between the government and the rebel factions led to a peace agreement. The Burundi peace negotiations culminated in the Arusha Peace and Reconciliation Agreement of 2000;[18] the Sierra Leone peace negotiations led to the Lome Agreement in 1999.

Both countries received regional or subregional intervention missions that were taken over by United Nations peacekeeping operations. The peacekeeping operations were, in turn, withdrawn and replaced by UN Integrated Offices. In Burundi, the United Nations Operations in Burundi (ONUB) replaced the African Mission in Burundi (AMIB) in June 2004. ONUB was in turn replaced by the Integrated Office in Burundi (BINUB) on January 1, 2007. In Sierra Leone, the Economic Community of West African States Ceasefire and Monitoring Group (ECOMOG), which intervened in March 1998, replaced the UN Peacekeeping mission (UNAMSIL) in November 1999. In turn, UNAMSIL was replaced by the UN Integrated Office in Sierra Leone (UNIOSIL) on January 1, 2006.

There are a number of economic similarities between Burundi and Sierra Leone: Both are among the poorest countries in the world, with a low Human Development Index (HDI) ranking, both depend on primary commodities for a substantial share of their exports, both are fairly

[18] Note that the Forces for Defense of Democracy (FDD), the National Liberation Forces (FNL), armed factions of the National Council for Defense of Democracy (CNDD), and the Party for the Liberation of the Hutu People (Palipehutu) did not sign the Arusha Accords. But CNDD-FDD signed the ceasefire and power-sharing agreements with the Government in 2003 and the Palipehutu-FNL signed a comprehensive ceasefire agreement with the Government in 2006.

reliant on official development assistance (ODA), and both have high economic vulnerability indices.[19] These structural vulnerabilities have several important implications. First, research indicates that poor countries typically face a high risk of reverting to conflict within five years of the ending of a prior conflict.[20] Second, according to Paul Collier, the "three economic characteristics that make a country prone to civil war are low income, slow growth and dependence upon primary commodity exports."[21] Third, these trends underline the need for the Peacebuilding Commission to pay particular attention and to help these two countries avoid a relapse into conflict.

Nature and scope of the Peacebuilding Commission's engagement with the first two countries on its agenda

To understand the performance of the Peacebuilding Commission so far, it is useful to explain its engagement with the first two countries under its consideration: Burundi and Sierra Leone. This is because engagement with these two countries is more advanced than the other two: Guinea-Bissau and the Central African Republic. In doing so, it should be noted that the nature and scope of the Peacebuilding Commission's engagement varies from country to country. This is because the underlying causes of conflict, the conditions under which each country emerged from war, and the stage of post-conflict recovery are different and require individualized treatment. The Peacebuilding Commission's engagement with the two countries has focused on supporting the development of integrated peacebuilding strategies, bringing together various actors in support of peacebuilding efforts, and offering assistance and encouragement to the governments to sustain the peacebuilding efforts.

[19] See the annex at the end of this chapter for a summary of the basic political, economic, and social facts on the two countries.

[20] The figure on the chances of reversal is rounded up to 50 percent in many reports and speeches, but the actual figure is 44 percent. However, a recent study has indicated that the authors of the original figures revised it down to 20 percent four years after the first study. The original study was by Paul Collier *et al.*, *Breaking the Conflict Trap: Civil War and Development Policy – A World Bank Policy Research Report* (jointly published by the World Bank and Oxford University Press, 2003), p. 83; for the reference relating to the revision, see Astri Suhrke and Ingrid Samset, "What's in a figure? Estimating Recurrence of Civil War," *International Peacekeeping* 14 (2007) pp. 195–203.

[21] Paul Collier, *The Bottom Billion: Why the Poorest Countries Are Failing and What Can Be Done About It* (Oxford: Oxford University Press, 2007), p. 32.

Supporting the development of the integrated peacebuilding strategy

An integrated peacebuilding strategy (IPBS) is the Peacebuilding Commission's instrument of engagement with countries under its consideration. The process of developing an integrated peacebuilding strategy for both countries has entailed intensive interaction between the Peacebuilding Commission in New York, on the one hand, and the governments, the UN country team, donors, and domestic civil society organizations, on the other. The process included a series of inter-related steps beginning with a discussion of the peacebuilding needs based on the presentations by senior government leaders from the two countries to the country-specific meetings of the Peacebuilding Commission in New York in October 2006. This led to an endorsement of the peacebuilding priorities for the two countries, followed by a series of thematic discussions on these priorities in the country-specific meetings.

As part of the preparatory process for developing the Strategic Framework, delegations from the Peacebuilding Commission visited Burundi in April 2007 and Sierra Leone in March 2007. These visits were carried out to exchange views on priorities, identify gaps in peacebuilding, set a framework for enhanced dialogue with the governments and provide a platform for advocacy and interaction with partners.

The instrument, developed in cooperation with the national government, is called the Strategic Framework for Peacebuilding in Burundi. The articulation of the Strategic Framework took place against the background of a series of policy frameworks that had been articulated by the government, in collaboration with its partners, to guide the process of its national reconciliation and post-conflict recovery and development. These frameworks included the government's emergency program, the poverty reduction strategy, and the UN common action plan and joint roadmap, including the various peace agreements.

Recognizing that peacebuilding encompasses political, security, and development issues, the Strategic Framework for Peacebuilding in Burundi,[22] adopted by the Government of Burundi and the Peacebuilding Commission on June 20, 2007, identified the following selected peacebuilding priorities: "promotion of good governance; supporting the Comprehensive Ceasefire Agreement between the

[22] See Strategic Framework for Peacebuilding in Burundi, UN Doc. PBC/1/BDI/4 (July 30, 2007).

government of Burundi and the National Liberation Forces (FNL); security sector reforms; justice sector reforms; promotion of human rights and action to combat impunity; ensuring land reforms and socio-economic recovery; mobilization and coordination of international assistance; sub regional dimension; and a gender dimension."[23]

The Strategic Framework also defined the mutual commitments (referred to as mutual engagements) between the Peacebuilding Commission and Burundi. The commitments made by the Peacebuilding Commission included providing sustained attention to, and support for, the mobilization of resources to Burundi in support of its peacebuilding priorities, advocating within the international community for support to the peacebuilding process; and attempting to transform the sub-regional dimension of peacebuilding in the African Great Lakes region into a commitment to Burundi.

Following the adoption of the Strategic Framework, the Peacebuilding Commission and the government of Burundi developed a Monitoring and Tracking Mechanism which outlines the institutional mechanisms as well as procedures for tracking progress in the implementation of the Strategic Framework and details relevant benchmarks. Crucially, the institutional mechanism for monitoring at the country level uses the existing institutional arrangement for monitoring the country's poverty reduction strategy developed by the government.

The integrated peacebuilding strategy for Sierra Leone called the Peacebuilding Cooperation Framework was adopted on December 12, 2007.[24] Developing the framework had slowed down in the lead-up to the presidential and parliamentary elections in August and September 2007 but resumed immediately thereafter. The development of the Cooperation Framework built on a series of policy frameworks that have been articulated by the government to guide the post-conflict recovery and development process. The main peacebuilding priorities reflected in the Peacebuilding Cooperation Framework include "youth employment and empowerment, justice and security sector reform, consolidation of democracy and good governance, capacity building, and sub regional dimensions of peacebuilding."[25]

In addition to making specific commitments to the main peacebuilding priorities, the Peacebuilding Commission undertook to support the

[23] *Ibid.*

[24] See Sierra Leone Peacebuilding Cooperation Framework, UN Doc. PBC/2/SLE/1 (December 3, 2007).

[25] *Ibid.*

implementation of the Cooperation Framework within the context of the governing bodies of international institutions. It advocated for a sustained partnership and an enhanced dialogue between the government of Sierra Leone and its international partners, including attempting to increase the number of international partners supporting peace consolidation efforts in Sierra Leone. Furthermore, the Peacebuilding Commission supported the development of a Sierra Leone National Aid Policy to ensure effective and timely implementation of aid effectiveness policies and good practices, such as the Paris Declaration. More significantly, the Peacebuilding Commission also committed to galvanizing attention and sustained levels of financial resources and technical assistance to support the implementation of the Framework.[26]

The biannual reviews of the Strategic Framework for Peacebuilding in Burundi and the Peacebuilding Cooperation Framework for Sierra Leone were conducted in June 2008.[27] The biannual reviews are six-monthly assessments of progress in the implementation of the peacebuilding priorities and commitments jointly agreed to by the Peacebuilding Commission and the government of the two countries as well as other stakeholders. These reviews are an important part of the sustained attention by the Peacebuilding Commission to the countries on its agenda and they offer an opportunity for course correction, depending on developments in the country.

Bringing together various actors in support of national peacebuilding efforts

The process of articulating the Strategic Framework for Peacebuilding in Burundi has been as important as the outcome itself. One of the strengths of the Peacebuilding Commission is its ability to bring various actors together into many facets of its work. This approach was used to good effect in the development of the Burundi Strategic Framework, where it brought together the government, donors, the UN country team and a wide variety of civil society organizations – including private sector organizations, women's associations, religious groups, and traditional

[26] *Ibid.* para. 26.

[27] The key findings are to be in Recommendations of the biannual review of the implementation of the Strategic Framework for Peacebuilding in Burundi, PBC/2/BDI/L.2 (June 19, 2008) and Conclusions and recommendations of the biannual review of the implementation of the Sierra Leone Peacebuilding Cooperation Framework PBC/2/SLE.2 (June 19, 2008).

associations. In so doing, the Peacebuilding Commission not only fulfilled the task entrusted to it in its founding resolutions but also built national and international consensus around key peacebuilding priorities. The significance of bringing the civil society organizations into this process is discussed below in the section entitled "Present and potential added value."

As in Burundi, the effort to develop a Cooperation Framework for Sierra Leone benefited from increased dialogue between the government and other stakeholders, in particular the donors, the civil society organizations and the UN country team. Such collaboration, especially with the development partners, will be critical in making progress on a range of programs. As the report of the Chairman of the Country Specific Meeting (CSM) mission to Sierra Leone in October 2007 noted, "The Peacebuilding Commission should play a pivotal role in strengthening dialogue between the Government and its international partners as well as broadening the donor base in Sierra Leone. A critical element for broadening the donor base and attracting non-traditional partners will be the development of government led sector-wide strategies and master plans in areas such as energy, physical infrastructure, water supply, and health and the private sector and flexible funding mechanisms and structures."[28]

Offering assistance and encouragement to governments to sustain the peacebuilding effort

The engagement of the Peacebuilding Commission extends beyond the development of the Strategic Framework and bringing the actors together in support of that effort. The Peacebuilding Commission also offers a helping hand to the governments in situations of real or potential crisis. The visit of the Chairman of the Burundi country-specific meeting to Bujumbura (the capital of Burundi) in early September 2007 provides a striking illustration of this kind of engagement. The visit was aimed at and enabled the Chairman to dialogue with the relevant stakeholders, in particular the government, opposition parties, and donors. The Chairman urged them to overcome the budgetary impasse, to break the parliamentary deadlock, and to end the withdrawal of FNL from the Joint Verification and Monitoring Mechanism that had been established to

[28] See Report of the Mission of the Chairman of the Peacebuilding Commission in Sierra Leone Configuration to Sierra Leone (October 8–15, 2007), pp. 2–3.

monitor the Comprehensive Framework Agreement of 2006. Following the visit, the Peacebuilding Commission issued a statement outlining a set of specific recommendations to all stakeholders.[29]

The need to improve energy supply in Sierra Leone has long been recognized and the new government has declared energy as an utmost priority. In its report on the October 2007 mission to Sierra Leone, the chair of the country-specific meeting on Sierra Leone recommended that "the Peacebuilding Commission should support the government's effort by galvanizing additional resources and commitments for an immediate response and holistic medium-term energy sector."[30] As a response, the CSM for Sierra Leone held a meeting on November 13, 2007 to examine how various actors can support the government's effort to increase energy supply. An efficient and reliable energy supply is critical to reviving the economy of Sierra Leone, in particular its agricultural, industrial, and commercial production.

The challenges

The new peacebuilding architecture faces a range of challenges. In its first annual report, the Peacebuilding Commission identified a few:

> The main challenge facing the Commission is to maximize its impact on the ground to make the United Nations peacebuilding architecture an effective instrument of international collaboration in support of countries emerging from conflict. The commission's future work will need to focus on ensuring that peacebuilding processes remain on track and that challenges and gaps are addressed in a timely manner by all relevant stakeholders … others will include further development of the Commission's working methods and monitoring mechanisms for the IPBS; enhancing operational relationships with other intergovernmental bodies and regional and sub regional organizations; and improving interaction with the field based on lessons learned during its first year of operations.[31]

[29] See Conclusions and Recommendations of the Peacebuilding Commission following the report of the Chair of the Burundi configuration in identical letters dated September 20, 2007 from the Chair of the Burundi configuration of the Peacebuilding Commission to the President of the Security Council, the President of the General Assembly and the President of the Economic and Social Council, UN Doc. PBC/2/BDI/2 (September 21, 2007).

[30] Report of the Mission of the Chairman of the Peacebuilding Commission in Sierra Leone Configuration to Sierra Leone (October 8–15, 2007), para. 9.

[31] See Report of the Peacebuilding Commission on its first session, UN Doc. A/62/137-S/2007/458 (July 25, 2007), p. 2.

Getting the process right is fundamental to the functioning and effectiveness of the new peacebuilding architecture, in particular the Peacebuilding Commission. More significantly, the Peacebuilding Commission's emphasis that it needs "to maximize its impact on the ground" reflects awareness that its operational success will be judged by whether its work enables war-torn countries to achieve durable peace and to avoid relapse into conflict.

Yet there are other challenges. One of these relates to the sequencing of financial allocation from the Peacebuilding Fund (PBF) and the development of the integrated peacebuilding strategy (IPBS). Burundi and Sierra Leone received funding from the PBF before the development of the Strategic Peacebuilding Framework for Burundi or the Sierra Leone Peacebuilding Cooperation Framework. In its report in March 2007, the Peacebuilding Commission mission to Sierra Leone noted that "many stakeholders in the country remain primarily focused on the disbursement of the US$35 million allocated to Sierra Leone by the PBF."[32] This has raised the question of whether the development of an IPBS should precede the allocation of resources from the PBF. The short-term catalytic nature of the PBF, however, requires that financial allocation be made as soon as possible to the countries. The IPBS should serve as the framework for more substantive long-term funding for peacebuilding.

This is linked to another challenge: the Peacebuilding Commission's ability to marshal resources to fund peacebuilding. It has been noted that "we must not confuse the peacebuilding fund (with a target of US$ 250 million) with funding for peacebuilding. If peacekeeping can draw on up to US$6 to $8 billion to fund its operations through assessed budgets, how can we ensure that the Peacebuilding Commission can develop the capacity to generate sufficient assured resources for peace building?"[33] The actual figure for the proposed budget for peacekeeping for 2008–2009 is US$7.3 billion.[34] The potential for individual Peacebuilding Commission members to contribute to that effort is discussed in the next section.

Although there is wide recognition that peacebuilding efforts span the entire conflict cycle, from conflict prevention to peacemaking, peacekeeping and post-conflict peacebuilding, there is an expectation that the

[32] See Report of Peacebuilding Commission mission to Sierra Leone from March 19–25, 2007, UN Doc. PBC/1/SLE/2 (April 23, 2007), p. 2.

[33] McAskie, "The International Peacebuilding Challenge," p. 16.

[34] See "UN Peacekeeping in the Line of Fire," *Financial Times* (May 17–18, 2008), p. 5.

Peacebuilding Commission should help in smoothing the transition from peacekeeping to post-conflict peacebuilding. It has been observed that "one of the main challenges for the Peacebuilding Commission will be to find ways of drawing down the current caseload of UN peace operations without precipitating a relapse to conflict. If it were able to do so in even just one or two cases initially, it would make an important contribution."[35] The Peacebuilding Commission, however, should focus on post-conflict situations that can benefit from peacebuilding.

The present and potential added value

There is a considerable diversity of perspectives concerning the areas where the new peacebuilding architecture, in particular the Peacebuilding Commission, can or should bring value added to its work. It is possible to make a distinction between its present and potential value added. We begin by examining some of the value added thus far.

Ensuring predictable financing for peacebuilding efforts is one area where the Peacebuilding Commission has made a good start. The involvement of the Peacebuilding Commission in the donors' roundtable through the Chairman of the country-specific configuration on Burundi was a contributory factor for the successful partners' Round Table held in Bujumbura at the end of May 2007. That meeting was co-sponsored by the Netherlands and Norway (the latter in its capacity as Chair of the Burundi configuration of the Peacebuilding Commission). Norway played a key role in mobilizing the international community for active participation in the Round Table, both through bilateral efforts and by linking it to the work of the Peacebuilding Commission. In this regard, it was noted that "the US$655.6 million in funds pledged from international donors to Burundi in May would probably have been much lower if it had not been for the Commission, in particular the influence of Norway's Ambassador to the United Nations, John Lovald, who chairs the Commission's Burundi Committee."[36]

The Peacebuilding Commission has also added value by assisting the countries under its consideration to "stay the course" and better manage political crises. In both Burundi and Sierra Leone, the Peacebuilding

[35] Salman Ahmed, Paul Keating, and Ugo Salinas, "Shaping the future of UN peace operations: is there a doctrine in this house?," *Cambridge Review of International Affairs* 20 (March 2007), pp. 11–28.

[36] Security Council Report (October 2007), p. 8.

Commission has contributed to helping the countries stay the course at critical political turning points. In early September 2007, the Chair of the Burundi configuration of the Peacebuilding Commission undertook a fact-finding mission, which resulted in the adoption of "Conclusions and Recommendations."[37] The recommendations are the outcome of a concerted approach by the international community to respond to three critical issues faced by the country, namely, a deadlock in Parliament that prevented the passage of legislative measures, the withdrawal of PALIPEHUTU-FNL from the Joint Verification and Monitoring Mechanism (JVMM), and serious economic governance problems that led to a delay in concluding a review by the International Monetary Fund (IMF). The completion of the IMF review was in part due to the efforts of the Chair of the Burundi CSM, which opened the way for resumption of negotiations between the IMF and the government of Burundi.

In Sierra Leone, a striking illustration of the commitment to galvanize international attention in support of Sierra Leone's Peacebuilding Cooperation Framework was provided by the convening of the High-Level Stakeholders Consultation on Sierra Leone in New York on May 19, 2008. That meeting brought together senior representatives of member states, the United Nations, the private sector and the civil society. During that meeting several participating international organizations and member states "expressed commitments to continue or increase their support to Sierra Leone in line with the Peacebuilding Cooperation Framework."[38] A specific example of the capacity of the Peacebuilding Commission to galvanize international attention on a particular peacebuilding priority is provided by the focus that the Sierra Leone CSM has turned on energy. The inclusion of energy among the peacebuilding priorities for Sierra Leone has enabled the government to attract assistance from a range of bilateral and multilateral partners for the rehabilitation of the power sector, including strengthening management capacity for the energy sector.

Moreover, the Peacebuilding Commission held three meetings on the 2007 Sierra Leone presidential and parliamentary elections, bringing together the government, the UN country team, donors, and civil society

[37] See Conclusions and Recommendations of the Peacebuilding Commission following the report of the Chair of the Burundi configuration in identical letters dated September 20, 2007.

[38] See Chair's Summary Statement on Peacebuilding Commission High-Level Stakeholders Consultation on Sierra Leone (May 19, 2008).

organizations. This was in response to the Security Council's request to the Chairman of the country-specific configuration on Sierra Leone to track progress on the main peacebuilding issues, including the presidential and parliamentary elections held in August 2007. The Peacebuilding Commission adopted a Chair's Declaration on the Presidential and Parliamentary Elections in which "members of the Commission advised of the need for all stakeholders to make every effort to ensure that the elections were conducted in a peaceful and orderly manner, in accordance with international standards for democratic elections."[39] As the Security Council Report has noted, "the Peacebuilding Commission's focus on Sierra Leone seems to have underlined to all parties the importance of agreeing to accept the outcome of the August 11, 2007 election. It may therefore have helped those involved in preparing for the election, in both the government and the UN, to be more alert to potential disruptions before and after the election."[40]

The engagement of the Peacebuilding Commission has created an environment at the country level for improved government–civil society dialogue. The work at the country level, both on the development of projects of the PBF and on the Strategic Framework for Peacebuilding in Burundi, provided an important opportunity to bring the Government and civil society organizations into dialogue. The National Steering Committee (Comité de Pilotage) brought together government representatives, the UN, donors and civil society organizations. The involvement of civil society organizations in such a process was ground breaking, and was a result of the process established by the Peacebuilding Commission.

The value of the PBF rests mainly in its unique capacity to fill critical funding gaps for peacebuilding. It channels resources for focused and time-limited activities deemed critical to the peace process, where funding is traditionally insufficient but contributes directly to peace consolidation, and funding for priorities in sectors that are usually difficult to finance. Sierra Leone provides an illustration of where the resources of the PBF proved critical in support of the national elections. The PBF provided readily available financing to the National Electoral Commission and the Sierra Leone Police, enabling them to manage the elections.

[39] See Chair's Declaration Adopted by the Peacebuilding Commission Country-Specific Meeting on Sierra Leone on the Upcoming Presidential and Parliamentary elections in Sierra Leone, UN Doc. PBC/1/SLE/4 (June 22, 2007).

[40] See Security Council Report (October 2007), pp. 8–9.

In certain emergency situations, such funding can provide immediate support to address an imminent threat to peace consolidation or reinforce the peace process. For example, the PBF has provided funding to support the peace process and political dialogue in the Central African Republic. More recently, the PBF has provided funding to Guinea Conakry for the national emergency program and reconciliation activities to bring all political actors together before the holding of legislative elections. The project will help restore confidence among the various political actors in Guinea and it will contribute to discussions on the country's electoral procedures, leading to the holding of credible elections.

The PBF has also added value in its unique catalytic role. In the preparation and implementation phases, the Fund not only kickstarts critical peacebuilding interventions – for instance to foster inclusive dialogue in Burundi or Côte d'Ivoire – it also attracts additional external resources from bilateral or multilateral sources. Several donors, thanks in part to the knowledge and cooperation built through the steering committees of the respective countries, intend to pursue and deepen certain initiatives launched in cooperation with the Fund. This catalytic impact is also visible within currently existing projects, such as in Burundi, where a $1.5 million project to support the reinforcement of mechanisms to fight corruption involved two government entities, the Ministry of Good Governance and the General Inspection and Local Administration, in addition to the Integrated Office in Burundi (BINUB) and UN Development Programme. Finally, by linking up and coordinating with other funding windows of UN agencies, the international finance institutions, and non-governmental organizations, the Fund helps to ensure that longer-term funding mechanisms will be able to take over after the initial catalytic impact of the PBF runs its course.

There are myriad ways in which the Peacebuilding Commission might potentially add value over time. One potential value added resides "in improving coordination between all national and international actors involved in peacebuilding and post-conflict reconstruction, helping to maintain a coalition of interests around a country in a post-conflict situation, contributing to bridging the 'relief to development gap' and generally improving the sequencing of various phases of peacebuilding efforts."[41]

[41] See, e.g., David Atwood and Fred Tanner, "The UN Peacebuilding Commission and International Geneva," *Disarmament Forum (UNIDIR)* 2 (2007), p. 29.

Building consensus around strategic peacebuilding frameworks in post-conflict countries is yet another way that the Peacebuilding Commission can add value. Burundi and Sierra Leone developed various policy frameworks before their respective engagements with the Peacebuilding Commission, because they were further down the road to post-conflict recovery and development than the typical immediate post-conflict country would be. Even so, the Peacebuilding Commission has developed peacebuilding frameworks and built consensus among the various stakeholders around the Strategic Framework for Peacebuilding in Burundi and the Sierra Leone Peacebuilding Cooperation Framework. Indeed, the strategic frameworks have proven useful in bringing together the political, security, and development dimensions into a single framework to support the transition from stabilization phase to long-term development. Thus, these frameworks have considerable potential to serve as essential guides to keep the countries on track for sustainable peace. The opportunities to use such frameworks as guides to international action will be potentially greater in countries immediately emerging from conflict. Though these umbrella peacebuilding frameworks may not replace existing structures, they can reinforce complex policy frameworks to support post-conflict recovery, reconciliation, and development. Examples include post-conflict needs assessment and poverty reduction strategy papers.

Marshalling resources is another area where the Peacebuilding Commission has great potential. Its influence within the constellation of UN intergovernmental bodies will depend among other things on "its potential to generate additional resources for a conflict-affected state whose perceived importance on the international agenda has receded."[42] The composition of the Peacebuilding Commission gives it considerable advantage over other options as to resource mobilization for post-conflict countries, and particularly for those under its consideration.

To appreciate the potential value added in this regard, one need look no further than the volume of official development assistance (ODA) provided by the Development Assistance Committee (DAC) members on the Peacebuilding Commission. The ten members of the Peacebuilding Commission that belong to DAC provided a total of $77.76 billion (75 percent) of the $103.65 billion in ODA given by

[42] See Richard Ponzio, "The United Nations Peacebuilding Commission: Origins and Initial Practice," *Disarmament Forum (UNIDIR)* 2 (2007), p. 8 at www.unidir.org/pdf/articles/pdf-art2627.pdf (last accessed August 6, 2008).

DAC in 2007.[43] When that amount is added to the resources that non-DAC and other developing member states of the Peacebuilding Commission give in aid annually, the enormous financial power that resides within the Peacebuilding Commission becomes evident. Among its members are Brazil, Russia, India, and China,[44] as well as OPEC members Angola and Nigeria.

It would be wrong to conclude from this, however, that a significant re-direction of ODA resources to peacebuilding can occur from Peacebuilding Commission members in a short period of time. Foreign policy considerations reinforced by domestic politics influence the amount, destination, and sectors to which donor countries allocate ODA. Still, in the long run, and provided that there is commitment among the membership of the Peacebuilding Commission to support post-conflict countries, there is considerable scope for Peacebuilding Commission members to offer financial resources and technical expertise to help countries under the consideration of the commission.

The assessments of the first year of the performance of the Peacebuilding Commission made by two groups of NGOs and of eighteen months' performance by a government-commissioned study provide us with a fitting conclusion to this section. The first group, ActionAid, CAFOD, and CARE International have noted that "the Peacebuilding Commission's impact has been largely positive and well received, but important challenges remain."[45] The Security Council Report – another non-governmental organization – has noted that "the Peacebuilding Commission has made considerable contributions in its first year, not only in terms of its own systems and processes but also in marshalling international resources and focusing attention on two countries that needed

[43] This is based on preliminary ODA data for 2007. See OECD: Table 1 on Net Official Development Assistance in 2007 – Preliminary data for 2007; released on April 4, 2008, available at www.oecd.org/dataoecd/27/55/40381862.pdf (last accessed August 6, 2008). The 10 members in the order of volume of their net ODA are the United States (US $21.75 bn), Germany (US$12.26 bn), France (US$9.94 bn), United Kingdom (US$9.92 bn), Japan (US$7.69 bn), the Netherlands (US$6.21 bn), Italy (US$3.92 bn), Norway (US $3.72 bn), Belgium (US$1.95 bn), and Luxembourg (US$0.365 bn).

[44] These four countries have been named the BRICs. The concept of BRIC was developed and popularized in Goldman Sachs, "Dreaming of the BRICs: The Path to 2050," *Global Economic Paper* 99 (2003). According to Jim O'Neill, who was the lead author of the 2003 Goldman Sachs report, BRICs, which are emerging as donors, now account for 15–16 per cent of the global output; see Jim O'Niell, "Dwindling US Trade Deficit Could Shape World Trade," *Financial Times* (September 26, 2007), p. 28.

[45] ActionAid, "Consolidating the Peace?" p. 2.

assistance in their transition from peacekeeping to development ... this will be a long process, but an important and valuable beginning has been made."[46] For its part, an independent analysis commissioned by the Permanent Mission of Denmark to the United Nations concluded that "the Peacebuilding Commission is a work in progress, but one that so far has proved the potential for its contribution. Continued focus on its performance by all stakeholders will be necessary if it is to (a) consolidate its positive impact on cases undertaken to date, and (b) extend its reach to new cases."[47]

An encouraging start

So much hope has been raised by the creation of the new peacebuilding architecture, in particular the Peacebuilding Commission, that there has been impatience for quick results. It is important to emphasize that the new peacebuilding architecture is in its infancy and much "learning by doing" is to be expected. It is not surprising, for example, that the Peacebuilding Commission, the linchpin of the new peacebuilding architecture, spent a good part of its first year addressing what the Chairman of the Peacebuilding Commission has called "critical organizational and methodological issues."[48] Still, there are some crucial tests of relevance to which the new peacebuilding architecture can be subjected, even at this stage in its life cycle. This test is based on some questions.

Do the first two countries on the agenda of the Peacebuilding Commission find the experience helpful to their peacebuilding efforts? As the first two countries to be referred to the Peacebuilding Commission, Burundi and Sierra Leone are the proving ground for the work of the new peacebuilding architecture. The Permanent Representative of Burundi to the United Nations has said that "[b]y selecting Burundi as the first beneficiary of its work, the Commission [has] demonstrated its commitment to building lasting peace and relaunching Burundi's national economy."[49] And

[46] Special Research Report No. 2, Peacebuilding Commission, p. 11.

[47] See "Taking Stock, Looking Forward: A Strategic Review of the Peacebuilding Commission – An Independent Analysis," NYU Center on International Cooperation and the International Peace Institute (April 2008).

[48] See Statement by Ambassador Yukio Takasu, Chairman of the Peacebuilding Commission, at the Debate at Security Council on the First Report of the Peacebuilding Commission (October 17, 2007), p. 1.

[49] See United Nations General Assembly Doc. GA/10635, statement by Mr. Joseph Ntakirutimana, Ambassador of Burundi to the United Nations (October 10, 2007), p. 3 at www.un.org/News/Press/docs/2007/ga10635.doc.htm (last accessed August 6, 2008).

the newly elected President of Sierra Leone stated in his inaugural address that the government of Sierra Leone "will continue to work with the United Nations in peacebuilding and will take full advantage of the opportunities provided by the newly established United Nations Peacebuilding Commission."[50] These are early encouraging affirmations that there is value in engagement with the Peacebuilding Commission.

Are more countries seeking to be considered by the Peacebuilding Commission? If countries emerging from conflict consider engagement with the Peacebuilding Commission useful, requests to be placed on the agenda of the Peacebuilding Commission will increase. The President of Timor-Leste, in his address to the 62nd session of the UN General Assembly, expressed the hope that "as the situation [in his country] progresses the Peacebuilding Commission will consider placing Timor-Leste on its agenda as a follow-up to the United Nations Mission in Timor-Leste (UNMIT)."[51] Following a request from the government of Guinea-Bissau in July 2007, the Security Council referred that country for consideration by the Peacebuilding Commission in December 2007. A country-specific configuration for Guinea-Bissau chaired by Brazil was created by the Peacebuilding Commission on December 19, 2007. Guinea-Bissau has thus become the third country under the consideration of the Peacebuilding Commission. In a sign of the increasing attractiveness of the Peacebuilding Commission for countries emerging from conflict, the Central African Republic requested in March 2008 to be considered by the Peacebuilding Commission, and was placed on the agenda of the Peacebuilding Commission on June 12, 2008. Côte d'Ivoire requested in April 2008 to be on the agenda of the Peacebuilding Commission and its request is under consideration by the Security Council, as of this writing.

Is the PBF responding to the peacebuilding efforts of countries in need? The PBF has also begun to respond to peacebuilding needs beyond Burundi and Sierra Leone, the first two countries on the agenda of the Peacebuilding Commission. These first two countries together with Guinea-Bissau have been declared eligible for and benefited from

[50] See Presidential Address delivered by His Excellency Mr. Ernst Bai Koroma, President of Sierra Leone and Commander-in-Chief of the Armed Forces of the Republic of Sierra Leone on the occasion of the State Opening of the Third Parliament, Freetown (October 5, 2007), p. 15.

[51] See Address by His Excellency Dr. Jose Ramos-Horta, President of the Democratic Republic of Timor-Leste to the 62nd session of the United Nations General Assembly (September 27, 2007).

funding from window one of the PBF. Since then, the PBF has responded to funding requests from other countries from the second and third (emergency) windows. Moreover, Liberia and Central Africa have received funding under the second window, while Nepal and Côte d'Ivoire have been declared eligible for these funds. Support from the emergency window of the PBF have been received from and approved for Burundi, the Central African Republic, Côte d'Ivoire, Guinea-Conakry, Haiti, Kenya, and Liberia.

Dag Hammarskjöld, the second Secretary-General of the United Nations, once remarked that the "United Nations was created not to lead mankind to heaven, but to save mankind from hell." He could just as well have been speaking of the new peacebuilding architecture and its role in post-conflict situations. The Peacebuilding Commission was not designed to provide early warning for impending conflicts nor to dissuade countries from resorting to war, but rather, it was designed to ensure that the countries under its watch achieve sustainable peace and do not relapse into conflict. Post-conflict peacebuilding is a complex and painstaking process, with the results not showing up in the short run. It is analogous to a marathon rather than a sprint. Nonetheless, the work of the Peacebuilding Commission during its first two years provides reason for hope and offers an encouraging start.

Annex

The Economic Vulnerability Index (EVI) reflects the risk posed to a country's development by exogenous shocks, the impact of which depends on the magnitude of the shocks and on structural characteristics that determine the extent to which the country would be affected by such shocks. The EVI is a combination of seven indicators: (a) population size; (b) remoteness; (c) merchandise export concentration; (d) share of agriculture, forestry, and fisheries in gross domestic product; (e) homelessness owing to natural disasters; (f) instability of agricultural production; and (g) instability of exports of goods and services.

Basic Political, Economic, and Social Facts about Burundi and Sierra Leone

Country	YoPA	YoFE	Pop. 2005	HDI Ranking 2006	GDP 2005	Net ODA/ GNI 2004–05	Commodities Export/Total Exports 2005	GDP Per Capita 2004: US$ GNI PPP	Economic vulnerability index
Burundi	2000	2005a	7.60 m	169/177	$0.79bn	50.9%	48.6%	90 677	59.9
Sierra Leone	1999	2002b	5.53 m	176/177	$1.20bn	32.0%	92.5%	190 561	63.7

(a) The next elections in Burundi are scheduled for 2010.
(b) Sierra Leone held presidential and parliamentary elections in August 2007 with a run-off presidential election in September 2007.
Note: **YoPA** = Year of Peace Agreement; **YoFE** = Year of First Election after Peace Agreement.
Sources: Economist Intelligence Unit: Country Profile for Burundi 2006; Country Report for Burundi, Feb 2007; Country Profile for Sierra Leone 2006; and Country Report for Sierra Leone, March 2007; UNDP: Human Development Report 2006; OECD: 2006 Development Cooperation Report vol. 8, No. 1; UNCTAD: DGDS/CSIRB Global Statistics Database 2007; World Bank: World Development Indicators 2007; United Nations Department of Economic and Social Affairs (2206): Overcoming economic vulnerability and Creating Employment: Report of the Committee for Development Policy on the eighth session (March 2–24, 2006).

9

The World Summit process and UN sanctions reform: between rhetoric and force

JEREMY FARRALL

The UN Secretary-General's High-Level Panel (HLP) proposed some broad and sweeping changes to the UN's collective security practices in its 2004 report to the General Assembly, *A More Secure World*.[1] As several chapters in this collection demonstrate, the bulk of the HLP's initial recommendations were seriously diluted in the two major documents that took the HLP's recommendations forward, Secretary-General Kofi Annan's report to the General Assembly (GA), *In Larger Freedom*,[2] and the GA's final product itself, the *World Summit Outcome*.[3] But sanctions reform represents an exception to this rule. A number of the HLP's more important recommendations are endorsed by the *World Summit Outcome*. Moreover, UN member states actually complemented the HLP's proposals with some additional initiatives of their own in the *World Summit Outcome*. Yet, despite the surprisingly progressive approach on sanctions reform exhibited in the *World Summit Outcome*, the final proposal could have been bolder still. First, the GA could and should have gone further in suggesting additional reforms to address failings of the UN sanctions system from a rule-of-law perspective. Second, although the appearance of reform proposals in the *World Summit Outcome* represents an important articulation of reform aspirations, the real question is what, if any, impact these proposals will have upon the Security Council's application and oversight of sanctions in practice.

This chapter traces the attempt to prompt UN sanctions reform through the process that began with the HLP's *A More Secure World* and culminated

[1] Report of the United Nations Secretary-General's High-Level Panel on Threats, Challenges and Change, *A More Secure World: Our Shared Responsibility* (New York: United Nations, 2004).

[2] A/59/2005, *In Larger Freedom: Towards Development, Security and Human Rights for All* (March 21, 2005).

[3] GA Res. 60/1/2005, *World Summit Outcome* (October 24, 2005).

in the General Assembly's *World Summit Outcome*. It begins by surveying post-Cold War developments in the UN Security Council's sanctions practice, identifying some of the major remaining sanctions shortcomings from a human-rights and rule-of-law perspective. The chapter then traces the progression of sanctions-related observations from *A More Secure World* to the *World Summit Outcome*. It considers the likely long-term impact of that progression on the Security Council's sanctions practice, and argues that the battle for sanctions reform is far from over. The chapter concludes by arguing that efforts to prompt Security Council sanctions policy reform via external regulation, whether by normative or institutional innovation, are unlikely to succeed. Rather, meaningful sanctions regulation must come from within the Council itself.

Post-Cold War refinements to UN sanctions policy

In the fourteen years between the end of the Cold War and the convening of the HLP, there was a considerable evolution in UN sanctions policy. During the Cold War the Security Council had only twice been able to muster the necessary consensus to employ its Article 41 sanctions powers.[4] Freed from its Cold War paralysis, the Council created eighteen sanctions regimes between August 1990 and late 2003, when the HLP first convened.[5] By the end of 2006, yet another five sanctions regimes had been established.[6]

4 In 1966 the Council applied economic sanctions against the illegal white minority regime in Southern Rhodesia. See SC Res. 232 (December 16, 1966), para. 2. In 1977 the Council imposed an arms embargo against South Africa. See SC Res. 418 (November 4, 1977), para. 2. Article 41 provides: "The Security Council may decide what measures not involving the use of armed force are to be employed to give effect to its decisions, and it may call upon the Members of the United Nations to apply such measures. These may include complete or partial interruption of economic relations and of rail, sea, air, postal, telegraphic, radio, and other means of communication, and the severance of diplomatic relations."

5 By late 2003, the following additional sanctions regimes had been applied (the number representing the Security Council resolution which initiated the regime): 661 Iraq, 713 former Yugoslavia, 733 Somalia, 748 Libya, 757 Federal Republic of Yugoslavia (Serbia and Montenegro) (FRYSM), 820 Bosnian Serbs, 841 Haiti, 864 (Angolan rebel group) UNITA, 918 Rwanda, 1054 Sudan, 1132 Sierra Leone, 1160 Federal Republic of Yugoslavia (FRY), 1267 Afghanistan/Taliban/Al-Qaeda, 1298 Eritrea and Ethiopia, 1343 Liberia, 1493 Democratic Republic of the Congo (DRC), 1521 Liberia.

6 Between late 2003 and the end of 2006, the Council created the following additional sanctions regimes: 1556 Sudan, 1572 Côte d'Ivoire, 1636 Independent Commission into Hariri Assassination, 1718 North Korea and 1737 Iran. For a list of all UN sanctions regimes established up until the end of 2006, see Farrall, Jeremy, *United Nations Sanctions and the Rule of Law* (Cambridge: Cambridge University Press, 2007), p. 468 (Table B). For summaries of all 25 UN sanctions regimes, see pp. 247–463 (Appendix 2).

UN sanctions have been applied around the globe, from Rhodesia to Yugoslavia and from Haiti to North Korea. They have targeted nations, rebel groups, and terrorist organizations.[7] When the Security Council applies sanctions it can choose from a range of measures, from comprehensive sanctions which prevent the flow to and from the target of virtually all products and commodities,[8] to simple measures that target specific items, such as arms, timber, or diamonds.[9] Sanctions regimes can also target particular activities, such as diplomatic relations or travel.[10] The Council has imposed sanctions in pursuance of a growing array of objectives.[11] Sanctions have been used to: compel an occupying state to withdraw its troops;[12] prevent a state from developing or acquiring weapons of mass destruction;[13] counter international terrorism;[14] stem human rights violations;[15] and promote the implementation of a peace process.[16]

[7] Rebel groups have been targeted in the Bosnian Serb, UNITA, Sierra Leone, and DRC sanctions regimes. The Taliban and Al-Qaeda sanctions regime targets terrorist organizations.

[8] Comprehensive sanctions were applied as part of the 232 Rhodesia, 661 Iraq, 757 Federal Republic of Yugoslavia (Serbia-Montenegro) (FRYSM), 820 Bosnian Serb, and 841 Haiti sanctions regimes.

[9] Arms embargoes have been applied as part of almost every UN sanctions regime. The following regimes, however, have consisted solely of an arms embargo: 418 South Africa, 713 Yugoslavia, 733 Somalia, 1343 Liberia, 918 Rwanda, 757 Federal Republic of Yugoslavia (FRY) and 1298 Eritrea and Ethiopia. Timber sanctions have been applied as part of both the 1343 and 1521 Liberian sanctions regimes. Diamond sanctions have been applied as part of the 864 UNITA, 1132 Sierra Leone, and 1572 Côte d'Ivoire sanctions regimes, as well as both the 1343 and 1521 Liberian sanctions regimes.

[10] Diplomatic sanctions have been applied as part of the 748 Libya and 1054 Sudan sanctions regimes. Travel sanctions or travel bans have been applied as part of the 232 Rhodesia, 661 Iraq, 748 Libya, 841 Haiti, 864 UNITA, 1054 Sudan, 1132 Sierra Leone, 1267 Taliban and Al-Qaeda, 1343 Liberia, 1493 DRC, 1572 Côte d'Ivoire, 1636 Hariri Commission, 1718 North Korea, and 1737 Iran sanctions regimes.

[11] On sanctions objectives in general, see Farrall, *United Nations Sanctions and the Rule of Law*, pp. 133–138.

[12] This was the initial objective of the 661 Iraq sanctions regime.

[13] Non-proliferation was an objective of the 418 South Africa, 1718 North Korea and 1737 Iran sanctions regimes, as well as the primary reason for maintaining the 661 Iraq sanctions regime after the conclusion of 1991 Gulf War hostilities.

[14] Preventing and responding to international terrorism was an objective of the 748 Libya, 1054 Sudan, 1267 Taliban and Al-Qaeda, and 1636 Hariri Commission sanctions regimes.

[15] Stemming human rights violations has been an objective of the 232 Rhodesia, 418 South Africa, 841 Haiti, 1160 FRY, and 1556 Sudan sanctions regimes.

[16] Promoting the implementation of a peace process was an objective of the Liberia, 864 UNITA, 918 Rwanda, 1132 Sierra Leone, 1493 DRC and 1572 Côte d'Ivoire sanctions regimes.

The UN's increasing use of sanctions has attracted staunch criticism. Critics have been particularly scathing about the use of comprehensive sanctions, denouncing them as at best ineffective,[17] and at worst as measures that galvanize opposition to UN intervention and strengthen the target's position of power.[18] Some critics have gone so far as to label sanctions "the UN's weapon of mass destruction,"[19] "a genocidal tool,"[20] or "modern siege warfare."[21] These concerns prompted international sanctions policy scholars to explore possibilities for sanctions reform.[22] Important intergovernmental meetings were also held on sanctions reform, coming to be known as the Interlaken,[23] Bonn-Berlin[24] and Stockholm[25] processes.

Partly in response to these initiatives, the UN Security Council has moved towards employing smarter, more targeted sanctions. Where possible, it has applied sanctions against particular individuals and

17 R. A. Pape, "Why Economic Sanctions Do Not Work," *International Security* 22 (1997), pp. 90–136.

18 Johan Galtung, "On the Effects of Economic Sanctions: With Examples from the Case of Rhodesia" in Nincic, Miroslav and Wallensteen, Peter (eds.), *Dilemmas of Economic Coercion* (New York: Praeger, 1983), pp. 17–60.

19 Denis Halliday, "Iraq and the UN's weapon of mass destruction," *Current History* 98 (1999), pp. 65–68; J. Mueller and K. Mueller, "Sanctions of mass destruction," *Foreign Affairs* 78 (1999), pp. 43–53.

20 Geoffrey Simons, *Imposing economic sanctions: legal remedy or genocidal tool?* (London: Pluto Press, 1999); George E. Bisharat, "Sanctions as Genocide," *Transnational Law and Contemporary Problems* 11 (2001), pp. 379–425.

21 Joy Gordon, "Sanctions as siege warfare," *The Nation* (March 22, 1999).

22 Cortright and Lopez have been particularly active analysts. See Cortright, David and Lopez, George (eds.), *Economic Sanctions: Panacea or Peacebuilding in a Post-Cold War World* (Boulder: Westview Press, 1995); Cortright, David and Lopez, George A., *The Sanctions Decade: Assessing UN Strategies in the 1990s* (Boulder: Lynne Rienner, 2000); Cortright, David and Lopez, George A. (eds.), *Smart Sanctions: Targeting Economic Statecraft* (Lanham: Rowman & Littlefield, 2002); Cortright, David and Lopez, George A., *Sanctions and the Search for Security: Challenges to UN Action* (Boulder: Lynne Rienner, 2002).

23 The Interlaken process sought to hone the tool of targeted financial sanctions. See *Targeted Financial Sanctions: A Manual for Design and Implementation. Contributions from the Interlaken Process* (Providence, RI: Watson Institute for International Studies, 2001).

24 The Bonn-Berlin process focused upon the design and implementation of arms embargoes and travel and aviation sanctions. See: *Design and Implementation of Arms Embargo and Travel Sanctions and Aviation-related Sanctions: Results of the Bonn-Berlin Process* (Bonn: Bonn International Center for Conversion, 2001).

25 The Stockholm process focused upon the question of making targeted sanctions effective. See *Making Targeted Sanctions Effective: Guidelines for the Implementation of UN Policy Options. Results from the Stockholm Process on the Implementation of Targeted Sanctions* (Uppsala: Uppsala University, 2003).

groups who represent a threat to international peace and security, rather than indiscriminately imposing them against collective populations as a whole. The Security Council's sanctions weapons of choice against such individuals and groups have been assets freezes[26] and travel bans.[27] Even when the Council has applied sanctions against nations, it has avoided comprehensive sanctions. Instead, it has employed arms embargoes and sanctions against natural resources such as diamonds and timber, whose illegal trade has fuelled conflict. In some cases, such as Afghanistan and Liberia, the Security Council has also sought assessments of the humanitarian impact of its sanctions.[28]

Yet despite these genuine improvements in sanctions policy, there is still considerable room for improvement. First, the Security Council's considerable discretion under Chapter VII has promoted an opaque approach to identifying the basis of a threat to the peace, breach of the peace or act of aggression.[29] Second, the Council often applies sanctions with vague goals, failing to articulate concrete objectives tied to specific conditions, the occurrence of which will result in termination.[30] Third, the Council's creation, oversight of and responsiveness to subsidiary sanctions bodies has also been haphazard to date. Sometimes the Council has created a sanctions committee at the same time it has imposed sanctions,[31] sometimes it has delayed before creating such a committee,[32] and sometimes it has created no committee at all.[33] Finally, although there has been an effort to improve the tailoring of sanctions

26 The Council has applied an assets freeze against individuals as part of the Iraq, UNITA, Taliban and Al-Qaeda, DRC, 1521 Liberia, 1556 Sudan, Côte d'Ivoire, Hariri Commission, North Korea, and Iran sanctions regimes.

27 Travel restrictions have been applied against individuals as part of the Iraq, Libya, Bosnian Serb, Haiti, UNITA, 1054 Sudan, Sierra Leone, Taliban and Al-Qaeda, 1343 Liberia, DRC, 1521 Liberia, 1556 Sudan, Côte d'Ivoire, Hariri Commission, North Korea, and Iran sanctions regimes.

28 For Afghanistan, see SC Res. 1267 (October 15, 1999), para. 6(c). For Liberia, see SC Res. 1343 (March 7, 2001), para. 14(g); SC Res. 1478 (May 6, 2003), para. 25(c).

29 Farrall, *United Nations Sanctions and the Rule of Law*, pp. 190–195.

30 *Ibid.*, pp. 196–202.

31 This was the case with the 661 (Iraq), 748 (Libya), 841 (Haiti), 864 (UNITA), 918 (Rwanda), 1132 (Sierra Leone), 1160 (FRY), 1267 (Afghanistan/Taliban/Al-Qaeda), 1298 (Eritrea and Ethiopia), 1343 (Liberia), 1521 (Liberia), 1572 (Côte d'Ivoire), 1636 (Hariri), 1718 (North Korea) and 1737 (Iran) Committees.

32 This was the case with the 253 (Southern Rhodesia), 421 (South Africa), 724 (Yugoslavia), 751 (Somalia), 985 (Liberia), 1518 (Iraq), 1533 (DRC) and 1591 (Sudan) Committees.

33 SC Res. 1054 created a sanctions regime in Sudan. No sub-committee was ever created to monitor that sanctions regime. For more on sanctions oversight and monitoring, see Farrall, *United Nations Sanctions and the Rule of Law*, pp. 163–180.

regimes, even targeted sanctions cannot escape charges of collateral human rights damage, as their application and administration can undermine the rights to property, due process and a fair trial.[34] Sanctions have also been criticized for their unintended impact upon the economies of third states. The Council has not taken genuine steps to fulfill the promise of Article 50 of the UN Charter,[35] despite symbolic recommendations concerning action that might be taken to mitigate the effect of comprehensive sanctions regimes upon the economies of third states.[36]

From the High-Level Panel to the World Summit Outcome

Most of the recommendations for reform outlined in the HLP report followed a similar trajectory. Starting as bold proposals for ambitious new doctrine, they were broadly endorsed by the Secretary-General in *In Larger Freedom*, before being heavily diluted, and in some cases unceremoniously discarded, by UN member states in the *World Summit Outcome*. In the case of sanctions, however, the progression followed a somewhat different trajectory. The HLP report outlined quite detailed sanctions recommendations, which were reduced and distilled by the Secretary-General into more concise proposals in *In Larger Freedom*. UN member states then expanded upon the Secretary-General's proposals, bringing the end-result close to, and in some ways even exceeding, the ambitions of the HLP's original recommendations. This section traces the evolution of sanctions reform proposals from the HLP report to the *World Summit Outcome*, highlighting key moments in their development and detailing exactly what criticisms the reforms sought to address.

34 See Iain Cameron, "UN Targeted Sanctions, Legal Safeguards and the European Convention on Human Rights," *Nordic Journal of International Law* 72 (2003), pp. 159–214; *Strengthening Targeted Sanctions Through Fair and Clear Procedures* (Providence, RI: Watson Institute Targeted Sanctions Project, 2006).

35 Article 50 provides: "If preventive or enforcement measures against any state are taken by the Security Council, any other state … which finds itself confronted by special economic problems arising from the carrying out of those measures shall have the right to consult the Security Council with regard to a solution of those problems."

36 The Council has made recommendations concerning potential action that could be taken by states and international organizations to mitigate the economic effect upon third states of the Iraq and FRYSM sanctions regimes. See Farrall, *United Nations Sanctions and the Rule of Law*, pp. 144–145.

Sanctions and the HLP Report

The HLP report stressed the critical importance of sanctions and suggested reforms designed to improve their effectiveness and enforcement.[37] It noted that sanctions were a "vital though imperfect tool" for dealing with threats to the peace.[38] Sanctions constituted a "necessary middle ground between war and words" when nations, individuals, and rebel groups violate international norms.[39] They were a useful instrument for putting pressure on leaders and elites with minimal humanitarian consequences. Moreover, they could both serve "an important symbolic purpose" and be "a powerful means of deterrence."[40]

The report's substantive suggestions were directed at the Security Council, sanctions committees, the Secretary-General, and donors. The Panel proposed that the Security Council should: (a) regularly establish monitoring mechanisms for every new sanctions regime and grant them the necessary authority, capacity, and resources to carry out high-quality, in-depth investigations;[41] (b) impose secondary sanctions in instances of verified, chronic sanctions-busting;[42] and (c) attempt to mitigate humanitarian consequences of sanctions.[43]

Sanctions committees, for their part, should: (a) be required to improve state reporting guidelines to ensure more effective sanctions implementation;[44] (b) improve procedures for maintaining accurate lists of the intended targets of sanctions;[45] (c) routinely assess the humanitarian impact of sanctions, with improved protocols for granting exemptions for humanitarian reasons;[46] and (d) establish review procedures for those claiming to have been incorrectly placed or maintained on sanctions target lists.[47]

The Secretary-General, for his or her part, should: (a) appoint a senior official to conduct analysis on how to most effectively target sanctions and coordinate their implementation;[48] and (b) ensure auditing of sanctions administration.[49] Finally, donors should devote more resources to strengthening the legal, administrative, and monitoring capacities of member states to more effectively implement sanctions.[50]

[37] High-Level Panel, paras. 180–182. [38] *Ibid.*, para. 178. [39] *Ibid.*
[40] *Ibid.* [41] *Ibid.*, para. 180(a). [42] *Ibid.*, para. 180(e). [43] *Ibid.*, para. 181.
[44] *Ibid.*, para. 180(b). [45] *Ibid.*, para. 180(b). [46] *Ibid.*, para. 181. [47] *Ibid.*, para. 182.
[48] *Ibid.*, para. 180(c). [49] *Ibid.*, para. 180(f). [50] *Ibid.*, para. 180(d).

Sanctions and In Larger Freedom

The Secretary-General's references to sanctions were shorter and his recommendations less detailed than those of the HLP. He repeated the HLP's view that sanctions were a vital tool for dealing with threats to the peace and constituted "a necessary ground between war and words."[51] He predicted that the use of sanctions, particularly to target "individuals responsible for reprehensible policies," would continue to be a vital tool in the United Nations' arsenal.[52] He then drew selectively upon the HLP's recommendations, proposing that, in order to ensure effective implementation, state capacity to implement sanctions should be strengthened. He focused on sanctions regimes, arguing they needed to be better structured and better monitored by well-resourced mechanisms, in order to protect their integrity and that of the institutions that oversee them, as well as to minimize the suffering caused to third parties, such as the civilian populations of targeted states.[53]

Sanctions and the World Summit Outcome

In the *World Summit Outcome*, UN member states outlined a number of general observations about sanctions, before articulating some basic recommendations. In the general observations, states underscored that "sanctions remain an important tool … to maintain international peace and security."[54] They expressed support for "efforts through the United Nations to strengthen state capacity to implement sanctions provisions."[55] Specifically, they resolved to ensure sanctions were carefully crafted and narrowly tailored to fulfill well-outlined objectives, and implemented in a way that balanced effectiveness against any negative socio-economic and humanitarian impact on innocent populations and third states.[56]

They also called upon the Security Council, with the assistance of the Secretary-General, to improve monitoring and accountability, and to develop mechanisms to address special economic problems arising from the application of sanctions.[57] Specifically, they suggested that the Security Council work to ensure that the procedure for placing individuals and entities on sanctions lists was equitable and transparent, with equally clear guidelines for removing individuals and entities, as well as

[51] *In Larger Freedom*, para. 109. [52] *Ibid.*, para. 110.
[53] *Ibid.*, para. 110; Annex, para. 6(k). [54] *World Summit Outcome*, para. 106.
[55] *Ibid.*, para. 110. [56] *Ibid.*, para. 106. [57] *Ibid.*, para. 108.

for granting humanitarian exemptions.[58] They also observed that sanctions regimes should only be kept in place as long as is absolutely necessary to achieve their objectives.[59]

A fairly even scorecard: the integrity of sanctions reform proposals from the HLP Report to the *World Summit Outcome*

In rhetorical and descriptive terms, the tempering effect of UN deliberation on the HLP's proposals is clear. In the early phases, both the HLP and the Secretary-General described sanctions as a "vital tool" for addressing threats to the peace and a "necessary middle ground between war and words."[60] By contrast, the *World Summit Outcome* is more restrained, describing sanctions simply as an "important tool" to maintain international peace and security.[61]

In substantive terms, it is true that certain HLP suggestions were adulterated or simply abandoned throughout the process. For example, its recommendation that secondary sanctions should be applied to chronic sanctions-busters[62] was not taken up by either the Secretary-General or UN member states. However, the *World Summit Outcome* did take up a number of the HLP's proposals, at least in broad terms. In the *World Summit Outcome*, member states agreed to the general principle, if not the precise detail, of the HLP and Secretary-General's recommendations that sanctions monitoring should be improved.[63] UN member states also resolved to implement sanctions in a manner sensitive to adverse socio-economic and humanitarian consequences.[64] They supported efforts through the United Nations to strengthen state capacity to implement sanctions.[65] They also followed the lead of both the HLP and the Secretary General, calling upon the Security Council to improve due process in sanctions administration by ensuring that clear, fair procedures existed for placing individuals and entities on and removing them from sanctions lists.[66]

In some areas the *World Summit Outcome* took even greater initiative than the HLP or the Secretary-General on sanctions reform. For instance, member states resolved: to ensure that sanctions were carefully

[58] *Ibid.*, para. 109. [59] *Ibid.*, para. 107.
[60] High-Level Panel, para. 178; *In Larger Freedom*, para. 109.
[61] *World Summit Outcome*, para. 106. [62] High-Level Panel, para. 180(e).
[63] *World Summit Outcome*, para. 108. [64] *Ibid.*, para. 106. [65] *Ibid.*, para. 110.
[66] *Ibid.*, paras. 108, 109.

targeted in support of clear objectives; to take care that sanctions had clear benchmarks; and to ensure sanctions were regularly reviewed and then terminated once objectives are achieved.[67] The *World Summit Outcome* also went further than the HLP report or *In Larger Freedom* in emphasizing the need to mitigate the adverse impact of sanctions upon third states.[68]

The *World Summit Outcome* and sanctions reform: could more have been proposed?

Although the bold spirit of the HLP's recommendations for serious reforms is embodied in the *World Summit Outcome*, neither the HLP's recommendations nor those of the *World Summit Outcome* reflected the full range of sanctions shortcomings and policy reform possibilities. The Security Council's sanctions practice still exhibits substantial shortcomings, particularly with respect to five basic principles of the rule of law – transparency, consistency, equality, due process, and proportionality.[69]

In terms of transparency, both the Security Council and its sanctions committees make their key sanctions decisions behind closed doors, and too often both the objectives of sanctions as well as the conditions that will lead to their termination are unnecessarily vague. As to consistency, the Council employs remarkably different approaches to different sanctions regimes. Its practice with respect to subsidiary bodies, such as sanctions committees and monitoring bodies, is bewilderingly varied. The principle of equality is undermined by the ability of some states to avoid sanctions when pursuing policies which, in other, practically identical circumstances, have triggered the application of sanctions. For example, sanctions were applied against North Korea and Iran to address nuclear proliferation, but not against India, Israel, or Pakistan. The principle of due process is violated by the invocation of sanctions against individuals not accorded the presumption of innocence until proven guilty. The problem is further compounded by the fact that individuals targeted by sanctions are not entitled to contest their blacklisting directly. Once inscribed on an assets freeze or travel ban list, those individuals must rely on their home state to take up their cause and petition both the state responsible for adding their citizen's name to the

[67] *Ibid.*, para. 107. [68] *Ibid.*, para. 108.

[69] For further analysis of the UN sanctions system from a rule of law perspective, see Farrall, *United Nations Sanctions and the Rule of Law*, especially chs. 2, 10, and 11.

list, as well as all other states on the relevant sanctions committee, to remove the individual from the list. Until all sanctions committee members agree that the individual should be removed, the individual remains on the list. This effectively accords the power of veto over this decision to all fifteen members of the sanctions committee. As for proportionality, both general and targeted economic sanctions continue to have a disproportionate effect upon innocent civilian populations and third state economies.

The *World Summit Outcome* identified some useful policy reform options to address some of these concerns, but some of these options raised as many new issues as they resolved. For example, it called for the Security Council both to improve its monitoring of the effectiveness of sanctions in achieving certain benchmarks as rapidly as possible, and to focus on mitigating special economic problems that arise from sanctions implementation.[70] However, it gave no specific recommendations for any permanent sanctions monitoring bodies. Presently, the Security Council establishes ad hoc committees, as it deems appropriate, to monitor sanctions regimes. If routine sanctions monitoring and humanitarian impact assessment are desirable, is the best way to achieve them to create new ad hoc monitoring mechanisms and to require fresh ad hoc humanitarian impact assessment capacity for each sanctions regime? Furthermore, given the checkered track record of sanctions committees in ensuring the protection of due process, and given the competing interests between making sanctions as effective as possible and avoiding unintended harm, are such committees the appropriate bodies both to monitor sanctions effectiveness and to conduct humanitarian impact assessments? Might there not be some virtue in abolishing ad hoc committees in favor of two newly created permanent bodies: a general established sanctions monitoring mechanism, which could build institutional knowledge and best practice to be applied uniformly to all the Council's many sanctions regimes; and a separate body to act as a balance, by conducting humanitarian impact assessments?

Several key areas of sanctions implementation in need of reform were not addressed at all by the process of deliberation from the HLP to the *World Summit Outcome*.[71] The transparency deficit in sanctions decision making in the Security Council and its sanctions committees was not

70 *World Summit Outcome*, paras. 107–108.

71 For my own sanctions reform policy recommendations, see Farrall, *United Nations Sanctions and the Rule of Law*, pp. 244–246.

seriously taken up. The obvious solution to the due process deficit, which would be to enable individuals to challenge their black-listing directly, was not proposed. There was no consideration of the potential of the unprincipled exercise of the veto power to undermine the credibility of UN sanctions, nor were potential strategies to mitigate the exercise of the veto canvassed. In that regard, one possibility might be a revival of the long-neglected P5 pact to exercise veto restraint, as originally articulated during the San Francisco conference in 1945.[72] Another might be a pact among E10 members to exercise their own effective veto to ensure that key components of sanctions reform, such as better targeting, setting clear objectives, and establishing time limits, are included in draft Security Council sanctions resolutions, no matter how difficult to enforce as a matter of *Realpolitik*.[73]

Looking to the future: treacherous normative waters

Above and beyond the question of whether the opportunity for reform created during the HLP to *World Summit Outcome* process was fully exploited, lies the more basic question of whether the process in fact represented an opportunity at all. The key barrier to meaningful sanctions reform has always been structural: the veto power of the permanent members of the Security Council. The veto remains one of the "rocks" upon which the United Nations was built, but it is also a rock upon which adventurous international normative explorations are destined to founder.[74] For the permanent members of the Security Council can veto any attempt to create normative limits upon the exercise of its Chapter VII powers. While the Security Council's sanctions practice has evolved considerably since the days of the Iraq sanctions regime, there is no normative structural barrier to prevent the Council from acting as it wishes. Historically, the Security Council has been extremely wary of attempts to promote normative principles that would tie its hands. Even in the realm of process, the Council has only been able to agree upon "provisional" rules of procedure.[75] The Council

[72] *Documents of the United Nations Conference on International Organization* (New York: UN Information Organization, 1945), vol. XI, 710–714. See in particular para. 8: *Statement by the Delegations of the four Sponsoring Governments on Voting Procedure in the Security Council.*

[73] See José E. Alvarez, *International Organizations as Law-makers* (Oxford: Oxford University Press, 2005), p. 199.

[74] Herbert V. Evatt, *The Task of the United Nations* (New York: Duell, Sloan, and Pearce, 1949), pp. 47–48.

[75] S/96/Rev.7, *Provisional Rules of Procedure of the Security Council* (December 1982).

is, therefore, unlikely to countenance formal normative steps that would restrict its substantive discretion to apply sanctions as and how it sees fit.

The *World Summit Outcome* demonstrates a widespread willingness among UN member states to acknowledge some of the past and present shortcomings in sanctions practice. But the articulation of general aspirations can do little to prevent the Security Council from acting as it sees fit when faced with intense political pressure to take immediate action to prevent or resolve a threat to international peace and security. In these high-stress situations the niceties of the principles outlined in the World Summit will not prevent the Council from falling into old patterns of action or from following worst rather than best practices, for the sake of expediency.

Despite this bleak normative landscape, international legal scholars have begun to explore whether and how the Council's almost unfettered power to take Chapter VII actions, such as instituting sanctions, might be regulated. These explorations tend to follow a two-step approach. The first step involves identifying the legal parameters within which Security Council action is legally permissible.[76] Sources for these parameters include the UN Charter itself, as well as extra-Charter principles of general international law. The second involves finding a mechanism to guarantee that the Council does not act in ways that exceed the legal boundaries of its authority – the favored mechanism being judicial review by such judicial bodies as the International Court of Justice (ICJ) and international tribunals established by the Security Council.[77]

[76] See, e.g., David Schweigman, *The Authority of the Security Council under* Chapter VII *of the UN Charter – Legal Limits and the Role of the International Court of Justice* (The Hague: Kluwer Law International, 2001); Erica de Wet, *The* Chapter VII *Powers of the United Nations Security Council* (Oxford: Hart Publishing, 2004); Alexander Orakhelashvili, "The Impact of Peremptory Norms on the Interpretation and Application of United Nations Security Council Resolutions," *European Journal of International Law* 16 (2005), pp. 59–88; Alexander Orakhelashvili, *Peremptory Norms in International Law* (Oxford: Oxford University Press, 2006).

[77] Bernd Martenczuk, "The Security Council, the International Court of Justice and Judicial Review: What Lessons from Lockerbie?," *European Journal of International Law* 10 (1999), pp. 517–547; Erika de Wet, "Judicial Review as an Emerging General Principle of Law and Its Implications for the International Court of Justice," *Netherlands International Law Review* 47 (2000), pp. 181–210; John Dugard, "Judicial Review of Sanctions" in Vera Gowlland-Debbas (ed.), *United Nations Sanctions and International Law* (The Hague: Kluwer Law International, 2001), pp. 83–91; Schweigman, *The Authority of the Security Council*; De Wet, *Chapter VII Powers*; Ioana Petculescu, "The Review of the United Nations Security Council Decisions by the International Court of Justice," *Netherlands International Law Review* 52 (2005), pp. 167–195.

Individual judges of the ICJ have, in deliberating on various cases before them, expressed the view that the Council's powers are limited.[78] The Court as a whole, in the ICJ advisory opinion on *Certain Expenses of the UN*, concluded that when the Security Council's actions were necessary for the maintenance of international peace and security, the presumption should be that it was not acting *ultra vires*,[79] and the International Criminal Tribunal for the former Yugoslavia, for its part, has found that the Council's powers under the Charter do not amount to an unlimited fiat.[80] However, none of the aforementioned bodies have had cause to explore the details of potential restrictions upon the Council's powers. Furthermore, even if the limits of Security Council power could be delineated, the ICJ has no true mechanism for binding judicial review.

The Article 96 procedure for advisory opinions approximates judicial review in some respects, but it is subject to severe constraints. First, only the General Assembly or the Security Council may request an opinion. Second, any opinions rendered are not binding in point of law and may be disregarded in point of fact.[81] When put in the context of reviewing sanctions policy, the power seems hollow, for how likely is the Security Council to request a review of its own sanctions decision making? The General Assembly might request such a review, but no mechanism exists for enforcing the Security Council's compliance with any advisory opinion rendered.[82]

Theoretically the ICJ's contentious jurisdiction offers a second manner in which the ICJ could review the sanctions policies of the Security Council. Under Article 34 of the ICJ Statute, which only allows states to be parties in such proceedings, the issue of the legality of a Security Council action could be presented as a preliminary or incidental question to some dispute between states.[83] Experience shows, however, that this is

[78] *Questions of Interpretation and Application of the 1971 Montreal Convention Arising from the Aerial Incident at Lockerbie* (*Libya* v. *UK*; *Libya* v. *US*), Provisional Measures (Orders of April 14, 1992), *ICJ Reports* (1992), 32 (Judge Shahabuddeen, separate opinion), 65 (Judge Weeramantry, dissenting opinion).

[79] *Certain Expenses of the United Nations (Article 17, Paragraph 2, of the Charter)* (Advisory Opinion of July 20, 1962), *ICJ Reports* 151(1962), p. 168.

[80] See, e.g., *Prosecutor* v. *Dusko Tadić aka "Dule,"* Case No. IT-94-1-AR72 (October 2, 1995), para. 28.

[81] Francesco Francioni, "Multilateralism à la Carte: The Limits of Unilateral Withholdings of Assessed Contributions to the UN Budget," *EJIL* 11 (2000), pp. 56–57.

[82] *Ibid.* [83] *Ibid.*

a path the Court has been hesitant to travel. In the Case concerning the *Application of the Convention of the Prevention and Punishment of the Crime of Genocide*, brought by Bosnia-Herzegovina against Yugoslavia, Bosnia argued that one of the necessary issues to resolve involved the compatibility of the Security Council's arms embargo with Bosnia's right of self-defense under Article 51 of the UN charter and under customary international law. The Court carefully avoided the issue, and did not grant the interim measures requested.[84]

Ultimately, there is no existing or emerging mechanism to force sanctions reform upon the Security Council, and attempts to coerce the Council into employing particular sanctions policies via the elaboration of norms designed to bring about external regulation of the Council's sanctions activities, such as independent judicial review, are unlikely to work. Because a policy shift cannot be extrinsically forced upon the Council, the challenge is to promote self-regulation from within the Council itself. Perhaps this could be done by framing the issue of sanctions reform as one through which the Security Council stands to have its power augmented rather than undermined.

Governments, non-governmental actors, policy makers, and others committed to improving sanctions policy should endeavor to illustrate to the Security Council that by taking a relatively small number of steps, including but not limited to those proposed by the HLP and the *World Summit Outcome*, the Security Council's sanctions powers would be made more effective, and thus augmented. Such an argument should not be too difficult to make, for when the Security Council applies sanctions, it relies upon the good faith and diligence of UN member states to take the necessary steps to implement them. A sanctions system which undermines human rights and the rule of law inherently cannot attract the kind of compliance and adherence that a regime that enjoys the confidence and cooperation of member states can.

84 *Ibid.*

10

The UN response to the evolving threat of global terrorism: institutional reform, rivalry, or renewal?

ERIC ROSAND[1]

Introduction

The use of terrorism as a tactic is not new, having been used for centuries by both states and non-state actors to further political ends.[2] What is new, however, is the dramatic increase in the number of terrorist attacks around the globe by stateless international terrorist groups, including Islamist terrorist groups such as Al-Qaeda and like-minded groups. While it may be tempting to explain away this increase by attributing it to partisan attacks in Afghanistan and Iraq, research has shown the phenomenon is truly global. There has been a 35 percent increase in the number of reported Islamist terrorist attacks outside those two countries with a 12 percent rise in fatalities related to those attacks.[3] With this upsurge in international terrorist violence, even the most economically and militarily powerful of countries now recognize that no single state or group of states can effectively fight this threat alone. As recognized by the Secretary-General's High-Level Panel on Threats, Challenges and Change (HLP):

> In today's world, a threat to one is a threat to all. Globalization means that a major terrorist attack anywhere in the industrial world would have devastating consequences for the well-being of millions in the developing

1 The author would like to thank Jason Ipe, Senior Analyst at the Center on Global Counter-Terrorism Cooperation, New York, for his helpful comments on an earlier version of this chapter.

2 For a discussion of the history of the terrorist phenomenon, see, e.g., Ben Saul, *Defining Terrorism in International Law* (Oxford: Oxford University Press, 2006), pp. 1–10 and Louise Richardson, *What Terrorists Want: Understanding the Enemy and Containing the Threat* (New York: Random House, 2006), pp. 3–38.

3 Peter Bergen and Paul Cruickshank, "The Iraq Effect: War Has Increased Terrorism Sevenfold Worldwide," *Mother Jones*, March 1, 2007, available at www.motherjones.com/news/featurex/2007/03/iraq_effect_1.html (accessed May 22, 2008).

> world … The erosion of State capacity anywhere in the world weakens the protection of every State against transnational threats such as terrorism … Every State requires international cooperation to make it secure.[4]

Worldwide cooperation thus becomes essential to ensure not only that all states have the necessary capacity to confront and prevent terrorism, but also the cross-border cooperation necessary to track funding, disrupt planning, prevent recruitment and stop future attacks as well as to investigate, capture, and prosecute terrorists and their supporters should preventative efforts fail.

The primary response to international terrorism has come from national governments, which carry primary responsibility for protecting their citizens. However, formal multilateral bodies and frameworks, and informal multilateral arrangements and programs at the international and regional levels do, when structured properly, make a substantial contribution as well. In fact, many successes in the campaign against terrorism have, to a large degree, been the result of cooperation and mutual support among governments around the world.[5]

In recent years, the traditional tendency to treat threats from non-state terrorist groups as a domestic concern has given way to an increasing focus on international and multilateral responses.[6] Nationalist or separatist terrorist groups such as the Kurdistan Peoples Party (PKK) in Turkey, the Tamil Tigers (LTTE) in Sri Lanka, or the Revolutionary Armed Forces of Colombia (FARC) generated only limited responses at the multilateral level. The emergence of transnational terrorism in the 1970s led to a spate of international law making to facilitate interstate cooperation in response to hijacking, hostage taking and other forms of terrorism. But only with the emergence of Al-Qaeda, with its extraordinary global reach, has the transnational threat posed by these non-state actors moved to the top of the agenda of international fora such as the United Nations (UN). More precisely, the terrorist attacks on the US on September 11, 2001 transformed the debate about international

[4] A/59/565 Report of the United Nations Secretary-General's High-Level Panel on Threats, Challenges and Change, *A More Secure World: Our Shared Responsibility* (New York: United Nations, 2004), executive summary, p. 1.

[5] William P. Pope, "European Cooperation with the United States in the Global War on Terrorism," remarks to the House International Relations Committee, Subcommittee on Europe and on International Terrorism, Non-proliferation and Human Rights, Washington, D.C., September 14, 2004.

[6] For the purposes of this chapter, "terrorism" is broadly defined as deliberate violence by non-state actors against civilians and other non-combatants for political purposes.

responses to terrorism. With global terrorism now at the top of its agenda, the US sought to ensure that it became a matter of central concern in multilateral institutions, particularly the UN.

The UN's efforts to formulate an effective response to the attacks of September 2001 and subsequent acts of terrorism perpetrated by Islamist and other non-state terrorist groups have been complicated by built-in limitations in the organization's design. As the HLP rightly points out, such global terrorist threats did not exist when the UN was founded and its charter was adopted more than sixty years ago.[7] Additionally, the UN system was designed in an era when the greatest threats to international peace and security emanated from states and not non-state actors, and when the state largely had a monopoly over the use of violence.

As stated by the G8 leaders at their 2007 summit in Germany, in offering support for the central role of the UN in global counter-terrorism efforts, "the UN is the sole organization with the stature and reach to achieve universal agreement on the condemnation of terrorism and to effectively address key aspects of the terrorist threat in a comprehensive manner."[8] Few would contest the notion that the UN can play a distinctive role in managing the threats posed by contemporary terrorism, because its global membership offers a unique basis for normative legitimacy and effective action. In contemplating the importance of the UN in monitoring and combating international terrorism, Anthony Cordesman of the Center for International Strategic Studies has gone so far as to conclude that "institutions like the UN … are the *only way* to cut across the fault lines that divide the world."[9]

Yet, the UN has been struggling with how to formulate an effective response to terrorism since well before 9/11, largely because of different perceptions among member states of what type and severity of threat terrorism presents. Many countries from the global South view the post-9/11 focus on terrorism as both a Western-imposed priority and as competition for resources they would rather see devoted to priorities such as poverty reduction, economic development, and combating organized crime.

On the one hand, the UN has used its norm-setting authority to provide a solid international legal framework for combating terrorism.

[7] High-Level Panel, Executive Summary, p. 1.

[8] *G8 Summit Statement on Counter Terrorism – Security in the Era of Globalization* Heiligendamm, Germany, June 8, 2007. Available online at: www.g-8.de/nsc_true/Content/EN/Artikel/__g8-summit/anlagen/ct-statement-final,templateId=raw,property=publicationFile.pdf/ct-statement-final (accessed August 10, 2007).

[9] Anthony Cordesman, "The Lessons of International Co-operation in Counter-Terrorism," *RUSI Journal* 151 (February 2006), p. 49.

The General Assembly and various UN agencies have adopted sixteen terrorism-related treaties, the Security Council has adopted a number of legally binding resolutions, and the UN Office of Drugs and Crime's Terrorism Prevention Branch has assisted scores of states with the drafting of domestic legislation necessary to implement them. Additionally, the UN's technical agencies such as the International Civil Aviation Organization (ICAO), World Customs Organization (WCO), and International Maritime Organization (IMO) have established counter-terrorism-related best practices or standards in their particular field.

On the other hand, the UN has been unable to reach agreement on a definition of terrorism that outlaws all indiscriminate attacks against civilians. Although scores of terrorist attacks are committed by a wide range of non-state actors, Al-Qaeda remains the only terrorist group the Security Council has explicitly declared a threat to international peace and security.[10]

According to international law expert, Ben Saul, "there are no clean lines between terrorism and other forms of political violence, and the debate about defining terrorism is also a debate about the classification of political violence in all its myriad forms: riot, revolt, rebellion, war, conflict, uprising revolution, subversion, intervention, guerilla warfare, and so on."[11] The lines become further blurred in a debate among 192 countries, many of whose ruling governments used political violence to overthrow dictatorships and other repressive regimes. Given these complexities in settling on a concrete definition, as well as the lack of consensus regarding the target of the UN counter-terrorism legal framework, and the divergent priorities among the global North and South, it is not surprising that many states have not been able to muster the political will to take the steps necessary to fully implement this framework.

A further feature of the UN's counter-terrorism efforts has been its reactive nature, adopting declarations, resolutions, or treaties or establishing committees or programs in response to individual attacks, instead of developing a coherent and coordinated response to the overall effort. Tensions among the three principal UN organs (General Assembly, Security Council, and Secretariat) that see (or do not see) themselves as having a key role to play in this area have also exacerbated the problem.

Few would dispute the HLP's broad conclusion that non-state terrorism is a threat to collective security. However, identifying the threat and designing an effective response in an organization with 192 member

[10] See, e.g., United Nations Security Council Resolution S/RES/1617, July 30, 2006.
[11] Saul, *Defining Terrorism in International Law* p. 5.

states and a wide range of member state bodies of different shapes and sizes are two very different tasks. In practice, the UN's attempts to address non-state terrorism have been redundant, ineffective, and sometimes counterproductive. This highlights the complexities of constructing a collective security regime that is able to take into account divergent perceptions of the threat and different views as to the appropriate target of such a regime. Unfortunately, the HLP failed to take these factors, which have plagued the UN's terror response, fully into account in its report.

Under the UN's current piecemeal approach, more than twenty different parts of the UN system currently deal with terrorism in one form or another. The Security Council's approach is particularly convoluted. Its hydra-headed counter-terrorism program, consisting of three committees, each with its own group of experts to support its work, has so far dominated much of the UN's post-9/11 response. The US, riding the wave of global sympathy that followed 9/11, pushed the Security Council to take control of the UN agenda, and faced little resistance. Many skeptics worry that with the United States at the helm of the Security Council, its attention is over-focused on the threat posed by Islamist terrorism and that, as a result, the Council's broader security agenda is being neglected.

After five years of a fragmented and ineffective Security Council-led UN response, seen by many as not representative enough and too narrowly focused on security-related and other preventative measures,[12] the wider membership of the General Assembly made its dissatisfaction known by adopting a first-ever UN Global Counter-Terrorism Strategy in September 2006. The Strategy also represents a response to the HLP's call for the UN "to develop a global strategy of fighting terrorism that addresses root causes and strengthens responsible states and the rule of law and fundamental human rights … [a]nd that incorporates but is broader than coercive measures."[13] Although it quite conspicuously avoided trying to define terrorism, the UN Strategy may have nevertheless forged the consensus and provided the normative framework necessary to allow for the creation of a more effective UN collective security regime that can address the full spectrum of terrorist threats, including that posed by non-state actors.

[12] For a critical overview of the UN's counter-terrorism efforts, see, e.g., Edward C. Luck, "Uninvited Challenge: Terrorism Targets the United Nations," in Edward Newman and Ramesh Thakur (eds.), *Multilateralism Under Challenge: Power, International Order and Structural Change* (Tokyo: United Nations University and the Social Science Research Council, 2006), pp. 336–355.

[13] High-Level Panel, para. 148.

After providing an overview of the Council's counter-terrorism initiatives, with a particular emphasis on its most far-reaching response to 9/11 – the adoption of Resolution 1373 and the Council's Counter-Terrorism Committee (CTC) – this chapter identifies some of the shortcomings in the overall Council effort. The second section provides a detailed account of the UN Secretariat's reaction to 9/11, tracing its evolution from initial ambivalence to active engagement during the last two years of Secretary-General Kofi Annan's tenure. The third section discusses the emergence of the General Assembly on the already crowded UN counter-terrorism playing field and how its adoption of the UN Strategy in September 2006 may signal a shift away from the Security Council as the central player. This chapter concludes by arguing for a broad-based UN-led response to terrorism, and by urging the Security Council to consider where its comparative advantage in the fight against terrorism lies.

It is the need for the above-mentioned broad-based response at both the normative and institutional levels which underlies much of the HLP's analysis. Yet this will be difficult to achieve so long as the Security Council, with its various committees and expert groups, continues to be the leading institutional actor within the UN. The chapter thus calls for the UN global counter-terrorism framework encapsulated in the UN Strategy to be implemented and assisted by a new UN counter-terrorism body that can provide the kind of institutional support necessary to make the UN a truly effective collective security regime. Even with this broader-based structure, the effectiveness of the overall UN effort may be undercut by its continuing inability to agree on a definition of terrorism (or, more precisely, the scope of its application), which, correctly stated by the HLP, "prevents the United Nations from exerting its moral authority and from sending an unequivocal message that terrorism is never an acceptable tactic, even for the most defensible of causes."[14]

The Security Council's post 9/11 response

The emergence of the Security Council as a central figure on the counter-terrorism playing field following September 2001 was a relatively new phenomenon. Like the rest of the UN, it had been reluctant to address international terrorism prior to the events of September 2001. During the Cold War, the prevailing attitude among states was that terrorism was largely a national problem and thus generally did not constitute the

[14] *Ibid.*, para. 157.

threat to *international* peace and security required for the Council to be seized with the issue under the UN Charter. In fact, previously the Council seemed to attach greater concern to the response of certain countries to terrorism than to the terrorist acts themselves. This attitude changed after decolonization and the end of the Cold War, when terrorism was no longer seen as a legitimate tool in the fight for self-determination or other political struggles.

The conclusion of the Cold War ended paralysis in Security Council decision making, allowing it to respond forcefully to the new brand of international terrorism that ignored national borders. In the 1990s the Council adopted Chapter VII resolutions imposing sanctions against Libya, Sudan, and Afghanistan for their alleged support of discrete acts of terrorism, such as the bombing of Pan Am flight no. 103 and the bombings of the US embassies in Kenya and Tanzania. These actions, robust as they may have seemed at the time, paled in comparison to the Council's post-9/11 response. The response in the years following 9/11 has centered on the Council's use of norm setting and institution building. Although generally carried out in an ad hoc manner and in reaction to particular terrorist attacks, the Council's approach has resulted in a broad, global legal counter-terrorism framework and the creation of a series of institutions to work with states and other stakeholders to implement that framework effectively.

Initial post-9/11 response: Resolutions 1368, 1373, and 1377 and the creation of the Counter-Terrorism Committee

The Security Council acted swiftly and unanimously after September 11, 2001. The day after the collapse of the World Trade Center, visible from the windows of many UN delegates' offices, the Council adopted Resolution 1368, which declared international terrorism to be a threat to international peace and security, and, adopting much of the wording from article 51 of the UN Charter, affirmed that a state victimized by terrorism was justified in exercising the right of individual and collective self-defense in response.[15]

Some two weeks after the adoption of Resolution 1368, the Council took a novel and innovative step by passing Resolution 1373, which enumerated a detailed list of mandatory measures that all member states must undertake as part of a global counter-terrorism campaign.[16] Rather

[15] United Nations Security Council Resolution S/RES/1368 (2001), September 12, 2001.
[16] United Nations Security Council Resolution S/RES/1373 (2001), September 28, 2001.

than being able to target non-state actors directly, the Council must rely on the cooperation of states to implement its measures within their respective jurisdictions against the relevant individuals, entities and groups. The Council, rather than merely urging or demanding that states generally do more to fight terrorism, decided to adopt a series of detailed legal obligations for all states. As bold as the Resolution was, the Council chose not to define terrorism in order to avoid the divisive definitional debate that had bogged down the General Assembly for decades. Resolution 1373's sponsors wanted something that would pass quickly, with one commentator going so far as to say that the resolution "was possible *only because* member states did not have to tackle the issue of defining terrorism ... Many among those voting for the resolution did not see eye to eye with the United States on such a definition."[17] Thus, each state would be allowed to determine against which individuals, groups and entities the measures should be applied.

Resolution 1373 also established the Counter-Terrorism Committee (CTC), which was modeled on the country-specific sanctions committees that the Council had established over the years, charged with monitoring state implementation of the Resolution's various requirements. The Resolution also asked the Secretary-General to appoint independent consultants to support the CTC's work. However, because it did not define the terrorist targets against which states must apply legally binding measures, it has been exceedingly difficult for the CTC to put political pressure on any state to implement the requirements of Resolution 1373.

In November 2001, recognizing the difficulties that most states would have meeting the complex requirements of Resolution 1373, the Security Council passed Resolution 1377, extending the CTC's mandate to include the development of technical assistance programs and the facilitation of technical assistance to states and international, regional, and sub-regional organizations.[18]

Resolutions 1390 and 1735: the Council's Al-Qaeda/Taliban sanctions regime

In January 2002, the Council decided to broaden the financial, travel, and arms sanctions it had imposed on Taliban-controlled Afghanistan

[17] Shibley Telhami, "Conflicting Views of Terrorism," *Cornell International Law Journal* 584 (2002), p. 35.

[18] United Nations Security Council Resolution S/RES/1377 (2001), November 11, 2001.

following the terrorist attacks against the US Embassies in Nairobi and Dar es Salaam to address what had now morphed into a global threat, with Al-Qaeda at its center (Resolution 1390). As part of its response to 9/11, the Council required all states to impose these measures on the individuals and entities listed by the Al-Qaeda/Taliban Sanctions Committee, the committee which manages and updates the list. The Council also asked the Secretary-General to establish a group of independent experts to monitor state implementation of this expanded regime. Once identified and approved by the committee, these individuals would be hired as UN consultants. Through a series of subsequent resolutions, most recently Resolution 1735 (December 2006), the Council has sought to strengthen and refine this sanctions regime, unfortunately with few positive results. The list is out of date, with most names having been added right after the attacks of September 11, 2001. The measures have not been adjusted to correspond with the evolving threat and state implementation efforts continue to lag.[19]

Support for the sanctions regime seems to be eroding as a result of concerns regarding both the quality of information on the list and the lack of fully transparent procedures for adding and removing names from the list.[20] The head of the expert group charged with helping the committee monitor state implementation of the regime (the Monitoring Team) has cited a number of reasons why fewer and fewer states are putting forward names for inclusion on the list, including the reluctance on the part of some to admit publicly to a "terrorist problem" by nominating their own nationals, the fact that forwarding the names of another country's citizens for listing can be seen as an unfriendly act and "misgivings about the fairness of a sanctions regime which can freeze people's assets without telling them why."[21]

[19] Colum Lynch, "UN, US Actions Sometimes at Odds on Afghan Policy," *Washington Post*, July 5, 2007, p. A10, www.washingtonpost.com/wp-dyn/content/article/2007/07/04/AR2007070401422_pf.html (accessed August 17, 2007).

[20] The committee has amended its guidelines, putting minimum evidentiary standards for submitting names and a more transparent listing process into place. It has also standardized mechanisms, including name transliteration and the use of reference numbers of all entries. "The 1267 (Al-Qaeda/Taliban) Committee and the 1540 (WMD) Sanctions Committee," *Security Council Report*, Update Report no. 5, January 16, 2006. Available online at: www.securitycouncilreport.org/site/c.glKWLeMTIsG/b.1355491/k.48B7/UPDATE_REPORT_NO_5BRThe_1267_AlQaidaTaliban_Committee_and_The_1540_WMD_Sanctions_CommitteeBR16_JANUARY_2006.htm (accessed August 19, 2007).

[21] Mark Tevelyan, "UN al Qaeda sanctions in need of reform," *Reuters*, July 26, 2007.

With respect to improving the procedures for removing names from the list, the committee has been trying to strike the right balance between its European members (and non-members), which generally favor greater transparency and providing those on the list with more rights, including possibly allowing them to approach the committee directly, and other, less forward-leaning members.[22] Even with the mounting controversy surrounding the due process issues, it still serves as the primary vehicle by which states are empowered to freeze the assets of suspected Al-Qaeda and Taliban members.[23] Whereas the asset freeze requirement has proved valuable in helping internationalize the policy of freezing terrorist assets, the travel ban and arms embargo have produced few tangible results.[24]

Implementation of the sanctions has also suffered, largely as the result of a lack of capacity on the part of some states but in certain instances as a result of a lack of political will. In December 2006, the Council directed the committee to identify possible cases of state non-compliance with the sanctions for the first time.[25] This call appears aimed at addressing the failure of the committee (and ultimately the council) to identify which states are not implementing the sanctions despite numerous reports of widespread non-compliance from the committee's Monitoring Team.

[22] Calls have been coming from all corners, including from world leaders at the 2005 World Summit, to enhance the due process rights of those individuals and entities seeking to have their names removed from the list. In response to these concerns, the committee established new de-listing procedures in December 2006, which include a request to the SG to establish a "focal point" to receive de-listing requests, and, where appropriate, to forward them to the committee. While the creation of a "focal point" in council Resolution 1730 is a positive step, it still leaves the ultimate decision for de-listing squarely in the hands of the Committee, and is thus unlikely to silence those countries and human rights organizations that have advocated for the creation of an independent panel of experts to consider de-listing requests.

[23] According to the Monitoring Team, as of the end of 2006, 34 states had frozen about US$ 91.2 million in financial assets, of which 74.2 percent was frozen by three states. *Written assessment pursuant to paragraph 17 of Security Council resolution 1617 (2005)*, December 20, 2006, copy on file with authors. As of December 2006, 45 states have still not reported to the committee on steps they are taking to implement the sanctions, as called for by the Security Council in January 2003.

[24] According to information provided to the Al-Qaeda/Taliban Sanctions Committee by member states, as of late July 2006, $91.4 million, mainly in the form of bank accounts had been frozen by 35 states under this sanctions regime. United Nations Security Council Al-Qaeda/Taliban Sanctions Committee, *Fifth Report of the Al-Qaeda/Taliban Sanctions Monitoring Team*, S/2006/750, at p. 21, New York, September 20, 2006.

[25] United Nations Security Council Resolution 1735, S/RES/1735 (2006), December 22, 2006, op. para. 21.

The team's reports have provided the committee with rigorous analyses of the threat and numerous recommendations not only on how existing sanctions measures could be adjusted, but also on what new measures should be adopted. Between 2004 and 2006, the team presented more than 200 recommendations in its various reports, most of which related to helping states improve their implementation efforts. Only a few, however, were endorsed by the committee, which has had difficulty finding consensus on most of them. As a result, the sanctions regime remains largely unchanged since September 2001 and has failed to keep up with the threat.[26]

Resolution 1456: combating terrorism while respecting human rights

In January 2003, the Council President (France) convened a meeting of the Council at the foreign minister level to show the body's continued commitment to addressing the global terrorist threat. Although a number of Council members, including the French and Russians, used this meeting to warn the United States about the perils of unilateral action in Iraq,[27] the meeting culminated in the adoption of another generic counter-terrorism resolution, Resolution 1456.[28] The annex to the Resolution mostly reaffirmed language in existing Council pronouncements on the issue, but more significantly it also included the Council's first ever call upon states to respect human rights while countering terrorism, using the following language that has since been repeated in a range of UN fora: "States must ensure that any measure taken to combat terrorism comply with all their obligations under international law, and should adopt such measures in accordance with international law, in particular international human rights, refugee, and humanitarian law."[29] Although not adopted under Chapter VII like Resolution 1373,

[26] For example, although the most recent resolution in this area (Resolution 1735) does contain language dealing with some of the newer aspects of the threat (e.g., use of the Internet to recruit and radicalize terrorists), it is merely preambular, with the Council failing to agree on what specific steps states should take regarding these areas.

[27] "Ministerial-Level Security Council Meeting Calls for Urgent Action to Prevent, Suppress all Support for Terrorism: Declaration in Resolution 1456 (2003) Adopted Unanimously Highlights Counter-Terrorism Committee's Role in Implementation," January 20, 2003. Available at: www.un.org/News/Press/docs/2003/sc7638.doc.htm (accessed August 8, 2007).

[28] United Nations Security Council Resolution S/RES/1456 (2003), January 20, 2003.

[29] S/RES/1456 (2003), Annex, para. 6.

this resolution has been frequently employed to push the CTC to give human rights concerns greater attention.

The Council's response to the Madrid bombings: Resolution 1535 and the establishment of the Counter-Terrorism Executive Directorate (CTED)

Between January 2003 and its next major counter-terrorism resolution, the Council continued its practice of adopting a resolution, presidential statement, or press statement responding to major terrorist attacks. Most famously, in its rush to show solidarity with Spain following the March 2004 Madrid train bombings, the Council adopted a resolution that both condemned the terrorist attacks and identified (incorrectly as it turned out) the radical Basque separatist group, Euskadi Ta Askatasuna (ETA), as responsible.[30] That error has never been corrected, which perhaps illustrates how little importance is now attached to what have become rather routine gestures from the Council.[31]

With the Madrid attacks still fresh in the minds of Council members, the Council was finally able to resolve the differences among its members on whether to create a larger and more professional expert group to support the CTC and what the structure of such a group should be. During the first two-and-a-half years of the CTC's mandate it had become clear to many Council and non-Council members that, given the breadth and long-term nature of the CTC's mandate, the committee needed a larger, more permanent and professional staff body to support its work. The differences had centered on the extent of control the Council (as opposed to the Secretariat) would have overseeing the day-to-day monitoring of states' efforts to implement Resolution 1373. Not fully trusting the Secretariat to handle what they perceived as the politically sensitive issue of terrorism, the US and other permanent members of the Council wanted to create a permanent structure to support the CTC that would be under the direct authority of the Security Council rather than in the Secretariat, as was the general practice. The elected members, however, were concerned over the precedent this might set for ceding control over the implementation of Council mandates away from

[30] United Nations Security Council Resolution 1530, S/RES/1530 (2004), March 11, 2004.

[31] For a discussion of this resolution and its implications, see Therese O'Donnell, "Naming and Shaming: The Sorry Tale of Security Council Resolution 1530 (2004)," *European Journal of International Law* 968 (2006), p. 17.

the Secretariat, which traditionally has responsibility in this area and is directly accountable to the more broadly representative General Assembly.

The compromise was to create a *sui generis* Secretariat body that, although technically reporting to the CTC through the Secretary-General, receives its policy guidance directly from the committee. Further, unlike with every other UN staff position, the Council rather than the Secretary-General would be given the final word on his or her appointment.[32] Yet, reflecting the significant concerns of the elected members of the Council (and the wider membership), the resolution establishing the CTED (1535) explicitly states that the creation of such a body is needed to help the Council address the extraordinary terrorist threat and is not to be seen as a precedent for other Council activities.[33]

Resolution 1535 not only established the CTED (with its 20 experts and a further 20 support staff), but for the first time explicitly authorized the CTC, via the CTED, to conduct site visits to states, with their consent, to discuss the implementation of Resolution 1373. This decision was triggered by recognition of the limitations of relying exclusively on written reports from states to assess implementation efforts.[34]

Resolution 1540: Council institutional and normative expansion continues

With a robust legal framework already in place – established by the above-mentioned resolutions and the various international conventions and protocols against terrorism – and a reinforced CTC intended to serve as a hub for the counter-terrorism programs at the UN and other inter-governmental bodies, the Council decided to continue to expand the framework and create additional institutional mechanisms, each time in

[32] United Nations Security Council Resolution 1535, S/RES/1535 (2004, March 20, 2004, op. para. 3 (requesting the Secretary-General, "to appoint [the Executive Director], after consultation with and subject to the approval of the Council").

[33] "*Bearing in mind* the special nature of resolution 1373 (2001), the continuing threats to peace and security caused by terrorism, the important role the United Nations and the Security Council must continue to play in the global fight against terrorism, the need to reinforce the Committee as the Security Council subsidiary body responsible in this area, and without setting a precedent for other bodies of the Security Council," United Nations Security Council Resolution 1535, March 26, 2004, S/RES/1535.

[34] See "Proposal for the Revitalization of the Counter-Terrorism Committee," S/2004/124, February 19, 2004 and "Report by the Chair of the Counter-Terrorism Committee on the problems encountered in the implementation of Security Council resolution 1373 (2001)," S/2004/70, January 24, 2004.

reaction to a specific attack or incident. The Council adopted Resolution 1540, motivated in part by a heightened sensitivity to nuclear security after revelations that the founder of Pakistan's nuclear program, Abdul Qadeer Khan, had been involved in an underground nuclear technology ring that supplied nuclear technology to Libya, Iran, and North Korea. The Resolution requires all states to take a series of legislative and regulatory steps to prevent weapons of mass destruction and their means of delivery from getting into the hands of terrorists. The resolution established yet another body answerable to the Security Council, "the 1540 Committee," charged with duties analogous to those assigned to the CTC in the context of 1373 implementation, such as: reviewing state implementation reports; identifying capacity gaps; liaising with relevant international, regional and sub-regional bodies; and serving as a switchboard between states in need of technical assistance fulfilling their obligations under the resolution and potential donors.[35]

As of February 1, 2007, the 1540 Committee had not yet received reports from nearly one third of the UN member states.[36] State reporting to the 1540 Committee has lagged for several reasons. First, there is the issue of reporting fatigue among countries burdened by their accountability to an ever-increasing number of counter-terrorism-related committees each with their own reporting requirements. During a February 23, 2007 debate in the Council on the work of the 1540 Committee, for example, South Africa's permanent representative said the Council "should acknowledge that the 1540 reporting requirements themselves were overly complicated and not suitable for many developing States."[37] In addition, the committee's day-to-day work has been impeded by cumbersome procedures for communicating with states. There is also a lack of agreement among its members on several critical points, such as: how to use the analysis being prepared by the committee's group of

[35] United Nations Security Council Resolution 1540, S/RES/1540 (2004), April 28, 2004. See also: "Security Council Committee Established Pursuant to Resolution 1540: Guidelines for the Conduct of its Work." Available online at: http://disarmament2.un.org/Committee1540/work.html (accessed August 18, 2007).

[36] "Cooperation between the Security Council and international organizations in the implementation of resolutions 1540 (2004) and 1673 (2006)," S/2007/84, New York, February 13, 2007.

[37] SC/8964 "Security Council affirms determination to strengthen cooperation aimed at countering nuclear, chemical, biological weapons proliferation," Presidential Statement Follows Day-Long Debate On Ways to Enhance Implementation of Resolution 1540 (2004), February 23, 2007. Available online at: www.un.org/News/Press/docs//2007/sc8964.doc.htm (accessed August 17, 2007).

experts (for example, whether they can be used by the committee and its group of experts to judge member state implementation); and how broadly to share the expert group's analyses; whether the group can use public sourced material (as opposed to only information provided by governments.

Resolution 1566: the Council reacts to Beslan

The Council's response to the seizure of some 1,200 hostages and the death of hundreds of civilians, including 186 children at a school in Beslan, Russia late in 2004 was emblematic of its broader efforts to address the terrorist threat. The desire to satisfy short-term political objectives of one or more Council members overcame the need to develop a more coherent Council counter-terrorism program. The Russian Federation, using the Council's forceful dynamic response to 9/11 as its benchmark, pushed the Council to adopt its strongest condemnation to date of attacks against civilians in Resolution 1566.[38] In fact, only last-minute objections of the two Organization of the Islamic Conference (OIC) members on the Council, Algeria and Pakistan, and the Russians' desire to maintain Council unity in its response to terrorism, stood in the way of the Council adopting its own definition of terrorism in this resolution and thus treading upon what most UN members view to be within the sole purview of the General Assembly.[39]

Although the resolution was not adopted under Chapter VII, it contained a number of diverse elements. Perhaps most significantly, it established another Council subsidiary body, "the 1566 Working Group," to consider a series of issues on which the Council could not agree during the negotiations of the Resolution, such as what practical measures should be taken to deal with terrorist groups other than Al-Qaeda and the Taliban, and the prospects for developing an international fund to compensate victims of terrorism. The group has met rarely and, not surprisingly, when it has the lack of a common definition of terrorism has made it difficult to reach consensus on any meaningful recommendations, including the establishment of a victims' fund.

[38] United Nations Security Council Resolution 1566, S/RES/1566 (2004), October 8, 2004.
[39] Saul, *Defining Terrorism in International Law*, p. 247.

Resolution 1624: the Council reacts to the London bombings

The Council's most recent addition to its counter-terrorism program came in response to the third major attack on one of the Council's permanent five members, the bomb attacks on London's mass transit system. The Council adopted another unanimous resolution, Resolution 1624, which calls on states to take action to combat incitement, strengthen their border security, and "enhance dialogue and broaden understanding among civilizations."[40] Although not adopted under Chapter VII (and thus non-binding), the Council nevertheless assigned the CTC responsibility for monitoring state implementation of its provisions and, as it did with Resolutions 1373 and 1540 as well as its Al-Qaeda/Taliban sanctions regime, it asked states to report to the Council on steps they were taking to implement the provisions of the resolution.

Assessing the Council's efforts: achievements and shortcomings

The above chronological survey of the Council's major post-9/11 counter-terrorism initiatives is revealing in several respects. On the one hand, the Security Council seems to have rushed into a new area without having first posed the antecedent question of whether it is capable of assuming a central, day-to-day role in the global counter-terrorism campaign. It has acted without determining what its institutional strengths are and where its comparative advantage may lie. Its initiatives appear to be ad hoc measures taken in response to the most recent major terrorist attack, rather than parts of a comprehensive strategy to address the global terrorist threat. In that vein, the Council has demonstrated a lack of regard for how each new initiative will fit with the existing Council programs.

On the other hand the Council, like the rest of the world, was faced with a situation that demanded immediate, robust action, and it was situated to organize the effort to internationalize the response to terrorism and stimulate other multilateral bodies to become engaged. Some six years later, more than 70 such formal and informal bodies are now involved in some form of counter-terrorism activity and a wide range of other UN actors are now committed to contributing in this effort. Even if it did act somewhat haphazardly, the Council is to be credited for acting to fill a leadership vacuum. After 9/11 the more representative

[40] United Nations Security Council Resolution S/RES/1624 (2005), September 14, 2005.

General Assembly condemned the attacks, but there was little hope here of effective leadership or substantive proposals given the differences in the definition of terrorism.

These Council bodies have succeeded in gathering unprecedented amounts of information from states on their efforts to implement their obligations; making some of that information public through their respective websites; establishing ongoing interactive dialogues with states on counter-terrorism; helping to identify and fill some of the capacity gaps; engaging with a wide range of international, regional, and sub-regional bodies; and, more broadly, highlighting the importance of international cooperation in the global counter-terrorism campaign. Yet, the committees and their expert groups have also faced a range of challenges that have limited their effectiveness to one degree or another.

The Council should also be credited for responding so quickly to fill normative gaps at the global level and for keeping the global threat of terrorism at the forefront of the international community's consciousness. When the Council adopted Resolution 1373 there was no global counter-terrorism legal framework in place. Although twelve international conventions and protocols against terrorism had been adopted in various UN fora over a period of nearly forty years, only two countries (the UK and Botswana) were parties to all of them. In fact, the Terrorist Financing Convention, then the most recent of these treaties, had only five states parties, well below the number required to have entered into force. The Council, however, using its Chapter VII authority to impose binding obligations on all states, took a number of the provisions in the financing convention and made them universally binding by including them in Resolution 1373.[41] In addition to imposing a series of legal obligations on all countries, Resolution 1373 called for all states to become parties to all of the international conventions and protocols against terrorism, which today number sixteen. Since the adoption of this resolution, the Council, including through its CTC, has continued to highlight the importance that all states join these instruments.

As a result of Resolution 1373 and the intense pressure from the Council and its CTC, the number of state parties has increased and

[41] It has been pointed out, however, that the Council did so "in blatant disregard of the other provisions [in the convention] ... particularly those concerned with the rights of the accused, which were part and parcel of the Convention negotiation." Andrea Bianchi, "Assessing the Effectiveness of the UN Security Council's Anti-terrorism Measures: The Quest for Legitimacy and Cohesion," *European Journal of International Law* 17 (2007), p. 914.

nearly one hundred countries are now parties to all of these same instruments.[42] Generally, as a result of the attention given to terrorism and terror-related issues by the Council more than seventy bodies are now involved in some form of counter-terrorism activity and a wide range of other UN actors are now committed to contributing to the effort. Many of the various new anti-terror bodies have succeeded in gathering unprecedented amounts of information from states on their efforts to fulfill their obligations. Much of that information has been made available to the public through the various bodies' respective websites. Some of those bodies have even established ongoing interactive dialogues with states on counter-terrorism. Others have helped to identify and fill gaps in state implementation and capacity. Finally, some of the new bodies have, through their engagements with a wide range of international, regional, and sub-regional actors, highlighted the importance of international cooperation in the global counter-terrorism campaign.

Already perceived by many as under-representative and in need of expansion, the Council's use of its Chapter VII authority to impose obligations on all UN member states and thus circumvent the traditional international law-making process, which is still based on the consent of states, has proven to be controversial. Many countries, particularly but not exclusively from the global South, have questioned the Council's authority to impose general, legal obligations. In addition to the legality of the Council's actions to act as a "global legislator," critics also argue that through its response, the Council usurped norm-setting powers that rightly belong to the more representative General Assembly.[43] Having the Council, a fifteen-member body unaccountable to the other UN organs, exercise this power has not only represented a threat to the balance of power between the Council and General Assembly as set forth in the UN Charter,[44] it has also alienated many UN member states, thereby discouraging their participation in global counter-terrorism efforts. Because so many states feel no real ownership of the counter-terrorism commitments and initiatives imposed by the Council, there have been difficulties in getting states to take the steps necessary to implement the Council's normative framework.

42 *Short ratification status*, July 31, 2008, prepared by UNODC's Terrorism Prevention Branch (copy on file with author).

43 Stefan Talmon, "The Security Council as World Legislature," *AJIL* 99 (January 2005), p. 175; Eric Rosand, "The Security Council as 'Global Legislator': Ultra Vires or Ultra Innovative," *Fordham International Law Journal* 28 (2005), p. 542.

44 *Ibid.*

As for the counter-terrorism-related subsidiary bodies created by the Council, the chief criticism is that often they were hastily established to respond to specific crises. In general, information sharing and other forms of cooperation between and among these groups have been inadequate. The result has been a proliferation of programs and initiatives with overlapping mandates, duplication of work, and multiple (sometimes confusing) reporting requirements for states. The wider UN membership, the Secretary-General, and the Council itself have recognized many of these shortcomings since 2004. In fact, the Council has repeatedly called for improvements in numerous resolutions and presidential statements, yet still has to take the steps needed to improve the situation.[45]

The decision-making processes of the Council counter-terrorism committees have also presented serious challenges. The practice of taking all decisions by consensus has significantly impeded their ability to take action in a timely fashion and at times diluted their work. The same consensus-based practice has made it difficult for any of the Council counter-terrorism-related bodies to identify non-performers ("name and shame")[46] or even to agree on a set of standards against which to measure performance.[47] The HLP report points out that the "Security Council may need to take additional measures to ensure compliance" in order to deal with states "that have the capacity to undertake their obligations but repeatedly fail to do so."[48] The HLP, however, fails to recognize how the procedures of the relevant monitoring committees create enormous obstacles to achieving this objective.

In addition, the political, administrative, and budgetary challenges of operating within the UN system have thwarted attempts by the Council's main counter-terrorism body, the CTC, to match donors and other technical assistance providers with those states it has identified as

[45] See, e.g., S/RES/1735 (2006); UN Security Council Presidential Statement (December 20, 2006), UN Doc. S/PRST/2006/56; S/RES/1617 (2005); S/RES/1566 (2004); UN Security Council Presidential Statement (January 18, 2005), UN Doc. S/PRST/2005/3; S/RES/1535 (2004).

[46] On a number of occasions, one or two committee members, including the one representing the region in which a targeted country is located, have successfully blocked any efforts to exert meaningful pressure on a particular country.

[47] There are examples of Council subsidiary bodies that do not operate by consensus, i.e., former Yugoslavia and The Hague ad hoc international criminal tribunals. Unlike the Council's sanctions and counter-terrorism subsidiary bodies, which are political, intergovernmental bodies, these are independent judicial ones where the judges are appointed and act in their individual capacities rather on behalf of a state.

[48] HLP Report, para. 156.

needing assistance or to assume a leading role in coordinating the work of the dozens of multilateral institutional actors on the counter-terrorism stage effectively.

In general, the Council's approach has been too narrow in focus, and has done little to address the broad range of human rights issues that often intersect with terrorism. There is a considerable body of literature highlighting the absence of any mention in Resolution 1373 of the obligation of states to respect human rights in the design and implementation of their counter-terrorism measures and the resulting lack of attention paid to rights issues by the CTC as it monitors states' implementation efforts.[49] Human Rights Watch produced a report in 2004, which highlighted the CTC's failure to take up human rights-related issues when responding to state reports from Egypt, Uzbekistan, Malaysia, Morocco, and Sweden, each of which described actions with human rights implications.[50] The HLP report commented on this problem, illustrating how it represents more than a normative failure, but actually undercuts the effectiveness of the UN's own counter-terrorism efforts. Specifically:

> Approaches to terror focusing wholly on military, police, and intelligence measures risk undermining efforts to promote good governance and human rights, alienate large parts of the world's population and thereby weaken the potential for collective action against terrorism. The crucial need … is to address not only [state] capacity but their will to fight terror. To develop that will – with States drawing support rather than opposition from their own publics – requires a broader-based approach.[51]

The CTC has reacted to pressure from its European and Latin American members, and various elements of the UN human rights system to increase its human rights focus. For example, it now has its own human rights expert and it includes human rights issues in its Preliminary Implementation Assessments of states' efforts to implement

[49] See, e.g., Jessica Almqvist, "Rethinking Security and Human Rights in the Struggle against Terrorism," paper presented at the European Society of International Law Forum in the workshop "Human Rights Under Threat," May 27, 2005. Available online at: www.esil-sedi.org/english/pdf/Almqvist09-05.PDF-search=%22human%20rights%20and%20terrorism%20CTC%22 (accessed February 19, 2007); "Hear No Evil, See No Evil: The UN Security Council's Approach to Human Rights Violations in the Global Counter-Terrorism Effort," *Human Rights Watch Briefing Paper*, April 10, 2004. Available online at: www.hrw.org/English/docs/2004/08/04/global9185 (accessed July 25, 2007).

[50] "Hear No Evil, See No Evil." [51] High-Level Panel, para. 147.

Resolution 1373. It also focuses on human rights issues during its site visits. However, the CTC's efforts have been tempered by some P5 members' concerns about diluting the Council's traditional security focus.[52] The resulting CTC response has been seen as overly slow, cautious, and conservative.[53] Yet, as noted above, it will be difficult to adopt such an approach so long as the Security Council, through its counter-terrorism-related bodies, remains the primary interface with UN member states on strengthening their counter-terrorism capacities.

The UN Secretariat

During much of the post-9/11 period, the UN Secretariat was largely a bystander as the Council seized the initiative. Although, in the immediate aftermath of 9/11, UN Secretary-General Kofi Annan forcefully spoke up against terrorism on various occasions, over time he rarely would use his "bully pulpit" to champion this issue. He also made a good-willed but ill-fated attempt in the months after 9/11 to prod UN member states to reach a breakthrough in the General Assembly in the negotiations on the draft Comprehensive Convention on International Terrorism, which were deadlocked over the scope of the definition of terrorism.

Shortly after 9/11, the Secretary-General had also established an inter-departmental Policy Working Group on Terrorism, composed of the Under-Secretary-Generals of key UN Departments, which produced a few months later a comparatively coherent report on the UN's role in counter-terrorism, the first ever attempt to produce a strategy on this issue in the Secretariat.[54] However, even the modest recommendations in this report saw no follow-up, and the Working Group met irregularly without any sense of purpose. In fact, the Secretariat's Department for Political Affairs, which chaired the Working Group and nominally acted as the UN Secretariat's "focal point" on counter-terrorism, never

[52] Rosemary Foot, "The United Nations, Counter-Terrorism and Human Rights: Institutional Adaptation and Embedded Ideas," *Human Rights Quarterly* 29 (2007), pp. 489–514.

[53] For example, OHCHR is still not included on the CTED's directory of technical assistance providers, and any exchange of information between CTED and the UN human rights mechanisms is still carried out on an ad hoc basis. Further, human rights continues to be noticeably absent from the CTED's directory of best practices for implementing relevant provisions of Resolution 1373.

[54] Report of the Policy Working Group on Terrorism, A/57/273, August 6, 2002.

dedicated any staff to the issue and senior Secretariat aides were openly critical of the US counter-terrorism agenda.[55]

Against this background, it was maybe unsurprising that the US and other permanent members opposed the idea of making the CTED an integral part of the Secretariat. As noted above, the Secretariat in turn objected to CTED's creation, pushing back against any attempt at diluting the Secretariat's influence. As part of its strategy, the Secretariat enlisted some of the elected members of the Council to fight its battles, which it characterized in terms of preventing P5 efforts to further expand the Council's role (at the expense of the General Assembly and Secretariat). The disagreements with the Secretariat, which continued during the first year of the CTED's existence, left scars and mutual suspicions between the CTC and Secretariat that have yet to heal fully.

With counter-terrorism ghettoized in the Security Council and the Secretariat largely marginalized, it was up to the latter to regain the initiative. The opportunity to do so came when the HLP urged the Secretary-General in its December 2004 report to take a lead role and promote a comprehensive global counter-terrorism strategy (and urged, *inter alia*, the General Assembly to resolve the outstanding differences that had prevented it from reaching agreement on a definition of terrorism).[56] On March 10, 2005, acting on the Panel's recommendation, the Secretary-General announced such a strategy, centering on what he termed the "five D's": (1) to dissuade disaffected groups from choosing terrorism as a tactic to achieve their goals; (2) to deny terrorists the means to carry out their attacks; (3) to deter states from supporting terrorists; (4) to develop state capacity to prevent terrorism; (5) to defend human rights in the struggle against terrorism.[57] These initial five D's were further elaborated a year later in a report entitled "Uniting against terrorism."[58]

The strategy tried to fulfill multiple and not easily reconcilable goals. On the one hand, the Secretary-General hoped that a UN promulgated

[55] Edward C. Luck, "The Uninvited Challenge: Terrorism Targets the UN." Available online at: www.sipa.columbia.edu/cio/cio/projects/LuckSSRCUNU.pdf at p. 15 (accessed August 18, 2007).

[56] Report of the Secretary-General's High-Level Panel on Threats, Challenges and Change, *A More Secure World: Our Shared Responsibility*, A/59/565, December 2, 2004, para. 148.

[57] "Secretary-General offers global strategy in fighting terrorism at Madrid Summit," March 10, 2005. Available online at: www.un.org/News/Press/docs/2005/sgsm9757.doc.htm (accessed August 13, 2007).

[58] Report of the Secretary-General, *Uniting against terrorism: recommendations for a global counter-terrorism strategy*, April 27, 2006. Available online at www.un.org/unitingagainstterrorism (accessed August 10, 2007).

strategy could both offer an alternative to the increasingly controversial US-led "Global War on Terror" and provide a comprehensive vision of a global and collective counter-terrorism effort in which all states could comfortably participate. On the other hand, the strategy was an effort to get skeptics among the Non-Aligned Movement (NAM)[59] countries to acknowledge that terrorism is indeed a serious threat to international peace and security requiring a concerted global response and, indirectly, to prove to the US that the Secretariat had the capability of engaging in the counter-terrorism discourse. Fundamentally, the strategy also was an effort to reestablish the Secretariat as a player in counter-terrorism and to provide the Secretary-General with a central message on which to focus attention.[60]

In order to ensure that the strategy would be more than mere rhetoric, the Secretary-General created the interdepartmental Counter-Terrorism Implementation Task Force in the summer of 2005. The Task Force brought together for the first time some twenty-four representatives from all departments and organizations of the larger – and confusingly fragmented – UN system, which were in some way involved in the UN's overall counter-terrorism effort, including the Council's expert bodies, key Secretariat departments, technical assistance providing agencies, as well as the World Bank, the IMF and Interpol.[61] Following in the footsteps of the now defunct Policy Working group on terrorism, the Task Force is chaired by a key policy adviser of the Secretary-General and meets periodically in multi-day retreats at the level of senior experts.

It is too early to tell whether the creation of the Task Force will lead to a more coherent UN response to terrorism. Supported by only minimal staff and without decision-making or enforcement authority (the Secretary-General has no directive authority over many Task Force members, who have separate and independent governing bodies), the creation of the Task Force can only be described as "institutional adaptation lite." It will face considerable challenges carrying out its limited mandate of ensuring that the UN's programs and operations are in line

59 The NAM, which was established during the Cold War, now consists of 115 developing states not formally aligned with or against any major power bloc. Information concerning the NAM is available on line at www.nam.gov.za/background/history.htm (accessed August 19, 2007).

60 Interview with Sebastian von Einsiedel, member of HLP secretariat (August 18, 2007).

61 For more information on the Task Force, including a list of members, see www.un.org/terrorism/cttaskforce.html (accessed August 13, 2007).

with the Secretary-General's strategy, promoting better coordination and strengthening information-sharing among agencies and programs.

Nevertheless, some permanent members of the Council eyed the developments in the Secretariat with deep suspicion. The US and others among the P5 were of course keen to keep the issue of counter-terrorism exclusively confined to the Security Council, where they could control the agenda. There was also a general attitude from the US side, particularly pronounced during the ambassadorship of John Bolton, that rejected the notion that the UN Secretariat was imbued with any institutional autonomy and instinctively opposed any policy initiatives emerging from the Secretariat.

But the US was by no means alone in that attitude, in particular vis-à-vis the Secretary-General's strategy. While European countries and some Latin American and African countries seemed to wholeheartedly support the subsequent strategies, many member countries from the OIC and from the NAM were skeptical. In particular, they felt that the issues of "root causes" and "foreign occupation" were not accorded sufficient emphasis. It was those states that declared that a strategy pronounced by the Secretary-General had no standing and insisted that the General Assembly would have to elaborate its own inter-governmentally agreed strategy. The September 2005 World Summit Outcome Document thus not only gave short shrift to the Security Council's counter-terrorism efforts,[62] but called on the General Assembly to develop the elements of a UN counter-terrorism strategy.[63]

The emergence of the General Assembly and the adoption of the UN Global Counter-Terrorism Strategy

Although the General Assembly has been unable to reach agreement on a definition of terrorism, the General Assembly (and other UN agencies) has managed to make several important contributions to the development of international norms against discrete acts of terrorism (although often not using the word "terrorism"). For example, the General Assembly adopted international conventions in response to a series of attacks against diplomats and the taking of US hostages in Iran in 1979. Its Ad Hoc Committee on Terrorism, which was established in 1994, has adopted three conventions aimed at suppressing terrorist acts: the

[62] Edward C. Luck, *UN Security Council: Practice and Promise* (Routledge: New York, 2006), p. 107.

[63] United Nations General Assembly Resolution 60/1, A/RES/60/1, September 15, 2005, paras. 81–83.

International Convention for the Suppression of Terrorist Bombings in 1997, the International Convention on the Suppression of Financing of Terrorism in 1999, and the International Convention for the Suppression of Nuclear Terrorism in 2005.

The International Convention for the Suppression of Terrorist Bombings appeared to break new ground by stating clearly that bombings are "not justifiable by consideration of a political, philosophical, ideological, racial, ethnic, religious or other similar nature."[64] In adopting the convention by consensus, it appeared that the General Assembly was taking a clear stand against indiscriminate violence toward civilians. Similar language was subsequently included in the International Convention on the Suppression of Financing of Terrorism. While using similar language represents progress, these steps forward need to be viewed alongside offsetting actions of certain states. The members of the OIC and the Organization of African Unity (now the African Union) have their own regional conventions with provisions that explicitly contradict provisions of the Conventions on Terrorist Bombings and Terrorist Financing by distinguishing between acts of terrorism and those committed in the fight against foreign occupation or for self-determination.[65] When ratifying the Bombings and Financing Conventions, several of these states, such as Pakistan, Syria, Jordan, and Egypt, reserved the right to continue to apply the distinctions and definitions from their regional conventions when implementing measures outlined in the UN Conventions.

Considering the few successes and the many complications outlined above, many observers were surprised that the General Assembly responded to the call in the *World Summit Outcome* document and adopted the first-ever Global Counter-Terrorism Strategy ("the Strategy"),[66] albeit after six months of sometimes difficult negotiations.[67] Many OIC and other NAM countries initially insisted on trying to include references to the distinction between terrorism and legitimate

[64] International Convention for the Suppression of Terrorist Bombings, December 15, 1997, Article 5.

[65] Convention on Combating International Terrorism, Organization of Islamic Conference, 1999, Article 2(a); Organization of African Unity Convention on the Prevention and Combating of Terrorism, July 14, 1999, Article 3.

[66] United Nations General Assembly, A/RES/60/288, New York, September 8, 2006.

[67] See, e.g., Associated Press, "UN General Assembly adopts counter-terrorism strategy," *International Herald Tribune*, September 9, 2006. Available online at: www.iht.com/articles/ap/2006/09/08/news/UN_GEN_UN_Counter_Terrorism.php (accessed August 10, 2007).

acts of political violence committed in the fight against foreign occupation in the Strategy. Once the expected global North opposition materialized, however, it became clear that there would be no consensus strategy with this language included. The adoption of a consensus document by the General Assembly, which could shift the balance of power within the UN away from the Council to the more representative General Assembly, was seen as more important than using the document as an opportunity to score points in the definition debate that was continuing to take place in another part of the General Assembly.

The General Assembly's Strategy calls for a holistic, inclusive, and nonmilitary-focused approach to counter-terrorism. By calling on all parts of the UN system as well as states and other international and regional bodies to contribute to its implementation, the Strategy provides an overarching framework, for a "whole of government" and "whole of system" approach to combating terrorism. It is based on an understanding that one of the best methods of countering terrorism effectively is prevention, and that the best form of prevention is early intervention to resolve conflicts before they are exploited by extremists and to alleviate the economic, social, and political marginalization of populations that, unchecked, makes such fertile ground for the spread of extremism. In so doing, it reinforces what many terrorism experts have long felt, namely that an effective counter-terrorism strategy must combine preventive measures with efforts to address both real and perceived grievances and underlying social, economic, and political conditions.

Given the universal membership of the General Assembly, the politically sensitive nature of many of the issues surrounding a threat like terrorism, and the different regional and sub-regional perspectives on the appropriate strategy for addressing the threat, it should come as little surprise that the Strategy consists largely of a series of broadly worded provisions that offer few specifics to help guide implementation. Yet the Strategy is significant for two important reasons. It brings these commitments together into a single document unanimously adopted by the 192-member General Assembly. Further, it represents the first ever truly global counter-terrorism framework and thus stands in sharp contrast to the Security Council counter-terrorism resolutions that many states view as having been imposed upon them without their consent.

Whether or not the Strategy is implemented effectively remains to be seen. One of the keys to implementation will be improving the coordination and cooperation among the twenty-four different parts of the UN system engaged in counter-terrorism and the numerous other engaged multilateral bodies and mechanisms. A lack of effective coordination and cooperation has almost come to define the UN's post-September 11 response, leading countries such as Costa Rica and Switzerland to call, as early as in 2004, for the establishment of a UN high commissioner for terrorism to coordinate all of these initiatives. The fourteen-country Group of Friends of UN Reform echoed these calls in 2005 as did the G8 heads of state when they called for a more coherent UN counter-terrorism program and response to the threat in their July 2006 summit statement.[68] To address the problems created by having multiple Council counter-terrorism bodies with somewhat overlapping mandates, the Secretary-General even recommended in March 2006 that the Council consider consolidating them into a single committee with a single staff body.[69] This recommendation was never considered by the Council, illustrating the difficulty in making headway in an environment where each of the several UN bodies, fearful of losing power or funding, is reluctant to coordinate or share information with the other bodies.[70]

Unfortunately, the Strategy does not address this power-sharing problem adequately. It calls for more cooperation within the UN but its provisions are largely directed to individual parts of the UN system, including the different Security Council counter-terrorism-related committees and their respective expert groups. The Strategy's primary remedy for improving the coordination and coherence of the UN's program is to welcome the Secretary-General's intention to institutionalize the Task Force within the Secretariat. Yet, partly reflecting the concern of some of the P5, which want the Council to remain the focus of the UN's counter-terrorism program, and the need to achieve consensus, the Strategy provides that the Task Force needs to conduct its work within existing resources.[71]

68 The Group of Friends consists of Algeria, Australia, Canada, Chile, Colombia, Germany, Japan, Kenya, New Zealand, the Netherlands, Pakistan, Spain, Singapore, and Sweden. See Group of Friends Non-Paper, "The Role of the United Nations in the Fight Against Terrorism," 2005, available at www.un.int/mexico/2005/Terrorism.pdf (accessed August 10, 2007).

69 "Mandating and Delivering: Analysis and Recommendations to Facilitate the Review of Mandates," A/60/733, Report of the Secretary-General of the United Nations, New York, March 30, 2006, paras. 122–123.

70 Curtis A. Ward, "Capacity-Building in the Asia-Pacific: The Role of the UN," delivered at Workshop on Implementing the UNGA Global Counter-Terrorism Strategy in the Asia-Pacific, New York, January 25, 2007 (text available on file with author), p. 2.

71 United Nations General Assembly, A/RES/60/288, New York, September 8, 2006, sec. III, para. 5.

In other words, despite the recognized need for improved coordination and coherence, the General Assembly did not provide the Task Force with the tools necessary to allow it to succeed in the long term. Lacking any resources from the UN regular budget, during 2006, 2007, and 2008 the Task Force has had to rely on limited, voluntary contributions from a handful of member states – all from the global North – to support its work.[72] In addition to inadequate resources, it remains to be seen whether the Task Force has the necessary authority to get the different parts of the system to share information, cooperate, and reduce overlapping mandates.[73]

A shift to a more inclusive, broad-based UN counter-terrorism program

For many of those UN members who have felt excluded from what they perceive to be a Council-led UN counter-terrorism effort that lacks legitimacy and inclusiveness, the adoption of the Strategy represents the reemergence of the General Assembly as the central player in the overall UN effort. The Strategy is also a response to the growing disapproval within the UN of the narrow Council-led approach that fails to try to tackle the root causes of terrorism that for many member states from the global South lie at the heart of any effective counter-terrorism strategy. These include "poverty, prolonged unresolved conflicts, dehumanization of victims of terrorism, lack of rule of law and violation of human rights, ethnic, national and religious discrimination, political exclusion, socio-economic marginalization and lack of good governance."[74]

Rather than reacting defensively to the Strategy as an attempt by the G77 to seize control of the UN's counter-terrorism agenda and undercut the Council's authority, the Council should welcome its adoption. It not only reflects legitimate concerns about the existing Council program, but can and should be used as a vehicle for strengthening it. By (explicitly or implicitly) incorporating the Security Council counter-terrorism framework, the consensus Strategy can help broaden the political constituency for the Council effort and help to narrow the divide between the Council

[72] This money has generally been given to fund the work of the Task Force's nine thematic working groups.

[73] United Nations General Assembly, A/RES/60/288, New York, September 8, 2006, sec. III, para. 5.

[74] Ibid., Sec. I.

and the General Assembly, and more fundamentally help to reconcile the security agenda of the global North with the development priorities of the global South.

Because of the long-standing tension and rivalry between the Council and General Assembly, which extend well beyond their counter-terrorism remits, one is unlikely to see too much benevolence from the Council. Nevertheless, the adoption of the Strategy, and the process leading up to it, may serve to highlight the insurmountable obstacles the Council faces in trying to spearhead the UN effort to design an effective collective response to the security threat posed by non-state terrorism.

As enunciated by the HLP, "the effectiveness of the global collective security system, as with any other legal order, depends ultimately not only on the legality of decisions, but also on the common perception of their legitimacy."[75] Yet, the Council continues to suffer not only from a perceived lack of legitimacy in its counter-terrorism activities, but the sense among the wider membership both that it is merely a tool of a handful of powerful states, in particular the US, and that it is no longer appropriate for the CTC, a Council body operating under Chapter VII of the UN Charter, to be at the center of global counter-terrorism capacity-building activities, trying to act as a "social worker" rather than the "police officer" that everyone expects from the Council.

Given the composition of the HLP, which included a respected national from each P5 country, including a prominent former US National Security Adviser, the HLP's goal of obtaining US support for its conclusions in the near term, and the likelihood that any criticism of the Council in this area would offend the US (and the other P5) it is not surprising that the HLP report fails to tackle this fundamental issue head on. Nonetheless, the report's call for a broader UN response to addressing the terrorist threat in paragraph 147 could be interpreted as an implicit criticism of the Council's efforts.

The time is right for the Council to (re)consider where its comparative advantage lies in the global fight against terrorism six years after the adoption of Resolution 1373 and the establishment of the CTC. To date, the Council's counter-terrorism contributions have primarily been in the areas of norm-setting, institution building, keeping terrorism on the political agenda, and engaging in dialogues with and stimulating the activities of states and multilateral bodies. It is not clear, however, that

[75] HLP Report, para. 204.

the Council's comparative advantage lies in all of these areas today and in the future.

In 2008, the Council still has an indispensable political role to play in keeping international terrorism on the world's agenda. It should remain as the final arbiter of non-compliance with the normative counter-terrorism framework it has established. Further, there may be times when a decisive and quick norm-setting response will be needed to address a normative gap that a new terrorist attack or uncovered plot reveals. The Council should tread cautiously in this area, however, given the continuing concerns regarding its use of its "legislative" authority. Continued Council activity here would be made more palatable if the expert bodies involved in overseeing implementation of the new (and existing) Council-imposed norms eventually became an integral part of the UN Secretariat, because then it would not look like the P5 were simply using the UN machinery for their own narrow national security interests instead of the collective security of all UN member states. There might be lessons that could be learned from the Council's involvement in and oversight of peacekeeping operations, where the day-to-day responsibilities of implementing the Council's mandates fall within the Department of Peacekeeping, which reports periodically to the Council, which in turn offers broad policy guidance.

In general, the Council is ill-suited to overseeing the more routine, day-to-day tasks of monitoring implementation, technical assistance facilitation, and engaging with states, multilateral bodies, and other stakeholders, as it lacks the legitimacy, technical expertise, and the attention span to sustain the momentum of a long-term capacity-building program and the multitude of tasks that are involved.

The significant rise in the number of multilateral bodies involved in counter-terrorism-related work since the passage of Resolution 1373, the adoption of the UN Strategy, the emergence of the Task Force (although under-funded), and the difficulties the Council's counter-terrorism-related committees and expert groups have had carrying out their mandates, particularly as they relate to capacity building, argue in favor of shifting the capacity-building work away from the Council to a more representative part of the UN.

Promoting and overseeing the implementation of the UN global counter-terrorism framework, which is now enshrined in the UN Strategy, requires a long-term and unwavering commitment and oversight from a member state body with broad legitimacy in both the global North and South. Specifically, such a body should be larger than

11

International justice and collective security: between pragmatism and principle

CARMEN MÁRQUEZ CARRASCO[1]

Some years ago, a prominent international scholar stated that "the administration of justice in the Community of States [would] not be complete until a criminal jurisdiction is established to cope with international crimes" and that the "necessity of such a jurisdiction [seemed] to be a fact established without reasonable doubt."[2]

At the time it was published in 1980, this quote was seen as an expression of idealistic fervor. In the 1980s, and even in the 1990s, the establishment of a permanent international criminal court seemed a long way off, if not impossible. However, international criminal prosecution of serious crimes, such as genocide, crimes against humanity, and war crimes, experienced unprecedented development during the 1990s. The establishment of the ad hoc international criminal tribunals for Rwanda and the former Yugoslavia proved to be an important catalyst because it forced the prospect of a permanent court back onto the international agenda. Once this happened, progress was astonishingly swift. Just over five years after the establishment of the International Criminal Tribunal for the former Yugoslavia, 120 nations voted to adopt the Rome Statute of the International Criminal Court (ICC) on July 17, 1998, a date that symbolically coincided with the fiftieth anniversary of the adoption of both the Convention for the Prevention and Sanction of the Crime of Genocide and the Universal Declaration of Human Rights, two instruments that

1 This chapter is a revised version of a paper first presented at the "The Reformed UN: Responses to Threats in a New Collective Security System" conference held in New York on December 3, 2005. The author would like to thank Horst Fischer and the other participants for their helpful comments and suggestions.

2 Benjamin B. Ferencz, *An international criminal court, a step towards world peace: A documentary history and analysis*, 2 vols. (Dobbs Ferry, New York: Oceana, 1980), vol I, p. xi.

recognized protection of human rights as the best means for safeguarding peace and security.[3]

Despite this progress, the prosecution of individuals responsible for serious international crimes has not been easy. Part of the problem is that, paradoxically, the UN Security Council's ("the Council's") objective of maintaining peace seems to conflict with the exigencies of international prosecution for serious international law violations. However, the Council's recent practices attempt to give effect to the famous aphorism "no peace without justice." The goal of international prosecution has fueled a search for solutions that are not only appropriately adapted to the specificities of the different situations confronting the Council, but also balance the needs of both peace and justice. In the course of this search, the Council created ad hoc tribunals, then "internationalized" or hybrid tribunals, and is now moving towards the establishment of truth and reconciliation commissions.[4] This evolution suggests that the Council is developing a new conception of the relationship between peace and justice in international relations.

Considering the potential impact of the apparent conflict between peace and justice on UN reform efforts, this chapter seeks to analyze the relationship between the Council and the ICC in the context of the evolving UN collective security system. In general terms, that relationship is structured around the two intersecting axes of peace and justice. More specifically, there are two conflicting logics behind the relationship between the Council and the ICC. On the one hand, there is a logic of coordination between the Council's maintenance of peace and security and the ICC's attempts to achieve international criminal justice, based on the fact that their objectives are complementary. On the other hand, in order to prevent the pursuit of justice from obstructing the Council's peace efforts, there exists a logic of subordination that places international criminal justice below the maintenance of peace and security. In the end, the Council's goal of maintaining peace and security is prioritized.

This chapter opens by tracing the evolving relationship between the Council and the ICC. The discussion continues with a closer examination of the conflicting logics underlying the relationship and the implications of their practical application. First, the chapter explores how the

3 Rome Statute, UN doc A/CONF.183/9 (July 17, 1998).

4 See C. Stahn, "United Nations, Peace-Building, Amnesties and Alternative Forms of Justice," *RICR* 84 (2002), pp. 191 ff.

Council's power to refer cases to the ICC and its role in ensuring state cooperation with the Court demonstrate attempts to align the institutions' respective objectives in accordance with the logic of coordination. Second, the chapter proceeds to explain how the Council's power of deferral and recent proposals regarding these institutions' roles in determining the crime of aggression tend to prioritize the Council's pursuit of peace over the objectives of the ICC, reflecting the logic of subordination. The chapter concludes with a preliminary assessment of these conflicting conceptions of the relationship in the context of the UN collective security system.

The evolution of the relationship between the Council and the ICC

The interrelatedness of peace and justice forced the Council and the ICC into an uneasy relationship. Issues regarding the relationship between the Council and the ICC have been the subject of profound debate and intense controversy since the inception of the Court at the Rome Conference.[5] While the connection between the two institutions is now secured by a relationship agreement in addition to linked objectives, the compromises enshrined in the current Rome Statute provisions governing the relationship represent "a delicate balancing act of international justice with international peace and security."[6] Today, striking a proper balance is especially critical in light of the importance of the Council and the ICC in the context of efforts to eradicate impunity and implement global justice.

There can be no doubt that the UN was actively engaged in efforts to create a permanent criminal jurisdiction and that the Council's current practices are a continuation of this project. These efforts culminated in the adoption of the Rome Statute and the establishment of the ICC at the Conference of Plenipotentiaries. While the ad hoc international criminal tribunals were subsidiary organs of the Council under Chapter VII, the ICC is legally distinct from the UN structure and boasts its own unique legal personality. The Rome Statute describes the ICC as an "independent permanent International Criminal Court in relationship

[5] See Christopher Keith Hall, "The First Five Sessions of the UN Preparatory Commission for the International Criminal Court," 94 *AJIL* (2000), p. 788.

[6] J. F. Escudero Espinosa, *La Corte Penal Internacional y el Consejo de Seguridad. Hacia la paz por la justicia* (Dilex, 2004), p. 25.

with the United Nations system."[7] Although the ICC is "organically separated from the United Nations,"[8] Article 2 of the Rome Statute states that the Court "shall be brought into relationship with the United Nations through an agreement to be approved by the Assembly of States Parties to this Statute and thereafter concluded by the President of the Court on its behalf."[9] In 2004, the UN and the ICC approved a relationship agreement in accordance with this mandate. This instrument provided for a reciprocal obligation to mutually respect the others' statutes and mandates in addition to recognizing a duty to cooperate with each other in order to facilitate the exercise of their respective responsibilities.

Despite the rejection of proposals to integrate the Court into the UN system, the Court still lacks complete autonomy because grave crimes that violate international law unquestionably "threaten the peace, security and well-being of the world."[10] Hence, the ICC and the UN are connected not only by the 2004 agreement that forms the legal basis for their relationship, but by the relatedness of their objectives. The 2004 agreement reaffirmed the links between the prosecution of grave crimes and the maintenance of peace and security. Even though their work is related, the autonomy of each institution is ensured by the Rome Statute, which does not interfere with the Council's powers in the field of peace and security, and the UN's obligation to respect the provisions of the ICC's Rome Statute under the relationship agreement.

Without a doubt, these links between the Council and the ICC play a central role in the relationship between the UN and the ICC. For instance, when the Rome Statute was adopted, there was major concern as to whether it was possible to establish a permanent and independent judicial institution that could operate free of political influence. Given the ICC's functions in the maintenance of international peace and security, it was necessary for the Rome Statute to explicitly articulate the Council's role under Article 24 of the UN Charter.[11] At the same time, to paraphrase a well-known article, it was necessary for the temple

[7] Rome Statute, Preamble, para. 9; Rome Statute, Article 4; see also L. Condorelli and S. Villalpando, "Relationship of the Court with the United Nations" in Cassese, A., Gaeta, P., and Jones, J. R. W. (eds.), *The Rome Statute of the International Criminal Court: A Commentary* (New York: Oxford University Press, 2002), p. 221.

[8] *Ibid.* [9] Rome Statute, Article 2. [10] Rome Statute, Preamble, para. 3.

[11] UN Charter, Article 24.

to rely on the police for enforcement of states' cooperation in the investigation and prosecution of crimes within its jurisdiction.[12]

The relationship between the Council and the ICC today has to be evaluated in the context of the ongoing international efforts to eradicate impunity and implement the principle of global justice. In the course of a cycle of World Summits, the UN has recognized the changing nature of the international community's structure and has proceeded to implement global governance. The process started with the Commission on Global Governance (1992),[13] continued with the UN Millennium Summit and its Declaration (2000),[14] and moved forward in response to a series of UN reports addressing collective security.

All three of these reports, either directly or indirectly, raised the issue of the Council's and the ICC's roles in a collective security system. First, the 2004 Report of the High-Level Panel on Threats, Challenges, and Change, entitled *A More Secure World: Our Shared Responsibility*, directly discussed the respective roles of the Council and the ICC in collective security and the challenge of prevention.[15] Regarding conflict between and within states, the Report stated that "the Security Council should be ready to use the authority it has under the Rome Statute to refer cases to the International Criminal Court."[16] Referring to the ICC, the Report highlighted the fact that "since 1945, an ever stronger set of norms and laws –including the Charter of the United Nations, the Geneva Conventions and the Rome Statute for the International Criminal Court – has regulated and constrained States' decisions to use force and their conduct in war."[17]

Second, in the 2005 Report of the United Nations Secretary-General, entitled *In Larger Freedom: Towards Development, Security, and Human Rights for All*, Kofi Annan reemphasized the importance of the ICC. He declared that "justice is a vital component of the rule of law"[18] and to ensure this justice he encouraged member states to fully cooperate with the ICC (and other international or mixed war crimes tribunals) by surrendering accused people to the Court upon request.[19]

[12] Martti Koskenniemi, "The Police in the Temple: Order, Justice and the UN, A Dialectical View," *European Journal of International Law* 6 (1995), pp. 325–348.

[13] See The Commission on Global Governance, *Our Global Neighborhood* (New York: Oxford University Press, 1995).

[14] See Millennium Summit, New York, September 6–8, 2000, *United Nations Millennium Declaration*, UN doc. GA Resolution A/55/2 (September 8, 2000).

[15] See High-Level Panel. [16] *Ibid.*, para. 89.

[17] *Ibid.*, para. 158. [18] *In Larger Freedom*, para. 138. [19] *Ibid.*, para. 18.

Third, in the 2005 World Summit Outcome document, the UN General Assembly reaffirmed its values and principles by recognizing

> the vital importance of an effective multilateral system, in accordance with international law, in order to better address the multifaceted and interconnected challenges and threats confronting our world and to achieve progress in the areas of peace and security, development and human rights, underlining the central role of the United Nations, and commit ourselves to promoting and strengthening the effectiveness of the Organization through the implementation of its decisions and resolutions.[20]

In this document, all of the governments represented in the General Assembly acknowledged that "collective security depends on effective cooperation, in accordance with international law, against transnational threats"[21] and that "peace and security, development and human rights are the pillars of the United Nations system and the foundations for collective security and well-being."[22] Furthermore, they recognized that "development, peace and security and human rights are interlinked and mutually reinforcing."[23]

Unlike the bold references to the ICC in the first two reports, the World Summit Outcome document not only failed to utilize strong language regarding the ICC, but the member states went so far as to avoid any express mention of it.[24] This omission was due to opposition from the US, particularly during the last round of negotiations.[25] As a result, the final Outcome document was less specific than its draft,[26] providing answers to only a few pressing needs.[27] These shortcomings of the World Summit Outcome document were overcome in 2006, during a meeting convened by the Council to consider "strengthening international law: rule of law and maintenance of international peace and security."[28] What had not been possible to achieve during the World Summit was accomplished by the Council President's statement on

20 World Summit Outcome, para. 6. 21 *Ibid.*, para. 7. 22 *Ibid.*, para. 9. 23 *Ibid.*

24 The document's only ambiguous reference to the ICC appeared in para. 134, which "[r]ecogniz[ed] the need for universal adherence to and implementation of the rule of law at both the national and international levels." *Ibid.*, para. 134.

25 Coalition for the International Criminal Court, Press Release, September 9, 2005, www.iccnow.org (last accessed October 10, 2005).

26 Draft of World Summit Outcome, para. 112.

27 See, e.g., Frederick L. Kirgis, *International Law Aspects of the 2005 World Summit Outcome Document*, American Society of International Law, www.asil.org/insights/2005/10/insights051004.html (last accessed May 22, 2008).

28 *Statement by the President of the Security Council*, UN doc. S/PRST/2006/28 (June 22, 2006).

impunity. Carefully avoiding any express mention of the ICC, the statement read:

> The Security Council emphasizes the responsibility of states to comply with their obligations to end impunity and to prosecute those responsible for genocide, crimes against humanity and serious violations of international humanitarian law. The Council reaffirms that ending impunity is essential if a society in conflict or recovering from conflict is to come to terms with past abuses committed against civilians and to prevent future such abuses. The Council intends to continue forcefully to fight impunity with appropriate means and draws attention to the full range of justice and reconciliation mechanisms to be considered, including national, international and "mixed" criminal courts and tribunals and truth and reconciliation commissions.[29]

Coordinating the objectives of the Council and the ICC in practice

Despite the uneasy origins of their association, two of the Council's practices establish links between peace and the international prosecution of grave crimes that particularly evidence the application of the logic of coordination to the relationship between the Council and the ICC. The first practice is referral, the power of the Council under the Rome Statute to refer a situation to the ICC in order to maintain peace. The second practice is the Council's fulfillment of its vital role in ensuring state cooperation with the Court.

The Council's power to refer cases to the ICC

Proponents of creating a permanent international criminal court asserted that such an institution would prevent the Council from utilizing its powers in the field of peace and security to establish new ad hoc international criminal tribunals.[30] Mindful of this desire to avoid more ad hoc tribunals, the delegates at the Rome Conference did not vehemently dispute the Council's power of referral, although some states did raise minor objections.[31] Instead, the Conference envisaged the

[29] *Ibid.*, at para. 4.

[30] International Law Commission, "Report of the International Law Commission," in United Nation International Law Commission, *Yearbook of the International Law Commission* (United Nations Publications, 1994), vol. II, p. 46.

[31] See P. Cargiulo, "The controversial relationship between the International Criminal Court and the Security Council," in Lattanzi, F. and Schabas, W. (eds.), *Essays on the Rome Statute of the International Criminal Court* (Rome: Il Sirente, 1999), vol. I, pp. 70–78.

Council's power of referral as a collective triggering mechanism parallel to the powers exercised unilaterally by state parties under Article 13(a) and by the Prosecutor under Article 13(c). The resulting Article 13(b) of the Rome Statute was fairly succinct as to the rules governing the Council's ability to trigger the ICC. It merely states that:

> The Court may exercise its jurisdiction with respect to a crime referred to in Article 5 in accordance with the provisions of this Statute if: (b) [A] situation in which one or more of such crimes appears to have been committed is referred to the Prosecutor by the Security Council acting under Chapter VII of the Charter of the United Nations.[32]

The Council's power of referral is not without limitations. The Rome Statute recognizes the Council's powers within the ambit of international criminal justice in accordance with the UN Charter. However, the Rome Statute cannot confer upon the Council any new competence. Such extensions of power would not only be politically inopportune but also legally impossible. Instead, the powers of the Council in this respect are limited to those envisioned in Chapter VII of the UN Charter. In order to implement any of the measures authorized by Article 41 *et seq*. of this chapter, the Council must determine the existence of a threat to the peace, a breach of the peace, or an act of aggression.[33] Of these three situations, threats to peace seem to be the best suited to the Council's purposes. For example, the Council determined that serious violations of international law constituted threats to peace before employing ad hoc tribunals and international prosecution in an attempt to end these threats. The Council's current practice seems to adhere to the same approach. For instance, in Resolution 1593 (2005), the Council considered the findings of the Enquiry Commission[34] and affirmed that "the situation in Sudan continues to constitute a threat to international peace and security."[35] As made clear by these examples, despite the restrictions on its power of referral the Council does retain broad discretion to determine which situations fall within the scope of its powers.

When the Council determines that there is a threat to the peace, a breach of peace, or an act of aggression, the Council also has broad discretion to determine the most appropriate measure for restoring peace and security. As recognized by the ICTY in the *Tadic* case, Article 41 of the UN Charter authorizes the Council to enforce its decisions by

[32] Rome Statute, Article 13(b). [33] UN Charter, Article 39.
[34] *Resolution 1593*, UN doc. S/RES/1593 (March 31, 2005). [35] See *ibid.*, preamble.

any means other than the use of armed force, thereby implicitly authorizing the Council to create international criminal jurisdictions.[36] Additionally, the debate about Chapter VII does not prohibit the Council's recourse to any jurisdictional institution available to it by virtue of an international treaty and agreement. However, the problem with the Council's attempts to enforce its decisions by these measures is that state parties do not have an obligation to cooperate. The Rome Statute's Article 13(b), recognizing the Council's power of referral, offers a solution to the Council's limited ability to enforce its decisions by introducing the possibility of coercive measures, albeit this possibility is itself limited by the voting procedure that allows the five permanent members of the Council to veto proceedings against themselves.

When the Council does decide to exercise its power of referral under Article 13(b), it is engaging in a measure primarily perceived as operational, not normative. As a consequence, a decision by the Council does not create a normative pattern of behavior for states, but instead institutes a legal regime opposable to all. Recognizing that after referral, the ICC will determine whether a crime within its jurisdiction was committed, many scholars have noted that Article 13(b) was designed "to empower the Court not the Council" by extending the ICC's jurisdiction to situations not normally within its domain.[37]

Regardless of these theoretical observations regarding the Council's power of referral, there are rules and procedures governing the exercise of this power. At the most basic level, Article 13(b) of the Rome Statute authorizes the Council to refer "a situation" to the Court, but this does not grant it the power to refer the individuals responsible for crimes. Such a power would contribute to the politicization of the ICC. This does not resolve the question of "whether the single case of an individual could sometimes have an impact on the entire situation addressed by the Council," with the consequence that "the impunity of specific individuals would constitute a threat to the peace."[38] However, any assertion that an individual's impunity could be a threat to peace is unlikely to succeed

[36] *Prosecutor* v.*Tadic*, Jurisdiction Appeal, no. IT-94-1-AR72 (October 2, 1995).

[37] F. Berman, "The Relationship between the International Criminal Court and the Security Council," in von Hebel, H., Lammers, J. G., and Schukking, J. (eds.), *Reflections on the International Criminal Court: Essays in Honour of Adriaan Bos* (T. M. C. Asser Press, 1999), p. 174.

[38] I. Prezas, "La justice pénale internationale à l'épreuve du maintien de la paix : à propos de la relation entre la Cour Pénale Internationale et le Conseil de Sécurité," *Revue Belge du Droit International* 1 (2006), 79.

because the identification of individuals fails to conform to the Council's previous practice. In any case, it does not affect the powers of either the ICC or the Prosecutor.

When the Council refers a proper situation to the ICC, the Prosecutor certainly has ample discretion regarding the disposal of the matter. It is up to the Prosecutor to decide whether or not to initiate an investigation. This decision must be based on one of the three considerations listed in Article 53: "(a) The information available to the Prosecutor provides a reasonable basis to believe that a crime within the jurisdiction of the Court has been or is being committed; (b) The case is or would be admissible under Article 17; and (c) Taking into account the gravity of the crime and the interests of victims, there are nonetheless substantial reasons to believe that an investigation would not serve the interests of justice."[39]

If the Prosecutor chooses not to investigate a referral, the Council does have some recourse. If the Prosecutor decides not to investigate a situation that the Council referred to the ICC under Article 13(b) on the ground that there is no reasonable basis to proceed, the Council can ask the Pre-Trial Chamber "to request the Prosecutor to reconsider that decision."[40] However, even if the Pre-Trial Chamber exercises its discretion to make the request, its action does not bind the Prosecutor according to the Rules of Procedure and Evidence if not the Rome Statute itself.[41] If the Prosecutor refuses to proceed with an investigation based on his or her belief that "[it] would not serve the interests of justice" or if the Prosecutor concludes upon investigation that there is not a sufficient basis for a prosecution on the same ground, the Council can appeal to the Pre-Trial Chamber. In this case, the Chamber may, on its own initiative, review a decision of the Prosecutor not to proceed. In such a case, the decision of the Prosecutor shall be effective only if confirmed by the Pre-Trial Chamber.[42] The difference between these two faculties of the Pre-Trial Chamber is based on the fact that, in this latter case, the Prosecutor acts in accordance with his or her discretion (principle of opportunity) and founds the decision on meta-legal considerations, while in the former case (the reasonable basis), the Prosecutor's decision is strictly

[39] G. H. Oosthuizen, "Some preliminary remarks on the relationship between the envisaged International Criminal Court and the Security Council," *Netherlands International Law Review* 46 (1999), pp. 313–342. [40] Rome Statute, Article 53.

[41] Rules of Procedure and Evidence, Rule 108. [42] Rules of Procedure and Evidence, Rule 110.2.

confined to the principle of legality and hence the Statute respects his or her autonomy and independence.[43]

Should its attempts to appeal the Prosecutor's decision fail, the Council has no further recourse because ultimately, referral is within the ICC's jurisdiction. Therefore, although the Council can determine that in a given situation there are enough grounds to initiate an investigation or prosecution, its decision is not binding on the ICC. The Rome Statute makes clear that the Court "shall satisfy itself that it has jurisdiction in any case brought before it."[44] This provision, which reflects a power generally recognized by jurisdictional organs (*Kompetenz/Kompetenz* principle), impliedly confirms that the ICC can control the Council's referral of situations to the Prosecutor. While the ICC's control of a referral's legality under the Rome Statute is not problematic, a more complex jurisdictional issue lies in determining the appropriate body to assess the legality of the Council's action under the UN Charter. The Council's powers under Chapter VII are most likely not subject to any legal control or judicial review.[45] Limiting the ICC to a formal assessment of the requirements with which the Council must comply under Chapter VII restricts the Court to examining the qualifications of the situation, a limitation that is inconsistent with its general judicial control.[46]

In any case, Article 13 of the Rome Statute clearly states that the ICC may exercise its jurisdiction with respect to crimes referred to in Article 5 and Article 17 confers solely upon the ICC the power to decide issues of admissibility. It should be remembered that the ICC and domestic courts have complementary jurisdiction according to Article 1 of the Rome Statute. The exceptions to this fundamental rule are provided for in Article 17 and are essentially related to the competent state's "genuine" unwillingness or incapacity to investigate or prosecute in a particular case. There are different interpretations among international lawyers as to whether the Council's referral of a situation under

[43] I. Lirora Delgado and M. Martín Martínez, *La Corte Penal Internacional. justicia versus impunidad* (Barcelona: Ariel Derecho, 2001), pp. 183, 199.

[44] Rome Statute, Article 19.

[45] See M. Wood, "The UN Security Council and international law. Second lecture: The UN Security Council's powers and their limits," Hersch Lauterpacht Memorial Lectures (University of Cambridge, November 7–9, 2006); Ioana Petculescu, "The review of the United Nations Security Council decisions by the International Court of Justice," *Netherlands International Law review* 52 (2005), pp. 167–195.

[46] I. Prezas, "La justice pénale internationale à l´épreuve du maintien de la paix," p. 77.

Article 13(b) constitutes another such exception.[47] In other words, this raises the question of whether referral by the Council can affect the complementarity principle. The Rome Statute does not envisage any restriction on this principle, confirming that the principle of complementarity retains its applicability no matter how the ICC's jurisdiction is triggered.[48]

Article 13(b) also has important implications for state consent to jurisdiction. When the Council refers a situation, the preconditions required for the exercise of jurisdiction by the Court delineated in Article 12 of the Rome Statute do not apply. This allows the Council to initiate a process leading to the prosecution of individuals who are either nationals of or have committed crimes in the territories of states which are not parties to the Rome Statute even if those states fail to consent.[49] Thus, the power of referral conferred upon the Council supersedes state consent, but it cannot override ICC decisions not to prosecute because the Court possesses the exclusive power to pronounce upon its jurisdiction and on the grounds of admissibility. Furthermore, Article 13(b) of the Rome Statute grants the Court a real universal jurisdiction.

Thus, the Rome Statute incorporates an important exception to preconditions for the Court's jurisdiction as set out in Article 12. Does it imply that the Council could authorize the ICC to act beyond its competence *ratione materiae* and *ratione temporis*? Except when an explicit derogation of the ICC's legal framework is provided for in the Rome Statute, it seems apparent that the Council cannot disregard the rest of the Statute's provisions governing the jurisdiction of the Court because

[47] See Oosthuizen, "Some preliminary remarks" p. 328; L. Arbour and M. Bergsmo, "Conspicuous absence of jurisdictional overreach," in von Hebel, Lammers, and Schukking (eds.), *Reflections on the International Criminal Court*, pp. 139–140; J. Cardona Llorens, "La Corte Penal Internacional y el mantenimiento de la paz y la seguridad internacionales" in Juan Luis Gómez Colomer (coord.), *La Corte Penal Internacional (un estudio interdisciplinar)* (Tirant Lo Blanch, 2003), pp. 68–69; M. Arsanjani, "The Rome Statute of the International Criminal Court," *AJIL* 93 (1999), p. 28.

[48] See Rome Statute, Articles 17, 19, and 53.

[49] V. Gowlland-Debbas, "The relationship between political and judicial organs of international organizations: the role of the Security Council in the new International Criminal Court," in Boison de Chazournes, L., Romano, C. P. R., and Mackenzie R. (eds.), *International organizations and international dispute settlement: Trends and prospects* (Ardsley, NY: Transnational Publishers, 2002), pp. 195–218.

the Council must respect the ICC's autonomy in accordance with their relationship agreement.[50]

The Council's role in ensuring state cooperation with the ICC

International criminal jurisdictions "lack an autonomous *police judiciaire* overriding national authorities. They are like giants without arms and legs, who therefore need artificial limbs to walk and work. These artificial limbs are the state authorities. If the cooperation of states is not forthcoming, these tribunals are paralyzed."[51] In order for the ICC to function effectively, it needs state authorities, but unlike the ICTR and ICTY, it lacks the force of a vertical cooperation regime and the enforcement power of the Security Council. The Rome Statute does not confer upon the Court any enforcement power. Thus, this temple needs the police indeed.

The Council's involvement in enforcement has had relevant consequences on the traditional model of judicial cooperation that is based on extradition conventions and from which no general obligation can be inferred. The Council has actually imposed a general obligation upon states to cooperate with the ad hoc international criminal tribunals. Likewise, the authority of judicial structures established in Kosovo and East Timor is grounded in the same logic because these international administrations of territory came about by virtue of Chapter VII of the UN Charter.

The Rome Statute adopts a mixed approach in the understanding that the general obligation of state parties to cooperate with the ICC comes from a conventional source. Part IX of the Rome Statute provides for a regime of cooperation that departs from mandating a general state obligation.[52] Under this regime, in cases of non-compliance, the ICC makes a finding and then can defer such instances of non-cooperation to the Assembly of States Parties or to the Security Council.[53] Deferral to

[50] See L. Condorelli and S. Villalpando, "Can the Security Council extend the ICC's jurisdiction," in Cassese, Gaeta, and Jones (eds.), *The Rome Statute*, vol. I, pp. 571 ff.; A. Zimmerman, "The creation of a permanent International Criminal Court" in Frowein, J. A. and Wolfrum R. (eds.), *Max Planck Yearbook of the United Nations* (The Hague: Kluwer Law International, 1998), vol. II, p. 216; D. Scheffer, "Staying the course with the International Criminal Court," *Cornell Journal of International Law* 35 (2001–2002), p. 90.

[51] Antonio Cassese, *International Law* (Oxford: Oxford University Press, 2001), p. 269.

[52] See A. Ciampi, "Obligation to cooperate," in Cassese, Gaeta, and Jones (eds.), *The Rome Statute*, vol. II, pp. 1607–1638.

[53] Rome Statute, Article 87.

the Council is inevitable whenever the Council referred the matter to the Court in the first place. While the Rome Statute does not expressly mention how this enforcement is to take place, presumably the Council could classify such refusals to cooperate as threats to the peace, breaches of peace, or acts of aggression under Chapter VII of the Charter and subject the non-compliant parties to all the consequences thereof.[54]

A Council resolution regarding uncooperative state parties under Chapter VII will not create a new obligation from a substantive point of view because that obligation is already prescribed by the Rome Statute. However, the Council resolution would have the effect of transforming a conventional obligation into a unilateral obligation. Non-compliance with this unilateral obligation could be considered a threat to the peace and eventually result in coercive action on the part of the Council. Regarding non-state parties (third states), the Rome Statute suffers from the ambiguities that result from making the Council's intervention dependent on state consent via an ad hoc cooperation agreement with the Court. Article 87 of the Rome Statute further complicates this situation by raising the question of whether the ICC should also notify the Council about non-party states that have not consented to such ad hoc agreement. Considering the Court's extended jurisdiction under Article 13(b), such notification would be logical.[55]

In any event, given that the Council has the power of referral with regard to non-state parties, it may be inferred that it also has the power to impose upon any state the obligation to cooperate with the Court. However, the Rome Statute remains silent as to the kind of action that the Council can adopt when non-party states fail to comply with that obligation. As a result, the Council's earlier practices, including ad hoc tribunals and the classifications of non-cooperation by non-parties as "threats to the peace" requiring appropriate response measures under Chapter VII of the UN Charter, have been very limited in actual practice.

Thus, a referral resolution by the Council can extend the ICC's powers when it enforces a general obligation of cooperation with the Court. For instance, Resolution 1593 (2005) on the Darfur situation states that the Government of the Sudan, like all other parties involved, has to cooperate fully with, and provide necessary assistance to, the Court and the

54 See ICTY, *Prosecutor* v. *Blaskic*. Judgment on Request for Review, IT-95-14 (October 29, 1997), paras. 26, 31, 33.

55 Oosthuizen, "Some preliminary remarks ..." p. 339; and Zimmerman, "The creation of a Permanent International Criminal Court," p. 216.

Prosecutor. However, the current lessons learned from this practice are not an invitation to optimism.

Subordinating the ICC's objectives to those of the Council in practice

At first sight, insisting on both peace and justice may seem paradoxical, raising at least two critical conflicts between the Council and the ICC.[56] First, according to certain hypotheses, the international prosecution of grave crimes can have negative repercussions for the peace process. Second, at a different level, the pursuit of both peace and justice results in conflict between the ICC's exercise of jurisdiction over the crime of aggression and the Council's powers under Chapter VII of the UN Charter. To resolve these clashes between the Council and the ICC, a logic of subordination is frequently applied to prioritize the Council's goal of maintaining peace and security. In practice, this translates into the Council exercising its power of deferral under the Rome Statute to obstruct the ICC's pursuit of justice and is reflected in proposals to grant the Council the power to determine acts of aggression thereby denying the ICC exclusive jurisdiction over such matters.

The Council's power of deferral

With regard to the power of deferral, Article 16 of the Rome Statute states that "no investigation or prosecution may be commenced or proceeded with under this Statute for a period of 12 months after the Security Council, in a resolution adopted under Chapter VII of the Charter of the United Nations, has requested the Court to that effect; that request may be renewed by the Council under the same conditions." This provision probably represents the first time that state parties to a multilateral treaty expressly consented to confer upon a political organ, such as the Security Council, the ability to force an international judicial institution to suspend an investigation or a prosecution.

The Article 16 power of deferral has been a source of controversy ever since it was proposed at the ICC Conference of Plenipotentiaries because

[56] See D. Sarooshi, "The peace and justice paradox: the International Criminal Court and the UN Security Council," in McGoldrick, Dominic, Rowe, Peter, Donnelly, Eric (eds.), *The Permanent International Criminal Court* (Portland, Oregon: Hart Publishing, 2004), pp. 95–120.

of its potential adverse effects on international justice. The drafting history of Article 16 shows that it was one of the most difficult and sensitive provisions to be included in the Rome Statute. It was permitted only after several other proposals had been rejected.[57] The problem confronting the drafters at the Rome Conference was the difficulty of crafting a provision which would be consistent with the Security Council's overarching responsibility for peace and security under the Statute but would not diminish the independence of the ICC that was mandated by Article 4 of the Rome Statute.[58] However, in the end, the power of deferral was justified by the fact that "at the fundamental level, the purpose of creating an International Criminal Court is to contribute to maintaining international peace and security, which obviously could not be done while inhibiting the operation of the Charter-established organ tasked with that very international peace and security."

Critics of deferral can take comfort in the fact that the Council does not wield this power unfettered. Article 16 requires the Council to act affirmatively to pass a resolution requesting the ICC to defer its investigation, an action that entails achieving the consensus of all five permanent Members of the Council. Presumably, the Council must also make a prior determination in accordance with Article 39, a prerequisite for any action taken under Chapter VII, including deferral resolutions. Moreover, the time limit, although subject to renewal, functions as an additional safeguard. Article 16 instructs that the Security Council may only defer the jurisdiction of the ICC over a particular matter for a period of twelve months. In light of the *travaux préparatoires*, this requirement should not be interpreted as the right to suspend *ad infinitum* the investigation or prosecution of a case before the Court. These restrictions have attenuated some of the Rome Conference delegates' concerns about deferral's potential to undermine the independence of the ICC by allowing for extensive control by a political organ. Furthermore, Article 16's restrictions

[57] See United Nations International Law Commission, *Yearbook of the International Law Commission*, vol. II, pp. 43–45; *Report of the Ad Hoc Committee on the Establishment of an International Criminal Court*, UN doc.A/50/22 (1995), para. 124; *Report of the Preparatory Committee on the Establishment of an International Criminal Court*, UN doc. A/51/22 (September 13, 1996), para. 141; L. Condorelli and S. Villalpando, "Referral and deferral by the Security Council," in Cassese, Gaeta, and Jones (eds.), *The Rome Statute*, pp. 644 ff.

[58] See also Condorelli and Villalpando, "Referral and deferral," in Cassese, Gaeta, and Jones (eds.), *The Rome Statute*, p. 644.

demonstrate the Rome Conference participants' commitment to gaining the support of states that oppose the ICC, particularly the United States.

But what is the exact scope of this provision? Given the Council's powers under Chapter VII of the UN Charter, in principle, it would not be legally necessary for the Council to adopt a resolution requesting deferral. In fact, the formulation of Article 16 seems to present a problem because the UN Charter does not envisage the kind of power that would allow the Council to suspend the activity of the ICC. Moreover, while the Council has the power to extinguish the ad hoc international criminal tribunals that it had established as subsidiary organs, it lacks both the judicial power and the authority to interfere with the tribunal's independence. As a result, the Council cannot impose its views upon tribunals. However, the ICC, established by an international treaty, cannot inhibit the powers of the Council under Chapter VII. Furthermore, the formulation of Article 16 makes *renvoi* to Chapter VII of the UN Charter and thus implicitly affirms the Council's priority.[59] Thus, the power of deferral must be strictly interpreted and exercised in light of the exceptional nature of the relationship between a political organ and a judicial institution.

In addition to these problems, at least four aspects relating to the scope of the Council's power of deferral under Article 16 remain unresolved. First, it is not clear how the Council would determine whether one of the situations specified in Article 39 of the UN Charter justified the suspension of ICC activity as a measure aimed at the maintenance of peace and security. This raises the questions of whether a threat to the peace under Article 39 must result from the ICC's investigation or prosecution or whether the Council "could refer to a larger factual or political background, related to the proceedings before the Court and placed in one of the categories described in Article 39."[60]

Second, the wording of Article 16 seems to concern only the Prosecutor's activities. Since the Council sends its requests to the Court, the correct interpretation should be that a deferral may intervene at any procedural stage. The Council and the ICC's relationship agreement provides that the Secretary-General should transmit requests to both the President of the Court and the Prosecutor.[61] Thus, it falls to the

[59] See Wood, "The UN Security Council."

[60] Condorelli and Villalpando, "Referral and deferral," in Cassese, Gaeta, and Jones (eds.), *The Rome Statute*, p. 647.

[61] Oosthuizen, "Some preliminary remarks ..." p. 334.

President of the ICC to identify which situations before the Court would be impacted by the deferral and to inform the Chambers of the Court accordingly.[62]

Third, another issue relates to the material scope of the deferral. While it seems apparent that the power to defer does not extend to the phase when the Prosecutor collects information prior to the formal opening of an investigation, it is unclear whether the ICC could take provisional measures in order to preserve elements of evidence.

Fourth, Article 16 also fails to clarify whether the Council's exercise of its power of deferral is subject to legal control or judicial review. Given that the Court is competent to pronounce upon its jurisdiction, in principle, the procedure envisaged in Article 19 would be applicable to the extent that the suspension can be regarded as a jurisdictional question *lato sensu*. In this case, as with the referral, the Council's control of compliance with the acts under the UN Charter is very limited in scope. Unlike referral, the conformity of a suspension with the Rome Statute could be subject to more extensive scrutiny. While the Rome Statute does not contain clear provisions to this effect, if the ICC decided to declare the deferral irregular, it is difficult to imagine how the Court will carry out its tasks if states are bound by that resolution not to cooperate with the ICC. Some scholars have argued that each state would have to recognize the regularity of the deferral and decide for itself whether to comply with the obligations envisaged by the Council's resolution.

While determining the scope of its powers under the ambiguous Article 16 is challenging, exercising the power of deferral can raise even more problems. For instance, the Council can request the ICC to suspend its activities by invoking one of the situations envisaged in Article 39 of the UN Charter. However, Resolution 1422 (2002),[63] like the homologous Resolution 1487 (2003),[64] failed to expressly reference any such situation, instead merely stating "that it is in the interests of international peace and security to facilitate member states' ability to contribute to

[62] Prezas, "La justice pénale internationale," p. 86.

[63] *Resolution 1422*, UN doc. S/RES1422 (July 12, 2002). See also M. El Zeidy, "The United States dropped the atomic bomb of Article 16 of the ICC Statute: Security Council power of deferrals and resolution 1422," *Vanderbilt Journal of Transnational Law* 135 (2002), p. 503; C. Stahn, "The ambiguities of Security Council Resolution 1422 (2002)," *European Journal of International Law* 14 (2003), p. 85; B. MacPherson, "Authority of the Security Council to exempt peacekeepers from International Criminal Court proceedings," American Society of International Law, www.asil.org/insights/insigh89.htm (last accessed May 24, 2008).

[64] *Resolution 1487*, UN doc. S/RES/1487(2003) (June 12, 2003).

operations established or authorized by the United Nations Security Council." The reference to the actual threat to peace that would justify deferring ICC action is conspicuously absent, unless one considers it a threat to peace for a state, here the United States, to fail to contribute its troops to peacekeeping operations when its nationals are not exempted. Even from this approach, a hypothetical threat to the peace consisting of the non-participation of one state's troops in peace operations seems to go beyond the particular character of the measures normally taken by the Security Council under the UN Charter. In other words, the Council is not empowered to adopt general norms in the absence of a concrete situation justifying its intervention, although its recent practice in the fight against terrorism raises some doubts in this respect.[65]

If the above-mentioned resolutions are of doubtful legality under the UN Charter, they are in blatant contravention of the Rome Statute. The formulation of Resolutions 1422 and 1487 raises a potential conflict between the Council's objective of maintaining peace and the ICC's activities. The resolutions also clash with the Rome Statute mandate requiring deferrals to be decided on a case-by-case basis. These tensions may explain why certain states have stressed the *ultra vires* character of the resolutions while others have claimed that they constitute an unacceptable and subverted way of modifying the Rome Statute.[66] For example, the European Union consistently denounced these resolutions as incompatible with the Rome Statute. The resolutions had stated that the Council "decides that Member States shall take no action inconsistent with paragraph 1 and with their international obligations." This statement seemed to refer to states' obligations under bilateral agreements with the US not to transfer any US nationals who may be found in their territories to the ICC. The European Union and other critics rejected the assertion of this conflicting obligation as a mere attempt to avoid state cooperation with the ICC presumably on the basis of Article 98.

While Resolutions 1422 and 1487 and others like them demonstrate the Council's ability to use its power of deferral to undermine the ICC's pursuit of justice, they do not exclude the possibility of states exercising their own powers of criminal prosecution. The Rome Statute affirms this

[65] See E. Rosand, "The SC as a 'global legislator': *Ultra vires* or ultra innovative?," *Fordham International Law Journal* 28 (2005), p. 101; see generally Wood, "The UN Security Council."

[66] See Security Council Meeting, UN doc. S/PV.4568 of (July 10, 2002), pp. 1–17; Security Council Meeting, UN doc. S/PV.4772 of July 12, 2003.

authority in its preamble, which declares that "it is the duty of every State to exercise its criminal jurisdiction over those responsible for international crimes." The recognition of each state's power is apparently an indirect acknowledgment of the principle of universal jurisdiction. However, the preamble of the resolutions specified that "States not Party to the Rome Statute will continue to fulfill their responsibilities in their national jurisdictions in relation to international crimes." This statement appears to conform with the intended effect of these resolutions, namely the exclusive jurisdiction of contributing states not party to the Rome Statute, an interpretation further supported by Resolution 1497 (2003).[67] The objective of such statements does not seem to be blocking the ICC but depriving UN member states of their criminal jurisdiction. As a result, the resolutions under examination enshrine an immunity regime for the benefit of a particular category of individuals. Under this regime, any eventual criminal sanctions for their acts would be solely dependent upon the will of the individuals' state of nationality.

It is not easy to carry out a legal assessment of the Council's practice of paralyzing the ICC's activity while at the same time aiming to disempower member states of their criminal prerogatives. The states' reaction and the power of the ICC to determine its own jurisdiction will provide precious clues indicating a sound response to these issues.

The Council's and the ICC's roles in determining the crime of aggression

Article 5 of the Rome Statute lists the crime of aggression among the crimes that form the ICC's substantive jurisdiction. Owing to disagreements among the participating states over the definition of aggression and the role to be attributed to the Council in this respect, the inclusion of the crime of aggression in the subject matter jurisdiction of the Court came about in the very last moments of the Conference of Plenipotentiaries' negotiation over the Rome Statute.[68] This central issue remains unresolved in the Rome Statute still. Instead, Article 5 of the Statute merely directs that "The Court shall exercise jurisdiction over the crime of aggression once a provision is adopted in accordance with Articles 121 and 123 defining the crime and setting out the conditions under which the Court

67 *Resolution 1497*, UN doc.S/RES/1497 (August 1, 2003).

68 See Press Release about this last session of the Rome Conference L/Rom/21 (July 17, 1998).

shall exercise jurisdiction with respect to this crime in accordance with the United Nations Charter."[69]

The countries that participated in the Rome Conference agreed to this compromise in order to secure the conclusion of the Statute after they had reached a deadlock over the crime of aggression.[70] Above all, the impasse resulted from the Rome Conference's inability to reach an agreement as to whether the ICC would be empowered to exercise jurisdiction in the absence of a Council determination that an act of aggression had occurred. The decision to postpone elaborating on the crime of aggression reflects an important divergence of opinions as to the precise notion of aggression – that is, whether it was a crime of a state or a crime that gave rise to individual criminal responsibility – as well as to the conditions for the exercise of jurisdiction. Surely, the definition and jurisdiction of the crime of aggression have always been extremely difficult issues to settle.

The search for an appropriate and effective definition and jurisdiction for the crime of aggression has raised both legal and political issues as the debate has evolved over time. Today's debate on the crime of aggression is probably the outcome of the international community's endless efforts since the establishment of the International Military Tribunal at Nuremberg. In fact, the circumstances under which the Tribunal was established at Nuremberg resemble the current situation regarding the crime of aggression under the ICC's jurisdiction, but there are two significant distinctions. First, at the London Conference in 1945, it was clear whom the Allies wanted to punish, but the punishers were unsure of the Tribunal's consistency with principles of international law. However, at the Rome Conference in 1998, there was less concern with the latter and more concern with the potential targets for prosecutions for aggression. Second, today, one superpower dominates international relations both politically and militarily, possibly making a consensus definition of the crime of aggression and the conditions under which it may be prosecuted more difficult than it would have been in 1945. In part, this difficulty stems from the fact that the concept of a common enemy has been obscured as terrorism became a more pressing issue. Despite these

[69] Rome Statute, Article 5, para. 2.

[70] Mohammed M. Gomaa, "The Definition of the Crime of Aggression and the ICC Jurisdiction over that Crime," in Politi, M. and Nesi, G. (eds.), *The International Criminal Court and the crime of aggression* (Aldershot, England: Ashgate Publishing, 2004), p. 55.

differences, the central problem is still to determine which organ is entitled to adopt a legally binding definition of aggression.

After the Nuremberg Tribunal, most legal work on the crime of aggression proceeded under the International Law Commission (ILC) at the request of the UN General Assembly. Both the ILC's drafts of State Responsibility and the Code of Crimes against the Peace and Security of Mankind dealt with the regulation of the "crime of aggression." The former draft conceived of aggression as an international crime that gave rise to the international responsibility of the state and the latter draft defined it as a crime against peace that gave rise to the criminal responsibility of individuals. The ILC decided not to articulate a general definition of crimes against the peace and security of mankind, instead leaving to practice the task of defining its exact contours. The distinction between state responsibility and individual responsibility, in connection with aggression, was recognized and well preserved in the work of the ILC. The ILC was seeking to define the crime of an individual who, in the case of aggression committed by a state, might be considered a leader or organizer of the crime and would therefore be personally liable for it. By characterizing aggression as an offence against the peace and security of mankind, the ILC relied on the formula used at the London Conference to prosecute individuals for aggression. Between 1954 and 1996, the ILC submitted three drafts of the Code, but the UN adopted none of them.

While there have been a few outbreaks since 1945 which could have been recognized as "wars of aggression," the Security Council has been extremely reluctant to find that any acts of aggression have occurred. Thus, many UN member states argued to the General Assembly the necessity of developing an instrument to define and confirm the act of aggression. By means of Resolution 378 B(V) of November 17, 1950, the General Assembly decided to refer the question of aggression's definition to the ILC and to later establish special committees to resolve this problem.[71] Consequently, several Special Committees on the Question of Defining Aggression were set up by General Assembly resolutions between 1952 and 1965. However, in spite of numerous efforts, no definition was approved.

Then finally, the last Special Committee, established by the Assembly in 1967,[72] was successful in drafting the definition that was provided by

[71] See *Official records of the General Assembly, Fifth Session, Annexes*, agenda item 72, document A/C.1/608.

[72] *General Assembly Resolution 2330 (XXII)*, UN doc. A/RES/2330 (December 18, 1967).

General Assembly Resolution 3314 (XXIX) and adopted by consensus on December 14, 1974. This definition has become the generally recognized definition of aggression, although constant debate persists on the issues of the legal content and the customary nature of the Definition of Aggression.

This definition, annexed to Resolution 3314, deals with aggression by states and not with the crimes of individuals. Article 5 is especially clear in distinguishing "war of aggression" from "aggression" in order to classify state responsibility and individual criminal responsibility separately.[73] The International Court of Justice (ICJ) has considered the Definition of Aggression as customary international law, referring explicitly to Article 3 as reflective of a customary norm in international law in its 1986 judgment concerning military and paramilitary activities in and against Nicaragua.[74] In any case, this Definition of Aggression serves as a simple guide for the Security Council in determining an act of aggression.

Despite the General Assembly's approval of the Definition of Aggression, the work to further define the crime of aggression has continued even after the establishment of the ICC. In accordance with Article 5 of the Statute and the Final Act of the Rome Conference, ten sessions of the Preparatory Commission (PrepCom) were held between February 1999 and July 2002. After the Rome Statute came into force on July 1, 2002, the Assembly of States Parties to the Rome Statute decided to establish the Special Working Group on the Crime of Aggression (SWGCA). At the time this chapter was drafted, this working group had held five formal sessions as well as several inter-session meetings.

The PrepCom mainly employed two approaches to the definition of the crime of aggression. The first one was the "generic approach," which proposed a general or abstract definition and the second one was the "list approach," which enumerated the specific acts constituting aggression. During its discussions, the PrepCom raised the possibility of combining these two approaches into a single definition. This proposed single definition would contain both an introductory paragraph of a general nature followed by a list of specific acts that constitute the offence.

While this issue is still open, it is the "generic approach," including a reference to the definition in Resolution 3314, that currently receives the most support in the context of the SWGCA's works. Based on a 2007

[73] Rome Statute, Article 5, para. 2.

[74] Military and Paramilitary Activities in and against Nicaragua (*Nicaragua* v. *United States of America*), Merits, *1984 ICJ Reports* 392 (June 27, 1986), p. 14.

discussion paper by the Chairman, the SWGCA's recent discussions have concentrated primarily on two components of the crime of aggression: the elements of the definition of the crime of aggression and the conditions that must exist before the ICC can exercise its jurisdiction. The SWGCA has focused on three elements of the crime: the leadership requirement,[75] the individual's conduct,[76] and the state's act of aggression.[77] Despite the delegations' fundamental disagreements over the definition, and particularly the consideration of the conduct of individuals, the discussions reveal agreement on the leadership requirement – that is, the fact that a state entity is the one committing aggression – and the required magnitude of the acts of armed force. However, there are several potential shortcomings that result from either the leadership requirement or the act of aggression element, not the least of which is the fact that acts of aggression committed by individuals not officially affiliated with a state entity cannot be subject to the jurisdiction of the ICC. Thus, terrorists and revolutionary groups that could possibly plan, initiate, and wage aggressive war would not be within the jurisdiction of the ICC.

Regarding the jurisdictional conditions for aggression, Article 5 of the Rome Statute indicates that the amendment "defining the crime and setting out the conditions under which the Court shall exercise jurisdiction with respect to this crime" should be "consistent with the relevant provisions of the Charter of the United Nations."[78] In principle, authorizing the Council to determine whether an act constitutes aggression would be most consistent with the UN Charter. However, this does not resolve certain ambiguities. Supposing that the Council determines that an act of aggression has occurred, the consequences are not very clear. Does it mean that the ICC is bound to respect the determination of the Council? The judicial function of the ICC renders the Court ill-suited for making the decisions of a political organ because such decisions would

[75] During the SWGCA's 2007 meetings, the majority considered the leadership clause a jurisdictional element and no longer part of the definition of the crime. See also UN doc. ICC-ASP/6/SWGCA/INF.1 (July 15, 2007), which presents the Report of the Informal inter-sessional meeting of the Special Working Group on the Crime of Aggression.

[76] Two approaches were discussed: the so-called "monistic approach" and the "differentiated approach," the latter of which received broad support.

[77] During the SWGCA meeting in June 2007, participants expressed broad support for defining the term "act of aggression" on the basis of Resolution 3314. See the Report of the Informal inter-sessional meeting of the Special Working Group on the Crime of Aggression, p. 8.

[78] Rome Statute, Article 5.

ultimately imply that the permanent members of the Council were shielded from the ICC's jurisdiction. Aside from that, making the Court's jurisdiction dependent on the Council determination could have the consequence of infringing upon the rights of the accused person and displacing the presumption of innocence because a different organ would have already attributed an act of aggression to the state.

As evidenced by the works of the Prepcom and the SWGCA, reaching an agreement on the jurisdictional conditions for the crime of aggression is a far more difficult task than agreeing on the definition itself. The various proposals submitted to the PrepCom go from extreme positions that defend the Council's exclusive responsibility for determining aggression of a state to those that argue that the Council has no role at all in this matter because the determination of aggression is a legal question that the UN Charter did not assign to the Council.

The essence of the arguments in favor of authorizing the Security Council to predetermine whether there was an act of aggression was well summarized by one PrepCom delegate who explained that:

> To ask the Court in the absence of a determination by the Security Council to decide that an act of aggression has taken place … would endanger … its judicial role and image … Imagine the immense difficulties that the ICC, a court of law, would face in dealing even with relatively simple acts of aggression … Is it equipped to consider such matters as historical claims to territory, maritime boundaries, legitimate self-defence under Article 51 or legitimate reprisals? … And is the competence of the Court, in any event, not limited to jurisdiction over natural persons? … We must now turn the ICC into a political forum discussing the legality of use of force by States.[79]

However, other delegates want to confer the power to determine an act of aggression upon an organ other than the Council. In the compromise proposals compiled in the 2002 Discussion Paper,[80] a failure by the Council to fulfill its responsibility to determine the existence of acts of aggression cannot make the jurisdiction of the ICC ineffective and nonexistent in practice because the responsibility of the Council is primary but not exclusive.[81] On this issue, the positions range from the radical, which propose authorizing the Court itself to make a ruling in the absence of a Council determination,[82] to the balanced, which prefer

[79] M. Lehto, "The ICC and the Security Council: About the argument of politicization," in Politi and Nesi, *The International Criminal Court*, p. 146.

[80] *Discussion paper proposed by the Coordinator*, UN doc. PCNICC/2002/WGCA /RT.1 / Rev.1 (July 10, 2002).

[81] *Ibid*., para. 4. [82] *Ibid*., para. 5.

to leave the determination of such a situation to another political organ like the General Assembly,[83] to a judicial organ like the ICC, or even to a mix of judicial and political organs like the ICJ and the General Assembly.[84] The debate continues with the recent addition of a Belgian proposal aimed to filter out politicized recourse to the ICC to the 2007 Discussion Paper, the basis of the SWGCA's current work.

These proposals have merit, but they also raise some problems. On the one hand, recognizing that the Court has an autonomous power to determine an act of aggression would bring about an expansion of the jurisdiction granted by the Rome Statute. The Court has jurisdiction over natural persons and in accordance with the Statute, "No provision in this Statute relating to individual criminal responsibility shall affect the responsibility of States under international law."[85] It is difficult to imagine how the Court could pronounce upon the responsibility of a state in order to determine the criminal responsibility of individuals without entering a field of competence that is not its own. On the other hand, it would not be wise to assign such a role to the General Assembly when the goal is to avoid politicization. In the end, the potential role of the ICJ with regard to the crime of aggression has more merit because it may contribute to re-enforcing legal security and to avoiding a conflict with the ICC. However, no matter which of these proposed solutions gains general support, it will need the acceptance of the United Nations organs.

Aside from the intrinsic power politics that will influence the outcome of the review conference that seems to have been postponed until 2010, the concern over the potential incompatibility between the Rome Statute and the UN Charter has contributed to the delay in reaching a compromise on the crime of aggression provisions. The delegations at the PrepCom and Special Working Group were quite aware that while the determinations by the Council on acts of aggression were based on political considerations, the ICC was required to review the situation by applying a totally different procedure in accordance with a judicial process. This difference in the assessment systems of the Council and the ICC may result in different findings. Therefore, any sound solution to the question of the relationship between the ICC and the Council will depend primarily on how it eliminates the possibility of inconsistency between the decisions of the two institutions. Surely, this has to be done with full respect for the Security Council's primary responsibility for maintaining peace and security and for the ICC's independence that

[83] *Ibid.* [84] *Ibid.* [85] Rome Statute, Article 25, para. 4.

enables it to fulfill its role in international justice. As acknowledged in a recent meeting of the SWGCA, "the Court and the Security Council have autonomous but complementary roles, which could be best advanced if both institutions have broadly compatible rules regarding the determination of an act of aggression."[86]

Conclusion

While practice does not seem to be sufficient to determine the adequacy of the preceding analysis, it does permit a few interim assessments. First, the analysis of referral to the ICC reveals an uncomfortable symbiosis of the Council's very exceptional regime with the Court's conventional regime, a tension caused by the Council's power. This affirmation holds despite the important role that the Council may play in ensuring member states' cooperation with the ICC. Regarding the competence of the ICC, the Council is heavily limited because even though it is the Court's prerogative to disregard non-member states' consent, it cannot arbitrarily modify its competence *ratione materiae*, *ratione temporis*, or *ratione personae*. The Council's activity is also constrained with regards to complementarity as this does not automatically affect the Court's appreciation of this condition. The ICC constitutes a resource servicing the maintenance of peace, but it modifies the rules of the game in the sense that from now onwards, it will not be exclusively defined by the Council. This strict regime may lead the Council to resort to other mechanisms, such as mixed or ad hoc tribunals.

Second, the enshrinement of the Council's powers to suspend the jurisdiction of the ICC clearly evidences the absence of an axiomatic link between the goal of maintaining international peace and security and that of achieving international justice, despite the Court's undeniable contribution to peacefully settling social relations that have been severely disrupted by grave crimes. In an international order where "peace" is not only a value to protect but also a legally structured mechanism (albeit within enormous political constraints), coincidence of these two goals may be perceived as contingent upon the conception of peace adopted by the casuistry of the Council, be it maintenance of peace vis-à-vis justice or temporarily favoring justice vis-à-vis peace. Even though there is an ongoing debate over the crime of aggression, the

[86] Report of the Informal inter-sessional meeting of the Special Working Group on the Crime of Aggression, p. 11.

uncertainty as to the application of Article 16 of the Rome Statute which results from the Council's practice evidences the scope of the difficulties the Court will face in the future.

Finally, the debate over the relationship between the ICC and the Council should not obscure the role that member states are called to play in the context of the Court, especially since the Council's actions in this matter will impact on them. The Court's efficacy in imposing criminal sanctions for grave crimes with international repercussions will be highly dependent on member states because beyond the potential legal control of the Council's acts by the ICC, member states are ultimately responsible for its political control. The General Assembly, dormant since the 1990s, would constitute an adequate forum for the political control of the Council's activities involving the maintenance of international peace and security, thus withstanding attempts to disguise unilateralism in the form of collective will.

PART IV

Perspectives on the ground

12

Developing security in the eastern Democratic Republic of the Congo: MONUC as a practical example of (failing) collective security

DENNIS DIJKZEUL

Introduction

The conflicts in the eastern Democratic Republic of the Congo (DRC) have caused the most deadly humanitarian crisis of our time. About 5.4 million people have died as a consequence of this crisis over the last ten years.[1] The crisis has often been referred to as "Africa's First World War," because at one stage eight African countries and many other international and transnational actors were involved. The United Nations Organization Mission in the Democratic Republic of the Congo (MONUC) has been active in the country since 2000. This chapter studies several aspects of the functioning of MONUC as an illustration of the opportunities, as well as the shortcomings, of a system of collective security.

The chapter first discusses the recent UN reforms and provides a brief overview of the conflicts and difficult peace process in the DRC. It subsequently analyzes MONUC's work as a concrete example of collective security in the eastern DRC. It goes on to show the closely related difficulties in creating a collective security system and improving security in current chronic conflicts and offers a grounded critique of international decision making and policy making concerning UN reforms and collective security.

UN reform

The UN reform process after the September 11, 2001 attacks on the United States generated a variety of reform proposals from a High-Level

[1] B. Coghlan, V. Nkamgang Bemo, P. Ngoy, T. Stewart, F. Mulumba, J. Lewis, C. Hardy, and R. Brennan, *Mortality in the Democratic Republic of Congo: An Ongoing Crisis* (International Rescue Committee/Burnett Institute, 2008), in mimeo and available at www.theirc.org (last accessed July 16, 2008).

Panel of Experts and the Secretary-General. The High-Level Panel Report, *A More Secure World: Our Shared Responsibility*, issued in 2003 concluded that the case for collective security today rests on three pillars: (1) that today's threats recognize no national boundaries, are connected, and must be addressed at the global and regional as well as national levels; (2) no state alone can make itself invulnerable to today's threats; and (3) it cannot be assumed that every state will be able or willing to meet its responsibility to protect its own peoples and not to harm its neighbors. The High-Level Panel called for a new consensus among nations to work affirmatively to assuage current conflict at all levels. Secretary-General Kofi Annan's report, *In Larger Freedom*, issued in March 2005 echoed the High-Level Panel's call for mutual responsibility among nations as the key to creating collective security.

Unfortunately, although Secretary-General Kofi Annan advised the member states to accept the bold reform proposals from *In Larger Freedom* in their entirety at the September 2005 World Summit, UN Security Council reform turned out to be the death sentence for such a package deal.[2] The lack of real champions for certain proposals, and also resistance by the permanent members and other states to Security Council enlargement, rendered the World Summit a disappointment.[3]

The Summit[4] "failed to address the toughest security issues: terrorism, use of force, non-proliferation [nuclear testing, disarmament], and Security Council reform."[5] Arab countries prevented incorporation of an unequivocal definition of terrorism as "politically motivated violence against civilians" so that no common international terrorism policy could be established.[6] On issues concerning nuclear testing, new weapons programs or production of fissile material, nobody "could even begin to agree on action either on the supply side (to constrain the availability of material and technology) or the demand side (to reduce the

[2] See Edward Luck, "The UN Security Council: Reform or Enlarge?," Paper prepared for *The UN: Adapting to the 21st Century* conference (Waterloo: Ontario, 2005); and "How Not to Reform the United Nations," *Global Governance* 11 (2005), pp. 407–414.

[3] P. R. Baehr, Ingrijpende Hervorming Verenigde Naties Opnieuw Mislukt, *Internationale Spectator* 59 (2005), pp. 586–590; and N. Soderberg, "The United Nations: 'Missed Opportunity'," *Financial Times* (September 14, 2005), www.crisisgroup.org/home (last accessed October 26, 2005); see also H. Versluys, "Verwaterde Conclusies VN-Top Teleurstelling voor Europa," *Internationale Spectator* 59 (2005), pp. 591–594.

[4] UN Doc, A/60/1.

[5] Soderberg, "The United Nations: 'Missed Opportunity'."

[6] Gareth Evans, "UN Missed the Chance of a Lifetime," *The Globe and Mail* (2005), www. crisisgroup.org/home/ (last accessed October 11, 2005).

motivation for acquiring weapons of mass destruction). The failure to find a new consensus on these issues is potentially quite disastrous, perhaps facilitating a new cascade of proliferation."[7]

Although the World Summit participants affirmed their commitment to achieving the Millennium Development Goals by 2015, the United States refused to be restrained by any binding obligations. Similarly, the goal for many developed countries to spend 0.7 percent of their Gross National Product by 2015 (and reach 0.5 percent by 2010) for official development assistance[8] was mentioned in the final report, but not enacted. In principle, at least half of this money should be allocated to "forgotten" crises in Africa.[9]

In the areas of peacekeeping and humanitarian affairs the *Responsibility to Protect* was incorporated despite objections by the United States. This responsibility – though not an obligation – entails that the "international community" should act when a state is unwilling or incapable to protect its population against genocide, war crimes, ethnic cleansing, and crimes against humanity.[10] It should do so collectively – with peaceful means where possible and force if necessary.[11] The *Responsibility to Protect* is a middle ground between traditional sovereignty, which protects states, and the *droit d'ingérence* (a concept originally formulated by Bernard Kouchner), which could lead to too low a threshold for interventions. The acceptance of this new norm of collective security marks a shift from just the protection of states to the protection of people.[12]

The member states also agreed to establish a Peacebuilding Commission – with a small Peacebuilding Support Office located in the Secretariat – to help conflict countries with rebuilding, reconciliation, and more sustainable development in order to prevent a recurrence of violence. The aim of the Commission was to help coordinate the manifold actors involved and extend the period of attention given by the international community to post-conflict recovery, as most donors shift to the next crisis too rapidly.

The humanitarian system was also reformed in light of suggestions made by the *Good Humanitarian Donorship Initiative*. A preparatory internal document of the UN Office for the Coordination of

[7] *Ibid.* [8] UN Doc. A/Res/60/1.

[9] Versluys, "Verwaterde Conclusies VN-Top Teleurstelling voor Europa," at 592. In the area of human rights, the discredited Human Rights Commission was replaced by the Human Rights Council.

[10] *Ibid.* [11] Evans, "UN Missed the Chance of a Lifetime."

[12] Gareth Evans, the former Australian Foreign Minister and current President of the International Crisis Group, has played an active role in both the High-Level Panel and the International Commission on Intervention and State Sovereignty (ICISS).

Humanitarian Affairs (OCHA) argued, "The international response to humanitarian emergencies has demonstrated that the present system does not always meet the basic needs of affected populations in a timely way." It suggested a "system upgrade" by providing more predictable and timely funding, strengthening response capacity, and improving coordination at the field and headquarters level. An expanded Central Emergency Response Fund (CERF) was to generate $500 million annually in advance of non-earmarked funds through public and private contributions, which would be allocated to UN agencies by the UN Emergency Response Coordinator during emerging crises.

In addition, the United Kingdom proposed common funding at the country level, linked to the Common Humanitarian Action Plan (CHAP) and the resulting Consolidated Appeal Process (CAP). It was hoped that such pooled funding would facilitate more strategic cooperation by the different actors – donors, UN organizations, international and local NGOs – involved. This new funding modality has been implemented in both Sudan and the DRC since January 2006.[13]

Simultaneously, the humanitarian response review identified gaps in response capacity in such sectors as health, nutrition, and logistics. In each of the sectors, the review proposed that a UN agency, for example the WHO in health and the UNICEF in nutrition, perform lead agency roles in a so-called cluster approach. By bringing together all actors present on the ground for each cluster under clearer leadership on a regular basis, this approach helps clarify their division of labor and define their roles and responsibilities. As a result, the approach provides more predictable action in analyzing humanitarian needs, jointly addressing priorities, and identifying gaps within and among sectors. The humanitarian review also aimed to strengthen the humanitarian coordinator position at the country level by improving selection procedures, strengthening training, and delegating authority (for example, with the help of the new financial tools).

In the end, the Summit failed to generate a grand resolution between the North and the South, as well as between the United States and the rest of the world, which encompassed the *In Larger Freedom* proposals. If the developed world had offered to commit 0.7 percent of GDP to development assistance, "ease trade barriers and slash debt in exchange for a

[13] HPG Briefing Note (November 2005); A. Stoddard, D. Salomons, K. Haver, and A. Harmer, *Common Funds for Humanitarian Action in Sudan and the Democratic Republic of Congo: Monitoring and Evaluation Study*, New York University Center on International Cooperation in collaboration with Overseas Development Institute (New York/London, 2006).

commitment by the developing world to implement good governance and get serious about ending support for terrorists and weapons proliferation," such a deal could perhaps have been reached.[14] Perceptions of threats, however, differed too radically to reach such a deal. The United States worried mainly about terrorism and weapons of mass destruction; the developing world feared the threats of underdevelopment, poverty, debt, HIV/AIDS, and other infectious diseases; while the Europeans took a middle position emphasizing comprehensive security that encompassed both the hard security issues and the soft threats resulting from underdevelopment. While the European concept came close to the UN's concept of human security, sidetracked by Security Council Reform, the Europeans failed to strongly promote their ideas of collective security.

To understand the actual impact of these limited reforms, and their implications for collective security, it is important to study security at the field level, such as in the DRC. Within the DRC, this chapter focuses especially on the Sud Kivu province, where the conflict changed with a haphazard peace process, more robust (armed) peacekeeping by MONUC in 2005, and democratic elections in 2006. The rate of success of MONUC's actions is contested by both the local Congolese and NGOs present in the war zones.

Conflicts in the eastern Democratic Republic of the Congo

This section discusses both the wars in the eastern DRC and the haphazard peace process.

The wars

In the early 1990s, attempts to limit President Mobutu's power and institute democracy failed. The already dire economic situation deteriorated further and ethnic tensions escalated. As a result of the Rwandan civil war and genocide in 1994, approximately 1 million refugees entered the eastern DRC. The refugee crisis intensified tensions among eastern Congolese population groups, led to serious environmental degradation, and prompted an influx of humanitarian organizations. The refugee camps were also used by the *Interahamwe*[15] as bases to regroup and re-arm in order to carry out attacks on Rwandan soil.

[14] Soderberg, "The United Nations: Missed Opportunity."

[15] The *Interahamwe* was originally made up of Hutu militia that played a central role in preparing and carrying out the Rwandan genocide.

In May 1996, Laurent Kabila's *Alliance des Forces Démocratiques pour la Libération du Congo* (AFDL) overthrew President Mobutu with strong support from the Rwandan and Ugandan armies. The Rwandans ostensibly intervened to foster the return of the refugees and attack the *génocidaires* in the camps. Many of the Rwandan refugees returned home, but the *Interahamwe* fled into the eastern Congolese forests, from where they plundered and raped the local population.

Over the next one and a half years, the alliance between Kabila and the Rwandan leadership frayed. In August 1998, the *Banyamulenge*[16] dominated *Rassemblement Congolais pour la Démocratie*[17] (RCD), with support from the Rwandan, Ugandan, and Burundian armies, started a second war – this time to displace Kabila's regime. This war, however, shortly reached a stalemate, as Kabila received support from Angola, Zimbabwe, Chad, and Namibia. Soon thereafter, Uganda and Rwanda grew apart over their differing economic interests and began supporting different rebel groups. As a result, the DRC was divided into three parts.

The RCD – supported by the Rwandans – maintained control over the eastern part, and the government forces, still loyal to Kabila, controlled the western and southern part of the country. The *Front de Libération du Congo* (FLC), led by Jean-Pierre Bemba and supported by the Ugandans, occupied the northern part of the DRC. Some of the people close to Bemba had also had close ties to Mobutu. In addition, a breakaway RCD group in Ituri, the Congolese Rally for Democracy-Liberation Movement (RCD-ML), led by Ernest Wamba dia Wamba, was also supported by the Ugandans.[18] In the meantime, the *Interahamwe* continued to destabilize and loot parts of eastern DRC, while various *Mai-Mai*[19] were also active in RCD- and FLC-held territory.

[16] The *Banyamulenge* are Congolese Tutsis, who have been living in the Mulenge Hills of South Kivu for more than two centuries. Some of their leaders, but certainly not all, are close to the Kagame government in Rwanda.

[17] The Rassemblement Congolais pour la Démocratie (RCD – Congolese Rally for Democracy) was the main rebel group fighting to overthrow President Kabila. It was initially a front made up of three political tendencies: Mobutist conservative resistance, anti-Kabila resistance and democratic resistance.

[18] K. Ilunga-Matthiesen, *Die Demokratische Republik Kongo – Eine Analyse aus staatstheoretischer, verfassungsrechtlicher und völkerrechtlicher Sicht* (Münster: Waxmann Verlag, 2005), p. 54.

[19] The *Mai-Mai* were originally formed as local self-defense groups to fight foreign occupation, but they increasingly turned into armed bandits that also raped and looted. Several different *Mai-Mai* groups exist that operate independently of each other.

Over time, these different warring factions and their international supporters became more interested in economic extraction and exploitation of natural resources like diamonds and coltan,[20] than in ending the war. As a consequence, it increasingly became unclear who was fighting whom.[21] Ugandans and Rwandans fought each other in Kisangani over economic and military interests.[22] The relationship between RCD and the Rwandans was also unstable.[23] Moreover, local ethnic conflicts – such as the deadly struggle between the Lendu and the Hema in Ituri – were spurred by Rwandan and Ugandan armaments.[24] As a result, the Congolese war broke down into "dozens of overlapping micro-wars" in which almost all the victims were civilians.[25]

Consequently, economic activity deteriorated rapidly, extreme poverty increased sharply, and the health system broke down. Many health centers became inaccessible and often people could not pay for remaining health services. Not surprisingly, the eastern DRC became an "unchecked incubation zone for diseases"[26] and the mortality rate skyrocketed.

[20] A colloquial term for a valuable type of metallic ore, which provides the raw material for capacitators in, for example, cell phones and computers.

[21] See, e.g., UN Doc. S/2001/357.

[22] For an overview of the main shifting alliances since 1996, see F. Reyntjens, "The Privatisation and Criminalisation of Public Space in the Geopolitics of the Great Lakes Region," *Journal of Modern African Studies* 43 (2005), pp. 587–607; G. Nzongola-Ntalaja, *The Congo: From Leopold to Kabila. A People's History* (London: Zed Books, 2003) and T. Turner, *The Congo Wars: Conflict, Myth and Reality* (London: Zed Books, 2007).

[23] In 2002, the RCD worked with some *Mai-Mai* groups with which it used to clash, while continuing to fight other *Mai-Mai* groups.

[24] Another example of the changing alliances concerns the positions of different Banyamulenge groups: "In 2002, the Banyamulenge community on the High Plateau of [Sud]-Kivu mobilized against the RCD[-Goma]/Rwandan forces, as increasing numbers of Banyamulenge came to the conclusion that being allied to Rwanda was counterproductive for them, especially regarding their goal of being accepted as Congolese citizens. They also felt that the RCD[-Goma] and the Rwandans were not doing enough to protect them from attacks by Congolese neighbors who viewed all Tutsis as Rwandan nationals. A Banyamulenge officer who defected from the RCD found substantial support on the High Plateau in 2001. In opposing the RCD[-Goma], he was able to forge an alliance between the High Plateau Banyamulenge and the ethnic Bembe and surrounding *Mai-Mai* groups." H. F. Weiss and T. Carayannis, "The Enduring Idea of the Congo," in R. R. Larémont (ed.), *Borders, Nationalism and the African State* (Boulder: Lynne Rienner Publishers, 2005), pp. 156–157.

[25] "Africa's Great War," *Economist* (July 4, 2002).

[26] L. Roberts, *Mortality in Eastern DRC: Results from Five Mortality Surveys*, Final Draft (New York: IRC Health Unit, 2000), p. 3.

The peace process

MONUC is one of the most complex operations in the history of UN peacekeeping. It also happens to be an illustration of collective security in action. MONUC's multinational and multidisciplinary design combines the functions of military, political, legal, humanitarian, and civilian police elements, and coordinates the UN family in the DRC. However, the political, operational, and logistical difficulties accompanying the peacekeeping efforts in the DRC have made the peace process slow.

After peace negotiations in Lusaka in 1999, MONUC was placed close to the front lines to facilitate the implementation of the Lusaka Accord. As a result, the warring factions partially withdrew: The Namibian and Chadian forces pulled out completely; the Burundians remained for some time but only to fight their rebel forces across their border; the Ugandans withdrew some troops, but later returned; and the Zimbabweans and Rwandans did not pull back to their national borders in order to protect their economic interests.

The assassination of Laurent Kabila in January 2001, and the subsequent entry into the presidential office by his son, Joseph Kabila, led to renewed diplomatic interventions to implement the Lusaka agreements of 1999. These agreements included the withdrawal of foreign forces and political negotiations to establish a transitional government and a process towards multi-party elections. In the meantime, the Security Council decided to increase the number of soldiers under MONUC's command.

In the spring of 2002, the inter-Congolese dialogue between the main parties to the conflict in Sun City broke down, but the Kabila government and the FLC were able to reach an agreement so that approximately 70 percent of the country's territory came officially under control of the Kinshasa government. In Pretoria in July 2002, an agreement was reached with the Rwandans about their withdrawal in return for renewed efforts by the Congolese government to facilitate repatriation of ex-FAR and *Interahamwe* irregular forces. By the end of 2002, most foreign forces had left the DRC, which considerably facilitated the peace process.

In December 2002, the inter-Congolese dialogue led to the Global and Inclusive Accord "between the government in Kinshasa and the RCD and the MLC rebel groups. This set out a framework for the establishment of a transitional national government (TNG),"[27] with four vice-presidents

[27] *Democratic Republic of Congo: DFID Country Engagement Plan* (London: UK Department for International Development, September 18, 2003), in mimeo.

representing the three warring factions and civil society. The TNG was inaugurated in July 2003. It was an internally divided government, but the process of national reunification that it represented was popular among most Congolese and the international donor community.[28] Its efforts to establish national policy made small progress. With the help of international donors, it reestablished a national health policy. It also integrated different warring factions (rebel movements and *Mai-Mai*) into the *Forces Armées de la République Démocratique du Congo* (FARDC) and deployed them mainly to the eastern part of the country; but the soldiers rarely received pay and increasingly preyed upon the local population.

Despite diplomatic and political progress, violence continued, especially in the eastern DRC. In the spring, 2004, fighting between FARDC and troops of a renegade *Banyamulenge* General, Nkunda, led to widespread looting and further gender-based violence in and around Bukavu.[29] Locally, this was called the *Mutebusi* war.[30]

Even after the successful elections in 2006, which made Joseph Kabila the first democratically elected President of the DRC, regular political killings and widespread impunity continued. Moreover, the FARDC and rebel forces – mainly *Interahamwe*, who call themselves officially *Forces Démocratiques de Libération du Rwanda* (FDLR) and local militias – continue to pillage and rape the local population.[31]

In 2007, General Nkunda, who had officially become part of the national army, started another rebellion in Nord Kivu.[32] Tens of thousands of people fled the violence and some FARDC positions were taken over by the FDLR. Neither MONUC nor the national government or international diplomats were able to prevent or suppress this rebellion. After negotiations, a shaky calm has been restored.

The ongoing violence has further weakened the remaining state institutions. Yet, when the warring factions can use state institutions in their quest for power and self-enrichment, they will opportunistically do so. The weakness of

[28] K. Ilunga Matthiesen, *Die Demokratische Republik Kongo – Eine Analyse aus staatstheoretischer, verfassungsrechtlicher und völkerrechtlicher Sicht* (Munster: Waxmann, 2006), p. 53.

[29] Bukavu is the capital of Sud Kivu.

[30] The rebels received hidden support from Rwanda. Reyntjens, F., "The Privatisation and Criminalisation of Public Space in the Geopolitics of the Great Lakes Region."

[31] In fact, the MONUC human rights observers held FARDC soldiers responsible for committing more than 80 percent of all human-rights abuses against civilians in the period from January to June 2006. See MONUC human rights report, Jan.–June 2006, as quoted in "A Fragile Future: Why scaling down MONUC too soon could spell disaster for the Congo," *Oxfam Briefing Paper* 97 (Oxfam International, February 2007), p. 7.

[32] In summer 2007, MONUC accused the Rwandans of supporting Nkunda.

the state, ongoing violence by various parties, the parties' firmly entrenched economic interests, and the breakdown of social norms and values have resulted in a chronic humanitarian crisis.[33] A study by the International Rescue Committee (IRC) has estimated that from 1998 to 2007, the DRC has had an excess mortality of 5.4 million people.[34] As conflicts continue, their total death toll may still surpass that of the holocaust.

In response, many humanitarian organizations have been active in the DRC. At an OCHA coordination meeting for Sud Kivu in Bukavu in mid-August 2005, twenty-eight different organizations, including NGOs, UN organizations and MONUC, attended. Diplomatic actors have also acted at national and international levels; just like the war itself, the international response constitutes a network of transnational and international elements stitched together. The warring factions, however, attempt to utilize the humanitarian and peacekeeping actors to their own benefit.

MONUC's functioning

MONUC began its operations in 1999 under a Chapter VI mandate, but its military observation role was insufficient to bring about peace. It "grew incrementally, constrained by doubts about the prospects of success and fear of a never-ending commitment of international resources."[35] However, "the signature of the 'Final Act' at Sun City on April 2, 2003, demonstrated a reinvigorated commitment by the Congolese to national reconciliation and the peace process. [Moreover,] the successful experience of the International Emergency Force (IEMF) in Bunia" cleared the air for an expanded role for MONUC.[36]

MONUC's tasks

In July 2003, the Security Council adopted Resolution 1493, "which increased … military strength to 10,800 and authorized MONUC to

33 For example, prostitution, rape, forced labor, community members betraying each other to militia and then sharing in the loot.

34 Coghlan, Ben et al. (2008).

35 Especially among members of the US Congress, doubts were raised about the costs and effectiveness of MONUC. See W. L. Swing, "Preface: The Role of MONUC and the International Community in Support of the DRC Transition," in M. Malan and J. G. Porto (eds.), *Challenges of Peace Implementations: The UN Mission in the Democratic Republic of the Congo* (Pretoria: Institute for Security Studies, 2004), p. x.

36 Malan and Gomes Porto, *Challenges of Peace Implementations: The UN Mission in the Democratic Republic of the Congo* (Pretoria: Institute for Security Studies, 2004), p. 11.

use all necessary means to fulfill its mandate in Ituri and North and South Kivu."[37] In short, it could undertake more robust, armed action under Chapter VII against violent armed factions that did not cooperate with the peace process. The reinforced MONUC was then organized around five key programs, as explained by William Lacey Swing, the Special Representative of the Secretary-General:[38]

1. *Peace and security*: to stop the killing and end the violence, the sine qua non for all that follows. The focus is on stabilizing Ituri and the Kivus; enabling 300,000 Congolese refugees to return; ensuring effective DDRRR/DDR;[39] enforcing the arms embargo; and promoting the normalization of regional relations.
2. *Facilitating the transition*: leading to free and fair elections. MONUC's Neutral Force has already filled the security void in Kinshasa, and we will now begin to focus greater attention on supporting the national electoral framework, and the … institutions of democracy. An electoral unit has been created in MONUC, and MONUC is already serving as convener of electoral assistance efforts.
3. *Establishment of the Rule of Law and Human Rights*: to end impunity and build stable institutions. Police training and criminal justice capacity building is underway in Ituri and will soon begin in the Kivus. MONUC is supporting the establishment of a National Human Rights Observatory and a Rule of Law Taskforce to coordinate security sector reform.
4. *Improve human conditions for sustainable peace*: the focus here is on programs that address the tragic legacy of war: humanitarian catastrophe; child soldiers; sexual violence; HIV-AIDS and support for the International Criminal Court (ICC) and for the establishment of a Truth and Reconciliation Commission.
5. *Support and management*: to reform and structure MONUC so that it can address all of the above effectively and efficiently.

Hence, MONUC was, and still is, an integrated mission combining civilian – developmental, humanitarian, and human rights – policing, and military tasks. It can thus be seen as a practical example of a more

[37] *Ibid.* at 67.

[38] Swingm "Preface: The Role of MONUC and the International Community in Support of the DRC Transition," pp. x–xi.

[39] DDRRR: disarmament, demobilization, repatriation, resettlement, and reintegration; DDR: disarmament, demobilization and reintegration.

comprehensive approach towards collective security by the UN. Most of its peacekeeping work focuses on the violent eastern part of the country: Ituri and the Kivus, as well as the Northern and Central Katanga bordering on Sud Kivu. To promote security, MONUC cooperates closely with the – now officially integrated – national army, the FARDC.

The following sections will discuss the progress with these five tasks in more detail. Given their central importance in the eastern DRC, the emphasis lies on peace and security.

MONUC's role in peace and security

The Secretary-General's reports on MONUC (for example, S/2005/603, S/2007/156) give the impression that the mission is making slow progress in a challenging situation and with very limited financial means. The reports, however, do not reveal that the local population and NGOs on the ground perceive such "slow progress" in a far more negative light.[40] In particular between 2002 and 2004, the local perception of MONUC in and around Bukavu, the capital of Sud Kivu, took a rapid turn for the worse.

The first blow to MONUC's reputation was the sex scandal. MONUC peacekeepers would use, and sometimes force, local women for prostitution. While previously there had been poverty-induced prostitution, such practice was generally limited. From 2002, prostitution became rampant in some discotheques frequented by MONUC soldiers. The local population talked about this in very disparaging terms. In particular, the fact that young girls, some only 14 years old, prostituted themselves raised opprobrium. Was this how the international community supported a war-torn society?

Second, in May and June 2004, fighting between FARDC and troops of dissident General Nkunda – the *Mutebusi* war mentioned above – led to looting and gender-based violence in Sud Kivu. Many humanitarian organizations had to close down temporarily and the local population felt that MONUC did not protect them sufficiently. When there was infighting among the rebels, fortunate government troops succeeded in retaking the town and MONUC was seen as helping *Banyamulenge* rebels rather than the local population. For the local populations, the

[40] In 2002, I visited several health facilities in the Kivus, where local children would always shout "Muzungu, Muzungu," which is Kiswhahili for white person. In 2004, I arrived in some of the same health districts, but this time the children said "MONUC, MONUC."

MONUC soldiers were pawns in the hands of the Rwandans and their supposed American backers.[41] After the *Mutebusi* war, the local population regularly threw stones at MONUC vehicles.

Third, the FARDC has yet to become an integrated force. In 2005, a *Mai-Mai* faction south of Bukavu was officially incorporated as part of the Congolese army, although the militia members never received any military training, and rarely receive pay. Perhaps not surprisingly, they continue to loot and rape the local population. MONUC is not able to force the local army commander to relocate the *Mai-Mai* faction to another part of the province. This is unfortunate, because such replacements in other parts of the DRC have tended to reduce the looting and other forms of violence.

Fourth, another challenge, with a long shadow, was that the FARDC and MONUC began fighting FDLR (*Interahamwe*) in the Sud Kivu province in 2005. A close reading of the following excerpts of a MONUC report highlights the inconsistencies in these actions.

Excerpts from the Nineteenth Report of the Secretary-General on the United Nations Organization Mission in the Democratic Republic of the Congo (S/2005/603) September 26, 2005

Disarmament and repatriation of foreign armed groups

30. Following the 16 July communiqué by the Transitional Government stating that it would take forcible action to disarm FDLR, consensus has been emerging within the Transitional Government on how to address the problem of foreign armed groups, and particularly FDLR. A meeting was held in Bukavu on 5 August between representatives of the Transitional Government, FDLR and MONUC to discuss modalities for encouraging the voluntary return of FDLR combatants to Rwanda, in accordance with the Rome declaration of 31 March.
31. Meanwhile, as described in paragraphs 20 to 23 above, the FARDC-MONUC joint operations in the Kivus continue to limit the ability of FDLR to maneuver in the more densely populated areas and to threaten civilians. This new resolve of

[41] Many Congolese believe that the Rwandans have only been able to gain such power in the eastern DRC because they are supported by the United States.

the Transitional Government to take more robust military action deserves to be actively supported by the international community, particularly by enhancing the military capabilities of the Armed Forces of the Democratic Republic of the Congo.

32. The Transitional Government should also be encouraged to take more decisive steps in using its own assets to help consolidate State authority and establish effective security mechanisms in areas where FDLR are no longer present. This aspect is becoming increasingly urgent, as the growing split among some FDLR commanders and preconditions recently posed by the group may further affect the implementation of the Rome declaration. MONUC has continued its efforts to take advantage of any opportunities for the peaceful repatriation of FDLR combatants and their dependants. The Mission is discussing with some Rwandan combatant leaders and with the Transitional Government the technical modalities of repatriation, and has publicized the decision taken by the Government of Rwanda that it would not prosecute any returning combatant aged 14 or younger at the time of the 1994 genocide.

At the time, the FDLR negotiated with the civilian leg of MONUC about its voluntary repatriation, and then without any advance notification to its civilian staff, the military leg of MONUC attacked the FDLR positions.[42] This caused several problems not indicated in the report by the Secretary-General:

- Negotiations with MONUC's civilian leg broke down, even though these talks had been making slow progress.
- FDLR soldiers had often taken up farming. Some international NGO staff members argued that the FDLR Hutus were frequently better farmers than the local population. Their agricultural surplus was sold on local markets, which fostered at least some local trade. This budding peaceful co-existence now broke down.
- FDLR rebels were forced deeper into the rainforest, where they had not been living before, and resorted to plundering the local population(s) so that the FDLR problem was moved to, and partly reinforced, in another

[42] The International Crisis Group (ICG) also called for such military action in an open letter to regional and international leaders in 2005.

area. Although some groups were happy to get rid of the FDLR, other groups (understandably) were less happy to receive them. As one local Congolese woman remarked: "If they want to fight the FDLR, I don't understand why they fight them deeper into the rainforest instead of straight to Rwanda?"

It appeared that MONUC was doing what the international community should have done when it failed to disarm the *génocidaires* in the Rwandan refugee camps in 1994 and 1995. The irony was that, unbeknown to most international observers, new alternatives for either local integration or peaceful return were opening up. Unfortunately, these alternative courses of action became more difficult to accomplish.[43]

During the same period, a local militia called the *Rastas*, made up of local criminals and renegade FDLR, began attacking and terrorizing local villages in the Walungu area south of Bukavu. They have their own informers in the local communities who tell them when there are goods to loot or persons to kidnap for ransom, which is economically a profitable way of life. The presence of both informers and *Rasta* members signifies a severe breakdown of social cohesion and traditional norms. People cannot trust their neighbors anymore. In the summer of 2005, the Mwami, a traditional chief of Walungu, threatened to kill everyone who worked with the *Rastas*. MONUC, however, did not want to attack the *Rastas* because they considered them a local problem. A local employee of an international NGO summarized the situation in the following way:

> En tout cas, à Walungu, ça ne va pas. On dénombre chaque semaine de nouvelles pertes humaines et curieusement, les ONG internationales ne s'en inquiètent pas. Comme si c'était normal que les Congolais meurent comme des bêtes pendant que les travailleurs des Nations Unies, présents sur le terrain, se promènent en véhicule dans les rues de la ville. C'est dans ces zones rurales où la MONUC est présente que règnent l'insécurité et les exactions. Qu'est-ce que cela veut dire ? En tout cas, ça n'est pas leur problème, cette paix tant attendue, ça sera à nous de les [*Rasta* et Interahamwe] chasser pour que nous puissions régler nous-mêmes nos problèmes (personal correspondence, November 6, 2005).[44]

[43] Before the 2006 election, the national government decided not to attack FDLR positions further, ostensibly in order to prevent obstructing the elections.

[44] "In any case, in Walungu things are not going well. Every week one counts new human losses and curiously enough, the international NGOs don't worry about them. It is as if it were normal that the Congolese die like animals, while UN staff members, present in the field, take a ride in the streets of the city. It is in the rural zones, where MONUC is

In 2007, the negative image of MONUC has been reinforced by accusations of weapons trading with General Nkunda's rebels by the Indian peacekeeping forces, and diamond smuggling by Pakistani forces, which also seem to proselytize and help build mosques. As stated, the violent stand-off with General Nkunda has further weakened MONUC's position. Not surprisingly, DDRRR has only made very modest progress.

It is clear from these examples that the local perceptions of problems and solutions, as well as sources of information, differ considerably from what is being discussed in the Security Council. Understandably, the local population perceives its suffering far more intensely than most MONUC staff and Security Council members realize. The local population views the international context of the conflict differently and tends to believe more in conspiracy-like theories of the roles played by the Rwandans, *Banyamulenge*, and the Americans.[45] MONUC's inability to address the problems with the FDLR, *Rastas*, FARDC, and general Nkunda's troops in the Kivus, in conjunction with corruption within MONUC itself, implies that the peacekeeping forces have often become part of the problem instead of contributing to a peaceful solution.

MONUC's role in facilitating the transition

Solid progress was made with voter registration for the elections in 2005. By the time of the elections MONUC forces had already increased to 17,000 soldiers and also received additional military support from a temporary European force. The elections were generally considered a success. Joseph Kabila became the first democratically elected President of the DRC.

Violence in the run-up to the elections was limited. However, after the election an armed stand-off occurred between forces loyal to Kabila and those loyal to his main challenger, Jean-Pierre Bemba. The latter fled the country. In this respect, a recent ICG report argued: "The new

present, that insecurity and exactions reign. What does this mean? In any case, it is not their problem, this long-awaited peace, it is up to us to chase them [*Rasta* and Interahamwe, DD] so that we can solve our problems ourselves." (Translation by the author.)

45 Simon Turner, "Under the Gaze of the 'Big Nations': Refugees, Rumors and the International Community in Tanzania," *African Affairs* 103 (2004), pp. 1–21 and Simon Turner, "Representing the Past in Exile: The Politics of National History among Burundian Refugees," *Refuge* 17(6) (1998), pp. 22-29 describe a similar political explanation of ongoing insecurity by refugees in refugee camps.

government's relations with the opposition have deteriorated sharply, raising the possibility of a drift to authoritarianism."[46]

These issues related to democratic transition show a chronic problem of peacekeeping operations and election support. With elections, the procedural aspects of democracy can be addressed. The substantive aspects of democracy, however, such as elite accountability and respect for other parties and minorities, are much harder to institutionalize.

MONUC's role in the establishment of law and human rights

Given MONUC's limitations, it is important to see whether alternatives exist in order to facilitate MONUC's operations and, more generally, foster collective security. Furthermore, enabling other means for establishing security is important because the quality of the judiciary and police also leaves much to be desired. Police officers are badly paid and often resort to corruption while those with access to riches continue to buy their own "justice."

MONUC has officially supported the ICC investigations. Three of those investigations can influence Congolese politics; they include investigations into Thomas Lubunga, leader of a Hema ethnic militia, indictments against Lord Resistance Army commanders hiding in a national park in the DRC, and the indictment of Jean-Pierre Bemba for his interventions in the Central African Republic as leader of the MLC rebel movement – but not for MLC crimes in the DRC![47]

"Concern about ICC's impact on the DRC political process is not so much that accountability measures will delay or derail peace efforts, but rather that ICC decisions will be exploited by local actors to advance their own political agendas."[48] Possible examples include further government accusations against the opposition and refueling Hema–Lendu tensions. An investigation into Nkunda or his men might become an even more explosive issue.[49] In any case, given the ICC's limited remit, it is at best only a small step in promoting justice in the DRC.

[46] ICG (2007) Congo: Consolidating the Peace, *Africa Report*, No. 128, July 5, 2007, International Crisis Group, Kinshasa/Brussels, p. i.

[47] At the moment, none of the Congolese political leaders has been indicted for war crimes carried out under their watch in the DRC.

[48] T. Carayannis, "The Impact of the ICC on the DR Congo (DRC)," Draft Report given at the *International Conference on Building a Future with Peace and Justice* (Nuremberg, June 25–27, 2007), pp. 1–2.

[49] For more information concerning these problems and Congolese perceptions of the ICC, see *ibid.*

In a similar vein, MONUC was also supposed to support the Truth and Reconciliation Commission. However, different donor priorities during the DRC's expensive election process meant that the "TRC never got off the ground."[50]

In the past, UN Security Council reports on the war economy also provided an alternative instrument to facilitate the transition. These reports exposed the economic interests of Uganda, Rwanda, and Zimbabwe, while also helping promote political change in the Kinshasa government (which led to the firing of several corrupt ministers who had been benefiting from the war). Uganda and Rwanda felt forced to withdraw – albeit at first only partially and temporarily – from the DRC. The reports named and shamed companies, governments, and individuals, such as Salim Saleh, President Museveni's brother. The reports, published three years in a row, showed the transnational nature of the Congolese "civil" war. Consequently, although Security Council member states were embarrassed by their national companies mentioned in the reports, they increasingly protected these companies' economic interests. Council members also feared that naming and shaming members of the then newly formed transitional government was becoming counterproductive.[51] As a result, the Security Council decided to discontinue the reports.

In fact, none of the recommendations of these three reports have been followed. Nor has aid policy become "conditional on accountability for Rwandan and Ugandan [and other countries and organizations'] activities in the DRC."[52] Nevertheless, the reports provided a crucial impetus for further research and advocacy by NGOs and academics to the war economy, and new diplomatic initiatives. It would be useful for MONUC if this form of reporting could be re-instituted as an additional and indirect instrument for its toolbox that can influence the behavior of the parties in conflict. At the very least, companies active in the DRC or engaging with its trading partners should be forced to respect the OECD guidelines on economic activities in conflict zones, and UN member states should develop their own legal framework for the prosecution of white collar crimes by their nationals

[50] *Ibid.*, p. 3.

[51] F. Grignon, "International Response to the Illegal Exploitation of Resources in the DRC," in M. Malan and J. G. Porto (eds.), *Challenges of Peace Implementations: The UN Mission in the Democratic Republic of the Congo* (Pretoria: Institute for Security Studies, 2004), pp. 43–52, especially p. 49.

[52] *Ibid.*, p. 51.

in war-torn countries.[53] "The regulation of resource exploitation in the Congo is a shared responsibility."[54]

If the Congo's natural wealth could be used in a productive way to fund the rebuilding of democratic state institutions, as well as infrastructure, the DRC would be able to turn its "resource curse" into economic growth. However, at the moment there are not sufficient safeguards for this to happen,[55] and good governance is still a long way off.[56]

MONUC's role in improving the human conditions for sustainable peace

Military action is not MONUC's only activity. Radio Okapi, for example, is a MONUC activity with the support of the Swiss *Fondation Hirondelle*. The radio station has been very successful in reaching the Congolese with objective news that has fostered peacebuilding and better understanding of the political situation.[57]

Yet, more problems continue to plague MONUC in Sud Kivu in the everyday execution of its tasks. Sometimes, MONUC just looks impractical. For example, in the dry season, road dust is a severe problem, because most roads are not paved. Owing to the omnipresent dust, many Congolese and expatriates suffer from nasal irritation. In 2005 MONUC operated water trucks that sprayed a little water on the roads to prevent dust; the water, however, evaporated rather quickly. Many local Congolese asked whether it would not be more practical to pave roads, even if only a very small part of the roads could be paved. In any case, they wondered whether the trucks could not be used better for other purposes.

A related, but more serious experience came from an international NGO that did emergency road reconstruction of dirt roads and bridges outside Bukavu in 2005. This is a cash-for-work project with local NGOs that also facilitates local access to health facilities and markets. Several days after the roads had been repaired, heavy military trucks from

53 Similar procedures should also be instituted and followed for corrupt MONUC soldiers.
54 Grignon, "International Response to the Illegal Exploitation of Resources in the DRC," p. 51.
55 "Who Benefits from the Minerals?" *The Economist* (September 20, 2007), p. 50 reported that an ongoing "review of mining contracts may well be a sham."
56 ICG Report, 2007.
57 J. N. Taunya, "Public Information and the Media: Radio Okapi's Contribution to the Peace Process in the DRC," in M. Malan and J. G. Porto (eds.), *Challenges of Peace Implementations*, pp. 53–65.

others' trucks are still able to destroy local roads, but if the roads are damaged, they are now repaired by people working for local NGOs.

Whereas the *Responsibility to Protect* is important from a legal and conceptual perspective, MONUC's action in the DRC was until recently an example of the difficulties of its implementation. One of the unforeseen advantages of the cluster approach in this respect is that it offers an instrument to help operationalize the *Responsibility to Protect* from the ground up. MONUC is now active in this protection cluster, which it co-leads with UNHCR. Although this initially sparked concerns about impartiality and neutrality with the humanitarian actors involved, the cluster provided a forum for strategic discussion and adaptation. According to Murthy, MONUC has helped the humanitarian organizations in the cluster with sharing its extensive security information, increasing deployments and patrols also on their request that reduced violations of the population, as well as with activities to tackle the problem of impunity, for example, with training the Congolese Army on basic human rights standards and professional military-civilian behavior.[63] Although the cluster approach can help bridge the gaps between relief and development and is off to a promising start, it deals mainly with humanitarian activities that are by their very nature short-term activities. While such activities are valuable, rebuilding and protection also require more long-term measures, such as institution building and international diplomatic support for dealing with the foreign militias. The advantage of the new humanitarian funding modalities and cluster approach is that they are geared towards implementation, although monitoring and evaluation still need to be developed further.

In sum, the UN reforms have been too limited to have a large, meaningful impact. While they are marginally beneficial, even taken together they do not constitute a new comprehensive collective security system. The disconnect between the reforms and the situation on the ground has only partially been overcome in humanitarian action and the elections, but rarely in other activities, which means that establishing peace and security in the DRC requires additional measures. Yet, there are

[63] J. Murthy, "Mandating the Protection Cluster with the Responsibility to Protect: A Policy Recommendation Based on the Protection Cluster's Implementation in South Kivu, DRC," *Journal of Humanitarian Assistance*, October 5, 2007, available at http://jha.ac/2007/10/05/mandating-the-protection-cluster-with-the-responsibility-to-protect-a-policy-recommendation-based-on-the-protection-cluster%e2%80%99s-implementation-in-south-kivu-drc (last accessed August 5, 2008).

many issues that MONUC can barely address, which is the topic of the next section.

The relevance of MONUC for the "New Collective Security System"

A lot can be learned about the proposed "New Collective Security System" from MONUC's involvement in the DRC. Looking at the MONUC experience, it is clear that organizational, funding, legal, and conceptual reforms of the World Summit alone are not enough to bring security in the DRC or by extension, in our world. This is mainly because the reforms fail to address the deeper systemic causes of the security threats in the Congo and other parts of our world. As a result, they also fail to address the manifold implementation problems sufficiently. The systemic causes can be divided into internal as well as external issues.

Issues external to MONUC

1. The self-sustaining political economy of war

First of all, neither MONUC nor any other form of intervention has sufficiently succeeded in addressing the self-sustaining political economy of war. The DRC has a fragmented war economy based on extraction of natural resources and exploitation of the local population. This conflict without borders can best be seen as a set of overlapping transnational networks of cooperating and competing criminal groups comprised of national and international business elites and state officials from different countries. These networks constitute a transnational oligopoly of violence and lawlessness. They sustain the ongoing conflicts, because this is a way to gain wealth and influence. Peace will marginalize many of these actors. They will bide their time till MONUC leaves, and in the meantime they will try to benefit from MONUC where possible, or weaken it if that strengthens their position. Put simply, these actors have no or insufficient incentives to cooperate with MONUC for peace.

2. Various local, national, transnational, and international conflicts interact

The description of the political economy of war already indicates that the problems are not only national, but also local and transnational. Put differently, there are many simultaneous conflicts that mutually reinforce each other.

MONUC, as well as the Security Council, have a hard time addressing the transnational effects of the war, because their focus is mainly on the state level. MONUC, after all, is only active within the DRC. The Peacebuilding Commission, regular reporting to the Security Council on the war economy, and international diplomatic support could in principle play a positive role in addressing these transnational and international aspects, but they are not or insufficiently used at the moment.

The fact that the peace process and MONUC focused mainly on the national government and the main rebel forces has also led to the relative neglect of the many localized violent conflicts, such as the *Rastas* or fights about land entitlements involving different ethnic groups, such as the *Banyamulenge*. The Security Council and MONUC urgently need to develop an approach to such local conflicts, because they have important transnational links, can refuel the national conflict(s), and hamper rebuilding.[64]

3. The breakdown of state institutions and civil society

Corruption within the Congolese elites is endemic. Members of the political elite benefited considerably from the violence. Several ministers of the transition government were leading different rebel movements and taking part in the transitional government allowed them to safeguard their interests under a more peaceful guise. This was the main reason why the transnational government postponed the elections several times.[65] After the elections, some of the factions that were part of the transnational government, especially the RCD, have lost political power. The recent fighting in Nord Kivu may also be a way in which certain RCD politicians, marginalized by the elections, are trying to regain some power. The institutions of the state, including the national army, are too weak to deal with this rebellion. According to Michel Kassa, "The most salient feature of the [ongoing crises] is the dilution of any sense of responsibility on the part of the many would-be authorities."[66]

[64] S. Autesserre, "D. R. Congo: Explaining Peace Building Failures, 2003–2006," *Review of African Political Economy* 113 (2007), pp. 185–202, and S. Autesserre, "The Trouble with Congo," *Foreign Affairs*, 87(3) (2008), pp. 94–110.

[65] Originally, the elections were planned for 2005.

[66] M. Kassa, "Humanitarian Assistance in the DRC," in M. Malan and J. G. Porto (eds.), *Challenges of Peace Implementations*, p. 7.

In addition, many institutions that mediate between state and society and can help enhance security are extremely weak. The DRC has a weakened civil society and misses a well-functioning judiciary, a professional army, a genuine police service, and a strong, independent civil service, while the health and education systems are in the early stages of reconstruction. Hence, the state institutions generally fail to mitigate the conflicts – and the national and local elites often purposely kept them this way. MONUC can help with security sector reform and some other tasks, but it can neither replace nor fully rebuild the other state institutions.

4. The breakdown of social norms and values

This breakdown of the state is reinforced by the fact that social norms and values that supported social cohesion have broken down: endemic corruption, widespread sexual violence, criminal gangs and militias such as the *Rastas*, human rights violations, and other forms of violence have not been stopped.

5. Ethnic violence

A special form of the breakdown of both the state and social norms and values is the manipulation of ethnicity and concomitant ethnic violence by elites and neighboring countries to legitimize military intervention, gain political power, and obtain economic access to resources. As stated, manipulated ethnicity in the eastern DRC also has important transnational aspects. At the same time, ethnicity is a type of loyalty that can compete with the institutions of a multi-ethnic state.

In particular, the twin problem of the FDLR and Nkunda rebels requires more diplomatic pressure on Rwanda to withdraw its hidden support to Nkunda, clarifying and protecting the position and rights of Rwandaphone people in the eastern DRC,[67] the return of Rwandan nationals from both the FDLR and Nkunda's rebel movement, and more ethnic reconciliation within the DRC. Even with a strong state, this would be a tall order. Such reconciliation – as well as rebuilding social norms and values – may take generations and thus requires a much longer time-horizon than MONUC's mandate provides or the World Summit reforms imply. Yet, if the international community does not succeed in simultaneously addressing the problems caused by the FDLR

[67] In particular, land and citizen rights of the Banyamulenge.

and Nkunda's rebels, the violent conflicts in the eastern DRC are bound to continue.

6. The lack of sustained international attention

For addressing the first five problems, MONUC strongly depends on the support from the great powers, and more generally national governments, with funding and diplomatic support. In particular, despite criticizing Rwanda's role in the DRC, MONUC alone is not able to lessen the intransigence of the Kagame government in Rwanda. It is simply not an international political actor that can hold neighboring countries accountable. This brings up the question whether MONUC is in the DRC to solve the security problems or just to contain them. Stronger international support is a sine qua non for a more successful MONUC.

The problems described above show that public space in the DRC has become privatized and criminalized.[68] In this context, MONUC is just one actor among many, engaged in a test of endurance with warring parties and unaccountable elites, who use violence and public power for private gain. The crisis in the DRC thus presents an extreme collective action problem, because there is no accountable state, civil society is weak, and international support is insufficient.

Issues internal to MONUC

Despite the fact that it is the largest UN peacekeeping force and can carry out more robust peacekeeping, MONUC is still a relatively small operation in comparison to the huge problems it confronts, such as the country's vast size, the weakened local institutions, the daunting logistical challenges of a deteriorated infrastructure, and a scattered population of IDPs. In other words, implementing MONUC's tasks is bound to be challenging and cost-intensive.

1. Stay above the fray?

The negative local perceptions of MONUC were reinforced by the violent conflict in Nord Kivu, where it often refrained from fighting.[69] Yet, Nkunda's rebels view the Blue Helmets as supporting the national army with the transport of munitions and troops, while in the eyes of

[68] F. Reyntjens, "The Privatisation and Criminalisation of Public Space in the Geopolitics of the Great Lakes Region."

[69] In Ituri, MONUC has been more forceful in disarming militias (Oxfam, 2007).

the local population they are complicit with "Nkunda's Tutsis and Rwanda" because MONUC does not take sufficient armed action.[70]

2. Breakdown of norms and values within MONUC

As the sex, weapons trade, smuggling, and other scandals have shown, MONUC's troops have often become part of the problems they are supposed to solve. These scandals, as well as operational decisions (not) to engage in fighting, determine the local perceptions of MONUC, which are often more negative than official UN reports show. It is very worrying, but not really surprising, that UN forces can become so deeply infected by the corruption of their local counterparts.

3. Getting the mandate right and getting money

The repeated problems in extending MONUC's mandate and providing sufficient funding and diplomatic support show, as stated above, that UN member states insufficiently provide such sustained attention and it is unlikely that they will do so in the future.

The internal problems mirror the external constraints in the DRC. The main lesson from MONUC's experience is that while it is one thing to intervene, it is quite another thing to intervene properly. The peace process has mainly focused on the national level, but frequent local violence, sometimes with transnational links, has received too little attention. Moreover, many other actors also bear responsibility for establishing security and good governance. And rebuilding reliable institutions takes much longer than MONUC's mandate allows. In the final analysis, MONUC alone cannot solve the DRC's collective action problems. Even the UN Forces themselves can become unaccountable, because Congolese actors or the Security Council cannot, or fail to, control them well enough. As a result, MONUC's role in establishing peace and security is actually limited, and at times counterproductive.

The state-based assumption

The external and internal issues highlight that the UN system is a state-based system that is only slowly and incompletely coming to terms with the challenges of state building, such as a transnational, self-sustaining political economy of war, manipulated ethnicity, a multitude of local conflicts, and the breakdown of social norms and values. All these

[70] A. Böhm, "Die Wunde Afrikas," *Die Zeit* (September 27, 2007).

problems transcend a traditional state-based perspective and thus require simultaneously additional local and transnational measures.

If MONUC does not receive sufficient support from the UN member states, in particular the permanent five and the DRC's neighbors, it will not be able to satisfactorily improve the situation in the DRC. The UN reforms as accepted at the World Summit were at best a tiny step in the right direction. The many operational problems of MONUC also imply that the successful implementation of the UN reforms will be a long-term affair, which will require continuous attention by member states for years to come. Taken together, the Summit reforms are too marginal to address the collective action problems of democratic state building and conflict mitigation on a sustained basis.[71] They therefore certainly do not constitute a credible international collective security system.

Put differently, both MONUC and the UN reforms suffer from the same shortcomings. At the World Summit, UN member states could not agree on the threats that face the world. In a similar vein, the crisis in the DRC is simply not perceived as enough of a threat to merit comprehensive international attention. This brings up the question what can be done to address this lack of agreement on threats.

Conclusions

The High-Level Panel on Threats, Challenges, and Change report, *A More Secure World: Our Shared Responsibility*, suggested that the central challenge for the twenty-first century was to fashion a broader understanding – bringing together issues of security, economic development and human freedom – of what "collective security" meant and of "all the responsibilities, commitments, strategies and institutions that come with it if a collective security system is to be effective, efficient and equitable." As stated, it concluded that nowadays the case for collective security rests on three pillars: (1) today's threats recognize no national boundaries, are connected, and must be addressed at the global and regional as well as national levels; (2) no state alone can make itself invulnerable to today's threats; and (3) it cannot be assumed that every state will be able or willing to meet its responsibility to protect its own peoples and not to harm its neighbors.

[71] Scholars of UN reform and collective security should thus study the actual field-level implementation of international policy and international law far more often. Criticism on legal or policy-making aspects of reforms is fine, but the litmus test for reform will be its implementation in the field.

The report thus stressed that in a world deeply divided by differences of power, wealth, and geography, what was needed was "nothing less than a new consensus between alliances that are frayed, between wealthy nations and poor, and among peoples mired in mistrust across an apparently widening cultural abyss." Yet, the World Summit outcomes were far less ambitious.[72] Moreover, as this chapter has shown, the Summit outcomes have had far too little impact on the ground. Nevertheless, the difficult collective security situation in the DRC is aptly summarized by the three pillars.

The case of MONUC makes clear that the current peacekeeping operation is often too fragmented, doing too little, too late. Additional measures with a longer time frame that incorporate both local and transnational issues can transcend the implicit state-based perspective.

In this respect, only the grand bargain as proposed in *A More Secure World: Our Shared Responsibility*[73] can create an enabling international environment to build more accountable and capable states, and carry out peacekeeping action by transcending the traditional state-based perspective. Even if such a bargain had been struck, it would still be very difficult to enhance security in the DRC. But at least MONUC would have had more tools and resources at its disposal and it would have received broader international support. In this way, the disconnect between the latest UN reforms and the dire situation on the ground could have been reduced.

In sum, unless a greater joint understanding of common threats is reached at the international level, no such North-South bargain – and concomitantly no groundbreaking UN reform – will be possible to overcome the large collective action problems in crisis countries. Only incremental reforms will then be made. If so, the world will often compartmentalize the threats in old ways and barely be able to address chronic crises such as the DRC.

Glossary

AFDL — *Alliance des Forces Démocratiques pour la Libération du Congo* / Alliance of Democratic Forces for the Liberation of Congo. The rebel force that brought Laurent-Désiré Kabila to power.

[72] The Summit would probably have made more progress if it had left out the issue of Security Council reform. Politicking about Security Council enlargement overshadowed decision-making on many of the other issues. Collective security reforms are probably more successful if they leave the Security Council untouched.

[73] Not including the portion on Security Council reform (see footnote 72).

FAR *Forces Armées Rwandaises*. The former Rwandan army that was implicated in the 1994 genocide.

FARDC *Forces Armées de la République Démocratique du Congo* / Armed Forces of the Democratic Republic of the Congo. The national army that was (officially) integrated during the transition.

FDLR *Forces Démocratiques pour la Libération du Rwanda* / Democratic Forces for the Liberation of Rwanda. Rwandan rebel group composed mostly of ethnic Hutus based in the eastern DRC.

FLC *Front de Libération du Congo*. Led by Jean-Pierre Bemba. Supported by the Ugandans. Occupied the northern part of the DRC. Transformed into a political party during the transition. Unexpectedly strong showing during the elections. Bemba is now indicted by the ICC.

Kabila, Joseph Son of late president **Laurent-Désiré Kabila**. President of the Congo since 2001. Democratically elected in 2006.

Mai-Mai Common name for the different local militias formed on the ethnic basis throughout the eastern DRC. Now officially integrated into the FARDC.

MONUC *Mission de l´Organisation des Nations Unies au Congo* / United Nations Organization Mission in the Congo.

RCD-Goma *Rassemblement Congolais pour la Démocratie–Goma* / Congolese Rally for Democracy–Goma. Main rebel group during the 1998 war. Supported by Rwanda. Controlled most of the eastern Congo. Armed fighters officially integrated into the FARDC. Transformed into political party during the transition. Lost the 2006 elections.

Rwandophones Kinyarwanda-speaking people. In the DRC context, the term often refers to the Congolese of Rwandan ancestry (both Hutus and Tutsis).

13

Indirect power: a critical look at civil society in the new Human Rights Council

ELIZABETH SALMÓN

The United Nations (UN) reform movement, as encapsulated in the High-Level Panel's *A More Secure World: Our Shared Responsibility*, Secretary-General Kofi Annan's *In Larger Freedom*, and the World Summit Outcome, employs a human rights-based approach in its examination of collective security.

The High-Level Panel on Threats, Challenges, and Change (HLP) was charged with examining the major threats and challenges the world faces in the broad field of peace and security, including economic and social issues insofar as they relate to peace and security, and making recommendations for a collective response.[1] The HLP defined the threats to collective security as threats to human security, thereby switching the object of collective security from member states to human individuals.[2] The HLP also recommended a structural change through the creation of a new human rights body, a free-standing Human Rights Council that would restore the effectiveness and credibility of the UN's devotion to human rights protection as outlined in the Preamble to the UN Charter.[3] In his report, Kofi Annan presented human rights protection as the means by which to achieve the ends of assured collective security.[4] Thus, following the advice of the HLP and Annan, the General Assembly voted to dissolve the Human Rights Commission and set up the new Council.[5]

1 The panel was appointed by the Secretary-General on November 3, 2003.

2 General Assembly, "A more secure world: our shared responsibility," Report of the High-Level Panel on Threats, Challenges and Change, A/59/565 (December 2, 2004), p. 11.

3 *Ibid.*, pp. 74 and 75 (paras. 283–284 and 291).

4 Report of the Secretary-General, *In Larger Freedom: Towards Development, Security, and Human Rights for All*, Fifty-ninth session, A/59/2005 (March 21, 2005), para. 14.

5 General Assembly Resolution A/Res/60/251 (April 3, 2006).

While the prescribed mission of the Council remains the same as its predecessor, it underwent various structural changes designed to make it more effective. First, the UN human rights body moved from a subcommittee of the Economic and Social Council that met once a year to a free-standing Council that meets at least three times a year and reports directly to the General Assembly.[6] Second, the method of electing Council members was modified such that countries are no longer elected as a member of a regional bloc, but rather, the General Assembly votes on each individual country after scrutinizing its human rights record.[7] Finally, the Human Rights Council instituted a mandatory Universal Periodic Review (UPR) for all the members of the General Assembly.[8]

In order to be effective, the reforms surrounding the creation and functioning of the Council must not only bring human rights closer to the average individual, but also facilitate the elaboration of a creative model to overcome past difficulties. The human rights-based approach offers a useful set of tools aimed at surpassing the dual citizen-state (petitioner-provider) scheme and developing a newly articulated system that recognizes the different rights and obligations of the various actors involved in human rights enforcement. These actors go beyond the traditional UN stakeholders (state governments) to encompass a variety of civil society organizations, such as public policy research centers, religious institutions, and media groups. More than any other UN body, the Council (and its predecessor, the Commission) promoted and embraced the involvement of these non-governmental organizations (NGOs[9]) and, in my opinion, allowing greater participation of civil

[6] General Assembly Resolution A/Res/60/251 (April 3, 2006).

[7] General Assembly Resolution A/Res/60/251 (April 3, 2006).

[8] Human Rights Council, 5th, A/HRC/RES/5/1 (June 18, 2007), Institution-building of the United Nations Human Rights Council.

[9] These rules of participation originated under Article 71 of the UN Charter, consolidated in Resolution 1296 (XLIV) (May 23, 1968), and later continued, with further improvements, in Resolution 1996/31 (July 25, 1996). ECOSOC Resolution 1296 (XLIV) (Arrangements for Consultation with Non-Governmental Organizations) (May 23, 1968) recognized NGOs with an international nature and allows only exceptionally the participation of those NGOs which lack this characterization. However, this situation changed some years later with the adoption of Resolution 1996/31 (July 25, 1996), which recognized NGOs acting at a national level in conjunction with those acting at an international one. It is worth mentioning that NGO participation within the UN has extended to other organs of the organization such as the Security Council and the General Assembly. In the former, it is becoming a common practice for ambassadors to meet routinely with the 20 or 25 of the most significant international NGOs, so that a "small number of NGOs including Amnesty International, Human Rights Watch, Oxfam, Save

society has contributed to the modernization and increased efficacy of the Council. Why? Civil society consists not only of the interests of the rights-bearers, but also includes the voices of the victims, and civil society organizations have the experience and technical capacity necessary to introduce topics and matters beyond the interstate agenda.

Permitting NGO participation was one of the most effective practices of the former Commission, a practice that the Council continues[10] as, fortunately, during the designing phase of the new reform, the Human Rights Council sought to retain the best elements of the former Commission, such as its special procedures and standard-setting mandates. However, the Council will greatly benefit from its new competition for membership, greater session frequency and flexibility, as well as the clear guiding principles and innovative Universal Periodic Review mechanisms. These additions provide the new body with a certain flexibility, giving it the potential to go above and beyond the work of the Commission. Despite its potential, however, the lack of political will surrounding the birth of the Council threatens to throw the Council back to an unwanted, yet familiar, situation: operating as an entity lacking the credibility or the authority to react to the needs of those suffering from the effects of grave humanitarian crises.

This approach to UN reform arises from a holistic view that collective security necessarily extends to human rights at the individual level and that a safe world requires that each and every one of its actors share the common goal of protecting human rights. This solid, peace-building scenario will replace the nominal one characterized by state rhetoric rather than action such that, hopefully, some states will cease to be a clear and present danger to global collective security. The participation of civil society at the international level is a crucial part of the collective security program for, in order for an integral concept of international peace and security to become a reality, civil society must be embraced by traditional stakeholders as an imperative actor.

the Children, World Vision, CARE and Médecins sans Frontières actively lobby the Council and meet with *individual* missions on a continuous basis." In reference to the latter, recently there have been numerous efforts to strengthen the relationship between civil society and the General Assembly, such as the Forum on General Assembly and Non-Governmental Organization Relations (November 21, 2006). For more see www.globalpolicy.org/security/mtgsetc/brieindx.htm (last accessed August 7, 2008).

10 See UN document: Resolution 1996/31, www.un.org/documents/ecosoc/res/1996/eres1996-31.htm (last accessed August 7, 2008).

NGOs and the basis for their participation in the Human Rights Council

A primary objective of UN reform is to provide greater visibility and protection of human rights issues.[11] Within the UN, Secretary-General Kofi Annan asked UN agencies to incorporate a human rights-based approach (HRBA) into their activities and to pursue interstate public polices which take human rights and their effective adherence into consideration. Beginning in 1997, Annan declared that the mission of the UN should be modified to include human rights enforcement as its ultimate objective.[12] In 1998, on the fiftieth anniversary of the Declaration of Human Rights, Annan, through the Office of the High Commissioner of Human Rights, asked all UN agencies to report on how they were contributing or could contribute to the enjoyment of human rights worldwide.[13] While it is not possible to assert that the most recent Council reforms have directly sought to promote this approach, it is true that the measures adopted will indirectly encourage increased participation and empowerment of international civil society in the work of the Council.

Although the UN's adoption of a human rights doctrine paved the way for the recognition of participation of the individual not only as an object but as a subject of international law, in reality, the structure of the UN does not provide a voice for individuals on the international level because states are the only official participants. Nevertheless, the protection and promotion of rights is not just a matter for the state because such rights implicated the concern of everyone interested in the protection of human rights. This is where NGOs come into play. NGOs have the power to serve as intermediaries between governments and individuals (rights bearers) and to promote the mechanisms by which the duty bearers of international law (the states) can be held accountable.[14] Thus, NGOs in

[11] A. Frankovits, "The Human Rights based approach and the United Nations system" (Paris: UN Educational, Scientific and Cultural Organization, 2006), pp. 28 and 54. See also Maria Luisa Silva, "The human rights based approach to development in the United Nations in the context of the new development goals," at www.unescobkk.org/index.php?id=6119 (last accessed August 7, 2008).

[12] UN Secretary-General, Renewing the United Nations: a Programme for Reform, UN GAOR, 51st Sess., UN Doc. A/51/1950 (1997).

[13] UNDP, "Integrating human rights with sustainable human development," UNDP policy document (January 1998).

[14] UN Population Fund, Human Rights-Based Programming, "What It Is" (New York: UNFPA, 2006), p. 1.

the majority of the members required in the former Commission). In the first two years of its existence, the Council has used both measures, holding a total of eight regular sessions and seven special work sessions. This number is significant if we recall that the Commission on Human Rights was only able to hold five special sessions in sixty years of existence. Nonetheless, what we wish to point out is that the greater frequency or semi-permanent nature of the Council is not sufficient guarantee that it will frequently respond to humanitarian crises, or, in other words, that the agenda will be conducted more effectively. In fact, the work completed so far has been even more frustrating given the lack of response to grave human rights violations taking place in other parts of the world.[42]

NGOs face concerns that, despite the availability of virtual channels of information, the growing number of meetings held at Council require either an increase in the available resources to travel to Geneva or a policy of NGO alliances that can guarantee minimum participation. This last option favors the most powerful NGOs and allows for a certain internationalization of their work, the results of which should be analyzed in the coming years. However, it seems inevitable that smaller NGOs, which tend to represent the interests of groups from underdeveloped countries, are being weakened in their lobbying capacities.

Looking at the original Council participation figures, although civil society is in fact participating actively within this organ,[43] such participation does not necessarily reflect the diversity of said society. Therefore, even though some NGOs do actually represent the needs of developing societies (among these we can find Comisión Colombiana de Juristas, Unión Nacional de Juristas de Cuba, and Al-Haq, among others), and some others represent the specific perspectives of the different

[42] The resolution adopted by G. A. Res. 60/251, also specifies the following: "(3) Decides also that the Council should address situations of violations of human rights, including gross and systematic violations, and make recommendations thereon. It should also promote the effective coordination and the mainstreaming of human rights within the United Nations system; ... (5) Decides that the Council shall, *inter alia*: ... (f) Contribute, through dialogue and cooperation, towards the prevention of human rights violations and respond promptly to human rights emergencies."

[43] During the first session of the Council, 154 NGOs participated; nearly half were non-Geneva-based. This number of attending NGOs is greater than the number in attendance at the closing session of the Commission on Human Rights in April 2006. In the first session about 50 written statements were submitted through NGOs, excluding other forms of written contribution, 58 oral statements were presented, half of which were joint statements; 22 parallel events were organized. See www.ngocongo.org/files/ngo_participation_at_Council_1st_session.doc (last accessed August 7, 2008).

geographic areas of the world (like the International Islamic Federation of Student Organizations, the World Islamic Congress, the Asian Forum for Human Rights and Development), in actuality, these organizations still represent a minority in comparison with NGOs from developed states. Moreover, some of the NGOs which represent developing countries (including the Europe–Third World Centre) are based and were developed in European states. However, it is possible to identify an increase in the number of NGOs coming from developing countries that participate in the Council's regular sessions (although the number was still below that of NGOs from developed countries).[44]

While it is still too early to determine any trends, we believe that the scant participation of NGOs coming from developing countries is a problem that must be addressed for the same reason that we must assure and guarantee the participation of civil society in the main human rights body of the UN. One option that is always available is to trust in the capacity of the NGOs to organize themselves, although not analyzing this information might risk their representativeness. Another option is to introduce innovating mechanisms such as a quota system or even a special fund – an experience that is not new to the organization[45] – in order to assure the inclusion of NGOs which would otherwise not have a chance to participate.

Nonetheless, at least on paper, the standing nature of the Council provides it with adequate mechanisms to address urgent human rights situations, and the frequency of its meetings should allow for a more focused and efficient approach in terms of its deliberations.[46] However, if

44 Human Rights Council, A/Council/2/9, Second Session. Report to the General Assembly on the Second Session of the Human Rights Council. Resolution 2/2; Human Rights Council, A/Council/3/7, Third Session. Report to the General Assembly on the Third Session of the Human Rights Council. Human Rights Council, A/Council/4/123, Fourth Session. Report to the General Assembly on the Fourth Session of the Human Rights Council. Resolution 4/1; Human Rights Council, A/HRC/5/21, Fifth Session. Report to the General Assembly on the Fifth Session of the Human Rights Council.

45 Breen, "Rationalizing the Work of UN Human Rights Bodies or Reducing the Input of NGOs? The Changing Role of Human Rights NGOs at the United Nations," p. 45. In support of the role of NGOs in drafting new standards with regard to the human rights of persons with disabilities, the Human Rights Commission invited governments, civil society, and the private sector to contribute to the United Nations Voluntary Fund on Disability, as well as to the voluntary fund established by the General Assembly in resolution 57/229, to support the participation of non-governmental organizations and experts from developing countries, in particular from the least developed countries, in the work of the Ad Hoc Committee.

46 See www.ngocongo.org/files/ngo_participation_background_paper_3_11.doc (last accessed August 7, 2008).

this design is not employed to its full advantage, it is already clear that this new structure itself will not automatically replace the political will and institutional cooperation necessary to allow the Council to trigger effective prevention and protection to those exposed to grave threats and violations to their basic securities.

For some people, it all boils down to the fact that international organizations were not created to face a global agenda and that the organization cannot be made more efficient because it was not created to this end.[47] Even if this were actually the case, a contemporary interpretation of the UN Charter does not permit us to assume this comfortable position. Quite to the contrary, the increased number of meetings held by the Council has the potential to keep the UN up to date with what is going on "in the field," despite the difficulties previously mentioned. In this sense, the work carried out by NGOs can be extremely useful inasmuch as the proximity between these organizations and the local realities have the ability to provide important information and better communication with groups that are the object, or the potential object, of human rights violations. By the same token, and even if we can discuss the possibility of creating or not creating a new ad hoc position at the UN,[48] we consider it significant that although this is no "guarantee of conflict prevention, exposure, publicity and world opinion can have an important deterrent effect on potential aggressors."[49]

Taking this into account, an exemplary measure has been the creation of the Council Extranet and the HCR orientation web page,[50] two services that were vocally praised by the NGO community as major steps forward in terms of accessibility to the Council, outreach, and transparency. This not only brings the UN and its work regarding human rights closer to the final beneficiaries, but also guarantees the right to information as a mechanism of inclusion and participation. Thus, the Office of the High Commissioner for Human Rights (OHCHR), as well as the collaboration of the Council with civil society

47 Modesto Seara Vàzquez (ed.), *Las Naciones Unidas a los Cincuenta Años* (Mexico: Fondo de Cultura Económica, 1995), pp. 388–389.

48 On the tenth anniversary of the Rwandan genocide, the Secretary-General announced the creation of this position, which involves the United Nations as a whole, linking the political and the human rights facets of the institution.

49 Walter A. Dorn, "An ounce of prevention: UN Early Warning System Needed," *SGI Quarterly* 8 (1997), pp. 24–25 at www.rmc.ca/academic/gradrech/dorn3_f.html (last accessed August 7, 2008).

50 www.ohchr.org/EN/HRbodies/Pages/HumanRightsBodies.aspx (last accessed August 7, 2008).

organizations, allowed for access to NGOs to all relevant documentation, both informal and official, concerning the ongoing work of the Council, its timetable, provisional agenda, lobbying information, accreditation, and events. Draft resolutions as tabled or under discussion, as well as written versions of the speeches addressed in plenary meetings and various communications, were displayed online and therefore available all over the world. This tool, as many NGO representatives stressed, was not only very helpful for participants of the Council, but even more specifically for all NGOs who were not able to be present in Geneva for the session. The webcast of the High-Level Segment was a powerful tool used to increase the visibility of the Council, particularly outside of Geneva.[51]

In any case, the Council's frequency and flexibility are measures that in and of themselves may be highly positive. However, current practice highlights the fact that a more continuous presence does not guarantee a more effective reaction or one that better meets the needs of the international human rights community as the defects of the former system seem to have found room to develop rather than diminish. Therefore, we call this a *neutral* measure because its ability to develop human rights protections will depend on the actor's self-control and/or on the pressure that civil society exerts to achieve a more effective and fair use of the assigned time for the Council's work.

Indirect empowerment: NGOs' contribution to the collective security project

The goal of the international system to protect human rights is meant to complement the activity of states, who are responsible for drafting public policy and ensuring human rights protection on the ground. The Human Rights Council employs two mechanisms intended to incentivize nations' adoption of policies that protect and enforce human rights at the national level: membership qualification and UPR. NGOs play an important role in the effectiveness of these mechanisms, not only as observers and watchmen of state behavior but also as sponsors at the international level of public policy standards to which all states should be held. Therefore, NGOs enjoy a unique position as advocates with one foot on the ground at the state level and the other foot inside the UN.

[51] See www.ngocongo.org/files/ngo_participation_at_Council_1st_session.doc (last accessed August 7, 2008).

NGOs' role in scrutinizing membership of the new Council

The new election process for the Council is more stringent than the process used for the Commission.[52] No longer are states elected as part of a larger regional bloc, but rather, states are elected directly and individually by secret ballot and must have a majority vote of the General Assembly (ninety-seven state votes). The General Assembly is instructed to review each and every candidate and to pay close attention to "the contribution of candidates to the promotion and protection of human rights and their voluntary pledges and commitments made thereto."[53] Furthermore, evidence that a Council member is responsible for gross and systematic violations of human rights during its tenure will lead to its suspension from the Council with a two-thirds majority vote of the General Assembly.[54]

The adoption of these eligibility guidelines has brought the Council closer to becoming a model of independent and impartial vigilance on human rights around the world while also carving out a distinct role for NGOs. In fact, without the research conducted by these international civil society organizations there would be no independent ground upon which to raise doubts or make demands of states regarding their human rights policy. States are not formally required to submit voluntary pledges

[52] The 47 member states of the new Council occupy seats distributed among the following regional groups: 13 to the African Group; 13 to the Asian Group, 6 to the Eastern European Group; 8 to the Latin American and Caribbean Group; and 7 to the Western Europe and Others Group. The election process is based on the Council's founding resolution, which established elections by secret ballot and where each member of the Council is elected directly and individually by an absolute majority of the members of the General Assembly, whether or not they are present and voting (which is a minimum of 97 members out of 192). Members can serve two consecutive terms of three years each, but shall not be eligible for immediate re-election after those terms (in order to prevent *de facto* permanent memberships).

[53] G. A. Res. 60/251, para. 8. For more detailed guidelines, see "Suggested Elements for Voluntary Pledges and Commitments By Candidates for Election to the Human Rights Council," Report of the United Nations Office of the High Commissioner for Human Rights at www2.ohchr.org/english/bodies/hrcouncil/docs/pledges.pdf (last accessed August 7, 2008).

[54] *Ibid.* This provision is vital to human rights reform given the re-election of Sudan to the former Commission on Human Rights in 2004, which greatly deepened the Commission's credibility crisis in the public eye. On the other hand, following the creation of the Council, the General Assembly's denial of membership on the Council to Belarus in the May 2007 elections was celebrated as a sign that the requirement to consider states' human rights records will be observed. However, the Council already consists of flagrant human rights abusers like Algeria, Cuba, Pakistan, Russia, Saudi Arabia, and China.

and failure to do so does not preclude a state from becoming a candidate for membership on the Council or from voting for new members.[55] NGOs provide the information on state conduct that General Assembly members use for their assessment of a candidate's eligibility and serve as monitors of the current Council member states to ensure that they are upholding the human rights record expected of them.[56]

However, so far there is no consensus among international civil society as to exactly what makes a country a human rights abuser. Some have proposed that the OHCHR should help to classify candidate countries and guide the election process, making it more transparent, and that it should publish a summary on the HR situation in all countries prior to the Council elections. Others have considered excluding those countries from running at all as extra insurance for the Council's credibility.[57]

The first proposed test for membership on the Council focused on the state government's ratification of the six or seven core human rights treaties adopted by the UN between 1965 and 1989. The second suggested criterion consisted of compliance with reporting obligations under the principal international human rights treaties, while a third criterion, not included in the Human Rights Watch list but suggested subsequently by the United States, was that countries that have been the subject of Security Council sanctions not be permitted to be a member of the Council.[58] It appears that the General Assembly adopted the first approach, although a lack of complete freedom from political constraints finally led to the establishment of a partial hybrid system. Nevertheless, the system does require that member states have a strong and clear commitment to the protection of human rights.

[55] Compare the absence of formal requirements to participate in the election process with the requirements demanded by the European Union, as discussed by Helen Upton, "The Human Rights Council: First Impressions and Future Challenges," *Human Rights Law Review* 7 (2007), p. 32.

[56] G. A. Res/60/251, paras. 8 and 9.

[57] Ladan Rahmani-Ocora, "Giving the Emperor Real Clothes: The UN Human Rights Council," *Global Governance* 12 (2006), pp. 15–20.

[58] However, there are a number of objections to this criterion. See W. Kalin and C. Jimenez, "Reform of the UN Commission on Human Rights, Study Commissioned by the Swiss Ministry of Foreign Affairs," (Political Division IV) Institute of Public Law (2003), pp. 8–9. See also Nazila Ghanea, "From UN Commission On Human Rights to UN Human Rights Council: One Step Forwards or Two Steps Sideways?" *International and Comparative Law Quarterly* 55 (2006), p. 699; and Philip Alston, "Reconceiving the UN Human Rights Regime: Challenges Confronting the New UN Human Rights Council," *Centre for Human Rights and Global Justice* Working Paper No. 4 (2006), pp. 10–12.

The first election of the Council has shown some positive signs. The fact that all candidates in the first election made voluntary pledges and commitments during the election process (most candidates included some substantive, serious, and forward-looking measures that can be monitored post-election by NGOs) is a step in the right direction, and one that has been warmly welcomed by civil society. In most cases, the pledges regarded actions to be taken during, rather than prior to, the course of Council membership as well as formal invitations to special rapporteurs for visits.[59] Civil society has the potential to play a vital role in the task of selecting new members to the Council as surveillance by NGOs has become the appropriate mechanism for overcoming the limitations of diplomacy.

The Universal Periodic Review mechanism

In addition to the new requirements for elections, members of the Council are required to "fully cooperate with the Council and be reviewed under the universal periodic review mechanism during their term of membership."[60] Kofi Annan's address of April 7, 2005 to the Commission described UPR as the evaluation of "the fulfillment by all states of all their human rights obligations." Although UN treaty bodies are only able to scrutinize the human rights record of states party to the treaty, in the case of UPR, every UN member chose to be subjected to a review process "whereby states voluntarily enter into discussion regarding human rights issues in their respective countries," with findings being implemented "as a cooperative venture, with assistance given to states" that need help developing their capacities.[61] The Council should not be a tribunal for naming and shaming but instead should be "constructive and non-confrontational."[62]

[59] Upton, "The Human Rights Council: First Impressions and Future Challenges," p. 32. Also see G. A. Res/60/251, para. 9: "Decides also that members elected to the Council shall uphold the highest standards in the promotion and protection of human rights, shall fully cooperate with the Council and be reviewed under the universal periodic review mechanism during their term of membership."

[60] G. A. Res/60/251, para. 9: "Decides also that members elected to the Council shall uphold the highest standards in the promotion and protection of human rights, shall fully cooperate with the Council and be reviewed under the universal periodic review mechanism during their term of membership."

[61] Excerpts drawn from Ghanea, "From UN Commission On Human Rights to UN Human Rights Council: One Step Forwards or Two Steps Sideways?," p. 704.

[62] *Ibid.*

UPR allows the UN to engage in self-evaluation and to determine the extent to which its membership actually practices the values of the UN Charter.[63] It is the job of the Council to monitor all UN member states to effectively detect and prevent human rights violations and the UPR enables an ongoing diagnosis of potential future members of the Council while also serving as yet another assessment of member states who are parties to the central international human rights treaties.[64]

Just as NGOs play an important role in determining Council membership, they are also central to the success of the UPR, since they gather information through an alternative network not always accessible by other member states or UN Rapporteurs. Recognizing the valuable service NGOs provide to the UPR mechanism, the UN highlighted the exact stages of the review process at which NGO involvement would be needed: the preparatory stage, conducting the review, decision making, implementation, and follow-up to outcomes.[65] NGOs are encouraged to participate throughout the UPR, through the formulation of questions, criticism, as well as proposals to the reviewed states.[66] NGO contributions enter the record of a member state and can form part of the evidence of commitment when they stand for re-election to the Council. Thus, by providing accurate information about member states' human rights records and making the UPR system more precise, NGOs have the potential to wield enormous power at the international level.[67]

[63] The innovation of UPR enjoyed wide support during the negotiations but questions arose as to whether the UPR should be the only means by which the Council addresses the status of human rights in member states as well as the standards according to which the performance of states was to be assessed. Ultimately, with Decision 1/103, adopted at the First Session of the Council, a consensus was reached as to: (i) the terms of reference/basis of review; (ii) the objectives and guiding principles of review; (iii) periodicity and order of review; (iv) the process and modalities of review; and (v) the outcome of the review and its follow-up. It should be noted that the attendance at the sessions was rather diverse, with the presence of the representatives of Member States to the Council, observers from non-Member States, agencies from the United Nations, International organizations, and NGOs.

[64] Felice D. Gaer, "A Voice not an Echo: Universal Periodic Review and The UN Treaty Body System," *Human Rights Law Review* 7 (2007), pp. 124–125.

[65] Second session of the inter-sessional open-ended intergovernmental working group to develop the modalities of the universal periodic review mechanism established pursuant to Human Rights Council decision 1/103. A/Council/4/CRP.3 (March 13, 2007), sect. 28.

[66] Information note for NGOs regarding the Universal Periodic Review mechanism at www.ohchr.org/EN/HRBodies/UPR/Pages/NoteNGO.aspx (last accessed May 16, 2008).

[67] Françoise J. Hampson, "An Overview of the Reform of the UN Human Rights Machinery," *Human Rights Law Review* 7 (2007), p. 18.

NGOs, Special Procedures and the Complaints Procedure

NGOs also provide an important service to the Council by contributing to both the Special Procedures and to the Complaints Procedure. Special Procedures "consist of independent experts sent to individual countries to monitor and respond rapidly and objectively to allegations of human rights violations."[68] Celebrated as a major achievement of the former Human Rights Commission, special procedures will continue under the Council as "the essential cornerstone of United Nations efforts to promote and protect human rights" and "the frontline troops that we turn to for early warning and protection."[69] On the other hand, the Complaints Procedure is the confidential complaint procedure granting permission to the Human Rights Council to read, review, and investigate any and all complaints of human rights abuses brought to the attention of the Council by individuals or groups.[70] In order for complaints to be heard by the Council's working group they need to be made in good faith (that is, they are free of abusive language and are not brought to the Council's attention for political reasons) and rely on substantive information (that is, contains a factual description of the circumstances and relies upon eye-witness accounts rather than mass-media reports).

NGOs are an important tool for the civilian population – complaints can be brought by NGOs on behalf of individuals or groups lacking the resources to do so and the NGOs can furnish the data or research needed to support such written complaints. It is necessary to engage with civil society organizations, which should not only be providers of privileged information but also important interlocutors, so that their work can take

[68] Scannella and Splinter, "The United Nations Human Rights Council: A Promise to be Fulfilled," pp. 58–59. Testimony to the importance of the special procedures in the protection of human rights was expressed by Minister Paulina Veloso of Chile. She testified to the value of the special procedures of the former Commission on Human Rights, in particular the Special Rapporteur on Chile, from her personal experience with the disappearance of her husband.

[69] Jeroen Gutter, "Special Procedures and the Human Rights Council: Achievements and Challenges Ahead," *Human Rights Law Review* 7 (2007), p. 105.

[70] The complaint procedure was reviewed June 18, 2007 by the new Human Rights Council. The original, procedure 1503, was adopted by the Economic and Social Council in 1970 and used by the former Human Rights Commission until its replacement by the Council in 2005. For more about the review process and the content of the current complaint procedure see www2.ohchr.org/english/bodies/chr/complaints.htm.

the questions and contributions of complaint proceedings into consideration. This should all be accompanied by working methods that are not only cooperation but also results-oriented, and which allow for subsequent follow-up discussions for both the recommendations and their subsequent implementation.[71]

[71] G. A. Res. 60/251, para. 12.

14

Collective security: a village-eye view

J. PAUL MARTIN AND BENEDICTO Q. SÁNCHEZ[1]

> I have named this present report "In Larger Freedom" to stress the enduring relevance of the Charter of the UN and to emphasize that its purposes must be advanced in the lives of individual men and women. The notion of larger freedom also encapsulates the idea that development, security and human rights go hand in hand.[2]
>
> Kofi Annan, 2005

In his 1945 film *Distant Thunder*, Satyajit Ray portrayed the interconnected nature of global affairs and the rhythm of daily life in a village in India. The film describes how the high prices being paid in Europe for rice and other staples during the Second World War brought starvation and death to the Indian village. Upon viewing the film in 2007, one cannot help but wonder how much greater the impact would be today, given the massive processes of globalization that have taken place since 1945. Considering the impact of globalization's complex set of interacting economic and political forces on ordinary people,[3] no discussion of collective security can be complete without examining its relevance to these "villagers," a population composed of the world's millions of impoverished rural and urban men and women who have little influence on the power structures and other factors that govern their daily lives.

1 We are grateful for the comments and suggestions of the editors and fellow authors in this volume and for research assistance from Ms. Annamartine Salick.

2 *In Larger Freedom*, para. 14, available at www.un.org/largerfreedom (last accessed June 23, 2008).

3 Arundhati Roy outlines a more analytical approach to this problem, describing the lives of ordinary people struggling with the scarcity of food as well as bodily and emotional stress and abuse. Arundhati Roy, *An ordinary person's guide to empire* (Cambridge: South End Press, 2004). See also Sadako Ogata, "From state security to human security," *Ogden Lecture*, Brown University, Rhode Island, May 26, 2002, www.humansecurity-chs.org/activities/outreach/ogata_ogden.html (last accessed May 14, 2008).

One region of such villages is Negros Occidental in the Philippines, a province where one of the authors of this chapter belongs to the non-governmental organizations (NGOs) Broad Initiatives for Negros Development (BIND), Human Rights Defenders Negros, and the coalition Mediators for Peace. The NGOs operate in a region where there are renewed armed encounters between New People's Army (NPA) guerillas and the military tasked by the national government to crush this rebellion by 2010. In his NGO capacity, the author works among the civilian rural hinterland populations on the sustainable mountain development projects recommended by the United Nations' Rio Agenda 21. Agenda 21 is a thorough and broad-ranging program of actions demanding new ways of investing in the future to reach global sustainable development in the twenty-first century. Its recommendations ranged from new ways to educate, to new ways to care for natural resources, and new ways to participate in designing a sustainable economy. The overall ambition of Agenda 21 is to create a safe and just world in which all life has dignity and is celebrated.[4] In Negros, theories of collective security are meaningful only so far as they are also embraced and understood by the local community members who are supposed to benefit from them. As a result, implementing collective security at the village level requires creating political, social, environmental, economic, military, and cultural systems that combine to give ordinary people the building blocks for survival, livelihood, and dignity. However, problems arise when NGOs attempt to implement this vision of collective security only to find that their principles, goals, and strategies collide with those of the state entities that are more concerned with "national security."[5]

This conflict between NGOs and states illustrates the need to examine the principles, goals, and strategies underlying the parties' views on collective security, human security, and national security. The priority to be given to the various threats and the methods for addressing them are strongly disputed in post-9/11 Negros. For example, during 2004 and

[4] See UN Conference on Environment and Development, Rio de Janeiro, June 3–14, 1992, Agenda 21, UN doc. A/CONF.151/26 (August 14, 1992) at www.un.org/jsummit/html/basic_info/agenda21.html (last accessed June 17, 2008).

[5] National security doctrine has been the subject of extensive academic research, notably with respect to Latin America. This research shows how easily national security can hide the interests of a political group or social class and how it is often based on secret if not suspect information and decision making. At times, the doctrine can conflict with human rights. See Kathryn Sikkink, *Mixed signals: US Human Rights Policy and Latin America* (Ithaca: Cornell University Press, 2007).

2005, the National Task Force on Convergence sought to harmonize the perspectives of the civilian agencies and state armed forces in order to fast-track poverty alleviation in conflict-ridden, impoverished and remote *barangays* (villages). While civilian agencies talked of "winning back, enhancing and transforming," the state's soldiers used the language of "eliminating, defeating and annihilating."[6] Considering these divergent mindsets, human rights defenders who hold peace building as their goal have to tread carefully in engaging government-initiated programs in conflict prevention and peace building.

Until the NGOs and the states succeed in reconciling their visions for collective security, the Negros community will continue to endure a myriad of security threats, three of which are of particular significance. First, as in many other situations of low-intensity conflict, the local population in Negros has to live with threats from the military and from the insurgents. Each side demands their loyalty, allegiance, and financial and material support, employing such means as "revolutionary taxation" and coupling their demands with credible threats to life and property. NGOs working in this rural area, especially among hinterland communities, can only offer limited assistance due to their own dilemma. While the NGOs fear being branded by the insurgents as counter-insurgency tools of the military,[7] they are also concerned about being portrayed as front organizations for the Maoist Communist Party of the Philippines.[8] By trying to stay neutral in internal armed conflicts, the

[6] Teresita Quintos-Deles, "Keynote speech" in Zuraida Mae D. Cabilo, Sharon M. Quinsaat, and Trina Joyce M. Sajo (eds.), *Defining the human security framework in the Philippine context: Proceedings of the Third World Studies Center Policy Dialogue Series 2006* (Third World Studies Center, College of Social Sciences and Philosophy, University of the Philippines, 2007), p. 97. See also L. Chen, S. Sakiko Fukuda-Parr, and E. Seidenstickers (eds.), *Human insecurity in a global world* (Cambridge, MA: Harvard University Press, 2004).

[7] In 2006, for example, the NPA insurgents burned one of the cargo trucks of the NGO Alter Trade and threatened to further punish the leading Human Rights Defenders activist Edwin Marthine Lopéz, and Norma Mugar: see www.philippinerevolution.net (last accessed June 17, 2008).

[8] See National Democratic Front (NDF) Chief Representative Luis G. Jalandoni, *Letter to Alter Trade* (July 28, 2007) (on file at BIND, Philippines). On the other hand, this chapter's co-author was accused by the armed communist splinter group, the Revolutionary Proletarian-Alex Boncayao Brigade (RPA-ABB) and a military ally, as a top cadre of the Maoist Communist Party of the Philippines-New People's Army. Its local commander warned him that he is in the order of battle of the RPA-ABB's national operational command. However, the top RPA-ABB cadre Veronica Tabara denied that there is such a list, indicating a loosening, if not a break, in the armed group's chain of command.

NGOs find themselves prime targets for violent attacks from both sides, and the local community suffers as a result.[9]

Second, the people of Negros face countless health threats. In seeking redress or healthcare, poor migrant peasants and indigenous communities in regions such as Negros Occidental have little access to government services. Courts and social services are to be found only in city and town centers. They are virtually absent in the hinterlands. The only government entities willing to penetrate the hinterlands are military units geared for combat against the Maoist insurgents. This short-sighted approach by the government is aggravated by the absence of local police forces to protect the villagers from other threats, such as armed bandits and cattle rustlers.

Third, the local Negros population witnesses the exploitation of its natural resources. During the 1970s and 1980s, lowland-based *hacienderos* (rich land-owners) used private armies to seize forestlands from migrant farmers, indigenous communities, and rival *hacienderos*. They then degraded lands with the logging concessions, deforesting the Northern Negros Forest Reserve (NNFR). The roads built by the multinational logging companies are still littered with unmarked graves of shoot-out victims, relics of the unrestrained struggle for control of the lands.

In the wake of these threats to security at the local level, armed propaganda units of the Communist Party of the Philippines have been able to exploit the villagers' discontent in order to recruit peasants for their "people's war" in the hinterlands. The NPA won the peasants' support by repelling the private armies and expelling the *hacienderos*. Within two years, the communist insurgents decided that mass support in the rainforest reserve was widespread and strong enough to launch guerilla warfare. Full-time company and platoon-size guerilla units were formed to launch tactical offensives. NPA attacks escalated from ambuscades of isolated Philippine Army squads to daring military operations against municipal centers and army company detachments.

The state military's response was just as intense. In 1989, the Armed Forces of the Philippines concentrated its activities on nine provinces, with Negros as one of the priorities. As part of its counter-insurgency operation,

[9] See International Consultant Paola Belloti, *Letter to President Gloria M. Arroyo* (September 4, 2006) (on file at BIND, Philippines). In concert with networking efforts of Alter Trade, the letter helped prompt the Philippine government, through its Office of the Presidential Adviser for the Peace Process, to hold a series of dialogues among various stakeholders such as BIND, Alter Trade Group, the RPA-ABB, the Philippine Army and the Philippine National Police. *Ibid.* See also Benedicto Q. Sanchez, "Armed conflict and sustainable mountain development," *Not by Timber Alone* 12 (May 2007), p. 4.

it also launched "hearts-and-minds" campaigns, using special operations teams to "counter-organize" the farmers into civilian volunteer organizations (CVOs). Those who refused to join the CVOs were forcibly evacuated and hamletted or resettled in controlled villages. Far-flung farms were declared free-fire zones, allowing them to be constantly and indiscriminately bombarded by artillery fire. Suspected NPA sympathizers were picked up and several local leaders became *desaparecidos* (the disappeared) or "salvaged," a Philippine military slang term for extra-judicial executions.

Such strong-arm militarist approaches, however, failed to quell the Maoist insurgency. The armed conflict waned, but did not die out. After more than a decade of relative calm, beginning in 2006, the NPA initiated a series of "tactical offensives" against the army and the police.[10] The northern Negrense towns and cities of Escalante, Toboso, Calatrava and San Cárlos witnessed massive military deployments responding to reports that the rebels were building strong popular support in those regions,[11] with military records showing an upsurge in the activities of the New People's Army in northern Negros.[12]

More recently the Philippine national government has veered away from defining the problem as national security and the only solution as military force. As threats to communities go beyond armed and physical violence and violence is perceived as rooted in broader structural and cultural causes, it is now recognized that establishing a just and lasting peace requires a multifaceted strategy, involving a collective approach with various actors working on different levels and addressing different aspects of the conflict. As the Office of the Presidential Adviser on the Peace Process (OPAPP) noted, the peace process cannot be determined by government alone, much less by the military. It needs the convergence of local, regional and national government entities and civil society actors. Thus, President

[10] Bayoran, Gilbert, "Paramilitary forces mobilized," *Visayan Daily Star* (January 22, 2007) at www.visayandailystar.com/2007/January/22/topstory4.htm (last accessed June 17, 2008).

[11] "Army operations to focus in Negros," *Visayan Daily Star* (January 3, 2008) at www.visayandailystar.com/2008/January/03/police.htm#police2 (last accessed August 7, 2008).

[12] Bayoran, Gilbert, "Teams sent to counter rebel fronts," *Visayan Daily Star* (September 15, 2007) at www.visayandailystar.com/2007/September/15/topstory6.htm (last accessed June 17, 2008). On the other hand, the Communist Party of the Philippines accused the government of "plaguing Northern Negros with brutal murders, abductions, tortures, warrantless arrests and coercions perpetrated by the military, police and CAFGUs [Civilian Armed Forces Geographical Unit, paramilitary units established in 1987 based on the notion of a citizens' armed force as expressed in the constitution]". See www.philippinerevolution.net (last accessed June 17, 2008).

Arroyo issued Executive Order 569 to facilitate bringing together the various sectors, especially at the local level. It mandates OPAPP to hold a series of workshops on Convergence for Human Security and Peace (CHASE) under the aegis of United Nations Development Programme's (UNDP) Conflict Prevention and Peace Building Program.[13]

Negros and other local communities across the Philippines can look forward to improved security in the future as this peace-building paradigm is developed further. During a recent local CHASE workshop, the co-author of this chapter argued for the convergence or collective security logic as a way to "civilianize" and "de-militarize" the hinterlands through civilian multi-stakeholder cooperation. In such a model, the military would play a secondary, back-up role to provide security for the civilian government and non-government agencies. The concept will be tested during the next two years and could prove an alternative to the previous paradigm that relied on the military to suppress the insurgency.

The approach is not new. The Broad Initiatives for Negros Development, the Filipino co-author's organization, cobbled a project-based memorandum of agreement with the Department of the Environment and Natural Resources, the community-based organization and the Philippine Army. The goal was to stave off threats from the RPA-ABB and armed illegal loggers which threatened implementation of the rainforest conservation and livelihood project. One of the signatories was Col. Victor Ibrado, then commanding officer of the 303rd Infantry Brigade. Now, Lt. General Ibrado is the current Philippine Army chief. The concept has been tried elsewhere on a more strategic basis in Mindanao, where civil society peace-making initiatives helped mitigate armed conflict between the government and military separatists.

The situation in Negros is illustrative of the problems encountered by villages around the world. This chapter endeavors to examine how the UN reform efforts relating to collective security respond to these problems from the perspective of villagers. It commences with an overview of the numerous security threats facing local communities. The chapter continues with an evaluation of the roles of institutions, such as international and local NGOs, foreign and national governments, and the local communities themselves, in minimizing security threats. Next, it describes the benefits of collective security as a model for such institutions. The UN's

[13] OPAPP, UNDP, Regional KALAHI Convergence Group, Iloilo City, 19–21 November 2007, *Background and rationale, Convergence for Human Security and Peace Workshop (CHASE PEACE)* workbook, p. 1.

unique position to develop this paradigm to the advantage of local communities is explored in detail. Finally, the chapter concludes by offering a proposal and recommendations for enhancing the effectiveness of these institutions' responses to security threats at the local level.

Security threats to villages

Collective security is "the institutions, policies, responsibilities and strategies necessary to ensure subsistence, physical security, fundamental freedoms and the acquisition of the knowledge and skills needed for sustainable communities."[14] In the world's impoverished communities, both urban and rural, the factors that can contribute to a lack of collective security are numerous. Of utmost concern are those factors that undermine survival needs, namely those associated with subsistence and health, such as sanitation, disease, food, drinking water, shelter, sources of livelihood, healthcare, and environment. The second tier of basic human needs and freedoms is associated with physical security including freedom from fear and violence. The third tier recognizes the human need to acquire the skills and knowledge necessary to cope with the basic responsibilities of adult life, including at least the ability to support a family and prepare offspring for their future lives.[15] Assuring these needs in a globalized world is complex, calling for resources increasingly outside those of the community, if not also outside those of many poor states.

Villagers, such as the Negros community, are the neediest of the "individual men and women" described in Annan's *In Larger Freedom*. They are the ones who face threats serious enough to determine whether they and their children will live or die. Often unheard and unassisted, it is the villagers who must deal with the polluted air and water, roving warring factions, and the lack of education and health facilities.

[14] This definition is a modification of one proposed in the introduction to this volume. It also emphasizes the inter-relatedness and interdependence of civil and political rights and economic and social rights. The Commission on National Security defines human security as the protection of the vital core of all human lives in ways that enhance human freedom and fulfillment. See Anna Lindley, "Human security now: Protecting and empowering people," *Journal of Refugee Studies* 17 (2004), pp. 244–246.

[15] Scholar Henry Shue identifies three groups of basic rights: subsistence, security, and liberty. Indeed the basic definition on which all his arguments are constructed reads: "A moral right provides (1) a rational basis for a justified demand (2) that the actual enjoyment of a substance be (3) socially guaranteed against standards threats." Henry Shue, *Basic rights: Subsistence, affluence, and US foreign policy* (Princeton: Princeton University Press, 1980), p. 13.

Aggravating the situation in many villages is the fact that fewer and fewer of their once-independent settlements, which could survive on subsistence agriculture or hunting-gathering in the case of some indigenous peoples such as the Atis in northern Negros, are now isolated from powerful negative forces originating from the outside. In the absence of government-provided security, they need weapons to defend themselves and their families from brigands if not from more organized insurgents. Suggestions to create zones of peace in conflict-riven areas of northern Negros seem impractical as most hinterland households are armed, keeping home-made *pugakhangs* (shotguns) or *paltiks* (improvised revolvers) for security against bandits.

To have access to healthcare or to buy goods from outside the villages, they must seek cash for the necessary payments, typically by leaving the community, taking wage-earning jobs in the towns and cities, and frequently never returning to their villages. This worldwide economic emigration results in thousands of rural communities without the young men and women able to support and rejuvenate them. Migration has also brought AIDS and other diseases to these villages. In many regions, massive extractive industries have become their neighbors, typically benefiting from minimal local controls to protect the environment and the local labor force. Few of these poor communities really benefit from the presence of industry, let alone have schools that could assure some of the literacy and other skills needed for more gainful participation in the new economy. Such threats add up to a high degree of insecurity. In both sending and receiving communities these circumstances can generate volatile and destabilizing segments. Unemployed or out-of-school youth, for example, can easily be recruited to protest, whether by the Maoist insurgents in Negros or in the impoverished *banlieues* of Paris. In such cases it is all too easy to persuade bored or frustrated youth to use violence to force radical change.

As outside influences increasingly compound the security threats to local communities, the village optic on collective security becomes more important than ever for three reasons. First, monitoring the conditions of ordinary communities provides indicators of the effect of national and international policies and practices. Second, as the building blocks of national society, the general health and well being of poor villages will, sooner or later, have an impact on the condition of the whole society. Monitoring them adds to and complements the bigger picture envisioned by Annan when he called for the UN "to advance the lives of individual men and women." Lastly, monitoring these conditions is a necessary step toward remedying them.

The list of potential threats that require monitoring is long:

- absence, incompetence or corruption of state institutions needed to assure personal security, criminal justice, dispute resolution, and social services;[16]
- presence of insurgencies and terrorist activities, especially if coupled with income-raising activities;
- tensions among ethnic, religious, or other social groupings, especially if coupled with actions or entities from outside the country;
- illegal activities such as drugs and arms dealing, as well as human trafficking;
- illegal or abusive exploitation of natural resources;
- presence of deadly viruses or other health epidemics;
- commercial activities with significant negative environmental or social impact;[17]
- overall emotional climate, long-standing popular grievances, social cleavages and mistrust.[18]

[16] This problem has been accentuated by post 9/11 legislation which increased police and military powers which in turn were used for other purposes. See Preeti Verma (ed.), *The People's Tribunal on the Prevention of Terrorism (POTA) and other security legislation* (New Delhi: Human Rights Law Network, 2004). Thus in the case of governments benefiting from the income of petroleum resources, communities where oil is extracted protest the lack of a share in the income by sabotaging pipelines and holding oil workers hostage. In other countries, notably recently Chad, civil servants have gone on strike in order to see increased wages that they believe are their rightful share of the increased national revenues coming from oil.

[17] Nigeria is a classic example. See Ike Okonta and Oronto Douglas, *Where vultures feast, Shell, human rights and oil* (London: Verso, 2003); Jedrzej George Frynas, "The oil industry in Nigeria: conflict between oil companies and local people," in Frynas, Jedrzej George, and Pegg, Scott (eds.), *Transnational corporations and human rights* (New York: Palgrave Macmillan, 2003).

[18] In the face of injustice, villager reactions can range from fear to anger and violence. In Venezuela, there is a village that is completely surrounded by the sea and massive haciendas. The owners of the haciendas have long refused to give even a few hectares to the village for a dump. The result is that the sides of the road into the village have become the garbage dump. The hacienda owners made it clear that any challenges to this situation will be met with threats to life, even those of outsiders. Fear is thus still the effective mechanism of control. Recently, Caitlin O. Mahoney and Tatiana M. Pinedo concluded that "Our results show that it is possible to measure the experience of human security, that this experience depends more on national emotional climate than socio-economic status, and that for community samples, a large part of human security depends on support from family and friends." Caitlin O. Mahoney and Tatiana M. Pinedo, "Human security in communities in Costa Rica and the United States," *Journal of Social Issues* 63 (2007), p. 353. Other articles in the same edition address the impact of the emotional climate on intergroup perceptions and relations.

The more threats present at once, the greater will be the overall impact, whether or not they are yet visible and acknowledged internationally. The more the threats are inter-related, the more complex will be the solutions. Civil conflict, for example, prevents villagers from farming and puts them at the mercy of opposing armed groups, marauding for food or possibly for their women and children.

Each of these threats is going to be visible to the villagers first and moreover the villagers, not the diplomats, policy makers, or scholars, will be the ones to suffer or die if their voices are not heard. The inability of poor local communities to make their voices heard or to change the complex forces that impinge on their lives is well illustrated with respect to arms sales, legal or otherwise. For example, during the Cold War, the US alone delivered over $1.5 billion worth of weaponry to Africa, arming states like Liberia, Somalia, the Sudan, and Zaire (now the Democratic Republic of the Congo), all of which are states that later witnessed some of the most devastating internal conflicts in Africa. In particular, the US supported the dictatorial and corrupt rule of Mobutu Sese Seko with over $300 million in weapons and $100 million in military training, buttressing Mobutu's repressive regime until the late 1990s.[19] According to the Stockholm International Peace Research Institute, companies in the United States and Western Europe accounted for 92 percent of all arms sales in 2005.[20] The net effect of these sales on poor communities is difficult to measure. Certainly, once so many of these arms find their way onto the black market, there is little villagers can do to defend themselves against firepower, whether from the government, private militia, rival clans, or local brigands. Ongoing intergovernmental and clandestine arms sales continue to fuel today's low-intensity conflicts in Africa and elsewhere. Typically it is the villagers who are dying. Faced with the consequences of the arms sales and similar forces beyond their control, the UN and UN reform seem far away to most villagers. Indeed, it is difficult for them to imagine how either could have an impact on their lives.

Unable to effectively advocate for themselves regarding issues such as arms sales, villages are dependent on other institutions to speak for them.

[19] See William Hartung and Bridget Moix, "Deadly legacy: US arms to Africa and the Congo War," *Arms Trade Resource Center*, New York, January 2000, at www.worldpolicy.org/projects/arms/reports/congo.htm (last accessed May 14, 2008).

[20] Gerard O'Dwyer, "SIPRI: World spent $1.2 trillion on militaries in 2006," *Defense News* (June 25, 2007), p. 4.

This can raise a number of problems as demonstrated by a major NGO dinner held at the UN a short time ago. The theme was bridging the gap between the rich and the poor. The list of invitees included twenty-seven experts who were seated at each table and discussed this topic with the guests. All but four of the experts were men and all but a few had salaries in excess of $100,000. One would suspect that the conversations would have been very different if the organizers had also placed at each table a person whose children went to bed hungry every night. What therefore does that say about the utility of the discussions that were held? The question is equally applicable to discussions about village security. This problem of representation was addressed during the Mountain Forum electronic conference on the Cusco Plan of Action[21] when a co-author explained that the Mountain Partnership,[22] a UN initiative, had to differentiate between members of mountain communities and members of the Mountain Partnership. The representatives of the mountain communities that have the most at stake in collective security lacked fluency in the official conference languages (English, French, Spanish, and even Italian), creating a huge obstacle to their meaningful participation in policy discussions. Moreover, even when the mountain communities participated in face-to-face meetings using interpreters, comprehension remained a problem. International conference delegates talk, discuss, and debate among themselves using another "foreign" language, one based on bureaucratic considerations and academic abstractions unknown to the local populations.

To overcome the problems associated with outsiders representing villages and to enhance their effectiveness, external development or peace-building organizations like the Mountain Partnership have to enlist local groups that have local experience, in this case, in mountain conservation, and that can speak and understand the multifarious "languages" of the communities, the scholars, and the bureaucrats. This role

[21] Mountain Partnership, *E-Consultation on the Cusco Plan of Action, second global meeting of the Mountain Partnership, August 30 – September 17, 2004*, at www.condesan.org/e-foros/CuscoActionPlan/bsanchez1.htm (last accessed May 14, 2008).

[22] Mountain Partnership, or the International Partnership for the Sustainable Development of Mountain Regions, is a voluntary alliance of partners dedicated to improving the lives of mountain people and protecting mountain environments around the world. Launched at the World Summit for Sustainable Development in 2002, the Mountain Partnership taps the wealth and diversity of resources, information, knowledge, and expertise of its members to support positive change in mountain areas. Mountain Partnership, *Welcome to the Mountain Partnership*, www.mountainpartnership.org/ (last accessed May 14, 2008).

is being played by civil society organizations, including the NGOs whose members work with the mountain communities, have college backgrounds, write proficiently in the official languages, and also have access to the Internet. Thus for the present, villagers need NGOs to represent them even in their own home regions.

Whether it is the villagers themselves or proxies such as NGOs or scholars, who work to minimize the threats to local communities, these advocates would agree with Annan's articulation of their objectives. They would recognize that Annan's freedom from want means at least access to healthy water, to an adequate diet, housing, sanitation, employment and healthcare. His freedom from fear means reducing the occurrence of conflict, wars and the use of coercion and violence, the capacity of the police, the courts and military to protect human rights and social order, and a degree of protection from major disasters such as highly contagious deadly diseases, earthquakes, volcanoes or tsunamis. Finally, Annan's freedom to live in dignity means access to basic education, to decisions that affect their lives, to legal redress, as well as to public information and the media. As summed up by Annan, "The notion of larger freedom also encapsulates the idea that development, security and human rights go hand in hand."[23]

The role of institutions in minimizing collective security threats to villages

Annan's laudable goals can only be attained, however, through effective institutions and appropriate strategies. Overcoming threats in sustainable ways depends on many institutional actors outside the village primarily because the causes of the threats and their remedies depend on institutions far from the village.[24] The distance between villages and these institutions can be both a question of time as well as physical distance. An example of distance in time is the spread of AIDS in present-day South Africa. Its roots are deep in early years of the European presence. Beginning in the 1830s, young men had been leaving their villages in and around South Africa to

[23] *In Larger Freedom*, para. 14.

[24] There is a large literature on poverty reduction. More recently this has focused on the role of the private sector and especially on foreign direct investment. General proposals in this field use aggregate material that identifies poverty alleviation within large segments and argues that overall growth within a country reduces the size of its impoverished population. See, e.g., Advisory Council on International Affairs, *Private sector development and poverty reduction* (The Hague, 2006). For example, there is no attention to job creation and other mechanisms operable and observable at the village level.

work in gold and diamond mines. In the process, they were required to stay for long periods and live in male-only communities far from their homes.[25] Today, when they return to their villages, many bring with them the AIDS virus. The dissemination of the disease is further aggravated if they return to find they have inherited the wife of a recently deceased relative with whom they have the right to cohabit.[26] Physical distance is well illustrated by the film *Distant Thunder*, in which the supply of rice in the Indian village was less than needed because the rules of supply and demand in a period of limited supply ensured that available supplies would inexorably go to those who could pay the most, in that case, Europe. With such causes deep in history and culture as well as across international economies, remedial action to deal with such threats calls for institutions that can address the complex patterns of the causes as well as related threats. International NGOs, local NGOs, foreign governments, local communities, and state governments play particularly pivotal roles in minimizing threats to villages.

The role of international NGOs

The external agencies likely to be most visible in a "village" are the NGOs.[27] Over the last twenty years and more, international NGOs such as CARE, Christian Aid, the Aga Khan Foundation, and the Open Society Institute have become major actors in development and the UN has been an important catalyst in their growth. Many of these NGOs benefit from the UN. Some run refugee camps for the UNHCR. The UN provides forums where local as well as international NGOs can gain support for change through their reporting and lobbying. In particular, the three major UN human rights conferences in Vienna in 1993, Beijing in 1995, and Durban in 2001 provided unique opportunities for NGOs from all over the world to get to know one another, to learn to work in concert, and especially to influence government officials. International NGOs brought to these meetings representatives from low-income

[25] A related phenomenon is the recent report of young men in the UK being recruited for terrorist training camps in Pakistan. Unemployed youth must be seen as a threat to security both in a dark local alleyway and as actors in a major international incident. Unemployment is thus a threat to collective security.

[26] Rangarirai Shoko, "Spouse inheritance continues in Zimbabwe despite AIDS," *Panafrican News Agency Daily Newswire* (January 24, 2001).

[27] Jude Howell and Jenny Pierce, *Civil society and development: A critical exploration* (Boulder: Lynne Rienner Publishers, 2001).

countries and countries with systemic human rights violations. At the meetings the representatives lobbied their respective governments and generally assured that final documents set strong guidelines and agendas.

There is also evidence to show that campaigns and lobbying by local and international NGOs help local communities by bringing threats to local security to the attention of the UN agencies. One recent example is the work of local groups concerned with the social and environmental impact of the Chad–Cameroon pipeline. A handful of local Chadian and Cameroonian advocates were able to mobilize international NGOs and scholarly resources in both Europe and the US. The latter were able to ensure that reports and social assessments on the impact of the pipeline on local communities reached the right desks, in this case, at the World Bank, the institution responsible for part of investment as well as for planning social benefits from the oil revenues.[28] No such reports reached the Bank from the two governments, the UNDP, or any other UN agencies.

Additionally, international NGOs help communities by asserting their political pressure against security threats. When the NPA burned the Alter Trade truck in Negros and threatened its managers with bodily harm, the fair trade organization mobilized its international partners, notably the German Bread for the World, the British Association of Fair Trade Shops, and even the Royal Norwegian Embassy.[29] The move compelled the Maoist umbrella organization, the National Democratic Front of the Philippines (NFDP), to respond and explain their side, first with a denial, and then a justification. The international outcry prevented the NDFP from carrying out their threat to "punish these NGO bureaucrats of Alter Trade Corp as equivalent to the exploitation, oppression and sufferings that ATC inflicted on the masses." In addition to providing financial support, the political pressure of the international organizations contributed significantly to easing the pressure of other non-state armed groups on local civil society organizations.

However, dependence on international NGOs and other outside agents in seeking to overcome poverty and other threats to human security has long bedeviled sustainable political and economic

[28] This project has been monitored by a number of groups in the US, notably the Environmental Defense. See, e.g., Environmental Defense Fund, *The Landowner Conservation Assistance Program*, www.edf.org (last accessed May 28, 2008); Bretton Woods Project, *Chad–Cameroon pipeline: Implementation, challenges and lessons learned*, www.brettonwoodsproject.org/art-552626 (last accessed May 28, 2008).

[29] See *Europe solidaire sans frontières* at www.europe-solidaire.org (last accessed June 17, 2008).

development.[30] Among the causes is the ephemeral nature of the aid, most of which is provided for individual projects with short timeframes, with outcomes defined by donors and their agents, and with the funds controlled by the external agency. Moreover, many of the international NGO partners need a share of the grants for their own support. In the case of security projects as such, the emphasis of donors tends to be on military means and thus the aid is more likely to go directly to government. The test of all these international aid models is their capacity to assure sustainable solutions once the external inputs, personnel, funds, and technology have been withdrawn. Thus, welcome as these external agencies are, they risk creating a level of dependence that lessens the efficacy of local groups once the external inputs cease.

The role of local NGOs

Like international NGOs, local NGOs work to reduce threats to villages. The limitations of strategies that rely on external agencies point to the need to develop the capacity of the local actors such as local government agencies and communities. In developing countries, especially those with failed or partially failing states, governments often claim that they cannot financially support the police and other services needed by their citizens. When local communities are thus left to themselves, progress must depend on their own resources and traditional leaders. In the ungoverned spaces in mountain hinterlands, ideological groups such as Al-Qaeda in Pakistan or the Maoist CPP-NPA are able to assume governance using their own set of policies, police, military, or even judicial functions. Where they are present, the contribution of the modern local NGOs is more limited as the latter merely supplement rather than take over other local services. One of local NGOs' supplemental roles is serving as conduits of information and, if necessary, alarm, to the larger society, a function that few local communities can perform.

Despite the importance of their role, the world of local NGOs in developing countries has yet to be mapped. Reportedly there are as many as 10,000 in some countries in Africa.[31] Closer attention, however, reveals substantial turnover and short life-spans for all but a minority of

30 See, e.g., Yash Ghai, *Human rights and social development: Toward democratization and social justice* (Geneva: UN Research Institute for Social Development, 2001).

31 On its website, the UN lists and provides details on NGOs across Africa, including over 120 such NGOs in Benin alone. See United Nations, *Networking: Directory of African NGOs*, www.un.org/africa/osaa/ngodirectory/index.htm (last accessed May 14, 2008).

these organizations. With the exception of those involved in conflict resolution, peacekeeping, and rural development, typically the majority of visible local NGOs are based in capital cities and in other major urban areas. While virtually every humanitarian or human rights NGO is dealing with one or more of the threats to collective security, as in Negros, this work is very likely to bring them into conflict with local government officials who are more responsive to national interests defined in military terms than to the needs of local communities. Moreover, local NGOs often have difficulty working with one another, in part because they are competing for the same limited funding and thus each needs to prove itself better than fellow NGOs.

To respond to these and other criticisms, more international aid agencies are adopting strategies that start with assessments of local needs in dialogue with local NGOs and the communities they serve.[32] The procedures also call for studying and comparing practices in neighboring communities with similar resources but where the outcomes, such as child health, are visibly different. These strategies that deal with individual threats are among the building blocks of collective security because they seek to mobilize local resources, and to enhance local problem-solving abilities and capacity. Popular demand for services that the states could not provide enabled the growth of civil society in Eastern Europe after the 1975 Helsinki Agreements, in the waning years of communist domination. The challenge therefore for the NGOs in poor communities remains their ability to identify, to represent to the wider society, and to respond to the needs of the communities they serve. As in Eastern Europe, one component of the strategy will be bringing the concerns to the attention of the international community. They are not in a position, however, to assume all the needed operations and services that are the responsibility of a national government, leaving space for more ambitious groups to function as quasi governments through a monopoly on the use of force and a full panoply of government services.

The role of foreign governments

NGOs are highly visible institutions in villages across the globe, but foreign governments contribute to minimizing threats in their own

32 See Andre Frankovits and Patrick Earle, *Working together: The human rights based approach to development cooperation* (Swedish International Development Cooperation Agency, 2001).

ways. Foreign government aid programs take two basic forms: economic and political development aid programs and arms sales. Unfortunately, with respect to their impact on collective security, development aid pales compared to the quantity of arms sold to many governments of developing countries and often, though perhaps more indirectly, to support one or the other side in an insurgency.[33] As indicated above, arms sales are big business for many governments in Eastern and Western Europe and North America, as well as for Russia, China, India, and Brazil. These arms have a very definite impact on "villagers" when a national government has defined its opposition as insurgency or terrorism, and adopts an exclusively military strategy. The official rationale on all sides, however, is always linked to national, if not also collective, security. On the ground, however, these and other arms quickly find their way to the black market, facilitating opposition groups' recourse to force. The willingness of foreign governments to sell the arms also defines the strategies a government uses to respond to opposition. Thus in a country like Chad, while foreign governments and the European Union support programs on rule of law for a few professionals, they are quite modest compared with the contributions the same countries make in the form of arms and even military personnel.[34] Local communities then find themselves in the middle. In communities such as Negros, far from the influence of foreign governments and indeed also from that of the UN and its agencies, security is determined by the military and militarized non-state players. Only recently have the strategies begun to move away from being exclusively based on firepower toward Annan's view that "development, security and human rights go hand in hand."[35]

The role of local communities

While local communities benefit from the efforts of NGOs and foreign governments, they should also play a vital role in ensuring their own

[33] This problem is monitored by agencies such as the International Committee of the Red Cross and Norwegian Initiative on Small Arms Transfers. See Norwegian Initiative on Small Arms Transfers, *Integrating small arms measures into development programmes*, www.nisat.org (last accessed May 28, 2008).

[34] The United States Congressional Research Service reported that France beat the United States, Russia, and China with respect to conventional arms transfers to Africa for the years 2002–2005. France's $900 million in arms sales dwarfed the United States with only $157 million. Richard F. Grimmett, "Conventional arms transfers to developing nations," *Congressional Research Service* (October 23, 2006), p. 50.

[35] *In Larger Freedom*, para. 14.

security against threats. Confronted by the limitations of the external actors and the tendency of weak governments to exercise control over their populations largely through the use of force, local communities have few options. Villagers in the Darfur region of Sudan and in some parts of the Eastern Congo, for example, could do little but flee. In other contexts, villages could better help themselves with appropriate outside technical assistance and financing. Local clinics need medicine and trained nurses and schools need textbooks and competent teachers. Every community also needs an economy and jobs to pay for these and other goods and services. Operationalizing Annan's freedom from want, freedom from fear, and freedom to live in dignity depends on job creation,[36] reliable food production, education, basic healthcare, sanitation projects, a stable public order, conflict and dispute management, and the local administration of justice. These cannot be achieved without a degree of social peace and without the support of public and private agencies and resources outside the village.[37]

The role of the state

Of all of these institutions, it is the national governments that have the most critical role to play. The Commission on Human Security thus called upon them for both the protection and the empowerment of people.[38] The implementation of international human rights takes place at the intersection between state sovereignty and the state's treaty obligations. In the words of the International Council on Human Rights Policy, Geneva: "States occupy a privileged position in human rights law.

[36] The need for job-led economic growth supported by adequate training and educational opportunities is underlined in Bremley W. B. Lyngdoh, "Skills for work in the future: A youth perspective," *Prospects* 35 (2005), p. 315.

[37] Collaboration between governments and NGOs is always hard. A village in Venezuela recently obtained the support of a multinational petroleum corporation to help build a fine clinic and maternity unit. Unfortunately, the local government then refused to provide a physician because it had not been consulted in advance.

[38] According to Sadako Ogata, "[p]rotection refers to the norms, processes and institutions required to shield people from critical and pervasive threats. It implies a top-down approach … States have primary responsibility to implement such a protective structure." However, international and regional organization, civil society and non-governmental actors, and the private sector also play a pivotal role in shielding people from menaces. As Ogata explained, "[Empowerment] implies a 'bottom-up' approach." It aims at developing the capabilities of individuals and communities to make informed choices and to act on their own behalf. Sadako Ogata, "Empowering people for human security," 56th Annual DPI/NGO Conference (September 10, 2003).

They have the monopoly of force; and by signing up to international human rights standards, they incur the primary duty to ensure that the rights of people under their authority are protected."[39] This normative statement has recently been re-emphasized by the international community as the responsibility to protect all persons within a given state from human rights abuses.[40] The human rights treaty obligations of most states come with internationally sanctioned monitoring and legal obligations. States fail to fulfill these obligations for many reasons. Weak states often portray themselves as powerless or lacking in resources. Today the villages in the Darfur region of Sudan, as well as many regions within the Democratic Republic of the Congo, are among the most visible illustrations of states that have been unable to protect their citizens from violence. In other cases, such as in Chechnya, Myanmar, and North Korea, the organs of the state itself may be the perpetrators of the violence. In recent years, the world community has also become more aware of internal displacements where the causes and remedies, such as restitution for losses of property, fall within the ambit of a single government, even when it is not the direct cause of the abuse and threats.[41] These situations point to the critical role played by the state apparatus in ensuring the physical security of its citizens.

As is discussed elsewhere in this volume, state sovereignty has lost its earlier aura of impermeability and impregnability.[42] In the context of collective or international security, for example, there is now a point when the way in which a state treats its own citizens calls for the attention of the international community and raises the possibility of humanitarian aid or other intervention. In other words, in question now is when do the violations of human rights permitted, perpetrated, or unable to be suppressed by a given state become serious enough threats to international security to merit UN action under Chapter VII, Article 39. From the point of view of villagers facing serious threats to their livelihoods,

[39] "Human rights after September 11th," *International Council on Human Rights Policy* (December 1, 2002), p. 52.

[40] "Each individual State has the responsibility to protect its populations from genocide, war crimes, ethnic cleansing and crimes against humanity. This responsibility entails the prevention of such crimes, including their incitement, through appropriate and necessary means. We accept that responsibility and will act in accordance with it." World Summit Outcome, para. 138.

[41] See, e.g., Dilek Kurban, Deniz Yukseker, Ayse Betul Celik, Turgay Unatan, and A. Tamer Aker, *Coming to terms with forced migration: Post-displacement restitution of citizenship in Turkey, Istanbul* (Istanbul: TESEV Publications, 2007).

[42] See chapters by George Andreopolous and Peter Danchin in this volume.

the first challenge is to get the message out. This calls for assembling data and finding the means necessary to make their case to the domestic authorities and, if that fails, to the international community. As virtually all such internationally visible current cases – notably Chechnya, Darfur, Myanmar, and North Korea, illustrate – purely humanitarian concerns, even systemic and major threats including human rights violations, are no sure trigger to galvanize forceful action by the international community. In each of the above cases, the states involved have been able to stave off all but nominal international action. Thus even though the concept of states' sovereignty has been eroded, for both theoretical and practical reasons, the security of citizens still depends substantially on the state.[43]

In the absence of threats to physical security, the rights of citizens can still be threatened when government presence is skeletal and ineffectual. This is the case in countries such as Liberia that are just recovering from civil wars, but it is equally true elsewhere where there has been no civil war, such as in Malawi or the Central African Republic. In such situations there is often little in the way of delivery mechanisms for basic human needs or for the protection of communities from other threats such as drug or people trafficking, arms trading, and the incubation of dangerous viruses and virulent diseases of which AIDS is only one. In other circumstances it might be the lack of protection from environmental hazards. Even in those communities where some government officials and services are present, their effectiveness is often undermined because the poorly paid personnel often resort to petty thievery and bribery.[44] In these cases, village communities must face the threats largely on their own.

Among the attempts by the international community to overcome poverty and to implement change beyond the standard development project is Millennium Villages, a model designed by Columbia University's Earth Institute. It uses the village rather than a single need or a development project as the defining parameter of the initiative. The aim is "to end extreme poverty by working with the poorest of the poor, village by village throughout Africa, in partnership with governments

[43] *In Larger Freedom*, para. 19. An interesting historical footnote is the role played in the early nineteenth century by the founding chief of the Sotho people in South Africa, Moshesh. Unlike all his neighbors, he was able to protect his people from marauding Ndebele invaders from Natal by gathering them onto the top of a flat mountain with vertical, easily defensible sides, called Thaba Bosiu. There his followers were completely self-sufficient year-round in terms of water, vegetables, and dairy produce.

[44] See, e.g., Shadrack Bo Gutto, *A practical guide to human rights in local government* (Carlsbad, CA: Butterworth, 1996).

and other committed stakeholders, providing affordable and science-based solutions to help people lift themselves out of extreme poverty."[45] Among the key science-based solutions are fertilizers and mosquito nets as well as special attention to the village schools. Jeffrey Sachs, the mind behind these villages, is committed to making improvements sustainable even in the face of the high cost of $110 per villager per year. The project focuses on meeting subsistence needs such as for food, health, and education, rather than a more inclusive concept such as collective security or economic and political development, but these are excluded. The villages chosen do not have major physical security problems. The project also seeks to work closely with government and local officials, choosing local trainers and local personnel wherever possible. Good governance issues are addressed in the context of fighting corruption. Human rights issues and the advocacy roles of civil society organizations are assumed rather than being one of the major objectives. Only time will tell whether these initiatives will overcome the limitations identified above, bringing, for example, the capacity building necessary for more sustainable outcomes than most other development projects initiated in Africa over the last fifty years. Critical to sustainability, however, will be the degree to which the services of the state are integrated.

Returning to the definition of collective security, namely "the institutions, policies, responsibilities and strategies necessary to ensure subsistence, physical security, fundamental freedoms and the acquisition of the knowledge and skills needed for sustainable communities," this chapter has argued for the central role of institutions and the state in particular. It is now necessary to ask how to compensate for the limitations of the state and of the other institutions in the face of the many truly great and urgent threats to subsistence, physical security, and fundamental freedoms faced by village communities all over the world. To which institution should "villagers" look for immediate assistance? If physical security and a degree of social peace are the first step, then Liberia is an example of an effective UN military presence. For the past four years UNAMIL, the UN mission in charge of security and peace building in Liberia, has assured Liberians of a period without major violence or conflict, creating space for the growth of the social and political institutions and the economy. In fact, UNAMIL is fulfilling the above definition of collective security. The UN presence has freed a resource-poor government of the

[45] See The Earth Institute at Columbia University, *Millennium villages*, www.earthinstitute.columbia.edu/articles/view/1799 (last accessed May 14, 2008).

responsibility of simply maintaining the peace. This situation differs substantially from one where an insecure government seeks to maintain its own power and relies on the military or the loyalty of one section of the population. The UN presence has avoided coercive patterns of social control that can easily result in restrictions with respect to speech, social action, and movement, limiting local political and economic initiatives as well as routine conflict and dispute resolution. However, as in Negros, when security is in the hands of the national military or a de facto vigilante group parading as a rebel organization such as the RPA-ABB and the task is defined as a fight against a violent opposition or insurgency, the principle is that of the classic paradigm of "dominate or be dominated," if not "eliminate or be eliminated." This leaves little space for negotiation and reconciliation. While a neutral UN presence demands an international consensus and funding that is difficult to attain, redefining the role of national militaries as peacekeeping agents to enable civilian agencies to function, like the UN model in Liberia, might open the way to more sustainable solutions.

The recent growth of domestic NGOs has presented a challenge to many governments.[46] While the level of mistrust and hostility is high in zones of conflict, government mistrust is often also fueled by the fact that many NGOs depend on sizeable funding from external sources. In question is whether the NGOs are constricted or instigated by their external donors on the basis of the latter's political goals, resulting in some states construing NGOs as actually undermining their national security.[47] Many states raise the broad question of the accountability of NGOs: who do the NGOs speak for? Who do they represent? To what degree to they represent the "villagers"? To what degree should they and their activities be coordinated, if not controlled by government? Who is accountable to whom?[48] This lack of trust makes NGOs slow to collaborate with government in putting in place the institutions, policies, responsibilities, and strategies necessary for a mutually acceptable form of collective security.[49] Today in Liberia this problem poses itself at the level of basic administration, more than as a question of physical

[46] Howell and Pierce, *Civil society and development.*

[47] These critiques come from both authoritarian and other regimes. See, e.g., Risto Karajkov, *N.G.O. bashing*, www.worldpress.org/ (last accessed May 28, 2008).

[48] J. Paul Martin, "The MDGs: How to achieve accountability," *Cooperation South 2005* (2005), pp. 12–21.

[49] See, e.g., R. A. Akindele (ed.), *Civil society, good governance, and the challenge of regional security in west Africa* (Agege, Nigeria: African Strategic and Peace Research Group, 2003).

security. Government ministries are able to do little more than watch as local and international NGOs with funds from the outside mount various social service initiatives. The resulting lack of coordination has long been the pattern in countries with undermanned governments. Impoverished governments like Liberia are not in a position to impose accountability on external agencies because they feel they are in such a needy position that they must accept anything that is offered.[50] None of this bodes well for long-term collective security.

Nevertheless, on account of the legal obligations assigned by both domestic and international law, their de facto institutions of governance, and states' monopoly on the use of force, states are central to responding to the threats to collective security faced by their citizens. The emerging doctrine seems to be that security can only begin to be achieved if the full collective security paradigm is a priority in national planning and it is operationalized on the ground.

The benefits of collective security as a development paradigm

The effectiveness of these institutions can be improved by adopting a collective security paradigm because this model offers a more inclusive view of development than either the national security or economic and political development aid paradigms that still dominate international development thinking. In comparison with current models for economic and political development, including the rights-based models, collective security appears to offer a superior action paradigm in that it includes the others and goes beyond them. Unlike other models, the first step in collective security is an assessment of *all* the threats at the level of the village. This bottom-up approach forms the basis for setting priorities based on the relative seriousness of the threats, on the available resources and on the norms set out above. This approach incorporates the goals identified by Annan and is consistent with his proposal that development, security, and human rights should go hand in hand as well as our definition of collective security. The principles implicit in this are derived largely from international human rights standards which not only provide criteria to distinguish between serious and minor threats, but also set action priorities.

50 Fernande Raine, "The measurement challenge in human rights," *SUR International Journal on Human Rights* 4 (2006).

The collective security paradigm proposed in this chapter calls for projects to be designed from the ground up rather than in an office in Europe or North America. The planning should also address rather than ignore the likely limited capacity of national governments to assume responsibility for all the elements of economic and political development as well as every capability within the "village." In calling for a full assessment of all the threats faced by the village and incorporating rights-based and sustainable paradigms for development, the model fits within the current 2005–2014 UN Decade of Education for Sustainable Development. Overall, once fleshed out, the development plans based on the concept of collective security proposed here call for designs and implementation that take into account all the key elements necessary for peaceful communities and sustainable development. This includes the often difficult negotiations between the military, NGOs, and local communities, such as those described above in Negros.

As the authors' proposed definition of collective security indicates, operationalizing such a vision requires enhancing the ability of the villagers to sustain and build on the changes after the withdrawal of the external inputs, whether the funds, technology, and human energy come from inside or outside the country. To what degree can these local communities become more effective agents in their own interests? It is one thing to be in the best position to know what is happening, but it is another to be able to analyze the threats and to seek and effect redress. To achieve these objectives, the "villagers" first have to bring information and analysis to the attention of agencies capable of response. So far this flow of information has depended on the presence of NGOs and the effectiveness of their advocacy and lobbying. A long-term solution, one that does not rely on NGOs, must depend on the services normally provided by the state.

Evaluating development aid projects has always been a challenge. Typically they are evaluated in terms of outcomes at the end of the project, as the external supports are being withdrawn. The collective security paradigm, however, calls for something more. It insists that a given project be more widely assessed, especially in terms of the *sustained* benefits to "villagers."

Thus a project that involves, for example, training primary school teachers is judged not by the number of teachers who graduate, but by the number of those teachers still in the classroom a given number of years later. Such criteria clearly call for more comprehensive planning as long-term outcomes, such as the number of teachers in classrooms, will depend on other factors, notably sufficient salaries, adequate working conditions, and freedom from violent conflict. Without those conditions, the teachers will not remain in the classroom and thus the goals of the training program will not be achieved.

A similar argument can be made for long-term planning and evaluation across the whole range of social services developed on a project-by-project basis by external agents. The collective security paradigm proposed in this chapter underlines the need for evaluation that assesses sustainability both in the original planning and design, and in terms of the de facto outcomes once the external inputs have been removed.

The UN's role in collective security at the village level

The UN and its associated agencies are not invisible or lacking influence in these various processes. Most obviously they are visible when the Security Council authorizes a peacekeeping mission such as in Liberia. In those cases, as indicated above, an effective mission can successfully reduce physical violence and create space for local political developments. In the context of development, the UN is also visible in capital cities and in a few rural areas, such as Negros, where UNDP training will be provided. History also reveals some other forms of presence. For example, in 1993 one of the authors met women villagers in Burkina Faso who talked about planning to attend the 1995 Women's Conference in Beijing and the author later met others who recounted their own or others' highly motivating experiences at the conference. More recently, the UN has successfully mobilized community support in the drafting and eventual approval by the General Assembly of the 2006 UN Convention on the Rights of Persons with Disabilities.[51] The resulting Convention calls for state parties to consult closely with and involve persons with disabilities and their representative organizations in the implementation and development of legislation and policies to give effect to the Convention.[52] The Convention incorporates also the capabilities approach that emphasizes the resources of an individual rather than his or her deficiencies. By seeing the affected community as necessary agents with their own resources and capabilities to seek remedies, this perspective provides a model for implementing the definition of collective security as

[51] *United Nations Convention on the Rights of Persons with Disabilities*, G. A. Res. 61/106, UN doc. A/RES/61/611 (December 13, 2006).

[52] See Tara J. Melish, "Perspectives on the UN Convention on the Rights of Persons with Disabilities: The UN Disability Convention: Historic process, strong prospects, and why the US should ratify," *Human Rights Brief* 14 (2007), pp. 37–47.

"institutions, policies, responsibilities and strategies [that] are necessary to ensure subsistence, physical security, fundamental freedoms and the acquisition of the knowledge and skills needed for sustainable communities."

The questions for the UN raised in this chapter are whether, as part of its reform, it *should* include more individuals from rural communities in low-income countries in its deliberations, just as it successfully included persons with disabilities, and if so, how? This goal calls for more frequent and systematic dialogue between "villagers" and international diplomats and policy makers. One of the proposals in the March 2005 report by Secretary-General Kofi Annan, *In Larger Freedom*, offers a framework to implement the ideals, decisions, and policies of the UN in ways that more directly impact on the lives of ordinary men and women. To assist this process the UN and its associated agencies should be better equipped to fulfill the following, largely facilitating, tasks: (a) communicating the vision of alternative futures and options to rural communities; (b) enabling the voices of those communities to be heard within its own halls; (c) assuring greater emphasis on the rights of the poor and the corresponding obligations on their governments; (d) using its convening power to improve communication and collaboration among actors working in rural communities; and (e) frequently evaluating its own capacity and that of its agencies to fulfill these tasks. Implicit in this approach is the need mentioned earlier in this chapter to bridge not only language differences but also the different cultures of the scholars, politicians, bureaucrats, and villagers. The UN would thus keep the issues on the table even if political circumstances did not permit an adequate international response.[53]

Enhancing the effectiveness of institutions' responses to security threats

To help the UN and other institutions reduce the gap between knowledge and action, the authors of this chapter propose a tool called a collective security index (CSI). This tool would be a step toward defining in some detail all the threats to local communities, in preparation for a discussion about remedies.[54] The CSI seeks both to work with and move beyond the

[53] See the chapter by Elizabeth Salmón in this volume.

[54] International Alert is one example of an NGO committed to monitoring situations likely to result in conflict. Its thematic work focuses on the role of business, humanitarian aid and development, gender, security, and post-conflict reconstruction in the context of building peace. International Alert, www.international-alert.org (last accessed May 15, 2008).

early warning indexes developed by different government and non-governmental agencies and scholars.[55] These various projects offer useful databases and computerized analyses that can be incorporated into the proposed model, but they remain focused on security defined by the needs of the state or government, rather than on how local communities, namely villagers, can participate. The voices of the villagers are not registered in these databases, although some of the NGOs focused on crisis alerts are better geared than others to respond to the interests and reflect the views of civil society in countries in crisis.[56] The proposed CSI seeks to remedy these limitations.

In proposing this CSI, the aim is to see it used routinely – that is, not just in relation to major crises – as a tool to identify and evaluate a wide range of indicators within a comprehensive normative framework, one that is more reflective of the threats to collective security as they might appear at the level of our metaphorical village. In setting priorities and seeking remedies, the model emphasizes the importance of local inputs such as by collecting data and using it to measure the threat.

The CSI would thus become the starting point for development based on the collective security model by prioritizing the needs of a given social unit, such as a village, town, or region, and evaluating its local capabilities in dialogue with the community. This would be the basis for communication with and planning across government ministries, between them and local officials, and with local and international NGOs. In some respects this process is nothing new to development thinking. The language of local participation is incorporated into many development grant proposals. Implementation, however, is a big challenge. One obstacle is simply a lack of time. Most development grants have short time spans, some as little as twelve months. Thus the external agencies administering the grants, to assure their own existence, have to show success in time to apply for the next grant. These outcomes tend to be measured through short-term rather

[55] There are several notable early warning indexes already in use. For example, USAID maintains a website dedicated to food security alerts. USAID, www.fews.net (last accessed May 15, 2008). The Integrated Crisis Early Warning System (ICEWS) of the United States Department of Defense "seeks to develop a comprehensive, integrated, automated, generalizable, and validated system to monitor, assess, and forecast national sub-national, and international crises in a way that supports decisions on how to allocate resources to mitigate them." Defense Advanced Research Projects Agency, *Integrated crisis early warning system*, www.darpa.mil/ipto/Programs/icews/icews.asp (last accessed May 15, 2008).

[56] The NGOs concerned primarily with crisis alerts include International Alert and International Crisis Group.

than long-term indicators. Moreover, if the grant is not renewed it is extremely unlikely that the agent can remain in the community.

Adopting the CSI requires identifying relevant indicators and a numeric intensity grade indicating the degree to which each item endangers collective security. This can then be further qualified by a factor (necessarily subjective) measuring the degree to which the community itself could or could not improve the situation. The primary categories for the index are the threats explained earlier in this chapter, including failure of state institutions, the presence of insurgencies and terrorist activities, group tensions, illegal activities, abusive exploitation of natural resources, existence of health epidemics, commercial activities with detrimental impacts, and the emotional climate.[57] This is not an exclusive list. In any given situation there may be other factors that endanger collective security. As a planning tool it provides both a framework for measurement and it flags the major factors that ought to be considered when planning, or seeking to contribute to, the development of a given community or set of communities.

The CSI identifies the threat and thus a situation that should trigger a government's obligation to protect the rights of all those within its borders. By focusing on local communities as well as states, the CSI encourages responses to threats that are more diversified and comprehensive than current models of humanitarian intervention under Chapter VII, Article 39 of the UN Charter. Such responses would not only encourage and empower both the state and the affected communities to be more self-reliant, but also promote closer cooperation and collaboration among the various external aid agencies by including representatives of the affected communities. As in the case of drafting the Convention on the Rights of Persons with Disabilities, the drafting and the planning would not be left just to international experts.

Conclusion

The basic recommendations of this chapter are (a) to support the usefulness of the concept of collective security at the level of local communities, and (b) to integrate the voices, resources, and capabilities of the "villagers" in debates and planning designed to respond to the threats they face. Implementing such a vision faces multiple institutional challenges on the part of the domestic and international agencies in a position to

[57] See *Journal of Social Issues* 63 (2007).

help, ranging from the UN to local government officials and local NGOs. Given the primacy that ought to be attributed to long-term sustainability, the authors have also argued that external aid ought to focus on capacity building in ways that enable communities to become more self-reliant, empowered, and thus more able to remedy threats in the future. Key to this process is building the capacity of national governments and the agencies that provide basic social services to the threatened communities. In the meantime local and international NGOs, limited though their resources and reach are, remain critical links in the chain to mobilize international consciousness.

As it thinks about reform, the UN can enhance the governments' effectiveness through its various sounding boards and convening powers, ranging from Security Council hearings and states reporting to the various human rights treaty bodies to occasional major conferences like those held in Vienna, Beijing, and Durban. In such contexts, the collective security model is not only a planning tool for economic and political development, it is a means to link threats in the "village" to those recognized by the world states as threats to international security. That said, given the asymmetries of power and interest among UN member states, there can be no illusions as to whose priorities will receive the most attention. The concept of collective security, however, might provide a common standard as well as a perspective showing relationships between, for example, abject poverty in the village and the major global threats such as terrorism or refugee flows.

BIBLIOGRAPHY

Primary Documents

2005 World Summit Outcome document, General Assembly Sixtieth Session, UN Doc. A/RES/60/1, September 16, 2005.

A More Secure World: Our Shared Responsibility, Report of the High-level Panel on Threats, Challenges and Change A/59/565, December 2, 2004.

In Larger Freedom: Towards Development, Security, and Human Rights for All, Report of the Secretary-General A/59/2005, March 21, 2005.

Books, Articles, and Reports

A Study of the Capacity of the United Nations Development System, DP/5, UN Geneva 1969, followed by General Assembly resolution GA 2688 (XXV) of December 11, 1970.

Action Aid, CAFOD, and CARE International, "Consolidating the Peace?: Views from Sierra Leone and Burundi on the United Nations Peacebuilding Commission," June 2007. www.actionaid.org/assets/pdf/peace_consolidating_the_final.pdf

Adamu, S., *The United Nations and the Agendas for its Reform*, www.ceddert.com/UN_and_the_agendas.htm

Advisory Council on International Affairs, *Private sector development and poverty reduction* (The Hague, 2006).

Ahmed, S., Keating, P., and Salinas, U., "Shaping the future of UN peace operations: is there a doctrine in this house?" *Cambridge Review of International Affairs* 20 (2007), pp. 11–28.

Akindele, R. A. (ed.), "*Civil society, good governance, and the challenge of regional security in west Africa*" (Agege, Nigeria: African Strategic and Peace Research Group, 2003).

AlertNet, "U.N. Summit Endorses Modest Reforms," *AlertNet* (September 17, 2005), http://alertnet.org/thenews/newsdesk/112693055950.htm, last accessed on October 26, 2005.

Allan, T. R. S., *Constitutional Justice: A Liberal Theory of the Rule of Law* (Oxford: Oxford University Press, 2001).

All Party Parliamentary Group on the Great Lakes Region and Genocide Prevention, *Cursed by Riches: Who Benefits from Resource Exploitation in the Democratic Republic of the Congo?* November 2002 (London, 2002).

Almqvist, J., *Rethinking Security and Human Rights in the Struggle against Terrorism*, paper presented at the European Society of International Law Forum in the workshop "Human Rights Under Threat," May 27, 2005.

Alston, P., "Reconceiving the UN Human Rights Regime: Challenges Confronting the New UN Human Rights Council," Centre for Human Rights and Global Justice Working Paper No. 4 (2006), pp. 10–12.

"Richard Lillich Memorial Lecture: Promoting the Accountability of Members of the New UN Human Rights Council," *Journal of Transnational Law and Policy* (2006), pp. 49–96.

"Reconceiving the UN Regime to Fit the Needs of the 21st Century," incomplete draft (2005).

Alvarez, J. E., "The Schizophrenias of the Responsibility to Protect," Panel Presentation at the 2007 Hague Joint Conference on Contemporary Issues of International Law: Criminal Jurisdiction 100 Years After the 1907 Hague Peace Conference (The Hague, Netherlands, June 30, 2007).

"The Security Council's War on Terrorism: Problems and Policy Options," in de Wet, E. and Nollkaemper, A. (eds.), *Review of the Security Council by Member States* (Antwerp: Intersentia, 2003), pp. 119–145.

"The Closing of the American Mind," *Reconciling Law, Justice and Politics in the International Arena*, proceedings of the 32nd Annual Conference of the Canadian Council on International Law, Ottowa, October 16–18, 2003.

"What's the Security Council For?" *Michigan Journal of International Law* 17 (Winter 1996), pp. 221–248.

Alvarez, Jose, *International Organizations as Law-makers* (Oxford: Oxford University Press, 2005), p. 199.

Anderson, K., "The Ottawa Convention Banning Landmines, the Role of International Non Governmental Organizations and the Idea of International Civil Society," *European Journal of International Law* 11 (2000), p. 110.

Andreopoulos, G., "The Challenges and Perils of Normative Overstretch," in Cronin, B., and Hurd, I. (eds.), *The UN Security Council and the Politics of International Authority* (London: Taylor and Francis, 2008).

Human Rights and Collective Security: "The Challenges and Perils of Normative Outreach," Presentation at the Columbia University Seminar on Human Rights, May 2006 (unpublished manuscript).

Annan, K. "Mandating and Delivering: Analysis and Recommendations to Facilitate the Review of Mandates," A/60/733, Report of the Secretary-General of the United Nations, New York, March 30, 2006, paras. 122–123.

"Uniting against terrorism: recommendations for a global counter-terrorism strategy," April 27, 2006.

"Speech at the Conclusion of the High-level Plenary Meeting of the General Assembly," UN Doc. A/60/PV.9 of September 17, 2005.

"The Secretary-General's Address to the General Assembly," New York, September 23, 2003; www.un.org/webcast/ga/58/statements/sg2eng030923.htm

"Secretary-General's Address to the General Assembly (New York, September 23, 2003), www.un.org/apps/sg/sgstats.asp?nid=517

"Report of the Secretary-General to the Security Council on the Protection of Civilians in Armed Conflict," S/1999/957, September 8, 1999.

"Report of the Secretary-General: Agenda for Development," UN Doc. A/48/935 of May 6, 1994.

"Two Concepts of Sovereignty," *The Economist* (September 18, 1999).

"Secretary-General's Address at the University of Bordeaux," UN Press Release SG/SM/4560 (1991).

Arbour, L. and Bergsmo, M., "Conspicuous absence of jurisdictional overreach," in von Hebel, H., Lammers, J.G., and Schukking, J. (eds.), *Reflections on the International Criminal Court* (T.M.C. Asser Press, 1999). pp. 139–140.

Arendt, H., "Truth and Politics," in Arendt, H. (ed.), *Between Past and Future* (New York: Penguin, 1968) pp. 227–264.

Arima, T., "Future Role of the United Nations within the Framework of Global Security: Japan's Perspective," February 13, 2005 (www.securityconference.de).

Arsanjani, M., "The Rome Statute of the International Criminal Court," *American Journal of International Law* 93 (1999), p. 28.

Association for Women's Rights in Development, "A Rights-Based Approach to Development," Women's Rights and Economic Change (2002), p. 3.

Atwood, D. and Tanner, F., "The UN Peacebuilding Commission and International Geneva," *Disarmament Forum (UNIDIR)* 2 (2007), p. 29.

Baehr, P. R., "Ingrijpende Hervorming Verenigde Naties Opnieuw Mislukt," *Internationale Spectator* 59 (2005).

Banda, M., *The Responsibility to Protect: Moving the Agenda Forward* (United Nations Association in Canada, March 2007).

Barnett, M., *Eyewitness to A Genocide: The United Nations and Rwanda* (Ithaca: Cornell University Press, 2002).

Bartelson, J., "The Concept of Sovereignty Revisited," *The European Journal of International Law* 17 (2006), pp. 463–474.

Beaulac, S., "Emer de Vattel and the Externalization of Sovereignty," *Journal of the History of International Law*, 5 (2003), pp. 237–292.

Beitz, C., *Political Theory and International Relations* (Princeton: Princeton University Press, 1979), pp. 74 ff.

Bellamy, A. J., "Preventing Future Kosovos and Future Rwandas: The Responsibility to Protect after the 2005 World Summit," Policy Brief No. 1, *Initiative:*

Ethics in a Violent World: What Can Institutions Do? (New York: Carnegie Council, 2006), pp. 12–13.

Belloti, P., *Letter to President Gloria M. Arroyo*, September 4, 2006 (on file at BIND, Philippines).

Berdal, M., "The United Nations at 60: A New San Francisco Moment?" *Survival* 47 (Autumn 2005), pp. 7–31.

Bergen, P. and Cruickshank, P., "The Iraq Effect: War Has Increased Terrorism Sevenfold Worldwide," *Mother Jones*, March 1, 2007, available at www.motherjones.com/news/featurex/2007/03/iraq_effect_1.html (accessed May 22, 2008).

Berman, F., "The Relationship between the International Criminal Court and the Security Council," in von Hebel, H., Lammers, J. G., and Schukking, J. (eds.), *Reflections on the International Criminal Court: Essays in Honour of Adriaan Bos* (T. M. C. Asser Press, 1999), p. 174.

Berman, H., "The Spiritualization of Secular Law: The Impact of the Lutheran Reformation," *Journal of Law and Religion* 14 (1999–2000), pp. 313–349.

Berman, N., "The Quest for Rationality: The Recent Writings of Tom Franck," *New York University Journal of International Law and Politics* 35 (2002–2003), pp. 339–362.

Berman, P., "Conflict of Laws, Globalization, and Cosmopolitan Pluralism," *Wayne Law Review* 51 (2005), p. 1105.

"From International law to Law and Globalization," *Columbia Journal of Transnational Law* 43 (2005), pp. 505–506.

Bianchi, A., "Assessing the Effectiveness of the UN Security Council's Anti-terrorism Measures: The Quest for Legitimacy and Cohesion," *European Journal of International Law* 17 (2007), p. 914.

Bisharat, G. E. "Sanctions as Genocide," *Transnational Law and Contemporary Problems* 11 (2001), pp. 379–425.

Bishop, D., "Lessons from Sars: Why the WHO Must Provide Greater Economic Incentives for Countries to Comply with International Health Regulations," *Georgetown Journal of International Law* 36 (2005), p. 1173.

Blair, T., "Doctrine of the International Community," Speech by UK Prime Minister Tony Blair to the Economic Club of Chicago, April 22, 1999, http://globalpolicy.org/

Blix, H., "Let Us Inspect Everywhere," *The Wall Street Journal* May 16, 2003.

Blokker, N. and Schrijver, N. (eds.) *The Security Council and the Use of Force* (Leiden/Boston: Martinus Nijhoff Publishers, 2005).

Bluemel, E., "Overcoming NGO Accountability Concerns in International Governance," *Brooklyn Journal of International Law* 31 (2005), pp. 146–147.

Bolton, J., "Is There Really 'Law' in International Affairs?," 10 *Transnational Law and Contemporary Problems* 1 (2000).

Bowett, D. W., *The Law of International Institutions* 4th edn. Library of World Affairs (London: Sweet & Maxwell, 1982).

von Bredow, W., "Herbe Enttäuschung. Die Vereinten Nationen bleiben, wie sie sind," *Frankfurter Allgemeine Zeitung*, (September 27, 2006).

Breen, C., "Rationalizing the Work of UN Human Rights Bodies or Reducing the Input of NGOs? The Changing Role of Human Rights NGOs at the United Nations," *Non-State Actors and International Law* 5 (2005), p. 118.

Bretton Woods Project, *Chad-Cameroon pipeline: Implementation, challenges and lessons learned*, www.brettonwoodsproject.org/art-552626 (accessed May 28, 2008).

Broms, B., *The Doctrine of Equality of States as Applied in International Organizations* (Vammala: Vammalan Kirjanpaino, 1959), p. 222.

Buchanan, A. and Keohane, R., "The Preventive Use of Force: A Cosmopolitan Institutional Proposal," *Ethics and International Affairs* 18 (2004), pp. 1–22.

Bull, H., "The Grotian Conception of International Society," in H. Butterfield and M. Wight (eds.), *Diplomatic Investigations: Essays in the Theory of International Relations* 51 (London: Allen & Unwin, 1966).

Bush, G. Sr., "Address before a Joint Session of the Congress on the Persian Gulf Crisis and the Federal Budget Deficit," September 11, 1990; http://bushlibrary.tamu.edu/papers/1990/90091101.html

Bush, G. W., "Prevent Our Enemies From Threatening Us, Our Allies, and Our Friends with Weapons of Mass Destruction," in *National Security Strategy of the United States of America* 13, 15 (September 2002).

Byrnes, J. F., *Speaking Frankly* (New York: Harper, 1947), pp. 34–35.

de Carvalho, B. and Schia, N. N., "UN Reform and Collective Security. An Overview of Post-Cold War Initiatives and Proposals," *Norwegian Institute of International Affairs*, 1 (2004).

Cameron, I., "UN Targeted Sanctions, Legal Safeguards and the European Convention on Human Rights," *Nordic Journal of International Law* 72 (2003), pp. 159–214.

Cargiulo, P., "The controversial relationship between the International Criminal Court and the Security Council," in Lattanzi, F. and Schabas, W. (eds.), *Essays on the Rome Statute of the International Criminal Court* (Rome: Il Sirente, 1999), vol. I, pp. 70–78.

Carty, A., "The Implosion of the Legal Subject and the Unraveling of the Law on the Use of Force: American Identity and New American Doctrines of Collective Security," *Revista Electronica de Estudios Internacionales* 11 (2006).

"The Black Hole of Modernity: From Sovereignty to International Legal Order and Back Again!" *Journal of the Philosophy of International Law*, vol. 1, iss. 1 (2006) pp. 7–37.

"Nietzsche and Socrates/Or the Spirit of the Devil and the Law," *Cardozo Law Review* 24 (2002–2003), pp. 621–634.

"Review Essay: 'The Concept of International Legal Personality: An Inquiry into the History and Theory of International Law, by Janne Elisabeth Nijman'

(The Hague: T. M. C. Asser Press, 2004)," *Melbourne Journal of International Law* 20 (2005).

Cassese, A., *International Law in a Divided World* (Oxford: Clarendon, 1986).

Cassese, A., Gaeta, P., and Jones, J. R. W. (eds.), *The Rome Statute of the International Criminal Court: A commentary* (New York: Oxford University Press, 2002).

Chandler, D., "New Rights for the Old? Cosmopolitan Citizenship and Critique for Global Democracy," *Political Studies* 51 (2003), pp. 336–340.

Charlesworth, H., "International Law: A Discipline of Crisis," *65 Modern Law Review* 377 (2002).

Charnovitz, S. "Two Centuries of Participation: NGO's and International Governance," *Michigan Journal of International Law* 18 (1997), p. 188.

The Charter of the United Nations, Hearings before the Committee on Foreign Relations, US Senate 79th Congress, 1st Session (Washington, 1945), p. 422. See also pp. 396, 416, 531, 585, 608, 654, 661, 707.

Chen, L., Fukuda-Parr, S., and Seidenstickers, E. (eds.), *Human insecurity in a global world* (Cambridge, MA: Harvard University Press, 2004).

Chesterman, S. (ed.), *Secretary or General: The UN Secretary-General in World Politics* (Cambridge: Cambridge University Press, 2007).

"Reforming the United Nations: Kofi Annan's legacy gets a reality check," Strategic Insights, Australian Strategic Policy Institute (May 2006).

"Reforming the United Nations: Legitimacy, Effectiveness and Power After Iraq," *Singapore Year Book of International Law and Contributors* 10 (2006).

"The Spy Who Came in From the Cold War: Intelligence and International Law," *International Law and Justice Working Papers* of the New York University Institute for International Law and Justice (2006).

"Just War or Just Peace After September 11: Axes of Evil and Wars Against Terror in Iraq and Beyond," *International Law and Politics* 37 (2005), pp. 281–301.

"Imposed Constitutions, Imposed Constitutionalism, and Ownership," *Connecticut Law Review* 37 (2005), pp. 947–954.

You, the People: The United Nations, Transitional Administration, and State-Building (Oxford: Oxford University Press, 2005).

"The Security Council as World Legislator?: Theoretical and practical aspects of law-making by the Security Council," Discussion Paper Based on Panel 1 of the series *The Role of the Security Council in Strengthening a Rules-Based International System* of the New York University Institute for International Law and Justice, 2004.

Chesterman, S. and Lehnardt, C., "The Security Council as World Judge?: The Powers and Limits of the UN Security Council in Relation to Judicial Functions," Discussion Paper Based on Panel 3 of the series *The Role of the Security Council in Strengthening a Rules-Based International System* of the New York University Institute for International Law and Justice.

Childers, E. and Urquhart, B., *Renewing the United Nations System* (Uppsala: Dag Hammarskjold Foundation, 1994), pp. 87 ff.

Chimni, B. S., "Alternative Visions of Just World Order: Six Tales from India," *Harvard International Law Journal* 46 (2005), pp. 389–402.

Chua, A., *World on Fire: How Exporting Free Market Democracy Breeds Ethnic Hatred and Global Instability* (New York: Random House, 2003), pp. 123–175.

Ciampi, A., "Obligation to cooperate," in Cassese, Gaeta, and Jones (eds.), *The Rome Statute*, vol. II, pp. 1607–1638.

Cilliers, J., and Malan, M., *Peacekeeping in the DRC – MONUC and the Road to Peace*, 66 (October 2001).

Claude, I., *Swords into Plowshares*, 4th edn. (New York: McGraw-Hill, 1984), p. 283.

"Comment on 'An Autopsy of Collective Security'" *Political Science Quarterly* 90 (Winter 1975–6), pp. 715.

"The Management of Power in the Changing United Nations," *International Organization* 15 (Spring 1961), pp. 219–221.

Coghlan, B., Brennan, R., Ngoy, P., Dofara, D., Otto, B., and Stewart, T., "*Mortality in the Democratic Republic of Congo: Results from a Nationwide Survey Conducted April-July 2004*" (New York and Melbourne: IRC and Burnett Institute, 2004).

Coll, A. R., "The Limits of Global Consciousness and Legal Absolutism: Protecting International Law from Some of its Best Friends," *Harvard International Law Journal* 27 (1986), pp. 599–620.

Collier, P., *The Bottom Billion: Why the Poorest Countries Are Failing and What Can Be Done About It* (Oxford: Oxford University Press, 2007), p. 32.

Collier, P. *et al.*, *Breaking the Conflict Trap: Civil War and Development Policy, A World Bank Policy Research Report* (jointly published by the World Bank and Oxford University Press, 2003), p. 83.

The Commission on Global Governance, *Our global neighborhood* (New York: Oxford University Press, 1995).

Commission on Human Security, "Human Security Now," New York, 2003. Available at www.humansecurity-chs.org/finalreport/English/FinalReport.pdf

"Comprehensive review of the whole question of peacekeeping operations in all their aspects," UN Doc. A/55/305 of August 21, 2000.

Condorelli, L. and Ciampi, A., "Comments on the Security Council referral of the situation in Darfur to the ICC," 3 *Journal of International Criminal Justice*, (2005), p. 59.

Condorelli, L. and Villalpando, S., "Relationship of the Court with the United Nations," "Referral and deferral by the Security Council," and "Can the Security Council extend the ICC's jurisdiction" in Cassese, Gaeta, and Jones, *The Rome Statute*, pp. 221, 644 *et seq.*

Convention on Combating International Terrorism, Organization of Islamic Conference, 1999, Article 2(a).

Cordesman, A., "The Lessons of International Co-operation in Counter-Terrorism," *RUSI Journal* 151 (February 2006), p. 49.

Corell, H., "Reforming the United Nations," *International Organizations Law Review* 2 (2005), p. 385.

Cortright, D. and Lopez, G. (eds.), *Economic Sanctions: Panacea or Peacebuilding in a Post-Cold War World* (Boulder: Westview Press, 1995).

Sanctions and the Search for Security: Challenges to UN Action (Boulder: Lynne Rienner, 2002).

The Sanctions Decade: Assessing UN Strategies in the 1990s (Boulder: Lynne Rienner, 2000).

Smart Sanctions: Targeting Economic Statecraft (Lanham: Rowman & Littlefield, 2002).

Covenant of the League of Nations, June 28, 1919, Article XVI, 1 Hudson International Legislation 1 (1931).

Cunliffe, P., "Making or Breaking the United Nations? The Antinomies of Analysing the UN," Draft Paper prepared for SAID Workshop, June 23, 2005.

Danchin, P., "Human Rights," in *A Global Agenda: Issues Before the General Assembly of the United Nations* (Lanham, MD: UNA and Rowman & Littlefield Publishers, 2003).

Defense Advanced Research Projects Agency, *Integrated crisis early warning system*, www.darpa.mil/ipto/Programs/icews/icews.asp (accessed May 15, 2008).

Delbruck, J., "Collective Security," in Bernhardt, R. (ed.), *Encyclopedia of Public International Law* (Amsterdam: North-Holland, 1992) vol. I, p. 646.

Delgado, I. L. and Martínez, M. M, *La Corte Penal Internacional. justicia versus impunidad* (Barcelona: Ariel Derecho, 2001), pp. 183, 199.

Delivering as One, Report of the United Nations Secretary-General's High-Level Panel on UN System-wide Coherence, New York, November 9, 2006.

Demeyere, Bruno, "Weapons of Mass Destruction in the Report of the Secretary-General's High-Level Panel: Renewing or Consolidating the Arms Control and Disarmament Regimes?" *International Law FORUM du droit international* 7 (2005), pp. 108–118.

Deng, F. M. and Minear, L., *The Challenges of Famine Relief: Emergency Operations in the Sudan* (Washington, DC: The Brookings Institution Press, 1992), p. 8.

Der Derian, J., Doyle, M., Snyder, J. L., and Kennedy, D., "How should sovereignty be defended?," in Bickerton, C., Cunliffe, P., and Gourevitch, A. (eds.), *Politics Without Sovereignty: A Critique of Contemporary International Relations* (London: Routledge, 2006).

Human Security Centre, *Human Security Report 2005*, University of British Columbia (2005).

Husketh, E. and Ulbrick, J. T., "Reforming the United Nations: The Use of Force to Safeguard International Security and Human Rights," *International Law FORUM du Droit International* 7 (2005), pp. 127–130.

ICTY, *Prosecutor against Tadic*, decision of the Appeal Chamber II, October 2, 1995.

ICTY, *Prosecutor* v. *Blaskic*. Judgment on Request for Review, IT-95–14 (October 29, 1997), para. 26, 31, 33.

Ignatieff, M., "Is the Human Rights Era Ending?" *New York Times* (February 5, 2002), p. A25.

Ilunga-Matthiesen, K., *Die Demokratische Republik Kongo – Eine Analyse aus staatstheoretischer, verfassungsrechtlicher und völkerrechtlicher Sicht* (Münster: Waxmann Verlag, 2005).

International Alert, www.international-alert.org (accessed May 15, 2008).

International Convention for the Suppression of Terrorist Bombings, G. A. Res. 164, U.N. GAOR, 52nd Sess., Supp. No. 49, at 389, U.N. Doc. A/52/49 (1998), entered into force May 23, 2001.

International Council on Human Rights Policy, "Human rights after September 11th," December 1, 2002, p. 52.

International Crisis Group, "Congo: Consolidating the Peace," *Africa Report* 128, July 5, 2007.

International Law Commission, "Report of the International Law Commission," in United Nations International Law Commission, *Yearbook of the International Law Commission* (United Nations Publications, 1994), vol. II, p. 46.

International Peace Academy, "The Future of UN State-Building: Strategic and Operational Challenges and the Legacy of Iraq," State-Building Project November 14–16, 2003.

"Weapons of Mass Destruction and the United Nations: Diverse Threats and Collective Responses," report from June 2004.

"Human Rights, the United Nations, and the Struggle Against Terrorism," conference November 7, 2003.

Investing in Development. A Practical Plan to Achieve the Millennium Development Goals. *UN Millennium Project* (New York: UNDP, 2005).

Jalandoni, L. G., *Letter to Alter Trade*, July 28, 2007 (on file at BIND, Philippines).

Jennings, W. I., *The Law and the Constitution*, 3rd edn. (London: University of London Press, 1943), p. xxxi.

Johnson, H. and Niemeyer, G., "Collective Security: The Validity of an Ideal," *International Organization* 8 (1954), pp. 19–20.

Johnson, J. T., *Morality and Contemporary Warfare* (New Haven: Yale University Press, 1999), pp. 41–42.

Joyner, D., "The Proliferation Security Initiative: Nonproliferation, Counter-Proliferation, and International Law," *The Yale Journal of International Law* 30 (2005), pp. 507–548.

Kadi v *Council & Commission*, September 21, 2005, nyr Case T-315/01.

Kaldor, M., *New Wars and Old Wars: Organized Violence in a Global Era* (Stanford: Stanford University Press, 2001).

Kalin, W. and Jimenez, C., "Reform of the UN Commission on Human Rights, Study Commissioned by the Swiss Ministry of Foreign Affairs," *Political Division IV Institute of Public Law* (2003), pp. 8–9.

Kant, I., *Critique of Pure Reason*, Smith, N. (trans.) (Edinburgh: Palgrave Macmillan, 1933).

Karajkov, R., *N.G.O. bashing*, www.worldpress.org/print_article.cfm? article_id=2298&dont=yes (accessed May 28, 2008).

Kassa, M., "Humanitarian Assistance in the DRC," in Malan, M. and Gomes Porto, J. (eds.), *Challenges of Peace Implementations: The UN Mission in the Democratic Republic of the Congo* (Pretoria: Institute for Security Studies, 2004).

Kennedy, David. "A New World Order: Yesterday, Today, and Tomorrow," *Transnational Law and Contemporary Problems* 4 (1994), p. 9.

"Theses About International Law Discourse," *German Yearbook of International Law* 23 (1980).

"Perspectives on International Law and Legal Humanism" Remarks for the closing plenary of the European Society of International Law, May 20, 2005.

"Losing Faith in the Secular and the Culture of International Governance," in Garber, M. (ed.), *One Nation Under God: Religion and American Culture* (London: Routledge, 1999).

"Speaking Law to Power: International Law and Foreign Policy Closing Remarks," *Wisconsin International Law Journal* 23 (2005), pp. 173–181.

Dinner Remarks at the New International Law Conference, Oslo, March 2007.

Remarks on International Legal Scholarship Law Reviews Dinner, Harvard Law School, April 20, 2005.

"Tom Franck and the Manhattan School," 35 *New York University Journal of International Law and Politics* (2002 2003), pp. 397–435.

Kennedy, Duncan, "The Structure of Blackstone's Commentaries," 28 *Buffalo Law Review* 205 (1979).

Kennedy, P., *The Parliament of Man: The Past, Present, and Future of the United Nations* (New York: Random House, 2006), p. 29.

Kindiki, K., "International Law on Trial: The Darfur Crisis and the Responsibility to Protect Civilians," Paper Presented at *Third World and International Law Conference*, April 21, 2007.

Kirgis, F., *International law aspects of the 2005 World Summit Outcome Document*, American Society of International Law, www.asil.org/insights/2005/10/insights051004.html (accessed: May 22, 2008).

"The Security Council's First Fifty Years," *American Journal of International Law* 89 (1995), pp. 506–539.

Klabbers, J., "Two Concepts of International Organization," *International Organizations Law Review* 2 (2005), pp. 277–293.

"Commissioning the Truth," *Ius Gentium* 8 (2002), pp. 57–67.

"Compliance Procedures," in Bodansky, D., Brunnée, J., and Hey, E. (eds.), *The Oxford Handbook of International Environmental Law* (Oxford: Oxford University Press, 2007), pp. 995–1009.

"Redemption Song: Human Rights Versus Community-building in East Timor," 16 *Leiden Journal of International Law* (2003), pp. 367–376.

"Straddling Law and Politics: Judicial Review in International Law," in MacDonald, R. and Johnston, D. M. (eds.), *Towards World Constitutionalism* (Leiden: Martinus Nijhoff, 2005), pp. 809–835.

Knipping, F., von Mangoldt, H., and Rittergerger, V., *The United Nations System and its Predecessors* (Oxford: Oxford University Press, 1997), vol. II, pp. 7–9.

Korb, L. and Wadhams, C., "A Critique of the Bush Administration's National Security Strategy," *The Stanley Foundation Policy Analysis Brief*, June 2006.

Koremenos, B., Lipson, C., and Snidal, D. (eds.), *The Rational Design of International Institutions* (Cambridge: Cambridge University Press, 2001).

Koroma, E. B., President of Sierra Leone and Commander-in-Chief of the Armed Forces of the Republic of Sierra Leone, Address on the occasion of the State Opening of the Third Parliament, Freetown, October 5, 2007, p. 15.

Koskenniemi, M., "What is International Law For?," in Evans, M. D. (ed.), *International Law* (Oxford: Oxford University Press, 2003), p. 89.

The Gentle Civilizer of Nations: The Rise and Fall of International Law 1870–1960 (Cambridge: Cambridge University Press, 2001).

"The Place of Law in Collective Security," *Michigan Journal of International Law* 17 (1995–1996), pp. 455–490.

"The Police in the Temple: Order, Justice and the UN: A Dialectical View," *European Journal of International Law* 6 (1995), pp. 325–348.

"Le Comité de Sanctions (crée par la résolution 661 (1990) du Conseil de Sécurité)," *Annuaire Français de Droit International* 37 (1991), pp. 119–137.

"The Politics of International Law," *European Journal of International Law* 1 (1990).

From Apology to Utopia: The Structure of International Legal Argument; (Cambridge: Cambridge University Press, 2006) [1989].

Kupchan, C. and Kupchan, C., "The Promise of Collective Security," *International Security* 20 (Summer 1995), pp. 52–53.

Kurban, D., Yukseker, D., Celik, A. B., Unatan, T., and Aker, A. T., *Coming to terms with forced migration: Post-displacement restitution of citizenship in Turkey, Istanbul* (Istanbul: TESEV Publications, 2007).

Lacey Swing, W., "Preface: The Role of MONUC and the International Community in Support of the DRC Transition," in Malan, M. and Gomes Porto, J. (eds.), *Challenges of Peace Implementations: The UN Mission in the Democratic Republic of the Congo* (Pretoria: Institute for Security Studies, 2004).

Landsberg, C., "The UN High-Level Reports and Implications for Africa," *Security Dialogue* 36 (September 2005), pp. 388–391.

Lauren, P., "The Commission on Human Rights: Protector of the Victims or Shield for the Violators?," A paper prepared for the Columbia Human Rights Seminar, April 6, 2006.

Lehto, M., "The ICC and the Security Council: About the argument of politicization," in Politi and Nesi, (eds.), *The International Criminal Court and the crime of aggression* (Aldershot, England: Ashgate Publishing, 2004), p. 146.

Le Mon, C. J. and Taylor, R. S., "Security Council Action in the Name of Human Rights: From Rhodesia to the Congo," *U.C. Davis Journal of International Law & Policy* 10 (2004).

Lindley, A., "Human security now: Protecting and empowering people," *Journal of Refugee Studies* 17 (2004), pp. 244–246.

Llorens, J. C., "La Corte Penal Internacional y el mantenimiento de la paz y la seguridad internacionales," in Juan Luis Gómez Colomer (coord.), *La Corte Penal Internacional un estudio interdisciplinar* (Valencia: Tirant Lo Blanch, 2003), pp. 68–69.

Locke, J., *Two Treatises of Government: Second Treatise* (W. S. Carpenter intr., 1984), sect. 183, 211 (London).

Lorimer, J., *The Institutes of the Law of Nations: A Treatise of the Jural Relations of Separate Political Communities* (1883), pp. 126–133.

Luck, E., "The Uninvited Challenge: Terrorism Targets the UN," available online at: www.sipa.columbia.edu/cio/cio/projects/LuckSSRCUNU.pdf (accessed August 18, 2007).

"Uninvited Challenge: Terrorism Targets the United Nations," in Newman, E. and Thakur, R., (eds.), *Multilateralism Under Challenge: Power, International Order and Structural Change* (Tokyo: United Nations University and the Social Science Research Council, 2006), pp. 336–355.

UN Security Council: Practice and Promise (New York: Routledge, 2006), p. 107.

"How Not to Reform the United Nations," *Global Governance* 11 (2005), pp. 412–13.

"The UN Security Council: Reform or Enlarge?" *Center on International Organization*, April 25, 2005.

Lukiyantsev, G., "Council to Replace Commission: Human Rights Problems in the UN," *International Affairs: A Russian Journal of World Politics, Diplomacy & International Relations* 52 (2006), pp. 51–56.

Lindley, A., "Human security now: Protecting and empowering people," *Journal of Refugee Studies* 17 (2004), pp. 244–246.

Lynch, C., "U.N., U.S. Actions Sometimes at Odds on Afghan Policy," *Washington Post* July 5, 2007, A10.

Lyngdoh, B., "Skills for work in the future: A youth perspective," *Prospects* 35 (2005), p. 315.

MacPherson, B., "Authority of the Security Council to exempt peacekeepers from International Criminal Court proceedings," American Society of International Law, www.asil.org/insights/insigh89.htm (accessed May 24, 2008).

Macrae, J. and Zwi, A. (eds.), *War and Hunger: Rethinking International Responses* (London: Zed Books, 1994).

Mahoney, C. and Pinedo, T., "Human security in communities in Costa Rica and the United States," *Journal of Social Issues* 63 (2007), p. 353.

Making Targeted Sanctions Effective: Guidelines for the Implementation of UN Policy Options. Results from the Stockholm Process on the Implementation of Targeted Sanctions (Uppsala: Uppsala University, 2003).

Malan, M. and Gomes Porto, J., *Challenges of Peace Implementations: The UN Mission in the Democratic Republic of the Congo* (Pretoria: Institute for Security Studies, 2004).

Maley, W., "UN Reform: Democratic Governance and Post-Conflict Transitions," *Chicago Journal of International Law* 6 (2006), p. 683.

Malloch Brown, M., "Holmes Lecture: Can the UN be Reformed?" annual meeting of the Academic Council on the UN system (ACUNS), June 7, 2007, p. 7.

"Power and Super-Power: Global Leadership in the Twenty-First Century," speech delivered at the Century Foundation and Center for American Progress, June 6, 2006.

Malone, D., "The United Nations and the Challenges of Building Peace in the Middle East," Lecture presented at the University of Utah College of Humanities Middle East Center on April 6, 2004, www.humis.utah.edu/humis/docs/organization_302_1130959428.pdf

Mamdani, M., "The Politics of Naming: Genocide, Civil War, Insurgency," *London Review of Books* vol. 29, March 8, 2007.

Manusama, K., *The United Nations Security Council in the Post-Cold War Era: Applying the Principle of Legality* (Leiden: Martinus Nijhoff, 2006).

Martenczuk, B., "The Security Council, the International Court of Justice and Judicial Review: What Lessons from Lockerbie?" *European Journal of International Law* 10 (1999), pp. 517–47.

Martens, J., "UN Reform and the Millennium Goals 2005," *Global Issue Papers* No. 16, March 2005.

McAskie, M., "The International Peacebuilding Challenge: Can New Players and New Approaches bring New Results," lecture delivered at Simon Fraser University School for International Studies (Vancouver, British Columbia, Canada, October 19, 2007).

McCoubrey, H. and Morris, J. C., "International Law, International Relations and the Development of European Collective Security," *Journal of Armed Conflict Law* 4 (1999), pp. 195, 199–200.

Mearsheimer, J., "The False Promise of International Institutions," *International Security*, 19 (1994/95), pp. 26–37.

Megret, F., "The Security Council," in Alston, P. and Meret, F. (eds.), *The United Nations and Human Rights: A Critical Appraisal* (Oxford: Oxford University Press, 2007).

Mertus, J., "Discussion Paper: Myths and Truths on the United Nations Human Rights Council," *United Nations Human Rights Reform: Breakdown or Breakthrough* conference held at Columbia University, April 27, 2006.

Miall, H., "The EU and the Peacebuilding Commission," *Cambridge Review of International Affairs* 20 (2007), pp. 29–45.

Military and Paramilitary Activities in and against Nicaragua (Nicaragua v. *United States of America)*, Merits, 1984 ICJ Reports 392 (June 27, 1986), 14.

Millennium Summit, New York, September 6–8, 2000, United Nations Millennium Declaration, UN doc. GA Resolution A/55/2 of September 8, 2000.

Morgenthau, H., "Positivism, Functionalism and International Law," *American Journal of International Law* 34 (1940).

Mueller, J. and Mueller, K., "Sanctions of mass destruction," *Foreign Affairs* 78 (1999), pp. 43–53.

Müller, J. (ed.), *Reforming the United Nations: The Struggle for Legitimacy and Effectiveness* (Leiden: Martinus Nijhoff, 2006), p. 93.

Muravchik, J., *The Future of the United Nations: Understanding the Past to Chart a Way Forward* (Washington, DC: The American Enterprise Institute Press, 2005).

Murphy, C., *The United Nations Development Programme: A Better Way?* (Cambridge: Cambridge University Press, 2006).

Murphy, S., "The Security Council, Legitimacy, and the Concept of Collective Security after the Cold War," *Columbia Journal of Transnational Law* 32 (1994).

Nardin, T., "Legal Positivism as a Theory of International Society," in Mapel, D. R. and Nardin, T. (eds.), *International Society: Diverse Ethical Perspectives* (Princeton: Princeton University Press, 1998).

Nevins, J., *A Not-So-Distant Horror: Mass Violence in East Timor* (Ithaca: Cornell University Press, 2005).

Newman, D., "A Human Security Council? Applying A 'Human Security' Agenda to Security Council Reform," *Ottowa Law Review* 31 (1999–2000), pp. 213–241.

Newman, E. and Thakur, R. (eds.), *Multilateralism Under Challenge: Power, International Order and Structural Change* (Tokyo: United Nations University and the Social Science Research Council, 2006).

Ngongo Taunya, J., "Public Information and the Media: Radio Okapi's Contribution to the Peace Process in the DRC," in Malan, M. and Gomes Porto, J. (eds.), *Challenges of Peace Implementations: The UN Mission in the Democratic Republic of the Congo* (Pretoria: Institute for Security Studies, 2004).
Nicholas, H. G., *The United Nations as a Political Institution 3rd edn.* (Oxford: Oxford University Press, 1967), p. 70.
Nicolson, N. (ed.), *The Harold Nicolson Diaries* 1907–1963 (London: Weidenfeld & Nicolson, 2004), p. 139.
Nissel, A., "The ILC Articles on State Responsibility: Between Self-Help and Solidarity," *New York University Journal of International Law and Politics* 38 (2006), pp. 355–371.
Noyes, J., "Christianity and Late Nineteenth-Century British Theories of International Law," in Janis, M. (ed.), *The Influence of Religion on the Development of International Law* (The Hague: Kluwer, 1991).
Nyamu-Musembi C. and Cornwall, A., "What is the rights-based approach all about?" Perspectives from international development agencies IDS, Working Paper No. 234, pp. 2–4 at www.ids.ac.uk/ids/bookshop/wp/wp234.pdf
Nzongola-Ntalaja, G., *The Congo from Leopold to Kabila: A People's History* (London and New York: Zed Books, 2002).
Oakeshott, M., *On Human Conduct* (Oxford: Clarendon Press, 1975).
"The Rule of Law," *On History and Other Essays* (Indianapolis: Liberty, 1999), p. 173.
OCHA, "General Talking Points for All OCHA Staff. Key Aspects of the Current Reform of the Humanitarian Response System," August 25, 2005.
"*Executive Summary*, Humanitarian Response Review."
"Sector Working Groups Update, Humanitarian Response Review," Geneva, August 19, 2005.
O'Connell, M. E., "The Counter-Reformation of the Security Council," *Journal of International Law and International Relations* (Winter 2005), pp. 107–120.
O'Donnell, T., "Naming and Shaming: The Sorry Tale of Security Council Resolution 1530 (2004)," *European Journal of International Law* 968 (2006), p. 17.
Office of the United Nations High Commissioner for Human Rights, "Draft Guidelines for a Human Rights Approach to Poverty Reduction Strategies," (2002), para. 23.
"Suggested Elements for Voluntary Pledges and Commitments By Candidates for Election to the Human Rights Council," www2.ohchr.org/english/bodies/hrcouncil/docs/pledges.pdf
Official records of the General Assembly, Fifth Session, Annexes, agenda item 72, document A/C.1/608.

O'Neill, J., "Dwindling US Trade Deficit Could Shape World Trade," *Financial Times*, September 26, 2007, p. 28.

O'Neill, O., *Bounds of Justice* (Cambridge: Cambridge University Press, 2000).

Oosthuizen, G. H., "Some preliminary remarks on the relationship between the envisaged International Criminal Court and the Security Council," *Netherlands International Law Review* 46 (1999), pp. 313–342.

Orakhelashvili, A., "The Impact of Peremptory Norms on the Interpretation and Application of United Nations Security Council Resolutions," *European Journal of International Law* 16 (2005), pp. 59–88.

Peremptory Norms in International Law (Oxford: Oxford University Press, 2006).

Orford, A., "The Gift of Formalism," *European Journal of International Law* 15 (2004).

Reading Humanitarian Intervention (Cambridge: Cambridge University Press, 2003), p. 202.

"The Politics of Collective Security," *Michigan Journal of International Law* 17 (Winter 1996) pp. 373–409.

Organization of African Unity Convention on the Prevention and Combating of Terrorism, July 14, 1999, Article 3.

Ott, D., "Chesterman: Destroying the UN to Save It," *Canadian Council on International Law Bulletin* 31 (2005).

Otto, D., "Nongovernmental Organizations in the United Nations System: The Emerging Role of International Civil Society," *Human Rights Quarterly* 18 (1996), p. 126.

Overseas Development Institute, "Humanitarian Issues in Ituri, Eastern DRC," *HPG Briefing Note*, November 2005.

"The Currency of Humanitarian Reform," *HPG Briefing Note*, June 2003.

Pahuja, S., "The Postcoloniality of International Law," *Harvard International Law Journal* 46 (2005), pp. 459–469.

Pape, R. A., "Why Economic Sanctions Do Not Work" *International Security* 22 (1997), pp. 90–136.

Perle, R., "Thank God for the Death of the UN," *The Guardian*, March 23, 2003.

"The Review of the United Nations Security Council Decisions by the International Court of Justice," *Netherlands International Law Review* 52 (2005), pp. 167–195.

Pogge, T. W., "What is Global Justice?," unpublished manuscript, Oslo, September 11, 2003.

Policy Working Group on Terrorism, Report A/57/273, August 6, 2002.

Politi, M. and Nesi, G. (eds.), *The International Criminal Court and the crime of aggression* (Aldershot, England: Ashgate Publishing, 2004).

Ponzio, R., "The United Nations Peacebuilding Commission: Origins and Initial Practice," *Disarmament Forum (UNIDIR)* 2 (2007), p. 8.